Understanding Global Cultures

This book is dedicated with fond memories to Mr. Francis P. Long, distinguished faculty member, Scranton Preparatory School, Scranton, Pennsylvania. I was very fortunate to have Mr. Long as an instructor in Latin, Greek, German, and English literature. He imbued in all of his young students a love of learning and taught all of us to see the beauty in widely divergent cultures, both ancient and modern.

Understanding
Global
Cultures

Metaphorical Journeys
Through 17 Countries

Martin J. Gannon
and Associates

SAGE Publications
International Educational and Professional Publisher
Thousand Oaks   London   New Delhi

For information address:

SAGE Publications, Inc.
2455 Teller Road
Thousand Oaks, California 91320

SAGE Publications Ltd.
6 Bonhill Street
London EC2A 4PU
United Kingdom

SAGE Publications India Pvt. Ltd.
M-32 Market
Greater Kailash I
New Delhi 110 048 India

Printed in the United States of America

Library of Congress Cataloging-in-Publication Data

Gannon, Martin J.
    Understanding global cultures: metaphorical journeys through 17 countries/Martin J. Gannon and associates.
        p. cm.
    Includes bibliographical references and index.
    ISBN 0-8039-5374-7.—ISBN 0-8039-5375-5 (pbk.)
    1. Cross-cultural studies. 2. Cross-cultural orientation.
    I. Title.
    GN345.7G36   1994
    306—dc20   93-37617
                                                                          CIP

94 95 96 97 98 10 9 8 7 6 5 4 3 2 1

Sage Production Editor: Yvonne Könneker

Contents

Preface: An Image of Thailand

This book introduces a new concept and method—the cultural metaphor—for understanding and comparing cultures around the globe. Before presenting the method briefly here and in detail in Chapter 1, I will describe personal and professional experiences that led to the concept's development.

During 1988 I was teaching at Thammasat University in Thailand. Given my previous visits and stays in foreign countries, I did what many long-term visitors to a culture do by way of preparation: I read intensively about Thailand's history and culture, and I studied the language. The visit was pleasant, but my intensive reading and study proved to be poor preparation for understanding Thais. For instance, "dos and don'ts" such as how to greet Thais and act in a *wat* (temple)—95% of Thais are Buddhists—were easy to understand, but authors typically presented them one-by-one without providing an overall framework or context into which they could be placed. Clearly such guides are important, but they are merely pieces in the puzzle of trying to understand the values, attitudes, and behaviors of Thais. Without a framework, visitors can even believe that they are acting properly when in actuality they are violating deeply held values and customs (see De Mente, 1990; Stewart & Bennett, 1991). In fact, the puzzle was especially intriguing, because Thais seemed so similar to, and yet so different from, their American counterparts. In both cultures there is a love of freedom, a dislike of pomposity, and a pragmatic outlook. But the differences are significant.

Midway in my stay I happened to read John Fieg's *A Common Core: Thais and Americans* (1976) (revised as Fieg & Mortlock, 1989). Fieg uses the image of a rubber band to highlight Thai values, attitudes, and behaviors. When the rubber band is held loosely between the fingers, its looseness is comparable to the manner in which most Thais interact with one another during the day. However, Thais also have a complex status system in which relationships are vertical and hierarchical. Once this status system is activated in any way—for example, a superior giving a direct order to a subordinate—Thais tend to respond immediately to its dictates, and so the rubber band tightens. As soon as the demands of the status system have been met, Thais can return to looser and more liberated behavioral patterns.

Fieg then says that Americans can be represented by a string that is held tightly between the fingers for most of each day. Periodically the string is loosened, but Americans do not enjoy the same degree of behavioral freedom that Thais experience—that is, the string can never be as loose as the rubber band. In the United States there are many external and internal controls that motivate individuals in this achievement-oriented society. Examples of external control include the numerous legal, accounting, and governmental forms that Americans routinely fill out. Imbuing children with the desire to work hard and to respond enthusiastically to the demands of the Protestant work ethic reflects internal control. Such internal and external control is present in Thailand to a much lower degree than in the United States. This image of Thailand, which serves as a partial metaphor, greatly increases our understanding of many diverse and seemingly contradictory behaviors.

With its population of approximately 57 million and a land mass about equal to that of France, Thailand is the only country in Southeast Asia that has never been colonized since its inception 800 years ago. *Thailand* means "land of freedom," and Thais tend to be a proud people at least in part because of this fact. They are also very individualistic—within limits. Like many other Asians, Thais are generally much more responsive to authority than are Americans. This response is manifested in the daily salutation of the *wai*: Thais hold both hands together as if in prayer and bow their heads when greeting one another. Supposedly this pattern emerged when a person conquered in battle would show the victor that he was not holding any weapons, and his bow to the victor exposed his head to any blow that the victor wanted to administer. This greeting is associated with another distinctive Thai concept, *krengchai*, which is very similar to the key Japanese concept of *amae* (see Chapter 14). Basically it means that an inferior in a relationship needs to show deference to the superior in order to put him at ease. In turn, the superior has an obligation to put the inferior at ease. In short, the first obligation to act comes from the inferior in a relationship, but it must be followed by appropriate actions of the superior. Thus "waiing" establishes a psychological relationship of dependency between superiors and subordinates or between peers, and the subordinate bends further when waiing to show deference. The subordinate also responds immediately to a superior's request or command, as the image of the rubber band would suggest. Adler (1991) suggests that American prisoners of war in Japanese war camps during World War II suffered much more than necessary simply because they refused to show subservience by bowing abjectly, thus violating the key cultural concept of amae or, in Thailand, krengchai.

There are many examples of krengchai that could be cited. Perhaps the best one involves the "flower day" that students at Thai universities observe annually. Although professors in Thai universities receive very low salaries, they are greatly respected, at least in part because Buddhist monks were the educators until around 1900. One day a year there is a flower ceremony at each Thai university that is unique and expressive of krengchai, as the following quote from an American Fulbright professor confirms (George, 1987):

> Today, students paid homage to their professors—a symbolic celebration of rather common significance to them. I found it an astonishing phenomenon.
>
> In a large auditorium, representatives from each department within the Faculty crawled up, in the manner of Asian supplication, and gave beautiful floral offerings to their "Aacaan" (professors). Their choral chants asked for blessing and showed gratitude. Their speeches asked for forgiveness for any disrespect or non-fulfillment of expectation. They promised to work diligently.
>
> In a moment of paradox, I remembered I must not forget to pay the premium on my professional liability insurance this year. (p. 5)

However, there are other key and competing or seemingly contradictory Thai cultural values. As Buddhists, Thais tend to have a gentle approach to life and view their current situations as transitory and superficial as they wend their way toward nirvana or the final state of peace and quiescence, which supposedly involves many different transformations of their beings over several centuries. Their word for "work," *ngan*, aptly expresses this attitude—it is also translated as "play." As a result, Thais highly value *sanuk* or a good time, and they punctuate their workday with such activity. Also, as Buddhists, Thais believe that time is circular rather than linear, and they experience difficulty using Western concepts such as proceeding logically and sequentially on a project from Point A to Point Z. Thais instead tend to begin a project at Point A, move to Point M, circle back to Point B, move to Point D, and so forth, finally arriving at Point Z after punctuating the entire activity with sanuk.

There are many critical features of Thai society that this image of the rubber band does not encompass, in large part because it does not contain a sufficient amount of complexity. Still, it is an excellent starting point for understanding Thai society. For instance, travel books frequently portray Thailand as the "Land of the Smile" in which people have "a warm smile and a cool heart." Indeed, Thais do tend to smile much more than do Americans, and the warm smile and cool heart reflect the Buddhist belief in the Path of the Middle Way—that is, be friendly to others but keep emotions under control, avoiding extremes of happiness or sadness. All of these ideas are consistent with the image of the rubber band, because Thais want others and themselves to be happy, and they accept a rigid hierarchy and an unquestioning reaction to authority or hierarchy of status in many situations at least in part because of this while still preserving their many periods of sanuk.

I have presented this description to illustrate how a simple image of a rubber band can help the visitor to a culture to go beyond the routine dos and don'ts and begin to understand how the values, attitudes, and behaviors in it are logically related to one another. However, rather than using just a simple image, I decided to use the concept of the cultural metaphor, which can serve as a guide, map, or beacon for connecting diverse and seemingly contradictory stimuli, attitudes, values, and behaviors so that understanding can be enhanced and interactions can occur smoothly.

Some cultural anthropology work bears directly on the concept of cultural metaphors, particularly Clifford Geertz's (1973) description of male Balinese society in terms of the cockfight. However, each metaphor in this book uses three to six characteristics of each metaphor to describe the culture of the nation being assessed. In the case of the Italian opera (Chapter 3), these are pageantry and spectacle, voice, exteriority, and the interaction between the chorus and the lead singers. Through the use of each metaphor we can begin to see the society in approximately the same manner as do its members. We can also compare societies through the use of these metaphors and their characteristics.

Although each metaphor is a guide or map, it is only a starting point against which we can compare our own experiences and through which we can start to understand the seeming contradictions pervasive in most, if not all, societies. Also, although we are describing a dominant, perhaps the dominant, metaphor for each society, other metaphors also may be suitable. In this book we do not address the issue of suitable alternative or supplementary metaphors. Further, our descriptions explicitly recognize and focus on the regional, racial, and ethnic differences within each country. Still, the unit of analysis in this book is the nation, because considerable evidence suggests that, at least for many countries, there are commonalities across regional, racial, and ethnic groups within each that can be effectively captured by cultural metaphors. In the United States, it is possible to gain some understanding of American racial and ethnic groups by studying the root culture from which they originated and their related cultures—for example, the Spanish bullfight for Spanish Americans.

As discussed in Chapter 1, there is one exception to the use of this unit of analysis, namely, applying the metaphor of the Chinese family altar to the Chinese in nations where they are an important or singular group. By and large, we found that the concept of the cultural metaphor works best when the unit of analysis is the nation. The Chinese are an exception to this generalization.

The first chapter describes three prominent approaches to *culture-general* understanding that emphasize a small number of factors or dimensions, such as time and space, to gain an understanding of cultural differences. The various chapters of the book are linked together through a discussion of these dimensions within each. However, it is our contention that relying solely on these culture-general dimensions provides an incomplete and relatively narrow view of a society's culture; that is, the dynamics of each nation's culture are expressed through the cultural metaphor and the many variables that each of them is able to encompass.

We used three criteria for selecting the countries in this book. The first was whether we could construct a metaphor for a specific country. In some cases we were unable to identify an appropriate metaphor; in other cases, we spent more than four years just identifying one suitable metaphor. We also wanted to describe countries whose citizens interact with Americans on an increasingly frequent basis. And, as suggested above, we sought to include countries from which specific racial and ethnic American subgroups have originated.

This book could not have been written without the help of individuals who are intimately familiar with the specific cultures for which we sought to construct metaphors. They served as coauthors of the various chapters. Our basic approach was for each coauthor to use the methods for constructing metaphors as outlined in Chapter 1 when writing his or her chapter, preceded and followed by intensive discussions both among the coauthors and with other knowledgeable individuals. Each chapter was rewritten in light of the suggestions offered by these individuals. I wrote Chapters 1 and 18 and was responsible for restructuring and editing the other chapters. The coauthors are Diana Liebscher and Eileen Fagen, Chapter 2 (Britain); Stefania Amodio and Lynne Levy, Chapter 3 (Italy); Douglas O'Bannon and Julie Kromkoski, Chapter 4 (Germany); Peter Brown and Sharon Ribas, Chapter 5 (France); Ana Hedin and Michelle Allison, Chapter 6 (Sweden); Amy Levitt, Chapter 7 (Russia); Stacey Hostetler and Sydney Swainston, Chapter 8 (Belgium); Katherine Feffer Noonan, Chapter 9 (Spain); Daniel Cronin and Cormac Mac Fhionnlaoich, Chapter 10 (Ireland); Amy Levitt, Chapter 11 (Turkey); Efrat Elron, Chapter 12 (Israel); Isaac Agboola, Chapter 13 (Nigeria); Diane Terry, Chapter 14 (Japan); Amit Gupta and Jeffrey Thomas, Chapter 15 (India); Hakam Kanafani, Chapter 16 (the United States); and Giuseppe Audia, Chapter 17 (China).

In addition to the authors, many others contributed to this book. Some coauthors interviewed several people, and each chapter was read and critiqued by several citizens or residents of the countries being described. We would particularly like to thank our colleagues at the Maryland Business School, University of Maryland at College Park, for their advice and suggestions, including Michael Agar, Mercy Coogan, Stephen Carroll, Edwin Locke, Sabrina Salam, Allyson Downs, Kenneth Smith, and Guenther Weinrach. We also want to thank the following for providing a supportive environment: Rudolph Lamone, former Dean of the Maryland Business School; William Mayer, Dean; Maryann Weikart, former Director of the MBA Program; and Mark Wellman, Director of the MBA Program.

Further, given both the scope and depth of this project, we were almost overwhelmed, not only with its complexity but also with its details. We have painstakingly attempted to eliminate any errors, however small, that would serve to detract from the general focus of the book. I accept responsibility for any inadvertent errors that might have occurred; if you encounter even a minor error, we hope that you will bring it and any suggestions for improving the book to our attention.

As usual, the staff at Sage Publications peformed its work admirably, and I am especially appreciative of the help that Harry Briggs, my editor, and others provided. These include Stephanie Caballero, promotion manager; Yvonne Könneker, production editor; and Abby Nelson, editorial assistant. Finally, my wife Doris, and our two children, Marlies and Reid, offered invaluable advice and suggestions. They patiently listened and responded to my rambling thoughts and concerns over the many years during which the concepts underlying this book gradually evolved. Without their support, this book might never have made the long journey from fragmentary insights into final form.

PART 1

INTRODUCTION

1

Understanding Cultural Metaphors

By broadening his conception of the forces that make up and control his life, the average person can never again be completely caught in the grip of patterned behavior of which he has no awareness. Lionel Trilling once likened culture to a prison. It is in fact a prison unless one knows that there is a key to unlock it.

—Edward T. Hall (1959, p. 187)

It seemed like such a small problem. Ed, a 24-year-old American who had recently joined the Hong Kong Orchestra as second bass, worked well with Tad, a 35-year-old Filipino who was the first bass, until Tad began to come late to practices or missed them completely. A symphonic orchestra demands some direction from the leaders of each of its sections, and Tad started to become ineffective in this capacity because of his tardiness and absences. At first only mildly annoyed, Ed began to assume the leadership of the bass section by default, but inevitably the section's performance started to decline. Ed expressed his annoyance to Tad in rather mild terms, at least from an American perspective. Tad simply did not respond in any way, and that included even responding directly to Ed's statements. Finally, Ed showed his annoyance at one rehearsal when the bass section was doing poorly, telling Tad—in a sufficiently loud manner so that a few other orchestra members heard him—that the bass section's performance had deteriorated because of his repeated tardiness and absence, that he needed to show some leadership, and that he was burdening him with work that was properly his own. Tad did not even look at him or acknowledge his presence or statement.

Visibly upset, Ed approached William, the manager of the orchestra, and asked that he, William, and Tad get together to "iron things out directly." A seasoned veteran of many cultural wars, William suggested an alternative meeting at which Tad; Min, a translator fluent in Tagalog (a major Filipino dialect) and English; John, the orchestra's conductor; and Ed sat from left to right in front of his desk while he conducted the meeting. The only dialogue was between William and each of the other participants at the meeting, and he subtly discouraged any cross talk. Ed wondered why a translator was present, because Tad spoke excellent English, but he did not openly raise the issue. William expertly managed the meeting, at the end of which Tad agreed to mend his ways for the good of the bass section and the orchestra, and Ed indicated that he would subdue his open criticisms. William and John seemed pleased, and the meeting ended.

In fact, Tad's behavior did change, and he was rarely if ever absent. However, he barely acknowledged Ed's existence and no longer even made a token gesture of friendliness or greeting. Such a show of impassivity was in marked contrast to Tad's warmth and geniality prior to the advent of the "small problem." They worked side by side for two more years and, although the bass section's performance improved, Ed became so miserable because of the deteriorated relationship that he finally quit and returned to the United States. In recounting this story years later, Ed still manifested the emotional damage he had incurred because of this small problem and indicated that it could have been easily avoided if he had only approached the orchestra's manager earlier before his outburst directly threatened the key Filipino cultural value of group harmony. Another key Filipino cultural value, not losing face or not being humiliated, was saved by William's skillful management of the conflict, but just barely, and Tad did not wish to become involved in any interactions with Ed because of the agony he had created and might again create.

As this story suggests, culture counts, and it counts quite a bit. To give but one example, Geert Hofstede (1980a, 1980b) completed a questionnaire study at IBM Corporation involving both its managers and employees in 40 countries in which he demonstrated that national culture explained 50% of the differences in attitudes; after additional data were collected, the study included 67 countries and

117,000 respondents. In fact, culture explained more of the difference than did professional role, age, gender, or race. A comparable but earlier study of 3,600 managers in 14 countries placed this figure at 30% (Haire, Ghiselli, & Porter, 1966). Given such studies, it seems that culture influences between 25% and 50% of our attitudes, whereas other aspects of workforce diversity such as social class, ethnicity, race, sex, and age account for the remainder of these attitudinal differences.

But the story also highlights other critical aspects of culture. Although Ed and Tad were sophisticated and had traveled and lived in foreign countries, their *cultural mindsets*—basic ways of thinking, feeling, and acting that occur simply because of the fact that people are members of a particular society—prevented them from addressing their small problem in an effective manner. Culture operates subtly, often on the unconscious or semiconscious level, and it has been aptly compared to a computer program that, once activated by a few commands or stimuli, begins to operate automatically and seemingly in an independent manner (Fisher, 1988; Hofstede, 1991).

As soon as Ed's outburst violated the key cultural concept of group harmony, the small problem became a major one that influenced Ed's thinking and emotional life even years later, at least to the extent that he still reacted emotionally when talking about it. But he was fortunate: Frequently when foreigners violate key cultural values, they are not even aware of the violations, and no one brings the matter to their attention. Foreigners are then isolated and begin to experience feelings similar to Ed's. As one American businessman in Asia aptly pointed out, one of the central problems in doing business in Asia— and, for that matter, in most if not all geographical regions—is that, once you make a major cultural mistake, it is frequently impossible to rectify it, and it may well take several months to realize that polite rejections really signify isolation and banishment. Sometimes a foreigner makes such a mistake and eventually leaves the country without even realizing or identifying what he had done.

Even genuinely small cultural mistakes can have enormous consequences. Many Germans, for instance, do not like to converse much during meals. Germans will ordinarily begin their meals by taking a sip of beer or soda and then picking up and holding knives and forks throughout the meal, putting them down only when they are finished eating. For many Germans eating is a serious business that is not to be disturbed by trivial comments and animated conversation. Many Italians, on the other hand, talk constantly during meals and wave their hands repeatedly. As a result, a German and an Italian dining with one another may feel aggrieved by each other's behavior, and much time is wasted negotiating acceptable rules of behavior that could otherwise be spent on substantive issues, including the development of trust.

Further, although technological and societal changes have been rapid in recent decades, cultures change only slowly and frequently at a snail's pace, and the influence of culture persists for centuries even after mass immigrations take place. The American Irish have the "gift of the gab," which befits a cultural heritage that has a strong oral tradition, and they are disproportionately represented in fields such as trial law and politics where this gift is an asset (see Chapter 10). The English and French in Canada think and feel differently in large part because of their respective cultural heritages, and these differences have threatened the very existence of the country.

Individuals from English-speaking countries are at a particular disadvantage culturally because the people of many non-English-speaking countries use both English and their own native languages. It is common for English-speaking visitors to a non-English-speaking country to assume cultural similarity when dissimilarity is really the norm. Today, approximately 800 million individuals speak English, which has become the international language, thus creating both opportunities and pitfalls for natives of English-speaking countries.

However, knowing a country's language, although clearly helpful, is no guarantee of understanding its cultural mindset, and some of the most difficult problems have been created by individuals who have a high level of fluency but a low level of cultural understanding. Glen Fisher (1988), a former foreign service officer, describes a situation in Latin America in which the U.S. team's efforts were seriously hampered because of the condescending attitude of one member whose fluency in Spanish was excellent. Fortunately, another team member helped to save the day because she showed a genuine interest in the culture and its people, even though she was just beginning to learn how to speak Spanish. Still, experts argue that it is impossible to obtain the deepest understanding of a culture if one is not fluent in its language.

Americans tend to experience difficulty in trying to understand the mindsets of other cultures because, at least until recently, they did not travel abroad in great numbers. They also tend to suffer from ethnocentrism, interpreting all they see only from an American perspective and negatively evaluating many aspects of a foreign culture because of this bias. (The same can also be said of the Japanese and other cultural groups, as we will see.) Even today American travelers follow a frantic schedule, sometimes visiting Hong Kong, Thailand, Japan, and Taiwan within the space of two weeks. To expect these travelers to understand these cultures in such a short period of time is unrealistic. Even fewer Americans spend any time residing in foreign countries; even when doing so, they tend to isolate themselves from the natives in their "golden ghettos." By contrast, Europeans speak two or more languages, including English, and experience great cultural diversity simply by traveling a few hundred miles from one country to another. Many Asians, because of their knowledge of English and education in Europe and the United States, are similar to Europeans in cultural sophistication.

This book describes a new method, *the cultural metaphor,* for understanding easily and quickly the cultural mindset of a nation and comparing it to those of other nations. In essence, the method involves identifying some phenomenon or activity of a nation's culture that all or most of its members consider to be very important and with which they identify closely. The characteristics of the metaphor then become the basis for describing and understanding the essential features of the society.

For example, Italians invented the opera and love it passionately. Four key characteristics of the opera are (a) spectacle and pageantry, (b) voice, (c) exteriority, and (d) interaction between lead singers and chorus (see Chapter 3). We use these features to describe Italy and its cultural mindset. Thus the metaphor is a guide, map, or beacon that helps the foreigner understand quickly that which a society's members consider very important. This knowledge should help foreigners become comfortable in a society and avoid making cultural mistakes.

Constructing Cultural Metaphors

Countless social scientists, particularly cross-cultural psychologists and cultural anthropologists, have devoted their lives to the study of culture. Our cultural metaphors are based partially on the work of cross-cultural psychologists and cultural anthropologists who emphasize a small number of factors or dimensions such as time and space when comparing one society to another.

The first of these dimensional approaches was described by two anthropologists, Florence Kluckhohn and Fred Strodtbeck (1961), although Kluckhohn is generally given credit for developing the original ideas. They compare cultures across six dimensions. However, they emphasize that philosophers, social scientists, and commentators interested in understanding cultural differences have focused attention on these dimensions for hundreds of years. These six dimensions are established by the following questions:

1. What do members of a society assume about the nature of people—that is, are people good, bad, or a combination?
2. What do members of a society assume about the relationship between a person and nature—that is, should we live in harmony with or subjugate nature?
3. What do members of a society assume about the relationship between people—that is, should a person act in an individual manner or consider the group before taking action (individualism to groupism or collectivism in terms of such issues as making decisions, conformity, and so forth)?
4. What is the primary mode of activity in a given society? Is it "being," or accepting the status quo, enjoying the current situation, and going with the flow of things; or "doing," or changing things to make them better, setting specific goals, accomplishing them within specific schedules, and so forth?
5. What is the conception of space in a given society—that is, is it considered private in that meetings are held in *private*, people do not get too close to one another physically, and so on; or *public*, that is, having everyone participate in meetings and decision making, allowing emotions to be expressed publicly, and having people stand in close proximity to one another?
6. What is the society's dominant temporal orientation: past, present, or future?

Kluckhohn and Strodtbeck note that each society has a dominant cultural orientation that can be described in terms of these six dimensions, although other, weaker orientations may exist simultaneously in its different geographical regions and racial and ethnic groups.

Another well-known anthropologist, Edward T. Hall, has spent more than 40 years developing and writing about a similar dimensional classification system (for a good summary, see Hall & Hall, 1990; see also Hall, 1959, 1966, 1976, 1983, 1987). He basically focuses on the communication patterns found within cultures, and he emphasizes four dimensions along which societies can be compared:

1. context, or the amount of information that must be explicitly stated if a message or communication is to be successful;

2. space, or the ways of communicating through specific handling of personal space; for example, North Americans tend to keep more space between them while communicating than do South Americans;
3. time, which is either *monochronic* (scheduling and completing one activity at a time) or *polychronic* (not distinguishing between activities and completing them simultaneously); and
4. information flow, which is the structure and speed of messages between individuals or organizations.

Hall then arrays societies along an overarching high-context and low-context dimension. In a high-context society, time tends to be polychronic, and there is a heavy investment in socializing members so that information does not need to be explicitly stated to be understood. Members of such a culture have known one another for long periods of time, and there is a strong agreement as to what is and is not expected. In the high-context Japanese society there is even an aphorism that expressly addresses this issue: "He who knows does not speak; he who speaks does not know" (see Chapter 14). Hence verbal communication is frequently not necessary and may well impede the transmission of the message. Also, members of high-context societies tend to have less physical space between them when communicating than do those in low-context societies.

As Edward Hall notes, high-context societies tend to require a strong leader to whom everyone else expresses submission or at least great respect. In Arabic countries, such a leader will sit in his office surrounded by people seeking his help and advice. He will not address the issues and people sequentially, as would tend to happen in monochronic countries such as the United States and Germany. Rather, he will deal with several issues and people as conditions seem to warrant, going from one group to the other in a seemingly haphazard fashion that takes into consideration their sensitivities and need to save face or avoid embarrassment.

Hall tends to array societies he has studied in the following way from high to low context: Japan, Arab countries, France (approximately the middle), the United States, and Germany. Clearly Hall has a bias against low-context societies, even though he recognizes that it is much easier to interface with a low-context society because information about rules and permissible behaviors are explicitly stated. To him such societies tend to be too mechanical and lacking in sensitivity to the needs of individuals. However, he does not critically analyze some of the problems found in high-context societies, particularly the overwhelming power of the leader that can be used indiscriminately, or the in-group bias that hinders relations with anyone outside the culture. Hall's system begins to break down when he talks about the "low-context" way in which the Japanese interact with foreigners but the "high-context" way in which they interact among themselves. Thus he seems to be describing the classic in-group and out-group phenomenon rather than an overarching dimension along which societies can be arrayed. Triandis, Brislin, and Hui (1988) have argued that the major dimension separating societies is that of individualism and collectivism in which the in-group and out-group distinction is critical, and it really seems to be this dimension that Hall is describing. However, as described in the various chapters of this book and highlighted in the final chapter, there are many different kinds of individualism and collectivism.

Still, Hall's work has been significant and insightful, particularly his treatment of time and space. Throughout this book we will use some of his basic concepts, especially the monochronic-polychronic distinction and that between a high-context and low-context communication.

The third major dimensional approach was developed by Geert Hofstede, whose work is cited above. He is a prominent organizational psychologist whose research is based on a large questionnaire survey of IBM employees and managers working in 40 different countries. Hofstede's work is especially significant because the type of organization is held constant, and it is the only large-scale cross-cultural study in which the respondents all worked for a multinational corporation that had uniform personnel policies. He develops empirical profiles of these 40 countries across four dimensions of basic cultural values:

1. power distance, or the degree to which members of a society automatically accept a hierarchical or unequal distribution of power in organizations and the society;
2. uncertainty avoidance, or the degree to which members of a given society deal with the uncertainty and risk of everyday life and prefer to work with long-term acquaintances and friends rather than with strangers;
3. individualism, or the degree to which individuals perceive themselves as separate from others and free from group pressure to conform; and
4. masculinity, or the degree to which a society looks favorably on aggressive and materialistic behavior.

The three dimensional approaches developed by Kluckhohn and Strodtbeck, Hall, and Hofstede have become enormously influential and, at the same time, controversial. Although they rely on a small number of dimensions so that profiles of various societies can be constructed, they by necessity leave out many features of the cultural mindsets that are activated in daily cultural activities, and they neglect the institutions molding these mindsets. These dimensional approaches are an excellent starting point for understanding cultures and providing an overall perspective on cultural differences, but an individual will experience great difficulty in applying them to daily interactions. In effect, these dimensions are instructive but somewhat lifeless and narrow because they leave out many facets of behavior.

The metaphoric method highlighted in this book supplements and enriches the three dimensional approaches so that a visitor can understand and, most important, begin to deal effectively with the flesh and blood of a culture. Although the metaphor itself cannot encompass all of the reality that is found within each society, it is a good starting point for understanding and interacting effectively with it. At the same time, the various chapters of the book are linked together through the use of the three dimensional approaches.

Throughout this book we have attempted to identify metaphors that members of given societies view as very important if not critical. However, we needed to identify metaphors that would be relatively complex so that we could make several direct comparisons between the metaphor and the nation it represents. Also, we wanted to have a metaphor for each society that would have several suitable features that we could then use to describe it. In addition, we sought to include numerous factors or variables such as religion and small group behavior when using the metaphor to describe the society, recognizing that some of them are important in some societies but not in others. For each society we used all of the dimensions of the three dimensional approaches described above. In addition, we focused on all of the following:

- religion;
- early socialization and family structure;
- small group behavior;
- public behavior;
- leisure pursuits and interests;
- total lifestyle, including work, leisure, and home and the time allocated to each;
- aural space, or the degree to which members of a society react negatively to high noise levels;

- roles and status of different members of a society;
- holidays and ceremonies;
- greeting behavior;
- humor;
- language, or both oral and written communication;
- nonoral communication such as body language;
- sports as a reflection of cultural values;
- political structure of a society;
- the educational system of a society;
- traditions and the degree to which the established order is emphasized;
- history of a society, but only as it reflects cultural mindsets or the manner in which its members think, feel, and act rather than a detailed history;
- food and eating behavior;
- social class structure;
- rate of technological and cultural change;
- organization of and perspective on work such as a society's commitment to the work ethic, superior-subordinate relationships, and so on; and
- any other categories that were appropriate.

Using all of these categories initially, we studied each society in depth and interviewed several natives. After an initial draft of a chapter was written, it was presented at seminars and reviewed by natives and long-term residents of the society being described. The chapter was then rewritten in light of the suggestions that were offered, and additional comments were solicited. This iterative process typically led to rewriting a chapter five or six times—and sometimes even more.

As this discussion suggests, we used a relatively straightforward method to construct our metaphors of different societies. However, several issues are related to metaphors that we need to address directly, and we do so in the final section of this chapter.

Worldview, Diversity, Stereotypes, and Sociotypes

Undoubtedly we can discuss many issues, but three seem of paramount importance: (a) the worldview that a cluster of countries may share, (b) diversity in the workforce, and (c) stereotyping.

As suggested previously, a society may be so large or complex that it is impossible to use only one metaphor to describe it. In fact, this problem seems to be impossible to overcome for some societies. It is also plausible that a society, regardless of its size, may contain so many ethnic and racial groups that it cannot be described adequately through the use of a metaphor. This problem can be overcome for many societies, as evidenced by the fact that there are cultural strands that unite the members of such groups within each of the societies presented in this book.

More important, it is quite possible that, while a given society may have a distinctive mindset, it is united to other similar societies by a cultural worldview that they all share. For example, even though some Arab countries such as Oman have a yearly per capita income of only a few hundred dollars and others such as Saudi Arabia are more than $20,000, the Arab countries still possess a common worldview that is different from their specific cultural mindsets.

Ronen and Shenkar (1985) have addressed this issue by reviewing eight rigorous studies, including that of Hofstede described previously, that have attempted to profile the values and attitudes of clusters of countries. They demonstrate that there are eight clusters of countries that hold common worldviews. For example, the Arab cluster includes Bahrain, Abu Dhabi, United Arab Emirates, Oman, Saudi Arabia, and Oman. Within each cluster, countries are united by three major factors: (a) a common religion or similar religions, (b) language, and (c) geography or land area. The only exception is the Anglo cluster, which has geographically separated countries through immigration but which has them culturally united by language and religion. Some countries are independent of clusters: Brazil, Japan, India, and Israel. Of course, Ronen and Shenkar recognize explicitly that there are differences between the countries in each cluster, and they relate these differences to the gross national product (GNP) and the stage of economic growth.

Clearly there are great differences between countries in each cluster, and these differences prevent us from understanding a specific country's mindset. Also, a metaphor that is appropriate for one country in a cluster is not suitable for another country in the same cluster; for example, American football cannot be applied to England. Hence our unit of analysis is the nation. Still, it must be recognized that such clusters do exist, and that they exert an enormous influence on the people within each of them.

One metaphor is an exception to this unit of analysis, namely, the Chinese family altar. This metaphor can be applied to several countries in which the Chinese are a critical or singular cultural group, and we devote one chapter to it because of the importance of the

Chinese not only in the United States but also in other regions of the world.

Further, while we will be analyzing cultural differences and similarities in this book, we would be remiss if we did not at least mention other sources of diversity, including social class, ethnicity, race, age, and sex. Their interactions are creating a new workforce in the United States and elsewhere. Thus native white males currently make up 41% of the U.S. workforce, but only 21% of the people entering the workforce between 1988 and 2000 will be in the same category.

Perhaps the most important of these factors is social class, at least from the perspective of this book. As a predominantly middle-class society, the United States does not like to emphasize social class differences. But they do exist, and their interaction with culture is fascinating. Research across several societies—Malaysia, Austria, Canada, France, Japan, Germany, and the United States—indicates that middle-class citizens behave differently than working-class citizens regardless of the society in which they live (Kagitcibasi, 1990). If there is a dinner party in these societies, middle-class children are asked to say a few words to the guests and to perform on the piano or another musical instrument. This practice leads to better preparation for school across these societies, because such middle-class children become self-assured when in the spotlight or in leadership positions. At 9 or 10 years of age, these children begin to talk to their parents in a very mature manner. By contrast, working-class parents across all of these societies tend to emphasize negative reinforcement of their children's behavior with the result that these children do not have high levels of self-confidence and self-worth. Thus, although culture tends to differentiate societies, social class identification tends to unite them.

The other aspects of diversity—ethnicity, race, sex, and age—are highlighted in the various chapters of the book. They tend to be culture-specific in that the manner in which different ethnic, racial, age, and sex-related groupings merge in everyday life varies dramatically from society to society.

The last of the three issues that needs to be addressed is stereotyping. More specifically, to what extent are the descriptions in each chapter stereotypical and inaccurate?

A *stereotype* is a mental picture that each of us possesses of different groups and their supposed characteristics and on the basis of which we tend to evaluate individuals from each group. Stereotypes can be erroneous and lead to unwarranted conclusions. However, all human beings use stereotypes because they are an easy shorthand way of classifying the multitude of stimuli to which we are exposed. The issue is not stereotyping itself, but whether the stereotypes are accurate.

Most of us take an extremely negative position on stereotyping. It can be very embarrassing to be accused of stereotyping, especially because it is frequently so difficult to refute the charge. In today's world the accusation is frequently raised and, as a result, it has become very difficult to discuss genuine differences. However, many social psychologists now take the position that there are real differences between groups and societies and that the negative connotations associated with stereotyping have led us to deemphasize these legitimate differences. From this perspective a stereotype represents only a starting point that is to be rigorously evaluated and changed as experience with groups warrants. Nancy Adler (1991) argues persuasively that it is legitimate and helpful to use stereotypes if they are descriptive rather than evaluative, the first best guess, based on data and observation, and subject to change when new information merits it.

In its worst or most inaccurate form, a stereotype takes the form of a universal syllogism that prevents undifferentiated thinking and exceptions. For example, all white American males are unethical; John is a white American male; therefore John is unethical. Stening (1979) points out that a stereotype built on a universal syllogism is quite different from a sociotype, that is, stereotypes empirically verifiable for the bulk of a population or group. Clearly metaphors are not stereotypes, but they do tend toward sociotyping in that they rely on the features of one critical phenomenon in a society to describe the entire society. There is, however, a danger that metaphors will include some inaccurate stereotyping, and we have attempted to guard against this possibility by having the various chapters of this book reviewed by natives of the societies being described or by long-term residents of them. In some instances we were unable to construct a metaphor that satisfied natives, residents, or ourselves. Hence this book includes only metaphors about which there is consensus.

Admittedly it is very difficult to test the validity of these metaphors empirically, at least at this point in time. Our tests are (a) consensus and (b) whether a metaphor other than the one we have selected increases our understanding of a particular society. Also, we have noted in many instances that not all members of a society adhere to the behavioral patterns suggested by the metaphor by using such phrases as "some Germans," "many Italians," and "the

Irish tend to." In effect, we are highlighting patterns of thought, emotion, and behavior that a society manifests and that are clearly and concisely portrayed by means of a simple and easily remembered metaphor. In this way the visitor can use the metaphor as a guide, map, or beacon to avoid cultural mistakes and to enrich cross-cultural communications and interactions.

Part 2 of the book describes 15 metaphors and the nations associated with each. We have selected these nations and metaphors because they represent a broad array of cultural mindsets that highlight both cultural differences and similarities. Part 3 contains two chapters, the first describing the Chinese in terms of the Chinese family altar. In the final chapter of the book we compare and contrast these societies in terms of three areas: (a) types of individualism and collectivism, (b) culture-creating mechanisms, and (c) cultural behavior.

PART II

CULTURAL
METAPHORS

2

The Traditional British House

We shape our dwellings, and afterwards our dwellings shape us.
—Winston Churchill (speech on rebuilding the House,
October 28, 1944)

A traditional British house is built to stand the test of time. It is almost always brick but can be made of stone or concrete. Houses hundreds of years old and a few buildings thousands of years old are still standing and functioning in their original capacity. These houses were neither built overnight nor meant to last just a short time.

Much of the essence of Britain and her people can be sensed from the fortitude and long-lasting style of their buildings. The design of a British house is traditional and blends with the others around it; the foundations are deep and strong; the floor plan does not vary and is unchanging over time. The walls have their own firm, fixed foundations so that the floor plan of the house is visible before the internal walls even go up.

Like the British people, there are no surprises in their traditional house. A British person could find his or her way around a three-bedroom "semi" (semidetached house or duplex) anywhere in the country.

They are all based on the same tried-and-tested design. Thus, based on the outside of a house, Britons know what the inside layout of the house is like—just as they know what to expect from one another.

The British way of life is reflected in their traditional houses. They are unchanging except for some slow chipping away or eventual weathering over the years. There is only one "right" way to do things, and most, if not all, citizens know what it is—no one has to be told.

Putting up a very modern California-style wood house with an open and unusual floor plan surely does not meet this need. In fact, a timber frame house of any sort would not tend to meet with approval and would make financing and insurance difficult to get. Some Britons would derisively term this type of house "ticky tacky," and a true British family would hesitate to rely on such methods for such a serious business as building a home. In fact, even when the population was sparse and forests abounded, houses were made of stone, not wood. A house, like a way of life, should have strong foundations, be familiar and unchanging, and be built in tried-and-tested ways.

For this reason and many others, the British seem to mystify Americans, and vice versa, although the sense of identification between them is strong. Margaret Thatcher, former prime minister of England, was fond of referring to Americans as her "first cousins," and Americans reacted positively to this and similar statements. In fact, this strong sense of identification is justified: Surveys focusing on many countries show that Britons and Americans tend to cluster together in terms of basic values and attitudes. This is not terribly surprising, because American law, government, and social mores are rooted in their British antecedents. However, there are significant cultural differences that surprise and confuse us when we consider our British cousins.

It will be helpful to examine the British culture in terms of the metaphor of the British house. We will examine the "laying of the foundation of the house" evident in their history, as well as today's political and economic climate. Next, we will look at the "building of the brick house," which naturally includes the various elements of growing up British. Finally, we will describe "living in the traditional brick house," including some of the cultural patterns in business and social situations.

History, Politics, Economics:
Laying the Foundations

First, let us identify Britain geographically. Several terms are used when discussing this area, including *the British Isles, Great Britain, Britain,* and *the United Kingdom.* We will be discussing *Britain,* which is synonymous with Great Britain and comprises England, Scotland, and Wales. These make up the larger of the two islands that lie off the northwestern coast of Europe. The smaller island comprises the Irish Republic (a separate country) and Northern Ireland, which remains under British rule. The term *United Kingdom* refers to England, Scotland, Wales (Britain), and Northern Ireland.

Although the issue is not stressed in this chapter, note that there is a great deal of disharmony in the United Kingdom with regard to Northern Ireland. Sectarian discrimination and violence in that area have resulted in the inability of Northern Ireland to govern itself. In the past, the laws of Northern Ireland deliberately discriminated against the Catholic minority; for example, property owners (largely Protestant) could actually vote twice. It was this institutionalized discrimination, among other things, that led to direct rule of Northern Ireland by London in the 1960s. Catholics initially welcomed British involvement; within the context of Northern Ireland, Catholics now have the same rights as all British subjects. The continuing British military presence is to enforce civil order, although some would argue that it is British stubbornness not to let things take their natural course. Embedded in the British notion of law and order, and basic civil rights, is the strong belief that no citizen should have anything less than full rights. In fact, ordinary citizens have the same inalienable rights as the king or queen (see also Chapter 10).

Britain's earliest history is a succession of invasions and immigrations from tribes such as the Celts, Romans, Angles, Saxons, and Jutes, many of whom were warriors, barbarians, and pirates. The date at which Britain was first inhabited is unknown, but parts of a woman's skull were found at Swanscombe in Kent and dated as approximately 250,000 years old.

However, Britain's history from the middle 1500s to the 1950s is a story of domination that many have tried to emulate without success. For many years, "the sun never set on the British empire" because it was so vast.

The British have left their mark in many of the foreign lands over which their flag has flown in a variety of ways. One of the most obvious is the fact that the accepted international business language around the world today is English. Many former colonies set up their parliamentary and legal systems to emulate the British system, including freedom of the press, and they still look to the British for advice and consent in their own affairs.

The rate of immigration into the "home country" of Britain from former colonies is approximately 1 million people per year, which roughly offsets the same number of emigrations each year; one quarter of the population of central London is now of African, Asian, or Caribbean origin. There is some resentment against these immigrants, many of whom settle in certain towns in which they set up small businesses and exhibit very "un-British" behavior such as keeping their businesses open longer at nights and on weekends than their British counterparts. However, these immigrants, much as in the case of the United States, have infused the British culture with new perspectives and approaches to life.

Most 19th-century Britons were better educated, better behaved, and far richer than were most other Europeans. Across Europe, people set out to dress like Britons, talk like them, and imitate their good graces. Even the fashion of wearing black, which survives in our contemporary evening wear, came from the British style of the 1830s. "It's their confidence," Aldous Huxley (1951, p. 38) said of them in *Antic Hay*, "their ease, it's the way they take their place in the world for granted, it's their prestige, which the other people would like to deny but can't" that made them admired models. The adoption of British ways was so universal that it was unquestioned. People automatically chose the best, and the best was British (Barzini, 1983, p. 36).

For hundreds of years, there was a tacit admission of British supremacy in almost every regard. Further, there was universal admiration and envy for the nation's wealth, power, sagacity, and brutal ruthlessness, whenever that was necessary. There was a certainty that Britain knew best; that its overwhelming power and wealth would take care of most of the world's military, political, and economic problems; that private problems could be controlled by the British moral code and rules of good manners; that Britain could prolong the status quo indefinitely; and that there was nothing to worry about (Barzini, 1983, p. 37). This is the heritage of the British people— the foundation on which the rest of the traditional house is built.

As noted in the first chapter, culture can vary along several dimensions, one of which is the conception of time, or whether a society is past, present, or future oriented. It is easy to see why Britons would emphasize the past. The antique pageantry and ceremony of the nation's political structure is built right into the walls and shell of the house; without it, the house would certainly not stand as tall and proud.

Britain's government is considered one of the world's most efficient and is based on acts of Parliament. There is a written constitution, although it is quite different from the U.S. Constitution because it is the acts of Parliament existing at any one time that are its basis. Within Parliament, the House of Lords basically acts as a review body and can delay, but not veto, acts passed by the House of Commons. Thus the real power rests with the House of Commons. Precedent or common law is used only when there is no legislation concerning a major issue or no clear legislative intent. Common law, however, is widely used. It is frequently assumed by the British that everyone "knows" the rules, and so the application of common law is positively received by most citizens. Contrary to the fundamental American assumption that supreme authority must never be vested in a single institution, the British Parliament exercises supreme power over both the figurehead monarchy and the courts. Like a load-bearing wall, it accepts full responsibility for governing in Britain.

In a very different way, the monarchy is a vital part of the political scenario; panoply and pageantry distinguish every ceremonial phase of royal processions. This enduring display of pomp simultaneously manifests and strengthens the people's unity. The official opening of Parliament involves a ceremony over which the queen presides, and each week she meets with the prime minister to discuss current national issues. The past, present, and future are united in the crown and the monarch. It is one of the things that makes Britain unique, and even many of its former colonies welcome the royal family with open arms and a unique respect. Without the presence of the royal family, some of the mortar that holds the traditional British house together would surely decay.

There are two main political parties in Britain: Labour and Conservative (Tory). From time to time, a third party emerges such as the Liberals or, more recently, the Social Democrats. Britain has a representative form of government. In a national election, people vote for their constituency's member of Parliament (MP). It is quite possible, and has happened, that the majority of votes is for a party that has a minority of seats in the House and so it does not win the election, because winning is determined by the number of party-affiliated MPs elected. Elections can be called by the government at any time within five years of the last election. This policy gives the party in power a political edge, because it can, within limits, arrange that an election take place when public support for the government is greatest. To offset this, a vote of "no confidence" in the prime minister and his or her party can force a reelection at any time.

Voting is strongly along party lines, and personalities are less important. Voting is also very much allied to social class, and so it is common to vote the way your parents did and the way your neighbors do. In addition, political parties are much farther apart ideologically than are U.S. parties, and changes in government can result in noticeable changes throughout the country. For example, the election of a Conservative government can result in nationalized industries being privatized, reductions in income taxes, and "reforms" of trade union legislation.

In addition to the elected officials, there exists a whole matrix of official and social relations within which power is exercised called the "Establishment." This elite web includes such diverse interests as Oxford and Cambridge Universities, the British Broadcasting Corporation (BBC), and wealthy, high-society individuals known as "the Great and the Good." It is a difficult network to break apart because of the different forms it may take under different circumstances. Some say that this network has lost some of its clout, whereas others feel that it just keeps changing shape.

Economically, Britain can be divided into two parts. The south (the area within a few hours drive of London) is considered by those who live there to be superior in sophistication, wealth, and social status. This is somewhat accurate because of the predominance of service, high-tech, and other growth industries in the south. The rest of Britain, the north, is associated with heavy industry, engineering, mining, and unemployment. High unemployment has plagued some parts of the north, where traditional industries such as steel, coal mining, and textiles have contracted in size. There is a strong popular feeling that the government should support these slowing industries with subsidies because the traditional ways, just like the traditional brick house, should be preserved.

In fact, there is a strong feeling that the entire population should be taken care of because so many services—health, education, and housing—are socialized and provided by the state. Socialism took heavy root in Britain after the ravages of World War II. Even though the British were among the victors, they had been badly beaten down as a people, with many of their cities destroyed, men lost, and food and other staples rationed. Of course, as a winner in the war, the British received no Marshall Plan or foreign aid to rebuild their country, and so they turned to socialism instead. This socialistic bias changed considerably in recent years because of the reign of the Conservative party, which has been moving away from socialism and privatizing many services, such as transportation and utilities.

Long after their empire was dissolved by granting independence to former colonies, the British were still considered the moral leaders of Europe. In World War II, they felt they had earned the right to be the third superpower in the world because the country had paid so dearly in terms of human life, destruction of property, and courage. However, in 1955, they stood aloof from or objected to attempts at unifying Europe. Although British opposition has softened in recent years, there is still strong resistance to the idea of a unified Europe.

Evidently Britain could have collaborated on many occasions to formulate the recommendations for a unified Europe in the nation's own interest, but many of its leaders found it unthinkable to join with other nations and risk losing full identity. Britain had always been a jealous guardian of its freedom of action, proud of its solitude. The British preferred at all times to be victims of their own mistakes rather than to trust the judgment of other people (Barzini, 1983, p. 61). Indeed, as Barzini tells it, if one asks a Briton point-blank, "Are you European?" the answer is usually "European? Did you say European? Er, er"—a long thoughtful pause in which all other continents are mentally evoked and regretfully discarded—"Yes, of course, I'm European." This admission is pronounced without pride and with resignation. Truly, they feel, if God had wanted to tie Britain with the rest of Europe, he would evidently not have dug the English Channel (Barzini, 1983, p. 59). It comes as no surprise that there is still dissension about the building of the underchannel tunnel or "chunnel" to connect Britain with France and the rest of Europe.

We have taken a look at the British character as exemplified in the traditional rigid, but long-lasting brick houses, and suggested that the strong sense of history is the foundation on which society rests today. Some of the traditions and shared beliefs represent the mortar that binds people in a national identity. Now we will look at the social mechanisms—socialization processes and the educational system—that sustain these feelings.

Growing Up British: Building the Brick House

Because of the prestigious foundations of their history, foreigners still expect the British to show something of their ancient firmness, resourcefulness, diplomacy, leadership, and, certainly, good graces. How do the British continue to instill some of these admired virtues in their society? How do they put the bricks together atop the foundation to grow up British?

It has been said that all Britons have a few ideas firmly embedded in their heads that exactly and universally give them the answers about how to be perfectly British. This has allowed them to know exactly what their countrymen would expect them to do and how to go about doing it throughout history. For the most part, there is only one "right" way to do just about anything—from greeting guests to waging war.

Above all else, the British bring their children up to behave. Inquiries about children will often be about whether they are well behaved rather than whether they are happy. It is assumed that they need to be controlled and not spoiled. A great importance is placed on learning proper manners.

The British are taught at an early age to control spontaneity, and because children can be embarrassingly spontaneous, the emphasis is on keeping them quiet and from bothering adults. For example, it is rare to see children in a restaurant: Most restaurants are just not set up to deal with them, and other diners would not approve because children do not yet know how to mind their manners. Children who do not know their place are thought to be precocious, and precociousness, which is equated with showing off or boasting, meets with disapproval. After all, children are meant to be seen and not heard. This emphasis on manners and knowing your place continues as one grows.

A result of this restraint is in the well-known British reserve in adults. Most, if not all, Britons have at least one thing in common: A respect and a strong desire for privacy. This sentiment is so strong that they often appear to others as distant and aloof. It is as if they are building walls between themselves and others to create their own space within the brick house.

This need for privacy is a defining factor and one of the dimensions along which cultures differ. The phrase "We like to keep ourselves to ourselves" is particularly British (Glyn, 1970, p. 176). Glyn notes that even in the case of child care, baby-sitters need to be hired because relatives will generally not help or interfere. He also observes that even on trains, the British will frequently not sit near someone when a more secluded seat is available. In a crowded fast-food restaurant, if people are forced to share a table, they will often act as though the other party is not even present. Striking up a conversation with a seatmate would generally be considered an invasion of personal space.

There are very practical reasons for the British insistence on private, personal space. Britain is a crowded country, and space must be used efficiently. Britain is about half the size of California, but its population of 57 million people exceeds that of California by some 30 million. In the European Community, the average population density is 146 people per kilometer, but in Britain it is 235. Although the British prefer houses and are not great flat (apartment) dwellers like other Europeans, their houses are small by U.S. standards and closer together than in the United States. And, just as there are partitions of rooms within the house, the British also grow hedges around their gardens to separate their space from neighbors and to keep out the eyes of passersby.

A good neighbor is one who is friendly at a distance—who does not intrude. Because physical distance is not possible, the only available protection of personal space is psychological distance. One should always phone ahead before visiting a British home: Dropping in unannounced would generally be unwelcome. Also, frequent social telephone calls tend to be regarded as an intrusion.

Emotional outbursts (except at times of genuine crisis) are seen as "soppy" or as evidence of an unstable personality. From childhood onward, the British are admonished to keep a "stiff upper lip"—referring to pursing the lips to prevent an outburst. Even good friends may never be as intimate as in many other cultures. However, this may apply differently to the different classes, with genteel restraint being seen as definitely more upper-class than lower-class British.

John Cleese (of Monty Python fame) made this point entertainingly in the film *A Fish Called Wanda* when his character told his American love interest, "Wanda, you make me feel so free. Do you have any idea what it's like being English? Being so stifled by this dread of doing the wrong thing, of saying to someone 'Are you married?' and hearing 'My wife left me this morning' or saying 'Do you have children?' and being told they all burned to death on Wednesday" (Shamberg & Crichton, 1988).

There is a lot of weight from their lofty heritage that the British must endure. Although the foundation is strong and deep, the walls and especially the exterior of the British house and personality must seem to be effortlessly indestructible and imperturbable.

Inside the house, private space is also cherished. The British do not generally like open-plan living areas. Instead, rooms are separated and divided by walls and doors that close. Although houses are relatively small, family members are thus ensured private space. Still, Edward T. Hall (1966) points out that the smallness of the houses effectively precludes children from having their own rooms, as is the norm in the United States. He argues that, as adults, the British do not have as great a need for separate offices as do members of other cultures. Even members of Parliament do not always have their own separate offices.

All of this discussion of privacy and reserve should not be taken to mean that the British are unfriendly. By and large they are friendly people and make gracious hosts. If you ask people for help, even on the street, most will give it cheerfully. Americans, on the other hand, are often seen by the British as coming on too strong and too gushing, as being insincere, and as becoming too personal too soon. The British need time to size someone up, because he or she could be as untrustworthy as a house with aluminum siding.

Although the British enjoy the privacy of their own small homes, they also enjoy the camaraderie of the local public house, or "pub." Nearly every large and small town throughout Britain has at least one pub, many of them hundreds of years old. This is where many British do most of their socializing with co-workers and friends. It is a favorite pastime to share a few beers together after work, even with bosses. In fact, pubs can almost be thought of as a substitute for the living room in a traditional house, because Britons do not entertain as frequently as Americans in their own homes.

Pubs generally serve various kinds of beer—ale, stout, lager (the British equivalent of American-style beer), or bitter—by the pint or half-pint. Women who order pints are regarded as unladylike; half-pints are better. Beers are served at room temperature, never cold, which disguises the flavor. Most other drinks are served without ice and, true to the British ideal of what is right, a request for ice will bring only a single cube.

Orderliness, patience, and unexcitability are hallmarks of British behavior. They prefer to see each task through until completion, regardless of the priority one might assign to it. For example, if you approach a hotel desk where a clerk is alone attending to paperwork, he or she will finish the current task unhurriedly before attending to you. There is nothing between the ordinary and a true state of emergency for most British, especially in the workplace—and a live customer is nothing to get excited about.

There is a wide range of living standards in Britain, from some of the worst slums in Europe to very grand estates. Roles and status are generally well-defined. Still pervading this stratified society are distinctions between the working class, the middle class, and the elite upper class. In numerous surveys over the past decades, the British themselves reinforce these divisions by assigning themselves more than 90% of the time to one of these classes without prompting. In a 1991 survey, 29% said they were middle class and 65% working class ("Tuning In," 1992). By contrast, most Americans, including many who would be considered working class in Britain, describe themselves as middle class.

One is born into a class, and it is difficult to move from one class to another. Once again, tradition rules, whether it be in one's house plan or social class. Family background, especially the accent and use of the language, will tend to determine the type of education and hence the qualifications earned for a career.

The British are experts at classifying each other by tiny details of speech, manners, and dress. George Bernard Shaw (1916) wrote in *Pygmalion* that "the moment one Englishman speaks, he makes another Englishman despise him" (p. 26). This statement was made so beautifully clear in the adaptation of this work into the musical comedy *My Fair Lady*. After hearing just a few words from any Briton, another generally can immediately classify him or her by social class and place of upbringing.

Although Shaw's writing spanned the turn of the century, the British still can identify regional accents and where a speaker is from and thus his or her class. The discrimination that this once produced may be fading because regional accents can now be heard in professions and walks of life that were once reserved for the upper class only. For instance, although there was a time when only "proper" upper-class English was heard on the airwaves, particularly the BBC, regional accents are becoming more acceptable and are heard in all areas of broadcast. This may be indicative of a broadening and deepening of the middle class in society, raising the level of some of the working class.

Even so, the use of the language (and other behavior) can still be telling of class. Alan Ross (1969) published a "popular" version of his article "Linguistic Class Indicators in Present-Day English" under the title "U and Non-U," referring to upper-class and non-upper-class language. Many of the distinctions have faded with time, but some are as true today as ever. For example, "I worked very hard" is U, but "I worked ever so hard" is non-U. "Half past ten" is U, but "half ten" is non-U. Rugs or a plain carpet are U, but wall-to-wall patterned carpet is non-U; putting milk into tea cups first is non-U, but offering it after the tea has been poured is U. Another non-U "Britishism" that tends to puzzle foreigners is saying "He wasn't half angry," which means he was extremely angry; or "He isn't half handsome" which means he was exceedingly handsome (Braganti & Devine, 1992).

Further, it is becoming increasingly difficult for outsiders to identify a Briton's social class. *The Economist* ("Little Class Game," 1992) asked a knowledgeable but anonymous Italian to describe how he makes such identification and, after admitting to the increased difficulty of doing so, he offered the following advice:

> So if you are in doubt, and you do not feel ready to play the Little Class Game with the professionals, go for the obvious. Some items of clothing still speak volumes about their owner. When you see somebody dressed as if he has stolen the trousers from an Italian two sizes bigger than he is, you assume he is middle-class, probably an estate agent. . . . And if you meet a girl with no stockings on in winter and navy-blue legs, you can still safely bet she is working-class. Some things, thank goodness, never change. (p. 64, © 1992 The Economist Newspaper Group, Inc. Reprinted with permission. Further reproduction prohibited)

Of course, the British seem to believe that Americans do not speak English at all and find their language only a sloppy adaptation. Other Europeans might tend to agree because they learn British English and sometimes find Americans more difficult to understand. Apart from the strict use of grammar and pronunciation, Britons and Americans can confuse each other with their use of different words. For example, in Britain, you will not hear "apartment," but "flat"; not "drugstore," but "chemist"; not "elevator," but "lift"; not "attorney," but "solicitor"; not "call" (that is, visit in person) or "phone," but "ring up"; and not "trunk" of a car, but "boot."

Some segments of the population have developed entirely different speech patterns that may not be easily understood by other British (or other English speakers). The most well-known is the working-class Cockney population—officially those born within hearing distance of the Bow Bells that ring from the Church St. Mary le Bow in London's East End. These people have developed Cockney "rhyming slang," some of which has passed into general usage. If a man talks about the "trouble and strife," he is referring to his wife. To say "I didn't say a dicky bird" means "I didn't say a word." Understanding Cockney rhyming slang is yet more difficult when the conversion is one step farther removed. For example, "loaf of bread" stands for head, but the whole phrase is not used, just "loaf." So if someone tells you to "use your loaf," you are being told to think clearly, or to use your head. Another popular expression is "Blimey!" which means "God, blind me if I tell a lie" and is used throughout Britain as a common exclamation.

Britons also do not tend to move too far away from their family homes and would most likely strive to live in houses very similar to those in which they grew up. They are not inclined to make changes simply for the sake of change; they prefer to stick with familiar and comfortable surroundings. Moving across town is not treated lightly, and one would need a good reason to move to another part of the country. Lack of work is often not considered to be a strong enough motivator to move away from one's home and roots. Britons tend to keep work and leisure completely separate, much as the living areas and bedrooms of the traditional two-story house are separated by downstairs and upstairs. They are therefore not likely to let their lives be dictated by their jobs or careers.

Given the importance of our metaphor for understanding British culture, it is ironic that a significant percentage of the population lives in housing where rents are subsidized by local governments. Housing is available on the basis of need, and waiting lists are maintained. This practice reflects the socialistic bias discussed previously, and it is also changing, because much of this housing is becoming privatized. True to innate British pride and independence, these changes are being welcomed by most people because the opportunity to own their own homes is a welcome prospect.

British educational policies have changed considerably over the past 20 years, but the effects of the old system are still evident. At age 11, British children were once required to take an examination that separated them into two groups. Members of the first group attended grammar schools that were academically oriented and focused on helping the students obtain admission to the universities. Members of the second group attended schools that provided an education with a more "practical" bias. It was possible for students in both groups to obtain admission to the universities if they passed major exams at age 16 and 18. However, the reality was that almost all members of the second group did not even attempt to go to a university.

Understandably, the "eleven plus" exam became very important in the minds of children and parents alike and often dictated where a family would choose to live. Schools with a reputation for high pass rates became very popular, and their surrounding neighborhoods tended to prosper. This is no longer the case, because these exams no longer exist: Many children attend American-style "comprehensive" schools for children of all abilities. Consequently, more young people have the opportunity to attend a university. The class system prevails, however, and even the newer "open university" that was created to give adults the chance to go back to school (and that has no formal entry requirements) and "red brick" universities do not attract as many working-class applicants as originally expected. This may be because of a lack of perceived need to further their education among working-class citizens. It is not currently necessary in working-class jobs to have a degree to get ahead, and going to school at night after working all day is not very appealing.

Just as grammar schools existed for the minority who were judged to be academically able, "public schools" (which Americans would refer to as "private") have existed for children of the financially able or those able to win scholarships. These were often founded by trades organizations—for example, the Merchant Taylors' boys school in London and both girls' and boys' schools founded by the Worshipful Company of Haberdashers. Others, including Harrow and Eton, are well-known and provide more than their share of entrants to the prestigious Oxford and Cambridge universities. The reputation of the school attended accompanies one through later life, and the more prestigious it is, the more doors it opens. These more prestigious schools often have ties or scarves with certain colors or patterns. Wearing them is considered an earned honor, and it would be a major faux pas to wear a tie or scarf to which one is not entitled.

Although there has long been a strong connection between church and state, outside Northern Ireland religion plays little part in the everyday lives of the British. Even though Henry VIII declared himself the equivalent of the pope when he created the Church of England, 35% of Britons claim to have no religion, which is the second highest number in Europe (after the Netherlands). The rest of the population, if pressed, would probably say that they are "C of E" (Church of England, or Anglican). The church services generally do not inspire enthusiasm, being rather serious.

Just as the mortar holds the solid British house together, so the socialization processes, class distinctions, and educational system described above represent the floor plan or design of the traditional British house. It is within this framework that the British people live, work, and play. But once any house has been built, people live in it in their own way. We will now look at some of the dimensions of British everyday life, such as work habits, etiquette, humor, social customs, and leisure activities.

Being British:
Living in the Brick House

Most travelers expect to find the British stuffy and starched. Indeed, that is one side of the coin: The gentleman wearing pinstripes and a bowler hat, carrying a furled umbrella, greeting another with "I say, old chap" and the like; and the oh-so-proper lady shopping at Harrods and having afternoon tea with dainty little cups and rich pastries. Flip the coin, however, and you may find orange- and green-haired punks with spike hairdos and other less noticeable eccentrics.

Further, you may offend the Scottish (or Scots) or the Welsh if you do not respect their differences. Many of the variances appear superficial, such as food preferences and specialties, but others are more substantial. For instance, Scotland has its own legal and educational system that is patterned after the German system (see Chapter 4), and Wales finds its identity in its own language.

Despite this wide spectrum, the British are considered a relatively homogeneous group of people. We will focus here on the similarities between them, not their differences. For instance, they all share the same constantly wet weather. The benefit of this is that it produces some of the lushest, greenest land in the world. Perhaps to enjoy this aspect of life, the Scottish invented the game of golf and still have some of the most desirable courses in the world.

Maybe this is what the British mean by "making the best of a bad lot." If things go wrong (or the weather happens to be lousy), the right thing to do is to make the best of it. This will be admired. The British tend to think highly of anyone who suffers setbacks and perseveres; whether success comes is less important.

Captain Scott of the Antarctic epitomized this, being beaten in the race to the South Pole by Roald Amundsen and dying in the attempt. The important thing was that he did the right and traditional thing, conducting a proper scientific expedition while his opponent really did not play fair, organizing his trip thoroughly and efficiently with the sole aim of reaching the pole first. As Anthony Glyn (1970, p. 29) said in his book *The British* in the chapter entitled "The Cult of the Loser," "Captain Scott of the Antarctic . . . had many problems to face, but public image was not one of them. It is hard to imagine a more perfect British hero."

"It is not whether you win or lose that is important, but how you play the game." The British really mean this and will even applaud the opponent for making a good play in a cricket match. Another expression in Britain is that "it's just not cricket" when something is handled unfairly. It is true that draws (ties) are quite acceptable and sometimes preferable in soccer and cricket matches. This is something that is totally disheartening and very rare in the United States, where the rules are often such that tie-breaking is essential. Also, the British heart tends to go to the underdog, the player who is in a lost and hopeless position such as that of the man playing for a draw in cricket, who must stay at his post until the close of play to deny the opponents their victory.

Whereas cricket tends to be a middle- and upper-class sport and very popular in public schools, soccer (called *football* in Britain) is a working-class sport. And, just as elite public schools, clubs, and universities have their own scarves or ties associated with them that are earned and worn with pride, scarves are available in soccer teams' colors. These may not be earned, but they can be seen trailing from car windows on Saturdays as enthusiastic fans travel to watch "away" matches. These same scarves are held aloft at the match in the stands as the crowd sways and chants in support of its players.

Regarding sports as a leisure activity, the British tend to be keener spectators than active participants. They invented many of the sports the world plays today: soccer, golf, tennis, badminton, and rugby. Indeed, the all-American sport of baseball is based on the old British city game of rounders. The British tend to be loyal fans and as sport mad as the Americans. They talk about it, read about it, gamble on it, and turn out in the worst weather to watch their local teams.

One major difference is that the British do not appreciate individuals who stand out; they prefer a well-trained team that works together in sportsmanlike fashion (Glyn, 1970). Glyn also notes that when games reach the international level, the British tend to lose interest; when things get that big and remote, the spirit of playing for pleasure is compromised. Perhaps this is why their international performance has been less than stellar.

Those who have the financial resources spend much of their leisure time "in the country." It is considered the utmost luxury to have a house in the country, and most Britons yearn for this. In the smallest towns and villages throughout Britain, houses may still be addressed by their "names" instead of street numbers. These names are usually descriptive and may include the name of the original owner: for example, Hawthorne's End or Cadbury's Cottage. This is a quaint carryover from the days when people referred to addresses this way and streets were unpaved and unnamed.

An important leisure priority for the British is a respect for nature in the form of the countryside and gardens. The British generally like to walk, sometimes around the block, but in a garden or country setting is better. Another way of getting close to nature is to create your own garden. However modest the patch of ground in front or back of the brick house, there is another traditional element—the English garden. It is not called a *yard*, which signifies a dusty concrete patch like a schoolyard, but *garden*, which implies flowers and grass. The British are renowned for beautiful gardens, which may be elaborate or small but usually consist of a patch of lawn surrounded symmetrically by colorful flowers and shrubs. Of course, these gardens do not suffer from lack of water and tend to be wonderfully lush.

The quintessential British leisure activity is afternoon tea. The tea time ritual is an important part of British existence; this indispensable drink restores the tired, consoles the weary, stimulates the exhausted, relaxes the anxious, warms the cold, encourages the appetite, and refreshes the thirsty.

Most Britons (like most Americans) start the day with either tea or coffee. Often it takes many cups to get the blood flowing again, but once up there will be more tea to keep the blood pumping. Tea may be a part of any meal. The usual way to take tea is with milk and sugar, and it is often accompanied by cakes or scones. A request for decaffeinated tea would be greeted with a slightly baffled but stern negative reply. Most inquiries about diet drinks or skim milk would be greeted with a laugh or quizzical expression.

The British tend to like their food bland, with no surprises. Lunch tends to be the larger meal, with dinner smaller, but this varies. A typical meal may be fish and "chips" (American french fries), bangers and mash (sausage and mashed potatoes), steak and kidney pie, or macaroni and cheese. The British also have Lord Sandwich to thank for coming up with the idea of putting a piece of meat or spread between two pieces of bread. And, in Britain, that is exactly what you will get—one, or at most two, pieces of meat between two slices of bread. Just as the traditional British house is built to please most of the people most of the time, so too British food is centered around being not too exotic for most people.

Ceremonies and holidays offer an interesting example of how the past-oriented British hold on to age-old attitudes and traditions. A large proportion of Britain's oldest surviving customs come from towns and cities and are bound with a long and complex history (Kightly, 1986). The celebrations are widespread; there are more than

7,000 fairs annually, and each village has a yearly festival celebrating the day of the patron saint to whom its parish church is dedicated. Founders' days are common as well, with institutions such as schools, hospitals, and alms houses honoring their benefactors annually. Such celebrations reinforce the same conservative traditions that the British house embodies.

One favorite tradition is Guy Fawke's Day, which is recognized each November 5 and is dedicated in memory of the fate of a traitor who tried to blow up the houses of Parliament. Bonfires are set, a straw doll symbolizing Fawkes is set atop it, and spectators cheer as it burns to ashes. At a Guy Fawkes bonfire, people chant the rather morbid poem, "Penny for the Guy, poke him in the eye, stick him in the fireplace and watch him die."

British humor seems to run the spectrum of possibilities. Despite their well-recognized reserve, the British have a basic aversion to seriousness and prefer to lighten most events with humor. On the one hand, there is the dry, satirical humor that one would associate with Noel Coward. At the other end of the spectrum, the British love the broadest slapstick, replete with rude jokes and outrageous behavior, such as in *The Benny Hill Show* and *Monty Python*. Even in dignified settings, such as the Parliament, high-spirited bantering finds its way into many otherwise dull negotiations. In one celebrated instance, an MP had to apologize to Parliament after its members voted that he must retract the statement "Half the members of Parliament are asses." He apologized by saying, "Half the members of Parliament are not asses," and then sat down. This skillful display of biting humor disarmed his adversaries.

Perhaps this love of humor comes directly from the British culture, in which a direct display of feelings is suppressed. Humor distracts from embarrassing or tense situations that might otherwise be difficult for Britons to handle. Just as the windows in a traditional home bring in light and fresh air, humor changes the atmosphere and relieves tensions.

In social and business situations alike, one should be right on time or up to several minutes late, but never early! The British institutionalized the idea of being "fashionably late"—usually interpreted as being 10 to 20 minutes late. If the British arrive early for an appointment, they will often wait in their cars or outside until the agreed-upon time.

The old notion of the British being unable to relate to another unless properly introduced by a third party is out of date. Increasing informality in this area is becoming more common, but British reserve may still shine through, giving the impression of coolness or indifference. Nevertheless, first names are used almost immediately in business and social situations among people of the same level. People of much lower business or social status usually will address their superiors by an appropriate title and surname. In some cases, men may be heard calling one another by their last names only, but this is simply a carryover from public school days and need not be imitated.

The phrase "How do you do?" is a very common greeting in Britain. It is not an inquiry, and it expects the same response and nothing more. To avoid sounding obviously American, say "Hello," not "Hi." Also, the British think the phrase "Have a nice day" on leaving someone is strange and a form of command. The British tend to be more circumspect in their conversations than do others. They avoid being direct for fear of offending someone. In fact, they often phrase definite statements as questions. For instance, they may say, "It gets dark in the evening, doesn't it?" No one is expected to answer the question.

Politeness and modesty are the hallmarks of the British in social conversation. Do not be surprised if, after giving a long recourse into the history of Poland to a new acquaintance, you find out much later that he or she is an expert scholar in this area. It would be impolite and immodest for the person to point that out to you at the time. Most likely you will have to learn these facts from another mutual acquaintance.

In all forms of communication, whether oral or written, subtlety, imprecision, and vagueness are typical. Exact facts and figures are avoided. Anyone can find obvious examples of this in the local newspapers, where trends are expressed in "more or less," but not answering the question, "How much more or less?" Such exacting details are seen as trivial, unnecessary, and somewhat distasteful.

Britons' view of work tends to be pragmatic. They are against regulations and prefer "muddling through," which usually results in finding the most expedient rather than the most innovative solutions. The French, who prefer to emphasize pure theory, sometimes experience difficulty understanding this muddling through perspective that their more empirically inclined British counterparts manifest. Further, in Hofstede's (1980a) cross-cultural study of 40 nations, the British clustered with those countries that seek to avoid uncertainty. Perhaps, as is evident in their legal proceedings, that is because they prefer to use tradition, precedent, and common sense to solve problems and have little need for drawn-out rules and regulations.

Paradoxically, the average Briton will obey any rules that are spelled out or stated in exacting detail. Their strong sense of order and tradition dictates that they do what is right as indicated by written instructions and legal signs. Unlike many other countries where rules and laws may or may not be obeyed depending on the circumstances, it is a common sight in Britain to see lines of people and cars waiting patiently in a way that would make members of other more hurried and anxious cultures cringe. It is understandable, then, that the British would shy away from having too many rules and written laws because they would tend to obey them strictly.

Most Britons prefer to work for other people rather than themselves. Only some 10% are self-employed. Overall, in the business environment there is more formality between different levels in the hierarchy, which is more rigid than in the United States, and formality in dealings between employee and superior is greater. Adler (1991) gave an example of an American executive who went to London to manage his company's English office. He noted with annoyance that visitors had to go through several people—the receptionist, the secretary, and the office manager—before seeing him. The English explained that this was usual procedure, and without it the executive's status would be compromised.

Similarly, Laurent (1983) studied diversity in concepts of management among businesspeople in 12 Western countries. Twice as many British as American managers felt that hierarchical structures exist so that everyone knows who has authority over whom, and twice as many thought that there was an authority crisis. The British were also more in favor of well-defined job descriptions, roles, and functions. This is consistent with living in the traditional British house, with its floor plan divided into many small rooms, each with a designated purpose.

Much as one can tell something about class and status from the size of someone's home, the company car is the most obvious symbol of rank within a company. It is a widespread "perk" used to avoid taxes, and thus, three quarters of new cars are bought by companies. Although the company fleet is usually of the same make, the cars are awarded based on their various options. The larger the car and the more the options, the higher the rank of its recipient. Of course, a chauffeur is a sign of absolute seniority (Mole, 1991).

Forty-seven percent of employees are trade union members as opposed to some 16% in the United States. The relationship between unions and management is generally adversarial, often resulting in strikes, some of which paralyze the country. Negotiations revolve around pay and conditions for the workers as opposed to long-term collaboration to ensure company success.

The most important abilities of managers are seen as conducting meetings efficiently and having good relations with subordinates. It is a convention that instructions should be disguised as polite requests. Combined with British reserve, this makes for a distant relationship in which both sides are constantly on their guard. Fairness is the most important arbiter of management style.

In general, meetings are a significant part of the workday in Britain. Business decisions are typically made jointly and usually discussed, ratified, or implemented at a meeting. These meetings are generally informal, beginning and ending with social conversation, and individuals are expected to make a contribution, even if it is only in the form of questions. Ideas and opinions are normally encouraged, but their value to the group depends heavily on the status or seniority of the person stating them.

In addition, Hofstede's (1980a) study points out that the British accept only small power distances between individuals and that all people should have equal rights. However, because there is a great emphasis on status and deference, subordinates are fairly comfortable being told what to do and are less likely to think of questioning an order from a superior of any type than are their American counterparts. For example, few people would consider questioning a doctor's advice or a teacher's wisdom.

Although the British are seen as being more individualistic than collectivist in Hofstede's study, "individualism" in the British sense tends to find its form in eccentricity and nonconformism rather than self-initiative and competition. They also are often uncomfortable and unwilling to take a stand unless they know that the group consensus will support them. A concern to avoid disharmony among group members will smooth over all but the most fundamental disagreement. For this reason, even as consumers, Britons will frequently accept indifferent treatment from businesses with little complaint. If a customer does complain, the response will quite likely bring a patient explanation of why the customer is wrong and how the business's actions are justified.

Britons also normally prefer to work in the security of a group within an established order with which they can identify. Motivation comes when they see the work as useful to themselves and others and that it strives toward a common goal. The basis of social control in Britain as in most Western nations is persuasion and appeal to the individual's sense of guilt at transgressing social norms and laws.

Indeed, this works particularly well in Britain because of the strong sense of tradition, the right way to do things, and "not letting the side down."

Most British will identify hard work, education, ambition, ability, and knowing the right people as the methods used in getting ahead. However, these factors often must be accompanied by regular company moves to achieve successful results. This is because of the fact that in many organizations, one must still wait for a higher-up to be promoted, move on, or pass away to make space for an employee promotion.

Women make up 45% of the workforce in Britain, which is much higher than in other European countries despite low maternity benefits and little or no child-care support. Economic necessities have driven women into the workforce. Because they are paid less than men and many are willing to work part-time, companies are happy to have them. Do not expect to find a significant number of them in the higher levels of management or in technical careers. However, one of Britain's strongest leaders in modern history, Margaret Thatcher, was a woman who was known throughout the world as the "Iron Lady." Women who find themselves in positions of authority can and do demand respect.

Speaking of respect, no one draws more than Queen Elizabeth. There is a magical and mystical quality about the royal family, especially the queen, that makes one stop and take notice. As might be expected in a tradition-bound society, the most glamorous and somber events involve royal processions. The queen's coronation was complete with decorative pomp and pageantry, the ritualistic anointment with oil and crowning.

More recently, however, the scandal pages and gossip newspapers have been captivated by the less noble actions of various members of the royal family. This is nothing new, because throughout the history of the royals (or any family so unrelentingly examined), there have been some demonstrations of less-than-perfect behavior. However, in a democratic society, it is also no surprise to find that there is a constant questioning of the necessity and future of the monarchy: Should the throne continue to exist? Should they pay taxes? And so on. In answer to these charges, one must remember that the queen embodies notions of history, tradition, civility, and national pride, and one third of Britons still dream of meeting her (Michon, 1992).

The royal family and the tradition of the monarchy are held very dearly in the hearts and minds of the British people, and the queen and her nobility are constant reminders of the brilliant past of the

British empire, the worldwide respect and awe afforded the nation throughout the world, and the hope and dignity of the future.

This concludes our discussion of the British. As it suggests, Britons tend to be steadfast and traditional in orientation, and the traditional British brick house is an apt metaphor for understanding the country and its people. Change does not come rapidly, and it must not do violence to the traditional, favored ways of the past. Because of this, there is a strong coherence among the people to a set of cultural values that are uniquely British, which have served them well in the past, and which—with modification—should help them adapt successfully to a rapidly changing world.

3

The Italian Opera

With a population of approximately 58 million, Italy is about the size of Florida, although less fertile and with fewer natural resources. The country is divided into two main regions. *Continental Italy* consists of the Alps and the Northern Italian Plain, whereas *Mediterranean Italy* encompasses the Italian peninsula and islands. The Appenine mountains run directly down the peninsula's center, and its northern range almost completely cuts off North from South. This geographical division has led to extreme regionalism, and many Italians view Italy as two separate nations: the wealthier industrial North and the poorer, more agrarian South.

Italy has been historically victimized by overwhelming natural disasters: volcanoes, floods, famines, and earthquakes. As a result, Italy exudes an aura of "precariousness" (Haycraft, 1985). Italians tend to accept insecurity as a fact of life. This acceptance may explain why they seem to be able to enjoy life more for the moment and are willing to accept events as they happen. Italians tend to feel that if something is going to happen, it will, and that not much can be done about it.

Italy's history is filled with many culturally rich and influential periods, including the Roman Empire and the Renaissance. The country emerged as a nation-state in 1861 as a result of the *Risorgimento* ("revival"), or national unification. Before unification, Italians never quite identified with the many foreign states that conquered and ruled them. This is a possible explanation for Italians' historic contempt for law and taxes. Even though Italians have been overwhelmingly influenced by foreign rule, they have managed to create a culture that is distinctly their own.

To understand Italy it is a good idea to look at opera, that art form Italians invented and raised to its highest level of achievement and that represents most if not all of the major features of Italian culture. The opera is a metaphor for Italy itself: It encompasses music, dramatic action, public spectacle and pageantry, and a sense of fate. It may be tragic or comic, intensely personal or flamboyantly public, with the soloists and chorus expressing themselves through language, gesture, and music, and always through highly skilled acting. A larger-than-life aura surrounds opera, and the audience is vitally engaged in the opera itself, showing great emotion and love toward a singer whose talents are able to express the common feelings that Italians tend to share. Operas and operatic songs reflect the essence of Italian culture and are embraced by Italians with an emotional attachment that less dramatic peoples might find difficult to understand. We thus choose opera as our metaphor to understand Italian culture.

Using this metaphor, we focus on four distinctive characteristics of opera and demonstrate how they illustrate Italian life:

1. the spectacle and pageantry itself and the manner in which the opera-like activities are performed in Italian daily life;
2. the use and importance of voice to express words in a musical fashion;
3. exteriority, which refers specifically to the belief that emotions are so powerful that an individual cannot keep them within and must express them to others; and
4. the importance of both the chorus and the soloists, which reflects the unity of Italian culture (chorus) but also regional variations, particularly between North and South.

Pageantry and Spectacle

On the surface, Italy is a land of pageantry and spectacle: extraordinary animation, vivid colors, expressive faces, revealing gestures, disorder, and loud noise. In public, people chat, whistle, swear, sing, weep, call to one another, and laugh. Pageantry and spectacle play such an important role in Italian life that people and things tend to be judged first and foremost on their appearance.

The surface of Italian life, playful yet bleak and sometimes tragic, has many of the characteristics of a show. First, it is usually moving, entertaining, and unreservedly picturesque. Second, all of its effects are skillfully contrived and graduated to convey a certain message to, and arouse particular emotions in, bystanders. Italians are frequently great dramatic actors, as we might expect of the creators of the opera. Scenes and expressions of sentiments become more elaborate when the public is present. Watch a typical Italian mother play with her baby. If she is alone, she is tender and solicitous like any other mother. As soon as somebody enters the room, she will immediately enact a tasteful impersonation of Mother Love. Similarly, an Italian businessman at a meeting will speak solemnly while checking to see the impression he is making on others (Barzini, 1964).

The first purpose of the show is to make life acceptable and pleasant. This attitude can largely be explained by the circumstances of history, both natural and those caused by humans: four active volcanoes; floods; and earthquakes; as well as continuous invasions by outsiders. All have created a sense of insecurity. Italians tend to make life's dull and insignificant moments exciting and significant by decorating and ritualizing them. Ugly things must be hidden; unpleasant and tragic facts are swept under the carpet whenever possible; and ordinary transactions are embellished to make them more stimulating. This practice of embellishing everyday events was not developed by a people who find life exhilarating but by a realistic group of people who tend to react cautiously because they believe that catastrophes cannot be averted but only mitigated. Italians prefer to glide elegantly over the surface of life and leave the depths unplumbed (Barzini, 1964).

The devices of spectacle do not exist because of the desire to deceive and bedazzle observers. Often, to put on a show becomes the only way to revolt against destiny and to face life's injustices with one of the few weapons available to a brave people: their imagination. To be powerful and rich, of course, is more desirable than to be weak and poor. However, it has always been extremely difficult for Italians, both as a nation and individually, to have both power and wealth.

This eternal search for surface pleasures and distractions is accompanied by *garbo*. Although this term cannot be translated exactly, it is the finesse that Italians use to deal with situations delicately and without offense. Garbo turns Italian life into a work of art. Italians tend to have a distinctly public orientation, are willing to share a lot, and are used to being on stage at all times.

As this description suggests, many Italians wish to portray a certain image to those around them. This is termed *la bella figura*, or the projection of "a confident, knowing, capable face to the world" (Brint, 1989). The importance attached to impressions is shown in the basic document of the Italian Republic, its constitution. In the American Declaration of Independence, the first of the self-evident truths is that all men are created equal. In the Italian constitution, the first basic principle is that "all citizens are invested with equal social dignity" (Levine, 1963). Most Italians would rather sit inside their home than go outside and make a bad impression. For example, Italians tend to leave the city for the seashore or country on holidays whenever possible, and it is said that an Italian who cannot afford the outing may stay home all day behind closed shutters rather than risk injury to his pride by being caught in the city (Levine, 1963).

A large number of Italians pursue la bella figura through material possessions. Giving a good impression—not only with demeanor but also with material wealth—is important. It is not uncommon for an Italian to keep a ski rack on his or her car during the summer months simply to impress the neighbors. One reason for the importance placed on la bella figura is that Italians tend to suffer from a national inferiority complex. This feeling is the product of their small, overcrowded, and scantily endowed land as well as of poverty throughout much of the land. The creation of a show through an eternal search for pleasures and distractions is an attempt to deal with the frightening realities of everyday life.

The Italian reliance on spectacle and garbo helps people solve most of their problems. Spectacle and garbo govern public and private life and shape policy and political designs. They constitute one of the reasons why Italians have excelled in activities in which appearance is predominant. During medieval times, Italian armor was the most beautiful in Europe: It was highly decorated, elegantly shaped, and well designed, but too light and thin to be used in combat. In war, Italians preferred German armor, which was ugly but more practical. Similarly, Rome was made to appear more modern, wealthy, and powerful with the addition of whole cardboard buildings, built like film sets, on the occasion of Hitler's visit in 1938.

Italians believe that "anybody can make an omelette with eggs" and that "only a true genius can make one without" (Barzini, 1964).

For example, warfare during the Renaissance, as it was practiced outside of Italy, consisted of the earnest and bloody clash of vast armies. He who killed more enemies carried the day. But in Italy it was an elegant and practically bloodless pantomime. Highly paid leaders of small companies of armed men staged the outward appearance of armed conflict, decorating the stage with beautiful props, flags, colored tents, horses, and plumes. The action was accompanied by suitable martial music, rolls of drums, heartening songs, and blood-chilling cries. The armies convincingly maneuvered their few men back and forth, pursued one another across vast provinces, and conquered one another's fortresses. However, victory was decided by secret negotiations and bribes. It was, after all, a very civilized and entertaining way of waging war. Although this approach often left matters as undecided as warfare elsewhere, it cost less in money, human lives, and suffering.

The operatic pageantry of Italian life also occurs in the rituals of the Catholic church. Italians prize these rituals for their pageantry, spectacle, and value in fostering family celebrations rather than for their religious significance. Many Italians view the church much like the opera: as a source of drama and ritual, but not authority. Although they do not attend church regularly, the church still exerts a strong cultural and social influence on their behavior, and almost all Italians identify themselves as Catholics.

Furthermore, the spectacle of Italian life is quite apparent in the area of communications. Italians tend to be skilled conversationalists. Conversations are easily followed by onlookers from a distance, for emotions on an Italian's face are read as easily as large-print words on a poster. Reading facial expressions is learned in childhood and is perhaps as important to an individual's survival as the art of reading print. Similarly, one can understand many of the actions that take place in an opera without fully understanding what the actors are singing.

Although Italians tend to be emotional and dramatic, decisions are influenced less by sentiments, tastes, hazards, or hopes than by a careful evaluation of the relative strength of the contending parties. This is one of the reasons why, when negotiating even the smallest deal, Italians prefer to look each other in the face. They read the opponent's expression to gauge his or her position and can thus decide when it is safe to increase demands, when to stand pat, and when to retreat.

Precision instruments such as speedometers and clocks are sometimes set incorrectly in Italy so as to increase the feeling of pageantry.

To give drivers a sense of pride in their driving skill, car speedometers may show a figure that is between 10% and 20% above the actual speed. Clocks in railway stations tend to be fast to encourage travelers to quicken their step. On the other hand, electric clocks on trains are often a few minutes slow to give the illusion of arriving on or ahead of time.

Transparent deceptions are used to give each person the feeling that he or she is a unique specimen of humanity and worthy of special consideration. Let an Italian simply shake hands with a prominent person, and he or she may claim the eminent one as a personal friend. Italians consider it a duty to cultivate this illusion not only for their fellow humans but also for themselves. In Italy, few confess to being "average." Instead, they persuade themselves that they are "one of the gods' favored sons" (Barzini, 1964).

The operatic Italians must always project a capable face to the world. Therefore, they prefer to engage only in work that will create the image of confidence and intelligence. In Italy, a middle-class person tends to work only when he or she has a profession, not while in high school or the university. In fact, many lower-level jobs such as waiting on tables are full-time in nature and not readily available to students. In the universities, students specialize immediately in their first year and do not dabble, as is the custom in the United States. However, there is no set term for most university careers—for example, four years devoted to undergraduate work and three years to law school—so many Italians spend more time in school than do their American counterparts.

Pageantry and spectacle also apply to business negotiations. When presenting ideas during such negotiations, a manager should ensure that the aesthetics of the presentation should be clear and exact; he or she should demonstrate a mastery of detail and language and be well organized. Polish and elegance count for a great deal. It is important for most if not all presentations to have the feeling of pageantry and spectacle. However, although pageantry is important in negotiations, Italians also tend to expect good faith bargaining.

Most Italians feel that it is infinitely better to be rich than to seem rich. But if an individual or a nation does not have the natural resources necessary to conquer and amass wealth, what is one to do? The art of appearing rich has been cultivated in Italy as nowhere else. Little provincial towns boast immense princely palaces, castles, and stately opera houses. Residents of some small coastal villages have completed elaborate paintings on the rocks that can be seen from the sea to give the illusion of wealth and prosperity. In spite of economic difficulties, many Italians wear good clothes, drive shining cars, and dine at expensive restaurants. However, some of these people own little more than the clothes on their back or the money needed to pay for the expensive meal. Decoration and embellishment are important so that the realities of poverty, uncertainty, and a scantily endowed land can be changed into a spectacle of illusion.

The pageantry of Italian life is highlighted by its lack of rigid social hierarchy. There is no permanent and rigid class structure in Italy. Rather, there are conditions on which a person is judged. These include occupation and the amount of authority a person has in that role, education, ancestry, and, in most instances, wealth. However, the major focus is placed on social behavior. Italians term this focus *civilità*, or the extent to which someone is acculturated to the norms of the area (Keefe, 1977). These norms include styles of dress, manners, and even participation in the local community.

Position in the social hierarchy can be clearly judged by the amount of respect shown to a person and his or her family by members of the community. However, respect is also associated with age and family position. A younger person will almost always show deference to older people, just as children show respect for parents.

Class consciousness and the social hierarchy will inevitably change as a result of industrialization, massive migration to urban areas, low birthrates, an aging population, and the so-called Americanization of Italian youth. However, certain titles still command much respect. These include doctor, lawyer, and professor. Many people feel honored to speak or have affiliations with someone holding such a title and will refer to him or her in a respectful, subordinate manner. For example, Italians rarely become impatient in a physician's waiting room because of their respect. Within a local Southern community, the title *Don* is given to the man for whom the people have the most respect.

One final example of pageantry is appropriate, especially because it shows how certain other cultures are similar to Italy (see Chapter 9). Once a year in every village and city there is a celebration in honor of its *santo patrono* (patron saint) in which a parade is featured. The statue of the saint is placed in the lead position in the parade, followed by the clergy, members of the upper classes, and then all other citizens. A celebration follows in the piazza or town center. This traditional festival and parade help to strengthen the feeling of solidarity and permit people to escape from the regular routine in a dramatic, spectacular, and fun-filled manner.

The reliance on spectacle must be clearly grasped if one wants to understand Italians. Spectacle helps people solve most of their problems and governs public and private life. It is one reason why Italians have always excelled in activities in which impressions are important: architecture, decoration, landscape gardening, opera, fashions, and cinema.

Voice

Italians tend to believe that their language is the most beautiful in the world. Much of the beauty of the Italian language derives from its higher proportion of vowels to consonants than in most languages, which gives it a musical effect. Italians place great emotion in their language, speaking with passion, rhythm, and changing tonality. It is the quality of the way people speak that is of utmost importance, and this bias is replicated in opera in that there are several strikingly different types of voice registers such as the soprano and the bass. And, like the opera, the sound and cadence of the communication play a role at least equal to the content of what is said in getting the message across. Italians are often much more interested in engaging and entertaining their listeners than in conveying their thoughts accurately.

In Italy, few people whisper, because everyone assumes that people are eager to hear the sound of their voice. Italians tend to talk louder than many other nationalities. At meetings or informal gatherings, individuals talk simultaneously and often shout without realizing that they have raised their voices. Stories are told with passion, anger, and joy. The air in Italy is filled with so many voices that one must frequently talk in a very loud voice to be understood, thereby increasing the total uproar.

Oral communication in Italy is something of a show itself. Speaking is punctuated by elaborate gestures, benefiting Italian operatic tradition. Whatever the section of the country, Italians talk with their hands. Quick, agile, expressive movements of hands, arms, and shoulders contribute emphasis and sincerity to spoken words and facial expressions. For instance, a man thinking about buying fish in a market empties his imaginary waist pocket when he is told the price, and walks away without a word (Willey, 1984).

However, the gestures are not, as many believe, unrealistically exaggerated. In fact, the gestures are so realistic that they may be unapparent. The acting of opera singers, directly derived from the Italian's natural mimicry, contributes to the erroneous impression of excessive exaggeration. In reality, Italian gestures are based on natural and instinctive movements and can therefore be understood by the inexperienced at first sight.

In addition to gestures, Italians sometimes use flattery and polite lies to make life decorous and agreeable. The purpose is to reduce the turbulence of day-to-day living and to make life more acceptable. Flattery somehow makes the wariest of men feel bigger and more confident, similar to the larger-than-life opera singer. This perspective accounts for the fact that Italians sometimes make promises they know they cannot fulfill. Small lies can be justified if they give pleasure, provoke emotion, or prove a point. This applies not only to the businessman who swears with soulful eyes that he will deliver his product on a certain day (and does so a month later) but also to men of government cabinet rank. Ministers will promise an appointment, will confirm and reconfirm it, but on the appointed day find an excuse for evading it. Casualness toward promises is part of accepted Italian behavior.

Contentiousness is generally not far below the surface of the Italian personality. This argumentativeness surprises many because it is discordant with the usual Italian demeanor. Yet the accusatory words shouted by offended drivers, the sidewalk conversations that often sound like arguments, and the tedious monologues by Italians reciting some imagined wrong they have suffered testify to their argumentative side. For most Italians, controversy is a hobby or sport, something in which Italians take immense pleasure (Levine, 1963).

Argumentativeness also will be displayed in the business environment when an employee bypasses his boss in the hierarchical line of work relationships. Most Italian managers believe that frequent bypassing indicates a poorly designed organization. Many Italians respond to this bypassing by reprimanding the employee or redesigning the reporting structure. The operatic Italians normally handle these types of incidents in a dramatic and emotional manner.

Italians are frequently portrayed as joyful people with an operatic song on their lips. This is not completely true. They can also be rather somber. This dark side is emphasized through humor that is more insulting than witty. Humor generally implies the ability to detach oneself from the object of wit. However, Italians tend to be passionate people who easily identify with what they are talking about.

Italians make up for this type of humor by analyzing everything around them through conversation. Talking is a great pastime for most Italians, who frequently meet in cafés to discuss the latest news. Privacy is usually lacking in any Italian community, even though Italians say they mind their own business. Unlike the reserved English citizen, the Italian is apt to tell an acquaintance of half an hour's standing all about his financial status, his family's health problems, and details of his current emotional attachments. The Italian love of conversation as a pastime usually limits the chances of something secret staying so for long, and it is this love of conversation (and voice) that is intimately related to exteriority, the third characteristic of the opera.

Exteriority

Exteriority refers specifically to the fact that feelings and emotions are so overwhelming that the individual cannot keep them to him- or herself but must express them to others. It also refers to the assumption that the event is more important than the actions of one individual, which is consistent with the Italian reaction to catastrophes and uncertainty described previously. The drama is of more significance to the viewers or community than to the individuals because of its symbolism and generality. This pattern of behavior is the opposite of that of the Anglo-Saxon, which emphasizes that a person should control emotions and not express them or, as the British say, keep a stiff upper lip (see Chapter 2). At Italian funerals, for instance, there is no shame in showing emotions, and both women and men cry openly and profusely to express what they feel. Some people even tear their hair out, whereas others jump on the coffin as it lies in the open grave. Such behavior is viewed as both acceptable and normal. Similarly, a major victory such as the World Cup championship that Italy won in 1982 is accompanied by excessive noise, large gatherings in piazzas, and communal festivities at which everyone talks excitedly and simultaneously. Although there will be some drinking, Italians do not tend to emphasize this aspect of victory as much as do Britons and Americans. However, if they lose, Italians tend to become subdued and mournful and will leave for home.

Given their emphasis on exteriority, it is generally not wise to ask Italians, "How do you feel?" Unlike Anglo-Saxons, who will usually give a cursory reply, Italians will describe in detail all of their aches and pains, what the doctors have prescribed for them, and even the most intimate details of any operations they have experienced.

Italians' excessive facility to express emotions is, strangely enough, a drawback for Italian actors. Perhaps because they are too richly endowed by nature, they may have more natural gifts and talent than necessary. Many Italian actors spend years trying to unlearn what their foreign counterparts have to learn—that is, how to express emotions. Orson Welles once observed that "Italy is full of actors, fifty million of them, in fact, and they are almost all good; there are only a few bad ones, and they are on the stage" (Barzini, 1964).

Because of the importance of drama in everyday life, Italians value the piazza as the center of every town and village. It is the stage on which people gather to share conversation and relate experiences. The actions that take place in the piazza are minor dramas of Italian life. Most people do not schedule meetings with others, but everyone knows that gatherings will occur at regular times at the piazza, usually around noon and at 5 p.m. or 6 p.m. after work, and it is easy to see old friends and acquaintances and make new ones. This pattern of strolling (*fare la passeggiata*) is in sharp contrast to the German *Spaziergang*, which occurs primarily on Sunday afternoons. Even in Italian cities where there is no central piazza, it is well-known that certain avenues serve as substitutes for them, and the village-like behavior is replicated along them. On these avenues there are many outdoor cafés at which people meet and greet one another, and sometimes there are even small open air areas with benches that are miniature replicas of the village piazza.

Italians tend to be great spectators of life. The show at the piazza can be so engrossing that many people spend most of their lives just looking at it. There are usually café tables strategically placed in such a way that nothing of importance will escape the leisurely drinker of espresso. A remarkable result of this pastime occurred when an old woman died at her window and three days passed before any of her neighbors thought that something might be wrong with the immobile figure.

Foreigners are frequently impressed by the fact that many Italians seem to be doing their jobs with wholehearted dedication and enthusiasm. This does not mean that these Italians do everything with efficiency, speed, and thoroughness. Rather, they frequently complete their jobs with visible pleasure, as if work were not human punishment. However, when visitors look closely at Italians' actions, they realize that many Italians have a theatrical quality that enhances but slightly distorts their actions.

In opera, the best example of exteriorization is the crowd scene. There are so many crowd scenes in Italian opera that some writers have identified them as one of its essential characteristics. Members of the crowd represent the chorus for the lead singers, and there is a dynamic interplay between the lead singers and the chorus. This interplay is analogous to the behavioral dynamics in a small village in which there is a problem and everyone will comment on it in the piazza.

There is no private life for most Italians. Everything of importance occurs in public or is at least discussed in public. There is no word for "privacy" in the Italian language, and information is widely shared. There are certain regional differences: Northern Italians tend to be more reserved than Southern Italians. However, once a person is perceived to be a member of the community, it is assumed that he or she will exteriorize when in public.

Business confidentiality can be a problem in Italy. Everyone discusses secret business negotiations with both friends and family as well as the press. Therefore, leaks are common for most large business deals. The media in Italy are volatile and speculation-prone because of people's interest in their neighbors' activities. That journalists accompany union members into negotiations with management shows that nothing is sacred in Italy, not even intricate labor negotiations. Even ordinary business dramas become theater for a large audience of spectators.

We have already indicated that dressing is important to Italians, because it represents pageantry and spectacle in the form of la bella figura. Dressing is also an aspect of exteriority, an outward expression of the emotions that Italians feel and want to convey. Italians dress differently in public than at home at least in part because of this. In the business environment, clothing is well tailored and sophisticated. Through their clothing, Italians exteriorize the feeling of confidence.

Many aspects of daily life yield endless opportunities for drama. A well-known example of exteriority is Italian driving behavior. In the larger cities such as Rome and Naples, the drivers blow their horns impatiently, swear at one another, gesture colorfully, and drive in a dramatic and seemingly reckless manner. To an Italian, such behavior is normal because it allows him or her to communicate with others even when behind the wheel. Even when two drivers get out of their cars to confront one another, they rarely come to blows, although their gestures, body movements, shouts, and torrents of words would lead the onlooker to the conclusion that blood will be spilled. The drama of the occasion is what gives Italians emotional satisfaction.

Even politics takes a dramatic and entertaining edge, especially during elections. Television coverage of such events is said to have something of a carnival atmosphere (Brint, 1989). Such an atmosphere reflects the Italian penchant for pageantry, voice, and exteriorization.

And, even though the Italian political system is changing radically (discussed below), such drama probably will continue to be part of the political process.

Feelings and emotions are expressed not only through direct communications but also through subtleties in Italian culture. The Italian history of natural disasters and foreign invasions has created a fear of the unpredictable. This fear can be detected behind Italians' peculiar passion for geometric patterns and symmetry that can be easily destroyed (Barzini, 1964).

Weddings are considered the highlights of life and constitute an excellent example of exteriorized behavior. In fact, the wedding scene is quite common in Italian opera. Italians often save for a lifetime to marry a daughter off in an appropriate manner. Guest lists frequently include the entire village. The wedding ritual is often something of a miniopera, beginning with the bridal party traveling in open automobiles to the church, with relatives and friends following. After the ceremony, the bride is pelted with confetti by her cheering friends and family. The success of the wedding ritual is judged by the number of cars, the size of the crowd, and the feast served. Parents are content to spend years of savings and even go into debt to correctly carry out the social obligations of a society that may, in the eyes of outsiders, be living at a subsistence level but that carries on ancient traditions with real satisfaction (Willey, 1984). Throughout the wedding ritual, the emotions of sadness and joy are expressed by all. It is not uncommon for both the bride and her father to be crying while walking down the church isle.

The family and the extended kinship group are the basic building blocks for exteriorization. Familial relationships tend to be close and emotional, and the behaviors found in the piazza are replicated within the family. The family is generally seen as one's greatest resource and protection against all troubles. For example, children are critically important, and normally everything is done for them, even to the extent of satisfying their smallest wishes. Parents often go without comforts to pamper their children and to see that they go to school and reach a higher rung on the social ladder. This attitude can be directly linked to the constant influx of foreigners who compete with Italians for jobs, rapidly changing governments, and the overwhelming natural disasters that have characterized Italian history. Of course, exteriorization plays a part in this support, because the family views its children as public expressions of its values and lifestyles.

Further, family connections are often extremely important for handling problems and getting ahead. Outside the family, official and legal authority is frequently considered hostile until proven otherwise. Closeness within the family is transferred to outside relationships and brings a personal edge to most social interactions. This helps to explain why Italians are so demonstrative and why men feel almost no hesitation to show affection to one another.

In the Italian business environment, family contacts tend to be necessary to run a successful company. An example of the importance of contacts is the general lack of hiring policies. Hiring is usually accomplished through personal connections and recommendations. Many corporations select a person not on the basis of his or her skills, but on the basis of their relationship with that person or his or her family.

The family remains the center and stronghold of Italian life, despite all modern trends, where the role of each member is understood and performed as elaborately as any Italian opera. Although men are the official leaders of the families, and women are subordinate to them, the reality of family life is much more complex. The main character in the family, who might be compared to the lead tenor, is the father. He is in charge of the family's general affairs. But although he holds center stage, his wife is an equally important figure, like the lead soprano. Although the Italian father is the head of the family, the mother is its heart. Although yielding authority to the father, she traditionally assumes total control of the family's emotional realm. She usually manages the family in a subtle, almost imperceptible way; she soothes the father's feelings while avoiding open conflicts. However, the woman of the house generally has the last unspoken word. The factors that determine the strength of the family are placed in the hands of women. Wives engineer appropriate and convenient marriages, keep track of distant relations, and see to it that everybody does the suitable thing, not for individual happiness, but for the family as a whole. That women form the predominant character of Italian life can be seen through many small signs. For example, popular songs frequently highlight the role of mothers, and in some years there are more songs devoted to her than to romance.

However, Italy tends to be a man's world. When a child is born, the proud parents tie a blue ribbon to the door for a son, but only sometimes do less proud parents of a girl put out a pink ribbon. The principle of male superiority is less strictly enforced in the North than in the South. For example, in Sicilian villages, unmarried women are supposed to sit indoors during the day when unchaperoned.

Divorce and abortion have recently been legalized in Italy. Legal abortion symbolizes the loosening of individual morals and the breaking of the hold of the Catholic church over the family. In 1974, civil divorce became legal, but it seems to be more a symbol of social independence than anything else. Not many marriages have actually ended in divorce, and Italy has a lower percentage of divorce than any other Western European country. For example, in 1987, there were only 18,000 divorces for the total population of more than 58 million. The number of separated couples, however, has increased significantly.

Many Italians view divorce as unacceptable because it chips away at the foundation of the family and entire clans. Others argue that it has not increased in popularity because of the fact that, without a husband, most women would be in dire financial straits. This argument is losing merit as industrialization ushers women into the workforce. Divorce, however, is still viewed seriously. If a man leaves his wife, it is not uncommon for the ex-wife to move in with the husband's family, while he is ostracized.

The family frequently extracts everyone's first loyalty. Italians raise their children to be mutually supportive and to contribute to the family. Separation from the family is generally not desired, expected, or easily accepted. Things that create conflict in Italian families may be sources of celebration in other cultures. Some normally joyful events that may cause operatic sadness are a job promotion that necessitates moving away from the family, acceptance into a prestigious university in a foreign country, and getting married (McGoldrick, 1982). Although these experiences may be sources of personal growth for the individual, they are likely to be experienced negatively if they weaken the collective sense of family.

Many Italians view education and vocational training as secondary to the security, affection, and sense of relatedness the family has to offer. Personal identity tends to be derived primarily from affiliation with the family, not from one's occupation or personal success. One Italian father expressed these thoughts regarding his daughter's university education: "What does she need an education for? I never had an education. She has a family, so what does she need Calculus for?" (McGoldrick, 1982). Learning is a threat to the family system if it means that a young person will be unduly influenced by outside authorities and perhaps leave home to work or study.

Family connections are extremely important for handling problems and getting ahead. Not wanting to work for outsiders, Italians often start their own family business. The business naturally adds to the solidarity of the family. Closeness within the family is transferred to some outside relationships and brings a personal edge to most social interactions. This helps to explain why Italians, like operatic singers, are emotionally passionate toward friends and extended family.

Sex for Italians, especially men, is seen as the essential life force (Newman, 1987). Although honor is a quality all strive to achieve, virility and potency are still the basis on which many men are judged. This is confirmed by the fact that an adulterous wife is considered to be a direct reflection of her husband's manliness. The ideal man is not necessarily intelligent or well off, but of good character and physically and sexually strong.

Most Italians do not put much faith in what others say. Everyone is considered to be an outsider except members of the family. It is not surprising that Italians, living as they have always done with the insecurity and dangers of an unpredictable society, are among those who found their main refuge among their blood relatives. This overall fearful, suspicious attitude may be partially because of a quality on which Italians place high value, namely, cleverness. Because of the constant change and struggle in the country, those who can survive through enterprise, cunning, imagination, and intelligence are held in high esteem by others around them. In other words, those who can create the most imaginative show are admired by many Italians. Minor deceptions, cleverly and subtly executed, are acceptable even if not necessary. Because everyone is trying to outsmart everyone else, the population as a whole is placed on the defensive.

Although the family is the group that above all else dramatically influences the individual, another important group, the political party, can be the difference between employment and unemployment. Italians move from group to group, feeling little remorse when doing so because they tend to be skeptical of all groups besides the family. Members of groups often create powerful coalitions that are used for gaining power and influence. These subcultures, groups, and parties allow for intergroup bargaining and dealing to gain coordination and cooperation between all involved.

Similar to Israel, Italy has had a political system since World War II that encourages the election of representatives from many minor political parties to Parliament. This system was put into place to guard against the rise of one-party rule, as happened under fascism. However, it tended to be extremely inefficient and, worse, corrupt. The worst example of corruption in Italy's history began to take form in 1992 and, as of spring 1993, more than 1,250 major political leaders, presidents of major Italian corporations, Mafia leaders, and at least three former premiers were being investigated or indicted for graft and corruption; several suicides and imprisonments resulted. As a consequence, Italy is beginning to move to a genuine two-party system that is normally associated with much less corruption. Still, the sense of family and coalition behavior is so strong in Italy that we can expect many of the behaviors described in this chapter to persist. For example, we can expect that many job referrals and recommendations will still be based at least in part on family connections—much more so than in the United States.

Exteriority also influences Italians' management style. There is little delegation of authority or effective communication between the different levels of management in most Italian firms. Employees have little say about decisions concerning the company or about their own work. In fact, superiors are very likely to cut off emotionally the ideas and suggestions of subordinates.

One final example of exteriorization is somewhat disturbing, because Italy is experiencing difficulty integrating the large number of legal and illegal immigrants flooding into the country, particularly those from the African nations of Morocco, Nigeria, Senegal, and Tunisia. The poorest Italians are most affected in feeling that these immigrants are taking jobs away from them. There have been disturbing events such as the burning of immigrants and the hanging of a 16-year-old immigrant. Many Italians are upset by this trend and, in true Italian fashion, have exteriorized it dramatically in newspapers, on television, and in the traditional piazza. Although such outbreaks of violence are common in many societies, these Italians are confronting the problem in an open manner involving everyone in the society, and solutions are gradually being implemented.

Exteriority is directly related to the mixing and balancing of diverse elements in both opera and Italian society. Because the entire community or audience is involved in the unfolding of the drama, several issues and factors come into play that involve numerous individuals. It is not an accident that Italians have not specialized in one-person stage shows or dramas. Thus Italy, although primarily stressing individualism, is strongly oriented toward specific aspects of groupism or collectivism. Although individuals might not give the country as a whole much consideration, they place great importance on local and regional affiliation. This is directly related to the next characteristic of the opera: the influence of soloists and the chorus.

Chorus and Soloists

Although a century of unification and decades of migrations have intermingled the Italian people, each region's inhabitants retain certain easily perceptible characteristics. Most Italians define themselves by the town where they were born, and there is a sharp contrast between Northern and Southern Italy. These regional differences are similar to the chorus and the soloists in operas. The soloists represent the regional differences in the culture, whereas the chorus is the embodiment of the overall Italian culture. Even though there are distinct regional differences, most Italians retain the cultural characteristics described above. Even the Northern League, which for years has advocated splitting Italy into North and South, now focuses its attention on fixing the political system and eliminating corruption, because the recent political scandal has involved all parts of the country.

Campanilismo (literally, "bell tower") is the word that expresses the idea of belonging first to a town, second to a region, and third to a nation. It refers to the fact that people do not want to travel so far as to be out of sight of the piazza church steeple.

Because of industrialization, Northern Italians have had the benefit of a thriving economy and a relatively prosperous existence. In contrast, Southern Italians, who have relied on farming for their livelihood, have tended to be poorer and less educated. The people from these two regions are similar in loving life and enjoying the illusion of a show. However, the difference between the people from these two regions is that Southerners tend to cling to the way of living in the past, whereas many Northerners look toward the future.

To most Northerners, wealth is the way to lastingly ensure the defense and prosperity of the family and close friends. Northerners are perpetually trying to acquire wealth in its various forms. They want jobs—good jobs and then better jobs. They also want the scientific and technical knowledge that will ensure better-paid employment and advancement. Most Southerners, on the other hand, want above all to be obeyed, admired, respected, and envied. They also want wealth, but frequently as an instrument to influence people. The Southerner is preoccupied with commanding the respect of the audience throughout the many operas of life. Most Southerners, be they wealthy or poor, want the gratitude of powerful friends and relatives, the fear of their enemies, and the respect of everybody. The Southerner seeks wealth as a means of commanding obedience and respect from others (Barzini, 1964).

In the South, the culture centers around death. Italians worry that the operatic drama of life will fall apart when a family member dies. The experience of dying and the fear of not being able to react properly to such an event has forced Southerners to create a complex strategy to enable them to face and conquer death (Willey, 1984). The strategy encompasses hundreds of beliefs, customs, and rituals. The purpose of these rituals is to reestablish contact between the living and the dead because, according to Southern beliefs, the family includes both the living and the dead. Each family member has reciprocal rights and duties. The dead have to protect the living and the living have to keep alive the memory of the dead; people tend to attach great value to these obligations. Thus in the early 1980s a parish priest in one Calabrian village thought he would discourage the long local funeral processions by levying a special fee per kilometer on the family of the deceased. His bishop promptly transferred him to another part of Italy (Willey, 1984).

This distinction between North and South can be easily found in Italian operas that tend to depict characteristics of various regions. For example, *Cavalleria Rusticana* by Pietro Mascagni represents a classic Southern opera with its emphasis on humble folk, suspicion, and revenge. *Tosca* by Giacomo Puccini, however, emphasizes the North; the opera takes place in elegant urban settings in which important personages display feelings that are more subtle and complex—although no less passionate—than those found among Southerners.

Education has been a major mechanism for bringing about the modernization of Italy and minimizing the regional differences. By diffusing the national culture through the teaching of one Italian language and raising literacy levels, Italians have stressed cultural unity and deemphasized regionalism to a greater degree than in the past. And, as suggested previously, the streamlining of the political system should help to accelerate such trends.

Although many of the differences between the "two Italies" have been defused and minimized through time, business dealings differ in the two regions. Working with people from Northern Italy, a low-context subculture that emphasizes written rules and agreements, is much like dealing with Americans or Germans. To negotiate effectively with Northern Italians essentially means communicating with them in a straightforward and sophisticated manner. Social talk should be kept to a minimum in order to get down to business. When negotiating with people from Southern Italy, a high-context subculture in which oral communication and subtle nuances are stressed, a visitor must spend time establishing rapport with his or her counterparts. Long-term relationships are important to Southern Italians and trust must be built before business dealings become truly effective.

In spite of these subtle differences, most Italians use a collaborative style of negotiating that continues a dialogue until everyone's needs are met. Part of this style results from the emotional nature of many Italians. Communication involves much more than words. The emotional nature of such Italians enables them to see past the words spoken and to the emotions felt. This insight helps them empathize and understand the needs of those with whom they negotiate. Such aggressive yet emotional Italians want to please everyone, including themselves. The collaborative style of negotiating thus is common throughout Italy.

Similar to the operatic importance of both chorus and soloists, the regional Italian differences combined with the overall Italian culture helped Italy gain economic strength during the 1970s and 1980s. This strength of Italy lies in the proliferation of small-scale commercial and industrial enterprises, which usually are family run. People whose families used to be Southern farmers brought their deep-rooted traditions to the North. Some of these traditions and skills enabled many Southerners to convert their families from farming into commercial markets. The tradition of keeping ownership within the family combined with the skills of managing a diverse product mix and willingness to work long hours makes the new entrepreneurs able to compete effectively with their European neighbors (Willey, 1984).

Italy is facing major economic problems, and its public debt is still bigger than its gross national product (GNP); the 1992 federal budget deficit was 11% of the GNP. Some governments in villages and even large towns do not have the money to manage critical services. To maintain a leading role in the European Community, Italy must change this situation.

The characteristics of the chorus and the soloists also can be applied to other aspects of Italian culture. Italians tend to be individualistic people, yet they place importance on the group and, as we have seen, the family is the primary group that influences individuals. Whenever important decisions are made, the individual usually consults with family members to get their opinions and evaluations of the situation. Although the family's opinions are important, the final evaluation is made by the individual. This is similar to the relationship between the chorus and the soloists in the opera. The chorus frequently gives the soloists the facts and opinions about the drama unfolding on stage, yet the soloists are the ones who dramatically decide how to handle the peril or situation.

The influence of the group is also felt in the business environment. In business meetings, people will exteriorize their feelings and opinions about a subject. They will listen to everyone's ideas and freely give their own opinions. Business meetings tend to be very productive in

Italy because of the openness displayed by everyone. However, like the chorus and the soloist, the decisions coming out of a meeting are frequently made by one or two dominant or domineering people. In spite of the influence of the group, Italians tend to be aggressive and materialistic individuals because of their bias toward spectacle and exteriorization.

Further, the vocal sections of the chorus are directly comparable to the many regional variations of the Italian language. Although each section is important to the harmony of the chorus, each has its own melody. The Italian history of invasions has produced many dialects, each the product of the particular regional invader. The language of Italy consists of both local dialects and Italian, a derivative of the Tuscan language. Although linguistic variations are disappearing to some extent because of the homogenizing effects of television and telecommunications, Italians still cling to the notion of having their own regional dialect.

In opera, there is inherent inequity in the amount of fame given to each soloist. The same is true in the Italian economy. Today, poverty persists in some areas, particularly in the South. Italian industry has become increasingly successful, but success is not shared equally by everyone. Because Northern companies believe there is a difference in the Northern and Southern work ethic, they are reluctant to locate branches in the South. The large migration of workers from South to North has left behind people who are not willing to give up customs and traditions that have been followed since early European civilization.

Although Italian culture consists of many regional subcultures, the modernization of Italy has begun to unify these subcultures. Italian culture is continuously changing to one where the melody of the regional soloists blends together into a harmonic chorus, as the political reforms described above confirm.

The Family Meal

One aspect of Italian culture, the family meal, is a microcosm of this entire operative culture. The characteristics of spectacle, voice, exteriority, and interaction between chorus and soloists all manifest themselves in the meal and the actions surrounding this Italian ritual. The daily dinner is the center of Italian life. It is the time when family members come together to enjoy one another and celebrate the family's emotional bond. It is critical that each member of the immediate family be present at this ritual. Even if a teenage child has too much homework or wants to go out with friends, the mother will usually insist that dinner takes priority.

The food served at this meal does not just consist of pasta but of soup, antipasto, pasta, and then the main course. Each day the mother orchestrates a spectacle of exquisite food. Italian food is beautiful to behold. The carefully coordinated colors of vegetables, pasta, and sauces create the background scene for the actions of the show taking place at the table. Every participant in the meal should be fully involved in enjoying the spectacle created by the mother. It is considered a serious breach of Italian etiquette to leave a half-full plate of food, and American guests to such a meal are sometimes astonished to learn that the large servings of food they have just eaten are merely prelude to the main courses, which their Italian hosts normally insist they attempt to eat.

Food itself is a source of emotional and physical solace. One of the main purposes of the family meal is to share a sense of love, unity, and stability. Emotions usually flow freely throughout the meal. Children are encouraged not only to discuss their daily activities but to share the feelings associated with those activities. The Italian trait of exteriority is frequently present throughout the meal. If a child has disappointed the family honor, parents and children will sometimes yell, cry, and express whatever emotion they are feeling. This atmosphere of open emotion is a critical part of the mealtime ritual. It enforces the feelings of family unity.

Still, the words spoken at mealtime are not as important as the gestures and emotions communicated. For example, the closing of both eyes in an otherwise immobile and expressionless face signifies resignation to an inevitable parental scolding or acceptance of a parental punishment. At times, if the family is discussing an important subject, everyone becomes involved and starts talking at the same time. From the outside, the noise level and emotional gestures create a show in which the tragedies of the day are being replayed.

Moreover, the principle of male superiority is evident during the meal. Men pay a great deal of attention to whether their wives can cook as well as their mothers. One Italian stated that his marriage almost broke up during the first two years until his mother taught his wife how to cook. Thus the wife's cooking ability is viewed as a reflection of her ability to care for the family, even though the father is the dominant force during the meal. Frequently he sits at the head of the table and controls the conversation. However, like the soprano, the mother also plays a critical part in this mealtime ritual by taking care of the emotional wounds of the children. It is also the mother who orchestrates the serving of the meal itself. At the surface level, the male superiority is played out during the meal. However, a look at the nuances of the emotional interplay shows that the mother is also a strong family force.

Because family relationships are one of the primary forces in Italian life, the education of children is a critical part of the family meal. This education is based on worldly events, family history, and plans for the future growth of the family business. The overriding theme to the learning is that the family is the primary source of unity in a harsh world. Consequently, the education given at the family meal is frequently considered more important than that provided by the schools. As noted previously, Italians are not trustful of outsiders, especially public servants. They tend to feel that nobody can teach their children as well as they can.

Tragedy, melodrama, emotions, learning, and the spectacle of food are all critical aspects of the family meal ritual. It is the cornerstone of family unity and also the means by which family values are passed down from generation to generation. Still, in spite of the cultural importance of food and the family meal, times are changing. People are beginning to eat less pasta and more frozen meals. Much of this change results from the increase of women in the workforce who do not have the time needed to cook elaborate meals every night.

In this chapter we have not explicitly treated the Italian orientation toward time, space, and the other culture-general concepts (see Chapter 1). As the discussion of the piazza suggests, Italians tend to be more polychronic than monochronic, performing many activities simultaneously. In Geert Hofstede's study of the cultural values of 40 countries, Italy clusters with those countries emphasizing a large power distance between groups in society; that is, Italians tend to accept the fact that some groups are and perhaps should be more powerful than others, and they act accordingly. Italians also try to avoid risk and uncertainty in everyday life, preferring friends over strangers and familiar over new or strange situations, as their behavior in the piazza and exteriorization would confirm. And, although family and kinship are important, Italy clusters with those countries that are more accepting of individualism and aggressive, materialistic behavior, all of which reflect the Italian exterioristic bias.

This, then, is Italy. It is still a grand and larger-than-life society whose citizens love pageantry and spectacle, emphasize a range of voices in everyday life, exteriorize emotions and feelings, and feel a commitment to the town and region of the country in which they were born. Italians have had a difficult history. The institutions have changed, rulers have come and gone, and people have to survive. And people do survive, thanks to their personal, unofficial relationships. In Italy life is the theater, each act carefully played out for everyone to witness. From this perspective, opera is not only helpful but also perhaps essential for understanding Italian behavior and culture.

4

The German Symphony

Germans, much like the Japanese, represent a major challenge to American understanding, even though the largest group (approximately 23% of the total population) of ethnic Americans is of German ancestry (*Statistical Abstract of the United States*, 1992). When Americans discuss Germans, they frequently describe them in terms of an emphasis on rules and order. Although such descriptions have some basis in fact, there are distinct differences between the southern and northern, and eastern and western parts of the country. In fact, over several centuries Germany has experienced significant increases and decreases in size because of wars and migration.

Contemporary Germany does not resemble any previous Germany, at least geographically. Created in fall 1990, Germany now combines the former East and West Germanies that were born of Allied negotiations after World War II. The reunited Germany borders many diverse nations, including France, Belgium, Denmark, the Netherlands, Luxembourg, Switzerland, Czechoslovakia, and Poland. Internally, the country is divided into smaller *Länder*, or states, and then into administrative districts, counties, and autonomous communes. Germany also includes islands located in the North and Baltic Seas.

Perhaps because of their history of shifting allegiances and borders, Germans tend to have a deep longing for unity. For many years after World War II, the West German government paid millions of dollars in ransom money to the East German government so that at least some East Germans could migrate to West Germany and be reunited with their families. This longing was visible most recently in their simultaneous joy and anxiety over reunification of East and West. Many West Germans felt incomplete without their brethren to the east but now have sacrificed much to welcome their poorer sibling back into the nation. Their joy is increasingly tempered by the realization that the former East German economy will require massive injections of capital to rebuild.

The unified Germany is not content to enjoy its accomplishments alone. Just as previous German leaders battled for control of Europe, so German leaders of today are forceful proponents of a peacefully united European Community (EC) in which all members are able to achieve lasting prosperity and stability.

The Symphonic Orchestra: Reflections on Germany

The essence of Germany can be experienced through the eyes and ears of the symphony. Symphonic music was created as an art form in Germany in the 16th century. What originally started out as chamber music or operatic accompaniment, with a few musicians and a relatively uncomplicated score, has matured into full sections of woodwinds, brass, strings, percussion, the occasional piano, and a long list of creative sound effects. Certainly the most enduring achievements of composers from all stripes of music have been accomplished in the symphony. This endurance has its analog in the staying power of German society and culture.

The music and their performers are brought together by the conductor. A skilled baton unites the disparate personalities and talents of the musicians so that they perform as one, at the literal level of the meaning of the term *in concert*. The various musical divisions of style and perspective, such as those between entire sections of strings and the brass, and between the individual flutist and percussionist, are melded and molded by the conductor to produce a unified sound. The symphony, rooted in the past and reined in the present by precision and synchronicity, makes an apt metaphor for modern Germany.

The orchestra, like the society, is made of individuals with their own likes and dislikes. However, for the greater good that is the music, individual preference is subdued to the wants of the conductor and the needs of the symphony. Everyone cannot be a soloist, nor do all wish to be. In any event, the soloist's time of improvisation is brief, and the conductor soon signals that it is time to return to the history of the piece. It is this discipline—the voluntary submission of the individual to the whole, the guidance of the conductor, and the shared meaning of the music—that allows the symphony orchestra to flower and flourish. Similarly "it is alright for the German business person to be ambitious and successful, though one must never be obvious about it—since it is bad to stand out. Assertiveness in business is permitted, but aggressiveness is considered in bad form" (Hall & Hall, 1990, p. 57). Like the soloist, the business person adds to the concerted efforts but is not the center of attention.

The symphony reflects the character of this nation. Germans love their music. Much like in the past, descendants of the aristocracy living in the old castles along the Rhine still arrange concerts of baroque and chamber orchestra music that is played in secluded rooms illuminated only by the intimacy of candlelight. These concerts are peaceful affairs that mentally transport the listener to an idealized Germany of old. Germans also frequent the symphony on a regular basis; the former West Germany with its population of 62 million boasts approximately 80 symphony orchestras. Frequently the visitor to small German towns and villages will be able to attend symphonic concerts given by local musicians in churches, typically on Sunday afternoons and weekend nights.

This societal and cultural love of music has produced some of the finest composers of classical symphonic music. In fact, many experts agree that the classical symphony reached its highest level of attainment and maturity in the works of Haydn and Mozart. The great German composers include Brahms, Schubert, and, of course, Beethoven and Bach. Further, Germany has produced several world-class conductors, including Herbert von Karajan and Rudolf Kempe.

Many Germans play musical instruments as a hobby, and of those, many belong to informal musical groups that carry forward the tradition. From the horns of the Alps to the brass polka bands, and up to the apex of the magnificent operas of Wagner, music is an integral part of German life. German music is not only integral but also serious; it is not generally an outlet for emotion and craziness as it is in the United States and other societies. Music is foreground, not background. It is meant as a collective experience intended to enrich life. Even the audience at German symphonies reflects this seriousness: Its members normally dress formally, listen intently to the music, and are silent until a major movement of a symphony is completed, at which time they tend to respond enthusiastically but with decorum.

German Leaders

If we examine modern German society, parallels with the symphony orchestra begin to emerge. The most striking of these is the relationship of the leader to this society. With the notable exception of Adolf Hitler, Germans historically have not reacted favorably to charismatic leaders who are intent on leading them to a new world order without any questioning of their authority. Rather, as Edward T. Hall and Mildred Hall (1990) show, some people such as the French seem to have a deeper longing for this type of leader than do Germans, who prefer a visionary leader who is mature and strong enough to delegate responsibility and decision making to competent subordinates throughout the hierarchy. Similarly, this is also the role that symphonic conductors fulfill.

In business organizations, for example, the French prefer top-down and autocratic decision making, and so it is essential for a visiting American executive to focus his or her attention on the top person in the organization. Conversely, an American vice president of marketing would be ill-advised to approach the top person or chief executive officer (CEO) of a German firm: The German CEO will generally tell the American to see his or her German counterpart responsible for making decisions in this area.

Those who helped to mold the modern German state are among the most famous rulers of world history, including Emperor Charlemagne in the 8th century A.D. and Otto the Great in the 10th century. Perhaps the most famous modern religious leader was Martin Luther, who began the Reformation when he nailed his 95 theses to the church's door at Wittenburg in 1517. But not until the rise of the Prussian state in the 18th century, ruled for 40 years by Frederick the Great, did the modern German state began to take shape. Frederick was a champion soldier, but his talent reached far beyond war. This colorful German leader also composed and played classical music that is still popular today. Frederick collected art, counted Voltaire among his friends, and preferred the French language to his native German. Ironically, he considered German culture worthless. Perhaps it was this disdain that motivated him to change and improve Germany. His nickname "the Great" came in recognition of both his military conquests (especially parts of Poland) and his selfless devotion to his subjects. The lasting legacy of Frederick, like the lasting legacy of the symphony, can still be seen in the Germany of today. His mark includes numerous reforms, many of which still survive, the most well-known of which is the German educational system, which is treated later in this chapter.

An interesting aspect of the political leadership in Germany is a recurring belief that great leaders are not really dead and will rise again to help the people in time of trouble. The beginnings of this myth have been traced to the death of Charlemagne (Russell, 1973). Later, King Henry II and his wife were canonized. After Frederick Barbarossa died, a legend formed around him that said that he was not dead but sleeping in a cave in the forest "seated between six knights at a table of stone until the day when, at last, he will deliver Germany from slavery and make her leader of the whole world" (Russell, 1973, p. 89). The myth continues to this day with rumors that Hitler did not really die in 1945. Christianity, which is based on Christ's death and resurrection, is an integral part of the history of Germany and may have been the catalyst for this perception of temporal leaders.

German Society, Education, and Politics

As a whole and in comparison, the German society is more collective than the American society but less so than most, if not all, Asian societies. Conformity is valued, and rules are many. Each person is expected to contribute to the extent of his or her talents. Similarly in the orchestra, each musician gives his or her gifts to create a seamless sound. Although the soloist is frequently allowed to improvise, the spirit of the symphony rests in the creation of mood and feeling through the combination of disparate sounds to create one sound. It is the voiceless description of a story, with each instrument providing its own perspective of the tale, but the same tale. So it is that in German society, each worker, each housewife, each street cleaner, and each solo violinist is expected to contribute to the success of the whole.

This sense of combined effort is fed and supported by the German educational system. This system epitomizes efficiency, with a place for everyone, but not much freedom to move from one place to another. Just as the oboist does not one day change to strings, the German society does not offer its labor force the mobility enjoyed in some other Western cultures. The educational system supporting this approach dates back to Frederick the Great and is based in large measure on the vision of Wilhelm von Humboldt, minister of education in early 19th-century Prussia. His vision included "a monopoly of education for a small elite, [and] an inferior system of education for the masses" (Dornberg, 1975, p. 110). Even the German government has admitted that its principal objective of encouraging every pupil to attain an education has only been partially achieved. The educational system is the one aspect of German society that remained almost untouched by the Allies after World War II.

Still, the German educational system has achieved remarkable results, and other nations have used it as a model for developing their own system; the United States is studying it closely because of the glaring deficiencies in its own system.

The educational system begins with the *Grundschule* or elementary school, where one teacher is sometimes assigned to the same group of children as they progress from Grades 1 through 4 or, in some states, 1 through 6; our discussion will assume Grades 1 through 4, although the total number of years of school is identical whether the Grundschule extends through Grade 4 or 6.

After graduating from the Grundschule, students are assigned to one of three different types of school. In some German states the teacher makes this assignment, whereas in other states it is based on the results of a standardized examination. Given the importance of this assignment, it is quite common for German elementary students to have tutors as early as first grade to improve their chances of success. This assignment largely determines each student's career, and no other society separates its children at such an early age. It is possible, but somewhat difficult, to change from one type of school to another after the fourth grade.

The first type of school is the *Gymnasium* or academic school designed for those who want to pursue university education. Students attend the Gymnasium from Grades 5 through 13, but they can leave after Grade 10 for a non-college-oriented career. If they pursue this option, their degree is equivalent to that of a *Realschule* (real world school) graduate (described below). Students in the Gymnasium are required to pass a very difficult exam, the *Abitur*, before they can be considered for admission to the university, which is not automatic but depends on the number of available slots. Even those who pass the Abitur and are admitted are not granted admission to the entire university, only to one of its faculties. Thus even these students have fewer opportunities than their American counterparts.

After Grade 4, other students continue their education at the Realschule through Grade 10. Some of these graduates then serve as apprentices for 2½ to 3 years while attending school 1 day a week. German industry subsidizes these apprentices and hires most of them after they have completed school. Other Realschule students attend the *Fachoberschule* (middle school) for 2 more years after the 10th grade and obtain a middle school degree, during 6 months of which they serve as apprentices. These students can attend the traditional universities either if they pass the Abitur or attend the *Fachhochschule* (specialized universities) for at least 1 year. Normally these graduates do not attend the traditional universities but continue to pursue a university degree in these specialized universities that emphasize four different concentrations: technical, social sciences, science, and business.

After the Grundschule, some students attend the *Hauptschule* (capitol school), and they can leave after Grade 9 without a degree. Most, however, leave with a degree and then serve as apprentices for 2½ to 3 years while attending school 1 day a week. These students also have the opportunity to attend the traditional universities or the specialized universities by going to school for 2 additional years (*Berufsoberschule*) and passing the Abitur examination.

This educational system reflects the German penchant for order. It is spectacularly successful and, as indicated above, provides some opportunities to move from one type of school and career to another. Although the United States is plagued with a population that is approximately 20% substandard in reading and writing skills, which limits their employability, almost all members of the German workforce possess these skills. Also, approximately 66% of the workforce has completed these apprenticeship programs, and there is an easy transition from school to work, something that is not true for many Americans. Further, some 10% of those certified in apprentice programs enroll in supervisory training programs in their late 20s, and this approach serves as an effective motivational tool for helping them to advance their careers. In addition, youth unemployment in the United States is typically double the general unemployment rate, but it is less than the latter rate in Germany.

There is no American counterpart to the German apprentice programs, and several American commentators have pointed out that it is one major reason why Germany has been so successful in business. However, critic John Dornberg (1975) echoes the thoughts of some

Americans who stress equality of opportunity: "It is hierarchical, elitist, class-oriented, authoritarian, and obsessed with imparting and acquiring prodigious amounts of encyclopedic knowledge" (p. 109). In 1972 major changes were introduced, the two most important of which were (a) the creation of 12 new universities to supplement the 48 traditional universities and (b) the elimination of the Abitur as a prerequisite for admission to these 12 universities. Even though the population has remained relatively stable since 1972 in the former West Germany, there are now five times more university students in that area of the country, a situation that indicates some improvement and opening of the educational system. However, the basic framework of the system, particularly the assignment of children to different types of schools after fourth grade, remains largely untouched.

Why do Germans cling so strongly to this system of education? As already indicated, it has worked spectacularly, as the German economy's performance before and since World War II illustrates. Just as important, Germans see themselves as integral parts of the whole society and, like musicians in the symphony, each must subordinate some individuality so that all of society may benefit. This is not to say that group identity is more important than individual identity. Rather, like orchestra members, they feel that it is important to do their individual parts to make the German effort successful. They believe in the importance of order and rules in society and that they have a responsibility to contribute their best efforts.

This idea of individual responsibility through group effort has led to the popularity of the Green party, the so-called *Bürgerinitiativen* (grass-roots movements), as well as various radical and sometimes violent political groups. Although not commonly viewed as emotional, Germans believe quite strongly that they know what is right and wrong. Those who mistake Germans for a cold, calculating people may mistake firm belief in a cause for lack of emotion. In *The New Germans*, John Dornberg (1975) writes,

> In the process these Buergerinitiativen may break the law, not to mention the holy principle of majority rule, but as Wolf Dieter Narr, a Berlin University political scientist, has stressed, "They do so only temporarily and not with anarchistic lawlessness in mind, but in order to have *better* laws." (p. 38)

On a lighter note, the *Baltimore Sun* ("Health Party," 1990) reported that the German Health party (the *Gesundheit* party) flew planes over the meeting place of German Chancellor Helmut Kohl and former Soviet President Mikhail Gorbachev to protest the food being served during a state visit to Deidesheim. It seems the party felt that the rich food being served endangered Mr. Gorbachev's health and that it was their duty to see that the menu was changed!

The presence of diverse interest groups in German government is a testament to the vitality of the political system. German government is based on a constitution, which provides for a president, a chancellor, lower and upper houses of Parliament, a central government, and state governments. Members of the *Bundesrat*, or upper house, are chosen by the state governments. The largest political party today is the Christian Democratic Union. This political system has enjoyed stability since it was fully realized in 1955, although there has been more unrest in recent years because of the unification of the former East and West Germanies and the large number of refugees—500,000 or more per year—since the fall of communism and the revival of ethnic unrest in Eastern Europe.

Of course, many Americans point out that this increased unrest, particularly the revival of nazism, is problematic. However, most Germans do not countenance this revival, and they have demonstrated in large masses against the depredations, killings, and assaults wrought by such right-wing groups; the German government has also taken strong action again them. Some Germans point out that the United States might even want to emulate the positive and strong actions that Germans have taken, given the high rates of crime, illegal drug usage, and unrest facing its own cities and towns.

Much has been made of the German passion for rules and order. To cite just one example, there is a place set aside and marked by signs in the woods near West Berlin where one is "permitted" to throw a stick to one's dog. Public signs everywhere in Germany describe the behaviors that are allowed, and those that are verboten or forbidden.

This sense of order is also reflected in the German respect for the clock. In both social and business life, tardiness is frowned on. Just as the soloist who comes in off cue may lose his or her position with the orchestra, the businessperson who comes in late for a meeting may lose a client. Most Germans are quite conscious of time and how to allocate it efficiently. For example, in one survey the German respondents had difficulty with the category "I had free time on my hands" when asked to indicate why they were seeking a part-time position. To many Germans, there is a sharp distinction between work and leisure, but in both cases they prefer that the time be used rationally and efficiently.

Those who disregard the rules can expect to be corrected by others, even by total strangers in public. In German society there is a clear right and wrong way to do almost everything, and true to the musical term *harmony*, conformity is absolutely necessary in symphony and absolutely expected in society.

The presence of detailed rule systems can be mistaken for a rigid hierarchy. Although rank distinctions are acknowledged and referred to in daily conversation in Germany, businesses commonly reach decision through consensus. Although there is certainly a hierarchy, businesses do not have the extreme centralization of decision making at the top of the organization found in many French or some American firms. The organization is extremely compartmentalized; information does not flow easily from one department to another. Likewise, responsibility usually stays within departmental bounds, and the departmental manager generally has much more authority than his or her American counterpart, even to the extent that he or she sometimes is portrayed as a tyrant (see Hall & Hall, 1990). This compartmentalization is illustrated in the German affection for closed doors and private space. Doors represent privacy and are not to be breached without invitation. The door is a psychological symbol, a protective barrier that separates the individual from the outside world, just as the stage separates the orchestra from the audience. These elements of compartmentalization and consensus management combine to make it difficult to reach a speedy decision. However, as is the case in consensus-seeking Japan, once the decision has been made, it is quickly implemented.

On the related issue of physical distance between individuals when talking to one another on a face-to-face basis, Germans keep more space between them than do individuals in nations such as France, Italy, and Thailand. Supposedly this distancing is a protective barrier and psychological symbol that operates in a manner similar to that of the closed doors. One German businessman became very aggravated by American visitors who moved their chairs closer to his desk as they talked. He solved this problem by nailing the chairs to the floor, thus frustrating the American visitors (Hall, 1966, p. 137). Similarly, it is remarkable to see some Germans vacationing on the seashore of the North Sea as they shovel sand on three sides to a height of four feet in order to define the space or sand cabin that they will occupy for a few hours.

In addition to physical distance, many Germans also possess a distinctive sense of aural distance. They tend to prefer a low noise level, and neighbors will post notices on apartments asking occupants to decrease the sounds coming from their dwellings. German law actually prohibits loud noises in public places on weekend afternoons. In one town some residents filed a suit against parents who allowed their children to play in the local playground during lunchtime and early evening. Germany, particularly its western part, is a crowded country, and the emphasis on both physical and aural distances is probably a reflection of this fact.

As might be expected, business meetings in Germany are lengthy and heavily laden with information. Contributors to the discussion often provide historical background and detailed analysis of their positions before making their actual point. One consultant who works both in Germany and the United States offered a telling example of the differences between the communication style of Germans and Americans. She was preparing a speech for her American clients but thinking in German, and she collected a great amount of background information, which Germans tend to love. However, she then realized that her American audience dislikes too much background information and eliminated so much of it that her speech was shortened by 20 minutes. The communication style of the German language often puts the action verb at the end of the sentence and the main point at the end of the talk. Much like many classical symphonies, meetings start slow, can last for hours, and ultimately build to a crescendo.

In addition, Hall and Hall (1990, p. 68) note that German negotiations are particularly time-consuming, with intonation, voice, and speech control being important elements to success. Thus, in business as in music, sound, tone, modulation, and timing are key to a successful performance. Still, some seasoned American executives who have lived in many countries prefer to negotiate and work with Germans rather than many other nationalities. According to these executives, Germans are well prepared and, although cautious, honor any commitments they make. It is also easy for foreigners to know how Germans feel on an issue, for Germany is a low-context society where subtle messages are not conveyed by silence and slight physical movements. For many American negotiators who have had to contend with such subtle, high-context behavior, Germany is a welcome relief.

The compartmentalization noted in the affairs of German business also spills over into private life. Just as the door to a businessperson's office protects his or her space, so too the German home protects the family from the outside world. An invitation to a German home is an invitation to share the family's private space and means the guest is most favorably regarded. Such invitations are issued much less frequently than in the United States.

Germans tend to be somewhat formal in social and business situations, introducing themselves by their family name. At one university a professor learned the first name of his secretary, who had worked for him for 30 years, at her retirement party. Germans reserve the familiar *du* (you) and first names for close friends and family. The emphasis is on *close* because in the early and even middle stages of getting to know another person, Germans make the clear distinction between friend and acquaintance. Even those people at work that an American would be quick to label a *friend* are usually referred to as *Kollege* (colleague) by the conservative Germans. And, unlike many Americans, most Germans do not socialize regularly with their co-workers after work.

This sharp distinction between friends and acquaintances may be related to the socialization process. Most Germans develop two or three close friendships during their early years that they often maintain throughout life. It usually takes a German much longer than an American to categorize someone as a friend, but once this determination is made he or she will treat this individual in a very special manner.

Along with privacy, the German family values the high quality of its possessions. However, because of legislated short shopping hours, this nation has little time for comparison shopping. This arrangement has clearly influenced commercial advertising in the country. Germans require detailed, accurate information in advertising to make the right purchasing decisions. Advertisers comply with this need by supplying information on product specifications, features, expected product life, and so on. This is in sharp contrast to celebrity advertisers, image, and lifestyle fluff so common in American advertising.

Once the purchase decision is made, the possessions are expected to last. Like the violinist who painstakingly cares for the craftsmanship in her Stradivarius, the German takes painstaking care of his or her possessions. Cars are conscientiously maintained, shoes are frequently polished, repairs are made promptly, houses are kept meticulously clean, and gardens are manicured regularly.

Germans have historically emphasized politeness, and this politeness is extended to acquaintances and strangers; for instance, a German sales clerk is very sensitive to the needs of all customers. Ironically, however, Germans are also known as a somewhat rude, abrupt people, both physically and verbally. A common complaint is that they do not stand in an orderly line but rather push and shove when waiting at a store. This aggressive behavior does not seem to be directed at anyone in particular; rather it is just that friendliness to strangers is not always seen as a positive quality in this society. Edward and Mildred Hall (1990, p. 43) attribute this behavior to German resoluteness.

There is a clear parallel between the German passion for order and the predictability and regularity of the symphony. In both societal rules and musical expression, there is a demand for regular beat and predictable form, coupled with a creative but somewhat bridled spirit. There is a formality to German society that is eloquently expressed in the symphony. Chronometer-like timing, precision, conformity, and an understanding of the individual's contribution to the greater score underlie both music and organizational activities.

This simultaneous emphasis on beauty and conformity is also illustrated in the German love for flowers. Most houses in Germany are lined with flowers in the window sills. The temperate climate of most of the country allows for the display of flowering plants in profusion in summer. Yet in any season of the year, a traditional gift to one's host is a bouquet of flowers. Gardening enthusiasts organize clubs and often tend communal plots. This love for nature, especially nature under control, is consistent with the German character; beauty, especially ordered beauty, be it a time-honored sonata or a newly bloomed rose, is most appreciated.

It is well known that Germans enjoy sports. In contrast to the practice in the United States, interscholastic sports are not sponsored and organized by the elementary and secondary schools. Rather, individuals must join sports clubs for such competition, and these are completely independent of the schools. The concept of the student athlete, which is stressed by many Americans who love football and other sports, is foreign to the German way of thinking. Soccer, of course, and tennis attract millions of participants and spectators. A complex card game called *Skat* and the increasingly popular *Volksmarsch* are informal and fashionable pastimes. Even though the climate can be unpredictable, two thirds of German families take a walk on Sunday (Burmeister, 1980, pp. 130, 134-136). There are hiking trails and maps for all parts of the country; one of the most enjoyable activities is to hike up to a mountaintop restaurant. Two common elements run through all of these activities. First, they are enjoyed at all levels of society; second, they tend to be organized into clubs or at least enjoyed in groups. There is a pattern of organizing pastimes in concert. These aspects of sport may provide relief from workplace stresses while providing the sense of group identity that Germans tend to enjoy.

The German worker has 30 paid vacation days per year, averages 37.6 hours per week at work, and earns $26.23 per hour, a situation that compares very favorably to the corresponding 12 days, 40.0 hours, and $15.49 for the American counterpart. The average number of work hours per year is 1,668 in Germany, whereas the comparable figure in the United States is 1,890 hours. As a result, Germans have ample leisure time, and they travel quite extensively: to the beach, the mountains, and famous spas such as Baden-Baden, as well as throughout Europe and the rest of the world. Recent prosperity has made it possible for many Germans to take lengthy trips; more than 45% of those who take vacations for more than a week go outside Germany. They incorporate their knowledge of all of these cultures into their daily lives; non-German restaurants, for example, are now quite common in German cities. In addition, the German language shares thousands of words with foreign languages, frequently English. *Manage, computer, arm, bank, extravagant, kandidat, salami, experiment, garage,* and *oboe* are among the terms that every American will understand when in Germany. Similarly, the German language has given English words such as *Gesundheit* (health), *Kindergarten* (children's garden or playground), and *Gemeinschaft* (community). Frederick the Great taught his people how to borrow and enjoy the best from other cultures, and the nation successfully learned and implemented this lesson.

Under Otto von Bismarck, Germany was the first nation to introduce a social security system, although he selected the age of 65 for receiving retirement income because most people died before reaching this age. Still, Germans have generous sick leave benefits and insurance plans that are far better than those of their American counterparts, and they use them to the fullest. In addition to doctor and hospital care, medical insurance also pays for spa rests and vacations. "Taking the cure" at a spa is popular in Germany, as evidenced by the sheer number of spas that exist: more than 600, some of which are centuries old. Germany certainly ranks as a world leader in the quality of medical care, which is provided by law to all.

Despite (or perhaps because of) these generous benefits for workers, the German is known as a dedicated and efficient employee. Certainly the achievements of the past 40 years could not have occurred without hard work at all levels of German society. German businesses are among the most successful in the world, especially in the production of cars, chemicals, electronic equipment, and machinery.

Agriculture continues to be a major source of revenue. Workers typically belong to a trade union and, unlike in the United States, these unions have kept strikes to a minimum. The success of this system may result partly from widely used participatory management techniques and *codetermination*—that is, the joint role that labor plays with management and government in setting German industrial policy. However, the labor costs associated with the German system are very high, and some German firms have begun to set up operations elsewhere, including the United States.

Still, many Germans guard jealously the number of hours they are required to work. One American computer consultant who was training German technicians was surprised that they included the time driven to the training center as part of their workday. Sometimes a clerk will stop waiting on a customer when quitting time comes.

An old tradition in Germany is that of folk festivals. They are held to celebrate all kinds of events, frequently the fall harvest and various church events. *Oktoberfest* and many wine festivals celebrate the earthly yield of crops. Likewise *Karneval*, which takes place before Lent, is marked by several weeks of costumed celebrators roaming the streets in search of the next party. Featured in these celebrations are fairs, street plays, dancing, music, parades, and abundant food and drink. At first it may seem that carefree festivals run counter to the dour German stereotype, but actually such communal activities are among the most popular and oldest of traditions, having been celebrated in the days when Mozart wrote his *Eine kleine Nachtmusik*, and they reinforce the feelings of group solidarity. Other traditions include a celebration in honor of the completion of a building and a children's holiday called *Laternegehen*, in which children parade through the streets carrying lanterns and singing traditional songs.

In addition to the above celebrations, which are rooted in paganism, Germans observe all of the Christian holidays. Christmas and Easter are celebrated for several days each. The Christmas season officially begins on the fourth Sunday before Christmas. Like Americans, Germans enjoy the tradition of Christmas trees or *Christbaum* (Christ tree), but unlike Americans some Germans do not dress their trees in colored lights. Rather, some prefer white electric candles, although most Germans opt for the more traditional and certainly more precarious adornment of hundreds of small burning candles arranged on the branches of the Christbaum. Although every year houses burn because of this practice, these Germans maintain this tradition and would no more think of changing it to meet modern times than they would think of rewriting Beethoven's Fifth Symphony.

Catholics and Protestants represent the bulk of organized religion in Germany today and exist in about equal numbers. More than 96% of Germans report that they belong to a church, although Germans are not frequent churchgoers. In 1933 there were 530,000 Jews living in Germany; through genocide and emigration, the number today is approximately 30,000.

The importance of Christianity to Germans fits easily into an examination of their character and into the symphony orchestra metaphor. Christianity involves the following of rules and doctrines. Christians believe that following these rules will result in an eternal reward in Heaven. Sin is considered a natural part of the human condition, which is to be regretted and forgiven only by God. The presence of strong leaders or bishops of the church, who are Christ's representatives, provides stability and comfort to Christians. We have seen that the German character desires the circumscription of rules for living and reveres strong but mature leaders. Just as the orchestra leader rules with a firm but fair hand, so God, in the person of Jesus and the bishops, rules over Germans.

Hofstede's (1980a) cross-cultural comparison of 40 countries in terms of four value dimensions supports the profile of Germans that has been highlighted thus far. Germany tends to cluster with those countries that are less accepting of an unequal distribution of power, status, and material rewards in society. Germany's vaunted social security system is merely one way in which Germans demonstrate this value orientation. Even though Germans cluster with other cultures that emphasize individualism, they are far less individualistic than almost any other country in this category, particularly the United States, which ranks first on this value dimension. As in the symphonic orchestra, individualism must be subordinated to the greater goal, and Germans are adept at accomplishing this objective.

Further, Hofstede shows that Germans are less comfortable with strange situations and newcomers than many other peoples, preferring to be surrounded by friends or at least colleagues whom they have known for a long time. This uncertainty avoidance is also characterized by a preference for minimizing risks, which most probably accounts for the extreme lengths to which German executives go when analyzing business opportunities before committing to them. And, as our discussion of the inconsistent manner in which Germans manifest politeness and aggressiveness suggests, they tend to cluster with those cultures that emphasize masculinity or aggressiveness; only 1 other of 11 countries—Switzerland—scores lower than Germany. It is difficult to explain this inconsistency and many of the other seeming contradictions noted in this chapter, but clearly the metaphor of the symphony helps to clarify why they exist simultaneously.

German Performance

Germany's boundaries have undergone many changes in the past 1,000 years. Like the diverse occupants of chairs in the orchestra, its citizens have been of many different ethnic backgrounds, each contributing their culture and outlook to the nation. However, although the country and its people have changed, for many hundreds of years there has been a central idea of the German nation, which is referred to as the "fatherland."

The fatherland is the focus of reverence and hope; it is the wellspring of desires for unity and the catalyst for many of the deciding events of German history. The fatherland of Germany can be easily differentiated from the motherland of Russia. It is a source of pride and of respect, a place that many expatriates recall with fondness. However, it lacks the nurturing element of a motherland; it is a harsher, more formal vision that inspires fierce pride and sometimes violence. Max Schneckenberger in *The Watch on the Rhine* (1840; in Morley, 1945, p. 573) captured these feelings of pride and respect:

So long as blood shall warm our veins,
While for the sword one hand remains,
One arm to bear a gun,—no more
Shall foot of foeman tread thy shore!
Dear Fatherland, no fear be thine,
Firm stands thy guard along the Rhine.

In recent years, many Germans have tempered this view with one that is more peaceful. Some surveys, for instance, indicate that a large group of Germans would like to see Germany's role in the modern world similar to that of peace-loving Switzerland. In many ways this orientation is parallel to that of Germany after the Thirty Years' War in the 16th century: The army did not engage in warfare for more than two centuries, and German soldiers gained the reputation of being ineffectual. Unlike other European powers at the time, Germany did not seek to colonize other nations.

Although the fundamental building blocks of "Germanness" have existed for hundreds of years, just as the orchestra changes and adds to its repertoire so the German state has changed and adapted to reflect the values of its leaders. During the reign of Frederick II in the 18th century, for example, German nobility attempted to re-create French culture. Bismarck, in the 19th century, created the famous military state of Prussia out of his own imagination and iron will and, with the assistance of the progressive Count Helmuth van Moltke, was able to rapidly improve the German soldier's reputation in the eyes of his enemies. Certainly Germans have both consciously and unconsciously imitated the United States since the end of World War II. The undercurrent running beneath the surface of this imitation is the German need to *be* something.

Regardless of one's viewpoint on nazism's relationship to the so-called German character, it is certainly true that World War II changed Germans in very material ways. The collective guilt over the atrocities that were committed has not been easy to address. Germany has made significant financial reparations, and many of the Third Reich's leaders were treated as criminals. However, certain cover-ups have come to light: Quite a few Nazis had risen to high public office in the postwar government and were removed from office only after they were exposed publicly. Nazis have found their way to South America, and others no doubt live quiet lives in Germany to this day. Considering the numbers of people who were involved in the war, tracking down and trying each one seems an impossible task. Instead, it is only those who rose to high office or who were discovered to have been particularly vicious who have paid the price. Those who were only foot soldiers are slowly dying off in ignominy. At first, Germans attempted to wipe the war from their collective consciousness and to start anew. They allowed the Allied powers to completely reorganize their country, and slavishly imitated American ways. The horrors of war were only vaguely mentioned in textbooks, and in 1959 Jürgen Neven-duMont caused an international scandal when he revealed that German students of that day were completely ignorant of the facts of the war. Germany was pressured to change its teaching methods and content in order to instruct a new generation about its past.

This cover-up might have been expected in any nation. However, Germans were so intent on leaving their past behind that they attempted to completely forget it in one generation. As before, they have tried to change into something else, to a Germany worthy of comparison to the Germany of old, proud and honorable. This is the part of German culture and society that creates fear in both its own citizens and in observers from other countries; the fear that the next manifestation of Germany might be worse than the last.

However, as some political scientists have pointed out, Germans have demonstrated that they have been responsible members of the consortium of advanced nations since the end of World War II, and this behavior should merit them full standing in the world community. In fact, it is somewhat ironic that Germany is now called a "wimp" because its citizens are so reluctant to participate in war (Fisher, 1993).

In short, Germans are like many other peoples who manifest inconsistent and contradictory values, and clearly their leaders have moved the country toward a stance that is acceptable to its allies. Most probably such inconsistencies cannot be eliminated in most, if not all, societies. Still, the Germany of today can be compared to an efficient and effectively led symphonic orchestra: Its citizens have enthusiastically accepted and implemented the democratic form of government that the Allies thrust on them after World War II. Although parts of Germany are changing, and other parts still cling to the past, the traveler to this country may be certain of one thing: In Germany, regardless of the economy or politics, there will always be a symphony.

5

French Wine

The French evoke strong emotional reactions in many short- and long-term visitors to their country. Frequently visitors complain about the rudeness that greets them in France, and they regale listeners with horror stories about the stubborn French who refuse to speak any language other than their own. However, many other visitors paint an opposite picture, describing the French as very concerned about visitors' feelings and welfare and going to extreme lengths to demonstrate hospitality and friendship. In fact, both portraits of the French have validity, especially if one uses the metaphor of French wine.

One legacy of French society that has remained integral throughout the development of French history is that of French wine. In looking back over the years, it quickly becomes evident that wine and France are inextricably bound together. Indeed, wine has been part of France's history since the Romans first conquered and settled in southern France and brought vine cuttings and the culture of wine with them.

Wine has played a vital role in determining economy, traditions, and attitudes. It has helped shape the country's disposition, weaving a common thread through all the varying walks of French life. Just as there are more than 5,000 varieties of French wine, so too there is a wide variety of French idiosyncracies and personalities. Beneath these differences, however, lies an industry and a people that work and grow together. Accordingly, wine appears an appropriate metaphor for describing and analyzing the French culture.

To focus this discussion within the metaphor of French wine, five principal elements of wine will serve as a guide: (a) purity, (b) classification, (c) composition, (d) suitability, and (e) maturation.

Purity

To more fully appreciate the metaphor, we must first understand what wine is, its origins, and how it is made. A wine's characteristics are the summation of its past as evidenced by the environment from which it develops. *Viniculture* is the precise and patient process that further shapes the destiny of the grape's transformation into wine. Fine wine is considered to be the distillation of 2,000 years of civilization. It is understandably viewed as an object of great pride, a survivor of nature's caprices and uncertainties, a product of patience and modesty and, most important, a symbol of friendship, hospitality, and *joie de vivre*.

Vital to the quality of the wine are the soil, climate, vine type, and viniculturalist who tends the wine-making process. The complex interplay of these factors determines whether pride or disappointment reigns once the wine flows from its bottled womb. Soil and climate nourish growth in mysterious ways that defy chemical analysis. Contrary to what might be expected, it is the type of soil on which little else grows that allows the vine to thrive. Climate and vine type must complement each other to produce healthy grapes, and the viniculturalist must be careful to make sure that the timing of harvest and maturation are meticulous and accurate.

Vines are also interbred, making it difficult to classify the wine produced because the offspring can resemble its parent or even display entirely new characteristics. Further, what is recognized as the world's greatest wine is grown only in a few select vineyards in France. The art and science of viniculture also influences the wine's personality. Experience, diligent patience, and effort are required to propagate the wine through its various stages of cultivation. The *vendage*, or harvest time, brings a sudden preoccupation with time. A delay of even 12 hours between harvest and preparation for fermenting can bring spoilage of both taste and aroma. After transfer from vats to bottles, the wine continues its aging process. Age, then, influences personality development, with great wines requiring more than 50 years to mature to perfection.

The French, much like Americans, have a romantic view of their country as special and unique. Like a flawless bottle of vintage wine, it is as if God had decreed that there be perfection in the land and people of France. They have mentally massaged the image of their borders into a hexagon that is perfectly situated midway between the Equator and the North Pole, balanced in soil and climate. Symmetry, balance, and harmony: It all coalesced in one great land because the French supposedly willed it. This perception of symmetry and unity in the physical dimensions of this geographically diverse land is more wishful thinking than reality.

The North and the South disagree even as to the origin of the French people. And in different parts of the country, people have different identities: The Northeast identifies with Germany and Switzerland, the Northwest with England, the Southwest with Catalonia and the Basque region of northern Spain, and the Southeast with Italy. Perhaps, then, the eternal struggle for unity has deep and stubborn roots in the past that dictate France's destiny as an aggregate of individuals struggling to forge themselves into a singular entity.

Thus the French tend to give the impression that France is the center of the universe around which the rest of the world rotates. One can quickly learn to resent the French belief in their cultural superiority and lack of immediate friendliness. But they readily defend their position in part by noting that international business and diplomacy were conducted in the French language until World War I and that French art, literature, and thought remain pervasive in modern education and society. They also band together by having shared a long and illustrious history of crusades, wars, and devastation.

The earliest traceable ancestry begins with the Celts, a Germanic people, who later became the Gauls. They planted an extensive empire that was subdued by the invasive Romans under Caesar in 52 B.C. For the next 500 years, the Gauls were repeatedly subjected to invasions by other Germanic tribes and finally by the Franks, who emigrated westward across the Rhine. From the Middle Ages and a feudalistic system emerged the Renaissance, (literally, "rebirth"), a time of increasing wealth and power for France and continuing turmoil.

A golden age burst forth in the person of Louis XIV, the Sun King, who proclaimed, "L'Etat, c'est moi" ("I am the state"). He orchestrated his rule from the extraordinarily lavish Palais de Versailles, and during his reign France expanded and built an impressive navy. Its language was spoken and its culture emulated all over Europe.

But the Sun King allowed a widening gap to develop between the wealthy and poor that, in an increasingly financially stressed economy, exploded into the French Revolution of 1789. The quest for "liberté, égalité, fraternité" first resulted in the brief rule of Napoleon Bonaparte, who allowed a more organized France to take shape by enforcing the Code Napoleon, which gathered, revised, and codified a vast, disorderly accumulation of laws, both old and new. Unfortunately, the oppressive restrictions that Napoleon placed on laborers, peasants, and women are still felt today.

Moving closer to the modern era, France was also heavily affected by the World Wars I and II. Although a victor in the first war, France lost nearly 2 million men. World War II still lives in the memories of many French people as a time of hopelessness and disgrace under German domination.

The history of French wine also has endured notable difficulties, one of which occurred from 1865 until 1895. During these years, a disease called *Phylloxera vastatrix* destroyed virtually every vineyard in France (Vedel, 1986). This tragedy of major proportions adversely affected thousands of wine growers. Even in such dire circumstances, the French did not lose their resolve. After toiling for months by trial and error, they discovered that a viable solution was to graft French vine strains onto American stocks that were resistant to the disease. Forced into a corner, the French came together to save the industry. In subsequent years the crops regained their health, and the wine industry flourished once again.

Even with this brief overview, it becomes apparent that the lives of the French people have been planted, uprooted, and replanted throughout history. It was the conquering Romans who left the French with an inherited sense of pageantry and grandeur as well as with an affinity for control and bureaucratic organization. They introduced the concept of centralization and a complex bureaucracy that have taken root in French hearts and minds. France's present concept of grandeur was first thrust on the French people in the time of Louis XIV. From this epic era there emerged the idea that the French were guardians of cherished universal values and that their country was a beacon to the world. The French saw themselves as favored, as possessors of ideas and values coveted and treasured by the rest of humanity. As Peguy wrote, "God loves the French the best."

It is true that the purest, finest wines must be grown in very special soil. In this sense the French consider themselves a very pure and proud country. Accordingly, those not born and raised in France need to guard against forming quick and negative first impressions without understanding past trials and tribulations as they relate to the formation of the French culture.

Classification

As noted earlier, France produces 5,000 varieties of wine precisely classified so that impostors cannot pass for superior wines. This incessant urge for nomenclature bestows a pedigree on wine that is displayed on each label. Through fermentation and the aging process in the bottle, wine will develop its final personality, blend, and balance.

Although wine is classified in excruciating detail, one who is not a connoisseur would be so audacious as to divide it into four major classes:

1. *appellation d'origine contrôlée* wines, which are the best and most famous;
2. respectable regional varieties, known as *vins délimités de qualité contrôlée*, that are quite good for everyday use;
3. the *vins de pays*, which are younger, fresher wines suitable for immediate consumption; and
4. the *vins de tables*, which are truly wine but lack taste and pedigree.

Similarly, French society is also clearly stratified and divided into four principal and generally nonoverlapping classes: The *haute bourgeoisie*, which comprises the few remaining aristocrats along with top business and government professionals; the *petite bourgeoisie*, or owners of small companies and top managers; *classes moyennes*, or the middle class—that is, teachers, shopkeepers, and artisans; and *classes populaires*, or workers.

Each person may know his place in society, but it does not imply that one person feels inferior to another. The French are comfortable accepting and living within the confines of this classification system rather than resisting it. The worker in the classe populaire is just as accepted for his or her contribution to society as the elitist official in the haute bourgeoisie class. This norm extends to attitudes of the French toward outsiders. Visitors to France sometimes have difficulty relating to the French, who can be just as ethnocentric as anyone else, because they tend to behave independently of others who mistakenly expect tacit cooperation from them in an undertaking. The reason for this outlook is quite simple. In the French mind, France and their own particular social class tend to come first. They interpret the phrase *tout le monde* (all the world) to mean all who are French or, even more specifically, all who are in their particular social class. Outsiders are countenanced but not openly welcomed.

Rules, regulations, and procedures give certainty, definition, and order to the French life along with guaranteeing the preservation of a particular quality and tradition to the lifestyle. It is *savoir vivre*—a certain way to do something no matter what the situation or how trivial it may appear—that facilitates life. It provides an avenue for security where a threat is presupposed and certainty where fears and doubts exist. Consequently, it leaves nothing to chance. Even as Napoleon codified civil law, another Frenchman codified gastronomy in 12 volumes. Nothing has been omitted or forgotten; even slavery was codified, which resulted in more humane treatment of France's slaves than of England's or Spain's.

On the other hand, savoir vivre can lead to preoccupation of form over substance, transforming every aspect of life into a ceremony. Preoccupation with form is evident in the French sense of style and fashion—and a flair for elegance. Some first-class French hotels have decrepit furniture, yet the rooms have such utter charm that all is forgiven and overlooked. Image, and the stress on the sensual, also is more important than the facts in business advertisements. French advertisements tend to be attention getting, concentrating on creating a mood or a response instead of informing (Hall & Hall, 1990). The advertising campaigns must first produce pieces of art before being efficient; this is why the French believe that American product advertising is not very good: It is too straightforward for French tastes.

That the French love classifying things is apparent not only with regard to wine but also with the classification of titles and their fastidiousness with and insistence on politeness and attention to social forms. Like labels pasted on wine bottles, those applied to people will stick. There is little room in French society for impostors, and little fluidity in crossing class barriers. They pay attention to status and titles and expect others to do likewise. Correct form must be followed. For example, when introductions are called for, the one who makes an introduction must be of the same status as the one being introduced. In a business meeting it is essential that the person with the highest rank occupy the middle seat. The importance paid to social standing is so great that even salary takes second place. Likewise, when honor is an issue, keeping one's word has more value than profit (Hall & Hall, 1990).

The following vignette depicts this typical but seemingly contra-dictory French behavior. Pierre B. showed his American guest the sights of Paris by car in a tour that culminated in a starlit evening in the hilly suburb of Montmartre. Making a swift right, Pierre gunned his car up a steep, narrow street. In choosing to ascend, he had deliberately ignored the one-way sign pointing downward, but no matter. He was about to reach the crest when spears of headlights turned downward and advanced on his tiny car. Thus obstructed, Pierre halted—as did the handful of cars. Faced with a headbeam-to-headbeam standoff, Pierre argued vigorously out the car window. The other drivers did the same. As the discourse generated increas-ing heat and passion, the American occupants in Pierre's vehicle began to feel uneasy, but he motioned assurances to them that he was in control. Then without warning, he leapt decisively out of the car as did the other drivers, and they all continued the escalating war of words in front of the interlocking headlights. Then, abruptly, it all ended. The drivers, in an unanimous movement, all piled back into their cars. Without a word, Pierre aggressively backed his car down the hill and lurched to a stop on the side street he had exited moments before. The handful of cars filed sedately past him and disappeared into the black night. Pierre paused a moment longer; then with silent resolution he revved the engine and gunned his car back up the same street. This time he reached the top and, once there, perched on the crest. Without a sliver of compunction he turned and looked smugly at his guests. He then sliced the air emphatically with his arm, and ejected a victorious, "Ah-HAH!"

Like the viniculturist, the French generally have a need to control and refine life and to order the universe. A significant portion of this desire can be attributed to the thinking of René Descartes, whose desire to make man the master of nature led him to ponder a rational meaning of the universe. Because he elected to discover this meaning without leaving his study because of his belief that "I think, therefore I am," his findings were not always accurate. But that did not matter to him as long as he was convincing. He has been described as the "intellectual father of the French preoccupation with form" (De Gramont, 1969, p. 318). One example of Cartesian thought is the general who devises a perfect battle plan with incomplete knowl-edge of the enemy's strength and capacity and suffers defeat—but with style and elegance.

One also can witness the legacy of the Cartesian method in life's most commonplace occurrences. Preoccupation with shaping, or-ganizing, and magically transforming raw material into a work of art is evident in food shop windows where displays of colorful and elaborately prepared casseroles and desserts could vie with the Louvre in terms of master-crafted creations. In sum, Descartes, who is frequently described as the founder of modern philosophy, left nothing unexplained, and neither do the French today.

French businesspeople are no less concerned with form in their business lives. Presentations are given from the heart so that the French display eloquence much more than do Americans. Their obsession with form shows in their belief that how one speaks makes as much an impression as what one says. The French love to discuss abstract and complex ideas spontaneously, in detail, and at length so that agendas, time factors, and conclusions appear to have less importance.

In addition, French business is highly centralized because of the long-lasting influence of the Romans. In a highly autocratic and bureaucratic way, the person atop the hierarchy is most important and wields power in many, if not most, decisions. This norm encourages the French to bypass the many intervening layers and to appeal directly to the pinnacle of power. The person in authority demonstrates it physically, for he or she is the person whose desk is placed in the center of the office. Those with the least influence are relegated to the far corners of the room. It is little wonder that change in French organizations tends to come from the top down, not the bottom up (Crozier, 1964).

Such a centralized social structure lends itself to the acceptance of autocratic behavior. Managers therefore display almost total control over their subordinates. In fact, French managers often are accused of not delegating authority, instead sharing vital information only within their own elitist network. As a result, it can be very difficult for lower-level managers to move up the corporate ladder.

This tight inner circle of upper management can be likened to the tight inner circle of the highest-quality wines that win awards year after year. Only those wines from the best regions, with the best color, brilliance, and taste, can gain the status of appellation d'origine contrôlée—the highest distinction available. In the same way, gaining a top management position frequently requires education at the finest of schools and upbringing in the most affluent regions.

This high level of centralization also can be regarded in a positive light, because it serves to maintain unity. The French remain a diverse people who tend to be proud of and loyal to their respective regions of origin. Throughout history the French have strived for unity, but they tend to detest uniformity, because they are a people who generally love to differ. De Gaulle once asked, "How can you govern a country that makes 365 kinds of cheeses?" The answer may be in the modern autocracy of centralization, where people who exist in a hierarchy of niches can find their own niche, security, and sense of belonging among members of the same social class.

This knowledge of France's hierarchical business structure can be instructive to American business managers. Just as we save the best bottle of wine for presentation only to the most distinguished guests, so we should save our most polished proposals for presentation to a top manager in a French corporation. Efforts to persuade lower- and middle-level managers may prove frustrating, because few final decisions can be made without approval from the top.

Another advisory note in business relations is to be aware of how the French handle the uncertainty of an unknown colleague at a typical business lunch. Uncertainty brings unease and implies a lack of control: It entails a threat that must be thwarted. The lunch thus gives the French colleague time and opportunity to reflect, study, and learn who the outsider is and how the person can be expected to behave in various situations. The French, who tend to be low risk takers, find it imperative to become familiar with the person with whom they do business. Pleasure and business are intertwined, because there is no better way in the French mind to open up communication and understanding than with a leisurely repast of food and wine (Hall & Hall, 1990).

Perhaps the best attempt to categorize and classify different types of French behavior was completed by anthropologist Edward T. Hall (1966). According to Hall, France is at the middle of his context dimension, with Japan and Arab countries having high-context behavior, whereas Germany and the United States have low-context behavior; that is, the French are high context because they frequently do not need explicit or written communication to understand one another. However, the French tend to emphasize low-context behavior in the form of excessive bureaucratic rules and regulations. This seemingly contradictory behavior reflects the Roman emphasis on centralization and bureaucracy as well as the innate French desire to know another deeply before transacting business.

Composition

Lichine states, "Wine is an extraordinary, intricate, and inconstant complex of different ingredients," and so it can be said of the French. Who they are has been determined by their ancestry, the region of the country where they were raised, and the social and educational systems that influence the kind of people they become. Their society is changing, and so are they. Perhaps their adaptability is an outgrowth of their complexity and inconstancy. The French tend to do many things at once, and they do them with alacrity—especially in an urban setting such as Paris, where the pace is rapid. In this sense the French are polychronic. This pace encourages quick decision making and contributes to their impetuousness where, in a highly centralized structure, businesspeople skirt cumbersome intervening layers of hierarchy to accomplish their objectives.

To the consternation of Americans trying to do business in France, the French tend to tolerate disruptions for the sake of human interactions because, to them, it is all part of an interrelated process. This toleration makes planning difficult, even for the French. After all, given life's uncertainties, one never knows what obstacles may prevent promises from being kept.

Still, Hall points out that the French tend to be monochronic— doing one activity at a time—once they have defined a goal they wish to attain. This simultaneous emphasis on polychronism and monochronism is another reflection of France's midpoint position along the high-context to low-context continuum. Given this intermediate position, it is easy to understand why foreigners have difficulty comprehending French behavior.

The French tend to work hard and prefer to be their own bosses, although few have the opportunity. In fact, too much entrepreneurial spirit is considered disruptive to normal business activity (Taylor, 1990). Sporadic 70-hour work weeks are not uncommon for some small-business owners. One prosperous flower-shop owner drives his small van more than 350 miles from Nancy in northeastern France to the southern coast to pick up his weekly flower supply. However, his business is quite seasonal; therefore, one can compare these arduous trips to the vendagelike intensity of the vineyards. The French pride themselves on such devotion to work and tend to believe that people in other countries do not work with such intensity.

On a typical workday the French rise early and have a simple breakfast of baguettes or croissants and butter or jam with café au lait. They work without a break until noon, when most stores religiously close for two hours. Lunch is a serious, unhurried meal: Some 60% of midday meals are eaten in restaurants. They work steadily from 2:00 p.m. to 6:30 p.m. and typically have a substantial evening meal, usually at home.

By law the French must devote five weeks, including all of August, to vacation—with approximately 40% of them migrating to vacation spots such as the Côte d'Azur. Holidays, like food and wine, are taken seriously, and the French tend to prepare carefully and meticulously for them.

Their weekends tend to be devoted to their families. Of the 85% who ascribe to Catholicism, only 15% attend Mass, usually on Saturday evenings or Sunday mornings. Saturday afternoons are often reserved for shopping. Some say that with regard to religion there is an anti-Church sentiment; others disagree, asserting instead that the French have no particular persuasion on religious matters—that they are more areligious than antireligious.

Geert Hofstede's (1980a) analysis of 40 nations in terms of four cultural dimensions tends to confirm the profile of the French and its apparent contradictions that emerge with the use of the wine metaphor. It is no surprise that the French tend to accept a high degree of power distance between individuals and groups in society and to dislike uncertainty, preferring to be in familiar situations and working with long-term colleagues. But they also tend to be individualistic and even iconoclastic, and so France clusters with other nations that value a high degree of individualism.

Still, Hofstede shows that France is a "feminine society" in which aggressiveness, assertiveness, and the desire for material possessions are of much less importance than the quality and pace of life. The French have deep-seated needs for security and getting along with insiders, colleagues, and family members. In short, the French accept centralization and bureaucracy, but only insofar as it allows them to be individualistic and buffers them from life's uncertainty so that a high quality of life can be maintained.

An integral part of maintaining this high quality of life in France is conversation. Like French business, however, conversation is not without classifications, rules, and hierarchical structure. Similarly, just as the wine-making process is complex, intricate, and meaningful, so is the art of French conversation. There is an innate restlessness in the French to explore every conceivable issue or topic through lengthy and lively conversation. Whether it be politics, weather, history, or the latest film, contrasts and controversy challenge the French intellect and heighten morale.

Many observers consider the French to be argumentative: None more so than the French themselves. They can be quick to criticize, but this is often only to stimulate discussion. Few French men or women are satisfied by mere superficial discourse. If a conversation is worth beginning, like the production of a tasty Burgundy, it is worth cultivating into a meaningful discussion.

For example, late one evening, in the small town of Dijon, an American stepped into a cab to save himself a 25-minute walk. No sooner had the American sat down when the cab driver quickly blurted out, "Ah, que vous êtes Americain?!" Not expecting such quick questioning, the American cautiously replied, "Oui, je suis Americain . . . pourquoi?" The cab driver responded excitedly that he had never been to the United States and wanted to learn more about it. Conversation continued briskly and was quite philosophical at times. The cab driver was mostly interested in comparing the respective styles and mannerisms of Americans and French. Meanwhile, time—and the money meter—were ticking away: 10 francs . . . 15 francs . . . 20 francs (some $4). The American knew pretty well the different ways to get home, and this was *not* one of them. Finally, after 20 minutes or so, the cab arrived at its destination. The American was a bit angry that the ride had taken so long and was worried that he did not have enough money. Just as he reached for his wallet, the driver said abruptly, "Arretez-vous! Je ne veux pas d'argent. Merci pour la conversation," and, after a pause, "Bonne nuit!" What did this mean? "Stop! I don't want any money. Thank you for the conversation. Good night!" Other Americans have had similar experiences.

The finest wines result from following very carefully a detailed, meticulous set of rules (Johnson, 1985). If one of these rules is forgotten or ignored, the quality of the wine will be greatly diminished. The same is true of speaking and conversation in France. Even small mispronunciations have the unnerving effect of fingernails scraping on a blackboard. It is a highly developed art and follows very specific rules.

It is no surprise that the French language is governed by a seemingly endless (and annoying, in many eyes) set of rules. For example, all French nouns are either masculine or feminine, and articles and adjectives must agree. Verbs have so many different endings and participles that they are almost impossible to remember. And, what is sometimes difficult for English speakers to understand, proper sentence structure often places the verb at the end of the sentence as opposed to its beginning or middle.

In conversational circles, there are two very different forms of addressing a person in French. The second-person singular, *tu* or *toi*, is reserved for only the closest of friends and family members of the same age or younger. *Vous*, which is the second-person plural as well as singular, is used on a more formal level. Care needs to be taken in using *tu* and *vous*, because the wrong usage can spoil a conversation or jeopardize a relationship at an early stage. Until a person is known well, the *vous* form should be used. As one becomes better acquainted, an occasional usage of *tu* is not considered offensive. But only much later, when friendships have thoroughly developed, should you use the *tu* and *toi* form regularly—but not with your elders or superiors.

A helpful guide to building a meaningful friendship in France is to recognize the parallels of this process to cultivating wine: Don't rush the process; allow quality to improve over time. In other words, approach the relationship in a high-context manner. For Americans venturing into France for the first time, it is important to acknowledge that the American conversational style is quite different from the French style. Although Americans tend to have many small conversations with many people, the French prefer fewer conversations at much deeper levels.

Another inherent conversational rule is that to smile at someone you do not know and say "Hello" is frequently considered provocative, not friendly. On the other hand, to pass a friend on the street or bump into family acquaintances without offering conversation would be considered rude (Taylor, 1990). These differing interaction styles for different "levels" of friends in France are not so common in the United States, where a friendly greeting and small talk are the norm.

Like a glass of vintage Bordeaux, the family tends to be important to the French because it is a source of acceptance, nourishing them in the midst of life's vicissitudes. The French often look to their families for emotional and economic support. Similarly, as when the horrible disease struck the wine industry in the late 1800s, wine growers look after one another in times of trouble. Relationships among family members are very close. Family bonds are strengthened by eating weekend meals and taking extended holidays together. These are times for catching up on family matters, planning, and simply enjoying one another's company.

Although the French can be very romantic about love, the concept of marriage and children tends to be approached in a businesslike, practical manner. Children are considered the parents' obligation, and children's behaviors directly reflect proper (or improper) upbringing. French parents are not as concerned about playing with the child as they are about civilizing him or her (Carroll, 1987). This parental guidance continues through adolescence and often through university. In fact, it is not uncommon for parents to help their children out considerably with housing or other expenses, even after marriage. One foreigner who had lived in France most of his life described this orientation: "The French support their children until they are stepping on their beards."

The French are very private with regard to their homes, so an invitation to dinner implies a high level of intimacy. The home is mostly reserved for family or very close friends. Restaurants are used for acquaintances and first-time get-togethers. Never ask to visit a French home if not invited, and if you want to stop by for some reason, telephone first.

Further, similar to a fine vintage selection patiently awaiting its proper time for opening and enjoying, the women's movement in France has been in no great rush for full equality in societal roles. The French woman sees herself, and is regarded as, the equal of man: equal but different. Presented with opportunities to play the same roles as men, she has shied away from doing so. Accordingly, many milestones in women's rights came about much later in France than in other countries. Only in 1980 did the Académie Française admit its first woman member. Until 1964, a wife still had to obtain her husband's permission to open a bank account, run a shop, or get a passport; and only in 1975 and 1979 did further laws remove inequalities in matters of divorce, property, and the right to employment.

Politically, women were given the vote in 1945, but they have not been overly eager to enter active politics. Even so, progress is being made, and in business most expectations about the ideal woman staying at the home have greatly diminished. In fact, women account for a higher percentage of the total labor force in France (39.2%) than in Britain (38.6%) or West Germany (36.7%) (Taylor, 1990).

So, given the French woman's tendency to prefer femininity over feminism, it is not surprising that the growth of the feminist movement has been relatively slow in France. This movement will most likely be just as or more successful in France than in the United States, but like the superior wines of France, its growth will be patient and organized.

Suitability

The most meaningful occasions in the French person's life often center around food and drink. Certain wines "marry" certain foods; furthermore, the type of wine served dictates the shape of the glass. The wine must be drunk properly with one's hand on the stem so as not to warm the liquid. A fine wine must be gently swirled, checked with a discerning eye for clarity, sniffed to detect bouquet, and tasted critically before it can be accepted for guests. Meals can linger for hours, consisting of several courses served in proper sequence and with appropriate wines to match each course.

This challenging and often controversial business of putting wine together with the proper food requires much mating and matching, contrasting and complementing (Johnson, 1985). In the same way, the French people constantly struggle to find a political system that matches best with the desires of the nation. During the Third Republic alone, from 1872 until 1940, France had 102 governments, whereas the United States had only 14. The 12 years of the Fourth Republic, from 1946 until 1958, brought 22 governments.

From 1986 until 1988, France was governed by what the French themselves called *cohabitation*: a president, François Mitterrand, from the leftist Socialist party, and a prime minister, Jacques Chirac, from the rightist "Rassemblement pour la République" party. The two were directly at odds with each other on many issues, particularly because Mitterrand advocated the nationalization of private industry, whereas Chirac was a proponent of privatizing several state-run organizations.

Part of the reason for such political instability is that the president, with the consent of the prime minister, has the power to dissolve the National Assembly at any time other than a crisis. This would be the equivalent of a U.S. president telling the 535 members of the Senate and House of Representatives that their jobs have been terminated. Such dissolution also can work from the other side; that is, the president and prime minister can each resign on their own free will, causing a new round of National Assembly elections to take place. Such upheaval and constant change make matching the government (wine) with the people (food) extremely difficult.

Internationally, France has guarded its sovereignty very carefully. For example, in 1966 President de Gaulle informed the North Atlantic Treaty Organization (NATO) that France was going to withdraw its land and air forces from NATO "to regain her whole territory and the full exercise of sovereignty." In 1982, when U.S. President Ronald Reagan was planning to deliver an air strike against Libya, French President Mitterrand refused to allow U.S. aircraft to fly over French air space. France's allies tend to react negatively to such controversial stances.

Ironically, governmental instability and the penchant for controversy is welcomed by the French people. They tend to be proud of their wide range of active political parties; there are six in all. Abundant political choice is consistent with the concept of French devotion to individual freedom. Further, the political process is helped along by a free press and a love of political discussion.

It seems that the French are determined to maintain their governmental system even though this may often result in controversy. Many observers point out that no matter where you set foot on French soil, you will find yourself engaged in political discussions. Although the wine and food of French politics are not always "suitable" to each other, it is their very unsuitability that stimulates conflict, controversy, and a spirited involvement of the citizens in the political arena.

The Maturation Process

The viniculturist strives for disciplined growth, tirelessly pruning and training the vines to conform to his or her will (Carroll, 1987). This disciplined growth is also reflected in the French educational system, which is strictly controlled by the state and where children begin their education at the age of six, with many enrolling in preschool by age two. Unlike countries such as Japan where promotion from one grade to another is generally automatic, students do not advance until they attain certain skills. The result is that children of widely varying ages are in the same class. French education is known to be rigorous, with 30 days of the school year tagged for examinations. But unlike the vendage and its intense preoccupation with accomplishing its mission in 12 hours, young students must focus their developing minds on 35 intense hours of instruction each week. Mercifully, it is also the shortest school year in the world.

For the child who continues in the French school system, controlled educational growth signifies growth that is directed toward a certain diploma. The teachers who tend their crops of young students make the decisions that guide their paths—and ultimately their careers. There is a tendency to stress mathematics, because proficiency in that area is seen as a key to success and guarantees treatment as a member of the elite. Today the most able children are being trained as scientists to operate in an international culture. Some observers are critical that this preoccupation with mathematics reaches into inappropriate realms of study such as music classes that also require such mathematics proficiency.

The destiny of less able or privileged children is to glean careers from what is left over. Parents of these children lack the education and influence to help them mold a bright future for their offspring. In a real sense, though, social status more than anything else determines a child's educational opportunity or fate. The elite, who understand the importance of education, begin to prepare their children early in life for entrance to the *grandes écoles* (elite universities similar to U.S. Ivy League universities) and universities or *facultés* (specialty colleges and universities; e.g., journalism), and this practice tends to reinforce the sharp social class differences. Still, although there is discrimination at an intellectual level (ability), there is none at a financial level, as occurs in the United States; tuition at the Sorbonne is the same as everywhere else in France.

Educational choices are limited in other ways. It is very difficult for those who do not belong to the upper social groups to have any freedom of choice in their vocations. Rather, the system early on categorizes them and shapes and defines their destinies. One young Frenchman, son of a successful flower shop owner who had built his business from selling flowers on the street, did not want to carry on the family business. Because of the intense competition in his country, he was convinced that he had no chance of going to the *lycées* (elite secondary schools) or universities, grandes éoles, and facultés that most privileged students attend. As a result, he pursued educational opportunities in the United States that were better than his choices in France. A somewhat similar situation exists for women who might wish to return to school after raising families or who might harbor thoughts of changing careers. Such opportunities are generally not realistic possibilities.

The French tend to take many things seriously, even life's joys. One of life's greatest pleasures are friends; therefore, friendship is taken seriously, as might be expected of a society emphasizing high-context behavior. Friendship must be carefully cultivated and tended over the years. The growth of friendship is a slow and deliberate thing. The French are critical of the quick and seemingly casual manner in which Americans make and discard friendships. Such behavior is uncouth—not unlike chugging down a glass of wine when a sip is properly called for. A friendship then is not to be taken lightly; like a carefully selected wine, it is to be savored and enjoyed to the fullest. A good wine and a good friend—they are the joie de vivre. For example, an American businessman had been in France just three weeks, working on a one-year project, when he came into contact with a French colleague who was critical to the project's success. The two businessmen naturally had to spend a great deal of time together. The American appreciated this opportunity to brush up on his French-speaking skills, because his colleague was a purebred Frenchman who supposedly did not speak English. The American did his best to communicate effectively, but often felt frustrated that he could not express himself clearly and feared that he might convey the wrong message unintentionally. Then suddenly, after four or five weeks of such effort, the two were preparing for a business meeting when the Frenchman said, "You can speak in English if you would feel more comfortable." The American was astonished. The Frenchman then explained that the French are very cautious in dealing with foreign business colleagues and are careful not to overexpose themselves before a more serious, respectful relationship is established.

Another area where maturation—as well as adaptation—appears in France is in the country's gradual response to the modern health and fitness craze sweeping the United States and much of Europe. Traditionally, the French have shown a disdain for such trends, choosing continued adherence to national pastimes such as fine wine and cuisine. But times are changing. Nowadays, joggers are everywhere: In the Parc de la Tête in Lyon, on the coastal roads of Brittany, and at the foot of the Eiffel Tower. Ten years ago, chances were that the person running along the Seine worked for the U.S. Embassy. Now he is likely to be a trader at the Banque Nationale de Paris (Thomas, 1992).

Smoking, which has been traditionally popular in France, has become decidedly less chic. According to the French Health Ministry, tobacco consumption has dropped sharply—nearly 8% following its peak in 1987—for the first time this century. The government has taken advantage of this social change by passing a law that makes smoking more difficult in public places.

By most accounts, the health craze began in approximately 1990. In 1979, the Gymnase Club opened its first gym. Today Paris alone has 18 Gymnase Clubs, all filled with people eager to trim down or get into and stay in shape. As if this were not enough, today's French are actually concerned about what they eat. They are subscribing to nutritionist services in record numbers, and the book *Eat Yourself Slim* was a bestseller for more than a year.

It is no surprise that the consumption of wine among the French has declined significantly from 137 liters per person in 1957 to 70 liters today ("Tuning In," 1992). But in true French fashion, this decline has been accompanied by an increase in the consumption of high-quality wines from 7 liters in 1957 to 20 liters today. Although this increase may reflect the greater spending power of the French, it also is consistent with the desire to make life more pleasurable and enjoyable.

Toward the Future

As our discussion implies, the French have a predilection to think in terms of greatness. This is understandable given the glories of their past. It also applies to the reputation the French have developed and maintained in the wine industry. French wines are the best—a fact that the whole world acknowledges. For the French, the assumption tends to extend to their other accomplishments and themselves. Assumption of greatness tends to be inbred in the French down to the most humble villager.

Undoubtedly, the French imagine greatness to be part of their future. In an era of technological upheavals, they are excelling in high-tech areas. Charles de Gaulle exhorted his fellow citizens to shape their own destinies independently of the United States, to find their own place in the sun and space, and to become a nuclear power in their own right. This they have done with lightning speed, making rapid advances in many areas of importance. They enjoy an impressive network of highways; 75% of the nation's energy is provided by nuclear power.

ADA, RITA, and ROMEO are all state-of-the-art computer systems that are used by the U.S. military. Minitel, the world's largest database, connects every conceivable service in Paris, and other cities as well, by computer. Moreover, the switch to Minitel has been accomplished in a short 20 years. With the building of the Concorde supersonic transport, the French married high-tech grace and excellence; it is, indeed, a work of art on wings. Ironically, the Concorde was a joint project with the British, but people commonly attribute the accomplishment to France, not Great Britain. Could it be because prestige and grandeur seem to be typically French concepts?

The famous train à grande vitesse (TGV) is the bullet-shaped orange train that streaks past vineyards and villages at more than 170 miles per hour. Riding the TGV at night with blackened windows is to experience complete absence of motion. To incorporate both transport and motionlessness in this train is a typical sort of French creation—a mastering of nature, a striving for perfection, a blending of unlikely and diverse elements.

In spite of its various wrinkles, the societal system in France functions quite well, giving its citizens a safety net that cuddles them like a blanket at birth and softens the unpleasant jolts that life can bring in old age. It provides 98% of its approximately 60 million citizens with a level of medical care and benefits unknown to Americans. Income is guaranteed to those over 65 even if they have never worked, and the wealthy also collect, because it is their right under the law. This is a system that the French would revolt for if it were to be taken away from them, and it is costly. At a yearly price tag of $250 billion, it is more than triple their defense budget. And, although its benefits are being cautiously pared to reduce a large accumulated federal deficit, it still gives pension benefits almost equal to an average wage and lavishes free care on mothers and babies alike in order to boost the sagging birthrate and to elevate standards of living. Such generous attention to families has succeeded in reducing the infant mortality rate to 7.6 per 1,000 in comparison to the United States' 10.4, and it gives parents access to day care centers at $14 per day. This price includes a well-trained staff and weekly visits by a pediatrician.

Even as wine has a maturation or aging process that alters its personality, so do the French. Also, just as the flavor of wine changes with different blends of ingredients, France's cultural composition is evolving. They have experienced many changes in their history, and more will follow. The population is growing: The French account for 60% of new births, and there are other contributors. One out of 12 people in France is a foreigner; 1 out of 20 is a Muslim. France is one of the few European countries that actually encourages assimilation by granting citizenship to all who are born on French soil. More recently, many people have emigrated from France's former colonies, with more than 1.5 million coming from northern Africa alone. Far more than 100,000 political refugees have been allowed into the country. There is resentment, prejudice, and discrimination against these newcomers, and some politicians such as Jacques Le Pen openly appeal to this xenophobic bias. Still, it is a fact that France is one of the few nations that has welcomed so many outsiders and refugees.

However, although the face of France is slowly changing in numerous and complex ways, short- and long-term visitors to this country will most likely continue to react to the French in strong emotional terms. The French most likely will continue to spend a great amount of time nurturing relationships, being wary of outsiders, being sensitive to social class differences, accommodating themselves to the centralized bureaucracy, and being individualistic and iconoclastic. Although such activities on the surface may appear to be contradictory, they reflect an approach to life that welcomes, and even thrives on, many different and contrasting ideals. The secret to being able to accommodate such difference is moderation—and wine offers good training in the exercise of moderation. Healthy in itself, it must be taken in proportion, because it is the excess of it that can cause serious problems.

In more than 2,000 years of wine cultivation, French winemakers have accumulated a wealth of experience from which they have established successful techniques and procedures. Throughout the history of vinification and cultural development in France, the quest for quality has mobilized their collective energy. Although nature ensures that each vintage will be different, it is the human element at each step along the way that determines the ultimate outcome. The best wines are objects of great pride and, at the same time, a lesson in patience and modesty. In this respect, the French obsession with rules, procedures, classifications, and form certainly help to develop a product—and culture—that is world renowned. Thus whatever paths the people of France choose to follow, the metaphor of composing a fine wine will continue to give insights into their fundamental motivations and system of values.

6

The Swedish Stuga

Sweden is one of the "three fingers of Scandinavia" and is located between Norway and Finland. It is just larger than the state of California. Thousands of islands line the coast and mountains form much of the northwest. Many rivers flow from the mountains through the forests and into the Baltic Sea. Sweden is dotted with lakes, and more than half the country is forested.

Although it rarely snows in the southern part of the country, the northern part has more than 100 snow days each year. The unique culture of the Swedes has been a result of the struggle to deal with and control harsh surroundings, and the outcome has been a stable society that, although it has experienced some difficulties in recent years, is economically and socially the envy of many others.

Sweden's population is 8.3 million and its annual growth rate is 0.2%. At least 85% of the people are ethnic Swedes. A small indigenous minority (approximately 15,000), the Sami, lives in the north. Known to some as *Lapps*, the Sami are nomadic and herd reindeer for a living.

In Sweden, approximately four of every five couples are unwed. Under Swedish law, couples have the same rights to property and inheritance whether married or not. If Swedes marry, it is generally on the birth of a child. The divorce rate is more than 50%. Sweden is a highly secular society. Although 95% of Swedes belong to the Evangelical Lutheran church, most people rarely if ever attend church.

The standard of living is very high in Sweden as indicated by the high ownership of telephones, television sets, and cars. Slums do not exist, and the crime rate is very low. Swedes have enjoyed almost full employment since World War II. Free, compulsory education has served to raise the literacy rate to 99%. There is such an appetite for books in Sweden that more than 5,000 titles are published annually for a Swedish population of 8.3 million, compared to only 50,000 titles published annually for 250 million Americans.

Sweden has a constitutional monarchy; the head of government is the prime minister. Members of parliament are elected for three-year terms.

An appropriate metaphor for Sweden is the *stuga*, or summer home. Before showing how this metaphor accurately reflects modern Swedish society and its cultural mindset, we need to provide background about its history and form of government.

Sweden's recorded history begins circa A.D. 500 with a series of unending minor wars and feuds. The Svea tribe, the largest at the time, gave its name to Sweden, or *Sverige*, which means "the realm of the Sveas." In approximately A.D. 1000 the famous Vikings formed a tribe of superb seamen known for their violence and success in ravaging Europe. But the Swedish Vikings soon turned their attention toward the east, setting up principalities in Russia and trading relationships with the Byzantine empire.

German domination of Sweden began in the Middle Ages. Missionaries from Germany arrived in Sweden during the 9th century but were not successful in converting Swedes to Christianity until the middle of the 11th century. German merchants conquered through commerce and gained almost total control over Swedish trade and politics in the 13th century. During the next few centuries, Germany ruled Sweden with a modified form of European feudalism. Still, Swedish farmers held tightly to their ancient rights and privileges under Norse "village ordinances" and Viking democracy, where the chief was only the first among equals.

Sweden, Norway, and Denmark were united in 1397 as the Union of Kalmar, which was formed because their leaders felt that all of Scandinavia should be ruled by the same monarch, Queen Margareta of Denmark, to fight against German domination. The union was successful in defeating the Germans in battle and stripping some of their power, but German political and commercial influence continued for several centuries.

During the early 1500s, Sweden took the first steps toward parliamentary government. A national assembly (the Riksdag) was formed with four estates: nobles, clergy, burghers, and peasants. Gustav Vasa accepted the Swedish throne in 1523 and began the Vasa dynasty, which continues to rule the country. Vasa's achievements were remarkable and far-reaching. He supported the Swedish Reformation to the Lutheran religion, succeeded in separating church and state for the first time, and strengthened the monarchy by making it hereditary. During the early years of the Vasa dynasty, Sweden became a major military power and sought to expand in trade and territory. The following years were filled with battles as Sweden became a formidable military power and took over various parts of Europe.

The 17th century ushered in the Age of Enlightenment, a time of scientific discovery, growth of the arts, and freedom of thought and expression. In 1769, the English traveler Joseph Marshall, reported that one could search "in vain for a painter, a poet, a statuary or a musician" among the Swedes, although he admitted that "they were unrivalled" in the natural sciences (Jenkins, 1968, p. 63). Swedish leadership in the sciences extended beyond the Age of Enlightenment because of the Swedish talent for orderly classification and systematization. The world's first systematic registration of population statistics was begun in Sweden in 1749, and the census is still taken every year. In 1819, traveler J. T. James commented, "On the whole, with regard to science, there is no country in Europe which, in proportion to her numbers, has contributed so largely to its advancement as Sweden, and none where it is still so steadily and successfully pursued" (Jenkins, 1968, p. 78). Scientists today visit Sweden to gain access to her remarkable compilations of data.

The Age of Freedom followed in the 18th century, during which the Riksdag introduced a constitution that limited the power of the monarchy. This Age of Freedom witnessed the start of a transformation of Sweden from an agricultural to a trading nation. In 1809, the Treaty of Fredrikshamn was signed with Russia, which resulted in the loss of Finland as part of Sweden. Norway separated into a sovereign state in 1905. In 1912, the three Scandinavian countries of Sweden, Norway, and Finland declared their agreement on a policy of neutrality, even during world wars.

Movement toward equality came fairly late in Sweden, but Swedes were much more progressive than their European or American counterparts after the movement began. In 1842, the Riksdag introduced compulsory education and elementary schools. Universal suffrage, including women, was proclaimed in 1921. In 1971, the Riksdag became a single chamber, and in 1974 a new constitution gave the ruling monarch purely ceremonial functions.

Sweden's late Industrial Revolution in the early 1900s contributed to its swift rise from poverty to prosperity. The country had already established solid educational and transportation systems that supported industrialization. There was also money for expansion into new industries because of Sweden's valuable timber and iron, which were in great demand in Europe. Sweden had discovered early that a partnership of private and public interests was the best combination both for achieving economic success and benefiting as many people as possible. The evolution into a social democratic system had started.

To understand modern Sweden, it is imperative to understand Swedish social democracy, which in Sweden is quite different from the socialism practiced until recently in the Eastern Bloc countries; it is a merging of the ideals of socialism and capitalism. This form of government is the hallmark of the Social Democratic party, which ruled the country from 1921 until recent years. Although the Conservative party won a recent election, it accepts most of the fundamental ideas of social democracy within the framework of a more capitalistic and privatized economy.

Furness and Tilton (1979) stress six fundamental values of Swedish social democracy: equality, freedom, democracy, solidarity, security, and efficiency (p. 38). This form of democracy is often called the "Swedish model" and sometimes "humane capitalism," and it relies heavily on close collaboration between business, government, and labor. Social democracy has created a society free of the inequalities of capitalism and many of the inefficiencies of authoritarian central planning.

The Swedish word *lagom* is key to understanding the rationale behind social democracy. Lagom is untranslatable but essentially means both "middle road" and "reasonable." This word is representative of the foremost characteristic of the Swede: unemotional practicality. Swedes tend to believe that all problems can be solved rationally and satisfactorily through the proper application of reason. Swedes have shown unusual thoroughness and ingenuity in translating their beliefs into social reality. The result of their efforts is a uniquely sensible way of life: a calm, well-ordered existence, part welfare, part technological advance, part economic innovation, and part common sense.

Still, because Sweden has experienced some economic difficulties in recent years, it has been reevaluating its unqualified commitment to social democracy, which requires tight central control of the economy. Today Sweden has begun to move toward a more competitive economy, a less-generous welfare state, and lower rates of taxation for individuals and business firms. For example, old-age pensions will start at 66 rather than 65, and workers' sickness benefits have been cut. Swedes seem to understand the necessity of these measures if the country is to remain prosperous and internationally competitive: 85% of them supported such measures in an opinion poll taken in 1992. Even the high rate of foreign aid per worker, of which Swedes are justifiably proud, has also been adjusted downward. Nevertheless, the social welfare guaranteed to every Swede is far higher than that found in most countries, an outcome that reflects the model of social democracy, or combining socialism and capitalism.

One advantage to this pursuit of lagom or rational thought and behavior is that arguments erupt less frequently than in most, if not all, other nations. When the rational Swedes begin the decision-making process, there is a strong tendency to find agreement. This allows Swedes to reach a consensus quickly and act to solve the awaiting problem. In fact, Swedes are so zealous and efficient at attacking perceived problems in their society that they often will import not only ideas to solve problems but also problems themselves! Thus John Kenneth Galbraith's (1984) *The Affluent Society* led the Swedish government to bigger and better spending programs to eliminate "public squalor," although it would be difficult to find anything in Sweden to fit Galbraith's depiction of American conditions.

Social democracy has been dubbed the "middle way" because it is a reasonable middle road between capitalism and socialism. Because social democracy is so consistent with the Swedish value of lagom, it has become much more than simply a model for economic planning. Social democracy is a functioning social system in Sweden as well as a political party. Thus, even when the Social Democratic party is not in power, Sweden is still a social democracy. As Kesselman et al. (1987) explained:

> Anyone who visits Sweden will quickly recognize that the influence of Social Democratic thinking extends beyond the 45 percent of the adult population who vote for the Social Democrats. To a remarkable extent, the Swedish Social Democrats have been able to define the problems on the political agenda and the terms in which these problems have been discussed by all major political parties. It is in this sense that social democracy might be described as the hegemonic force in postwar Swedish politics. (p. 529)

The interesting paradox in Swedish social democracy is the seemingly contradictory goals of equality and efficiency. Modern Sweden, though, is a society that has found a viable mean between equitable distribution of profits and economic performance. Milner (1989) believes that the "institutionalized social solidarity around them enables Swedes to feel secure and thus prepared to follow the market in the promising directions it opens up" (p. 17).

The ability to achieve equality and efficiency may be a result of certain circumstances in Sweden that are conducive to a successful social democracy. Sweden's small size and relative cultural homogeneity allow for social and cultural consensus. International competitiveness is valued universally but is also seen as the means to secure the cultural value of equality.

The Swedish Summer Home

The dream of most, if not every, Swede is to spend the summer in the family *stuga*, or summer home. The typical summer home is a small wooden house, painted the traditional reddish brown that is a by-product of copper mining. There are white trimmings around the door and windows, the facilities are modest, and the furniture is plain and simple. Only the necessities are found in this home. Often there is an outhouse, but otherwise there is no disturbance to the surrounding area.

More than 600,000 stugas are scattered everywhere, around the lakes and in the countryside. There are no fences or "No Trespassing" signs to be found. Usually, other houses cannot be seen from a stuga, but sometimes there are clusters of homes making a small community. Most Swedes are only a generation or two away from the farm, so many can return to the old family home. Some Swedes must rely on the summer homes of friends or relatives, and others may have access to a stuga owned by their company.

The ideal vacation is spent at the stuga in June or July communing with nature. Outdoor activities range from river rafting to walking, or just sitting underneath a tree and reflecting on life. Swedes usually like to spend time alone or in small family groups at the stuga. The idea is very different from the American "the more the merrier" vacation or the German vacation during which activities take place on a regular and predictable basis so that no time is wasted. Swedes want to use this time to get away from it all, be alone with their thoughts, rejuvenate themselves, and refresh their ties to nature.

One Swedish graduate student in the United States began to wax enthusiastically to her American friends about her upcoming vacation in Sweden. She planned to spend an entire month by herself at her family's stuga, taking along only a few small necessities, a radio, a small rowboat, and several books she wanted to read. The Americans were incredulous, and one expressed the unspoken but unanimous group opinion when she said that the month sounded more like a prison term than a vacation. Although many Americans react this way, Swedes generally nod knowingly and approvingly when another Swede offers such an enthusiastic description of an upcoming vacation.

As this discussion intimates, Swedish culture and values are mirrored in the metaphor of the Swedish summer home. The following characteristics of the stuga clearly reflect Swedish culture: love of untrammeled nature and tradition, individualism through self-development, and equality.

Love of Untrammeled Nature and Tradition

The national hymn in Sweden is "Du gamla du fria," which does not concentrate on glory, honor, or warfare but on a land of high mountains, silence, and joyfulness. In his 1910 book on Swedish national culture, statistician Gustav Sundberg discussed this issue:

> The most deeply ingrained trait in the Swedish temperament . . . is a strong love of nature. . . . This feeling is equally warm among both high and low—albeit not equally conscious—and this strong attachment to nature, which in some cases may produce wild unruly emotions, is on the other hand the most profound explanation of the indestructible power and health of the Swedish nation. (p. 104)

Swedes' love and respect for nature is a strongly held value that has led to many laws that protect wildlife, parks, and waterways. The country has been termed a "green lung"—that is, a place where one can breathe and enjoy the untouched countryside. Swedes were environmentalists long before it became fashionable, probably because of their intense love of nature and the desire to preserve it as it was when families lived on the farm. Ironically, Rachel Carson's (1962) Silent Spring caused an uproar in Sweden, in large part because of the Swedish love of untrammeled nature. In contrast, Germans prefer a controlled nature as represented by the flowers that adorn their homes (see Chapter 4). In the United States, there are fierce debates over the utility of environmentalism that, to many Swedes, seem irrational.

This preoccupation with nature stems in large measure from a centuries-long battle against the hostile elements in a vast, damp, cold, and sparsely settled land. It is not surprising that the engineer is held in high esteem in Sweden: His or her efforts are directed toward combatting and controlling the forces of nature. Similarly, the Nordic invention of orienteering is a result of this desire to combat the forces of nature. The orienteer is set down in a remote, unfamiliar location and challenged to find his or her way out with the help of only a map and a compass.

One of the least densely populated countries in Europe, Sweden has the space to provide ample outdoor activities, whatever one's pleasure. Walking is a favorite pastime of Swedes, and a long walk on the lakeshore or in one of the many national parks is a preferred way to commune with nature. Fishing and picking flowers, berries, or mushrooms are also on the back-to-nature agenda. It is quite fashionable to return to Stockholm on Monday morning with the stain of berries on your hands. For those more daring, a variety of water sports are abundant at the country's many lakes. River rafting, canoeing, and sailing are very popular.

For a true back-to-nature experience, Swedes like to go north with a backpack and walk in the mountains for days. Some hikers follow well-established trails and stay overnight in cabins provided for them. Other hikers prefer to stay overnight in tents that they carry, and these hikers use only a map and a compass to guide them. In effect, they orienteer. Another back-to-nature experience that Swedes love is rafting. The journey starts at one end of a lake where there are many logs from the huge timber industry in Sweden. For a fee, you make your own raft from the logs and make your way downstream to where the logs are returned for use in the timber mills. The trip takes several days, and the riders stop the raft at shore at night to make camp. This experience is the essence of the idea of getting back to nature and the old days of living off the land.

Until relatively recently, Sweden was an agriculturally based society. Ninety percent of the families lived on farms until the Industrial Revolution in the early 1900s brought workers to the cities. Sweden has moved very quickly into an industrialized, city-based country, with only 2% of the population employed on the land. Thus many Swedes remember life on the farm or have certainly heard many stories about it. The ties to the farm are strong and deeply personal. Regardless of everyday city life, most Swedes are still peasants at heart who could easily return to the ways of their ancestors, for the past is not too distant. Back-to-the-farm and nature romanticism constitute a major part of the culture. Swedes long for an escape to the country, where they can remind themselves of a simpler time.

Further, Swedes generally value tradition and still have a village culture. They deal with this paradox by spending the summer back in the traditional village setting of the old family home. As Arne Ruth (1984) relates:

> The [Swedish] model presents the paradoxical spectacle of a nation possessing more of the outward trappings of modernity than any other society, yet at heart remaining the incarnation of Tonnies's mythical *Gemeinschaft*. With the cushions of tradition gone, the brutally modern forces of *Gesellschaft* throw the society's delicately balanced social structure out of gear. (p. 63)

Geert Hofstede's (1980a) 40-nation study of cultures indicated that Sweden clusters with those countries emphasizing a small power distance between individuals and groups in society, a pattern that is typically found in a village setting. Hofstede also noted that Swedes exhibit weak uncertainty avoidance—that is, they do not feel threatened by ambiguous situations.

Swedes have traditionally had the characteristic of practicality and rationality. When there is a conflict between practicality and other values, practicality tends to win. This can be seen repeatedly in the setting of national policy. Staunchly neutral since her last war in 1814, Swedes can be said to avoid war largely because they view it as impractical and ultimately not beneficial to any participant. Likewise, although the Social Democrats ruled Sweden for more than 70 years and built a gigantic welfare system during that time that would be the envy of any socialist country, they never nationalized industry simply because it is not rational, and being rational is obviously more important than being strictly socialist.

Individualism Through Self-Development

The summer home is a place to go for solitude and quiet individualism. A Swede will escape into the nature surrounding the summer home to spend time reflecting on life and getting in touch with the inner self. In the untouched countryside, a person can stroll for miles without coming across another human being. Great value is placed on this time for self-development. Managers complain about the unwillingness of workers to put in overtime so that they can pursue such activities. Most Swedes are now entitled to five weeks of vacation a year, which they generally prefer to take in the summer. Absenteeism and excessive use of sick leave are problems for Swedish managers. Workers in Sweden take an average of 27 sick days per year, or more than five times the U.S. average of 5 sick days per year.

Swedes must work to afford to pay the high national sales tax, and a dual income is essential to maintain the desired quality of life. Although Sweden is a "doing" culture and Swedes are achievement oriented, they tend to prefer jobs where they can develop as people, and they frequently look for jobs that are intrinsically interesting or that allow them to spend more time away from work. Decentralized decision making is valued and consistent with the ideals of equality and independence. Swedes are highly committed to quality of life and thus tend to value private time alone or with family more than, or at least equal to, work.

Much of the emphasis on self-development is motivated by individualism. There is a common misperception that Sweden is a collectivist society because it is a welfare state. Swedes pay high taxes to fund a system in which education, housing, health care, and many other programs are available to all. It is true that Swedes value equality, but they have come a long way from the farm. Modern Swedes tend to place individual interests before collective interests. Sundberg also observed in 1912 that "we Swedes love and are interested in nature, not people" (Jenkins, 1968, p. 154).

In Hofstede's (1980a) multinational study of cultural values, Sweden also clusters with those nations emphasizing individualism, but it is obviously more collectivist than the United States, which ranks first on this measure. Swedish individualism is different from American individualism, however, because Swedes desire individualism to develop as people, whereas American individualism is more competitive.

The emphasis on community and family has eroded with the increased industrialization of Sweden. As a visiting American observed, "Officially Swedish ideology is very good. Their attitude toward society as a whole and the world is generous. But the funny thing is that people don't care much about their neighbors. Swedes are so insular, self-contained. It's easy to be lonesome here" (Heclo & Madsen, 1987, p. 4).

This American experienced the process by which visitors to Sweden are cordially and generously welcomed and then enthusiasm quickly ends. At heart, Swedes are basically loners who are unaccustomed to thinking in terms of other individuals. After the initial courtesies are over, it is usually difficult to pursue the relationship at a deeper level.

Ironically, the success of the social welfare programs has fueled the move toward individualism. Many Swedes feel that paying taxes absolves them of responsibility to other generations and to the needy. Likewise, teenagers in Sweden are encouraged to be independent, and they frequently travel outside of the country with friends. As a result, Swedish teenagers tend to be much more mature than the typical American teenager. Thus a weaker bond between generations has resulted. As Hans Zetterberg (1984) explains, "The milk of human kindness therefore flows less frequently from one human being to another; instead, it is dispensed in homogenized form through regulations and institutions" (p. 77).

A large number of organizations in Sweden exist to promote the interests of their members in a variety of areas. An apparent contradiction exists between Swede's preference for working toward a goal as a group and the individual isolation that is typically characteristic of him or her. The organizational system is accepted only because it is seen as the most practical and efficient way to get things done. Interactions between members are generally kept on a formal basis, thus preserving the individual's isolation.

Because the views of a single person are seldom voiced without first being digested by a group, organizations tend to promote conformity. It has even been argued that the end result is a lack of individual initiative and creativity. Indeed, the generally placid temperament of Swedes might be offered as proof of this hypothesis. However, it is a difficult jump in logic to state that organizations preceded the typically reserved affect of the average Swede. Rather, it is more likely that the organizations have allowed the natural temperament of Swedes to be retained while satisfying the practical need for a public voice for their concerns.

Swedish individualism is further supported by the insistence on individual rights, which seem to extend even to trivial levels. If it is raining and a passing car splashes a Swede, rules give him or her recourse. One takes the license number of the offending vehicle to the police station and files a complaint, indicating that, say, a suit was damaged. If the court finds that the driver did not take appropriate precautions, he or she would be ordered to pay damages (in this case, to have the suit cleaned). Sweden has a form of legal welfare that allows even those who cannot afford court costs to pursue a civil case.

Equality

The summer home brings into focus most of the important values in Sweden, including equality. The ancient tradition of *Allemansratt* ("Everyman's Right") permits anyone, within reason, to camp anywhere for a night, or to walk, ski, or paddle his canoe anywhere. Fishing is generally free, but licenses, permits, or papers are frequently required. Allemansratt also allows Swedes to pass over any grounds, fields, or woods regardless of their ownership. Swedes are careful not to abuse this right and generally do not disturb the areas close to an individual stuga. They use common sense, but it is not illegal to pick berries, mushrooms, or flowers from any source. There are no laws of trespass, and "Keep Out" and "Private" signs do not exist. Equal access to greatly loved nature is representative of the value of equality in other aspects of Swedish life.

The egalitarian passion that has been almost as important as moral force is termed *jamlikhet*. Success in the creation of an egalitarian society hinged on rapid economic growth and social democracy, and the national wealth resulting from the Industrial Revolution was distributed to all citizens through the guidance of Social Democratic policies. The goal was to organize society much as Swedes would construct a machine. In pursuit of this goal, Swedes are constantly looking for new approaches or ideas that will make the societal machinery run better.

However, the Swedish machinery designed to achieve such goals is quite complicated. Sweden could not be described as a simple and efficient machine. Rather, it is more like a Rube Goldberg invention: Highly complicated and inefficient in the sense that there are many unnecessary steps and processes that must be followed, but nevertheless the goals are eventually achieved.

The expression "krangel-Sverige" (roughly, "red tape Sweden") connotes a bewildering assortment of complications, regulations, procedures, and channels of authority. This does not imply that the system has broken down, but merely that it is inconvenient for the person who must deal with it. Swedes feel that the main function of the system is to operate; whether it gives pain, irritation, or pleasure to someone along the way is irrelevant to the main reason for its existence. Thus the Stockholm trams regularly pass would-be passengers if they are behind schedule, because the function of a tramway is to meet the established timetable; serving the public is only secondary. Similarly, the medical care system is intended to deliver medical care. Because waiting in line does not seriously interfere with this goal, long waits to obtain medical care are not viewed as worthy of discussion.

In the past, the legendary Swedish *titelsjuka* (title sickness) resulted in telephone listings that included a Swede's title. Today some 50% of the listings have titles following the names, but this is done for the practical reason of distinguishing people. That the practice has declined is evidence of the desire for a society of strict equality. Almost everyone now labels him- or herself as middle class. The principle of universality means that all Swedes, regardless of social position, rely on the same network of services. Thus all have a stake in the quality and accessibility of services.

Historically, Sweden has had very high tax rates, and the resulting taxes are used not only as a leveling device but also to pay for the extensive social welfare system. The government provides programs to make jobs available to all who wish to work, pensions for the elderly, sickness benefits for all workers, housing allowances, free education through college and university, almost-free medical care, and subsidized dental care. Unemployment benefits are generous, but they are not designed to encourage laziness.

Family benefits, a current issue of debate in the United States, are abundant in Sweden. A year or more of parental leave is available to both parents on the birth of a child. In Sweden, men's attitudes have changed much faster than in other parts of the world, and some 20% take some parental leave. The government provides general child allowances for all children and gives advance payments for child support. Day care centers, *dagis*, are provided by local authorities. These benefits are important in Sweden because 85% of all Swedish women of working age are employed outside the home.

Equal pay for equal work is another feature of egalitarianism in Sweden, even though many occupations are clearly divided by gender. Swedish women face the same problems as those in the United States in trying to move up corporate ladders. Sweden is also struggling with providing equality to its more than 1 million immigrants. Most of them are in the country for political and humanitarian reasons, and they have difficulties achieving the same standards of living as native Swedes. The government has made tremendous attempts to integrate the immigrants and to offer equal opportunity, but Swedish racism has surfaced and is growing despite public disapproval.

On Hofstede's masculinity-femininity scale, Sweden is extremely feminine when compared to other nations in that 40-nation study. *Femininity* is defined as the extent to which the dominant values in society emphasize relationships among people, concern for others, and the overall quality of life. The characteristic of femininity is descriptive of Swedes, but in some respects the society is changing. Relationships among people are becoming more distant, and concern for others is eroding because of increased individualism.

As the election of a conservative prime minister after decades of rule by Social Democrats suggests, there has been a change in ideological climate, although not in the moral content of Swedish social policies; the issue is really the extent of the state's prerogatives versus individual and family rights. As early as 1984, Ruth pointed out that the ideals and policies espoused by Social Democrats needed to be updated and reinforced by new models:

> A rationalistic futurism took the place of religion; social and technological change was felt to be not only unavoidable, but morally imperative. Antitraditionalism became, paradoxically, the dominant tradition. . . . Industrial organization and technological innovation are among the oldest and most formidable currents in Swedish culture. . . . [T]here will need to be a new source for the cultural myths necessary to release once again the social energy that has for so long characterized the Swedish model. (Ruth, 1984, p. 93)

Thus the opposition to the Swedish model by the new breed of Swedes appears to result from a lost sense of community and heritage that occurred because of rapid industrialization. Sweden is now preoccupied with such domestic problems as high taxes to support the welfare system, energy sources, a declining work ethic, and the physical and social environment. Still, the unity of the Swedish mindset is remarkable, as is the Swedes' devotion to untrammeled nature. We can expect that Swedes will continue to emphasize the values and attitudes associated with their summer homes, particularly those of love of nature and tradition, individualism expressed through self-development, and equality.

7

The Russian Ballet

January 1, 1992, marked the formal dissolution of the Union of Soviet Socialist Republics (USSR) and the recognition of separate republics as independent and sovereign nations. The largest of these republics in both geographic size and population is the Russian Federation, more commonly known as Russia. With a landmass of more than 6.5 million square miles and a population in excess of 140 million at the end of 1991, Russia dominated the former Soviet Union. After years of unification as a superpower, it is relatively easy to refer to these republics by a new name, the Commonwealth of Independent States. Yet each republic has its own identity, culture, and dominant language. Foreigners often fail to appreciate the significance of the differences, no matter how subtle they may be. For example, *Great Russians* is the term used to differentiate native Russians from neighboring Ukrainians (*Little Russians*) and Byelorussians (*White Russians*). Together these Slavic nations account for 70% of the population of the former USSR. Our focus, Russia, also shares common borders with Estonia, Latvia, Lithuania, Moldavia, Turkey, Georgia, Azerbaijan, Kazakhstan, Mongolia, and China.

As the ruling nationality of the old Soviet Union and home to its capital, Moscow, Russia received the lion's share of attention from everyone, including the other republics. Attesting to this fact is the emphasis placed on studying the Russian language, which was required in all schools throughout the USSR. The predominant religion of the Great Russians (and the White Russians) remains Russian Orthodox Christianity, although the Islamic population is increasing significantly. The capital of the Russian Federation, Moscow, is in the western region of the country. St. Petersburg, known as Leningrad during the years of the Communist regime, is northeast of Moscow.

Russian ballet provides a beautiful metaphor for gaining a cross-cultural perspective of the country. In order to better understand Russian culture, we will take a look at three important characteristics: (a) echelons, (b) theatrics and realism, and (c) the Russian soul. These elements also apply to our metaphor and help to distinguish this art form from its counterparts in other lands. With a quality larger than life, Russian ballet represents the complexities of Russian culture: the grand expression of aristocracy and the gentle beauty of a countryside.

Russian ballet means many things to many people. Some consider it the type of instruction given at the famous Bolshoi and Kirov academies; to others, specific ballet companies come to mind. Those who witnessed the sumptuous performances of Sergei Diaghilev's Ballet Russe ("Russian Ballet") in the early 20th century surely identified his productions as *the* Russian ballet. And audiences familiar with specific works such as *Swan Lake* and *The Sleeping Beauty* proclaim these magnificent dance programs as Russian ballet. Essentially, all of these definitions are correct. As we will soon learn, the words *Russian ballet* evoke feelings of tremendous joy to anyone who is familiar with the finesse and style of the assured dancers associated with any part of this form of art.

A brief background on the evolution of ballet in Russia gives us insight as to why the ballet remains so important to Russians today; it also explains why Russian ballet enjoys its excellent reputation throughout the world. Ballet in its modern form originated from court dancing in Italy during the Renaissance. Although many Americans today think of ballet as a feminine occupation, in the 17th century male dancers dominated the spectacles for the onlooking Italian nobility. Ballet emerged in the next century as a pantomime-dance to the fascination of wealthier Europeans. In France, royalty participated in this form of entertainment by assuming starring roles. As ballet gained popularity throughout Europe, its performances became theatrical and were enjoyed by the public at opera houses. Like Louis XIV who established an academy in France to improve the art, Peter the Great during the 17th century encouraged the development of social dance in an attempt to increase Russian awareness of the outside world. His determination to modernize Russia into a powerful empire was achieved by using Western Europe as a model. Russians have always had a great love of dancing, and when ballet was introduced in Russia in the 17th century, they responded enthusiastically to it. The monarchy emphasized the arts by paying salaries for dancers who became known as "artists of his Imperial Majesty."

One of the most significant changes in Russian ballet during Peter the Great's reign was the elimination of cumbersome robes to permit freer dance movements. In 1736, St. Petersburg, then the Russian capital, became home to the Imperial Russian Ballet. Two years later, Empress Anna, who was also fond of ballet, sponsored the first school at her Winter Palace with the goal of developing professional Russian dancers.

Ballet flourished in the 18th century with the assistance of French and Italian choreographers in St. Petersburg, Moscow, and Warsaw. Perhaps the most influential of those who staged ballet compositions was French-born Marius Petipa, who in the late 1800s created such masterpieces as *Swan Lake, The Sleeping Beauty,* and *The Nutcracker.* Among the legacies of the Russian ballet is its tradition of brilliant composers, such as Peter Tchaikovsky, who collaborated with Petipa to create the music of those well-known ballets, and Sergei Prokofiev, who wrote the stirring music that accompanies the ballet *Romeo and Juliet.*

Although ballet lost much of its vitality in Western Europe during the 19th century, Russia preserved the tradition and elegance of the art form for the rest of the world. In 1909, Diaghilev revived the splendor of classical ballet with his Ballet Russe for Parisian audiences. His company was hailed as the "most exciting artistic force in Europe for the next twenty years" (Clarke & Crisp, 1976, p. 27). Sadly, Diaghilev's extraordinary Ballet Russe did not survive his death in 1929, because of the lack of either a school to develop new talent or a permanent theater to call home.

After the Russian Revolution in 1917, the "artists of His Imperial Majesty" in the former St. Petersburg adapted to the socialist way of life as did the rest of Russia's citizens. Russian dancers became employees of state-owned companies. The world-renowned Maryinsky Theater in St. Petersburg became the famous Kirov Theater in Leningrad. Likewise, the Petrovsky Theater, home of the Imperial Ballet in Moscow, was renamed Bolshoi, signifying something big or grand.

In fact, ballet became even more popular than ever as the government discovered that ballet could express the problems and ideals of a socialist state. Soviet promotion of socialist realism emphasized all types of artistic creativity, and citizens were encouraged to attend cultural events.

To match the public fervor of ballet, an infrastructure was developed for its expansion. A. Y. Vaganova, a legendary ballerina from the old Imperial Ballet, was called upon to create a training program for dancers, and it eventually produced the finest dancers in the world. She was responsible for much of the physical richness of Russian ballet, and her method of teaching is still widely used throughout Russia. Other maestros such as George Balanchine and Mikhail Fokine inspired eager students, including the magnificent Anna Pavlova, Vaslav Nijinsky, and Galina Ulanova. More than 40 new ballet companies were formed, and theaters were built throughout the Soviet Union. Gifted female pupils hoping to become prima ballerinas were provided with free academic and artistic support. Soviet teachers also searched for boys with strength, agility, and stamina who wished to pursue careers as members of a ballet troupe. Even today, a retired Russian male dancer usually retains his special status as premier danseur. One of the reasons male Russian dancers are attracted to a career in ballet is that financial security in the form of a state pension is available on retirement.

Even today Russian ballet serves as the standard for the rest of the world. This measurement is based on its fine traditions of classical ballet and intense national commitment to preserving and improving the art form.

Echelons of the Ballet

Clear echelons of status and privilege exist within the ballet company. At the very top is the prima ballerina, the prominent star of the troupe. Years of schooling and practice alone do not set one dancer apart from others. The principal dancer must possess a natural gift of virtuosity and inner beauty. As is true in other nations around the globe, Russian citizens revere such accomplished individuals as national heroes. Russian children look up to these dancers as demigods in much the same way as American children idolize Olympic champions and great sports figures. Although she is the most famous personality within her industry, the ballerina does not necessarily receive the largest salary. However, her status as premiere dancer allows the ballerina much greater privilege than almost any payment could. Similarly, the producer, choreographer, and conductor belong to a special *klass* with access to better goods and quality of life in general. As members of the elite, they enjoy such luxuries as fresh oranges and other produce, stylish clothing of durable fabrics, spacious flats, and, most important, connections. Like the varying levels of status dictated by the position held in the ballet company, all Russians are members of a class or social ranking in their society. David K. Willis (1985) describes it in his book *Klass: How Russians Really Live*:

> The advanced and the backward rub shoulders at every turn. . . . They search for whatever benefits or privileges or social status—klass— might be hidden on the factory floor, in military barracks, in Party and government offices. . . . In fact, there exists an elaborate, calibrated, semihidden framework of privileges and benefits at almost every echelon. (p. 32)

Currently, there is a great effort to privatize the former Soviet economy, and at publication, the conflict over this effort has not been resolved. In fact, the Russian government is planning the largest privatization the world has ever seen: More than 6,000 of its largest and middle-sized companies. During the 1980s, only some 8,000 firms were privatized throughout the world. Although a small number of Russians seems to have benefited from this movement, most have suffered grievously. A basket of goods costing 100 rubles in December 1990 sold for 8,688 rubles in 1993. Under such circumstances, the importance of klass has most probably increased.

The next level within the ballet company consists of the director, set designer, and costume designer, revered not only for the titles they hold but also for their personal reputations. According to the Willis framework, these experts in their respective technical fields could be considered *military officer class*. Those who report to the director—specifically the production, stage, company, and wardrobe managers; musical arranger or director; set design assistant; makeup director; light designer; and dance captains—form the *rising class*. Many of these individuals possess the ambition and potential to become experts or even members of the elite. Below the rising class is the *corps de ballet*, or the members of the ballet company who perform dances. In keeping with Willis's terminology, these dancers represent the *urban class*, which is by far the largest class. Finally, supporting musicians and various technicians, who specialize in everything from lighting to makeup, are at the bottom of the hierarchy. As one would expect, this *rural class* sustains the other classes both within and outside of our metaphor.

Perhaps klass can be best measured by the quality of the food each class eats. Members of the top class are welcome to dine in posh private restaurants and to order consignment groceries from food-delivery services. High-quality beef, black caviar, fresh fruit, imported candies, and liqueurs are all standard fare for those with access to such luxuries. Kremlin officials, famous writers, and high-ranking scientists are among those who enjoy the privileges of top rank. Elite food shops are quietly tucked away on unpretentious side streets, and members of the top class are able to pay the high prices for the items offered for sale.

Hidden wealth and discreet private consumption of the Russian privileged class is recognized at other levels as well. Instead of complaining, Russians tend to work to acquire their own piece of the treasure through upward mobility. When an individual moves up to the top class, he or she is welcome at luxury shops that previously served him or her indifferently. Those at the military class level may shop at smaller stores with fewer exotic commodities and less variety. Military class members fully recognize that the privileges they enjoy are associated with their rank; they are truly grateful for those privileges. Such individuals are "entitled" to purchase fresh salmon, red caviar, canned crabmeat, canned orange juice, and sausage without filler ingredients. Moving down the hierarchy, members of the rising class often belong to clubs with restaurants. At this tier, Russians can enjoy well-cooked foods such as boiled chicken, pork liver, and canned vegetables. At many club restaurants, patrons are also allowed to purchase food to carry out. The majority of citizens, however, still spend much of their time in long lines waiting to shop at drab state-run or private stores with limited selections. Carrots and potatoes are sold unwashed and unwrapped. Butter, fruit, milk, and flour are often unavailable, and ordinary fatty meat or pressed meat can be inedible unless it is boiled for several hours. Even at offices and factories, it is typical to have three separate dining areas for the various levels of workers.

As is true in other nations, status symbols reflect a person's level in Russian society. Symbols for the top class can range from a chauffeur-driven Volvo to a Western toilet imported as a replacement for the usual white commode that continually drips, lacks a seat cover, and is made of plastic. Sophisticated Russians seek foreign-made items for fashion's sake alone, even if the items are basic. Services and intangibles also reflect an individual's status in Russia. Center lanes of major roads are reserved for those who have klass; police officers regularly clear traffic away so that foreign vehicles may quickly travel through.

Top grades of vodka are normally available for export and the elite. The best vodka costs more than a day's wages for the average laborer. Blat or influence is a trading privilege for difficult-to-get items, which is a constant and pervasive factor of Russian life. Friends will buy for friends, and many memorize the most personal preferences of members of their circle. At times, bottles of vodka are used as a currency to pay for the services of individuals who can influence the system and reduce the red tape. The function of the middleman is akin to that of the Brazilian despachante. Both are guides who know the bureaucratic intricacies, although Russians do not typically retain a lone trader permanently for transactions.

Similar to the Irish in material wants, spiritual intensity, and strong personal relationships, Russians tend to possess a strong sense of dignity and composure. Even though the lower classes may never experience the thrill of a performance, Russians share a great pride for the reputation of their form of ballet as both an enchanting magic and a symbol of magnificence. The very Westernness of ballet reflects Russian dignity and superiority, regardless of class status. The most prestigious of dance companies is the Bolshoi Ballet, which tours from the Bolshoi Theater in Moscow throughout the world. The Moscow Academic Choreographic Institute, better known as the Bolshoi School, is formally affiliated with the ballet company and is located adjacent to the theater. Less famous but sharing an equally superb tradition of dancers, teachers, and choreographers is the Kirov Ballet Company. This company and its school descend directly from Empress Anna's imperial school and ballet company and still make their home in the same building in St. Petersburg.

Drama and Realism

Audiences throughout the world recognize Russian ballet as the most spectacular form of dance. No other art form requires such a combination of elegance and simplicity: Russian ballet is distinctive from ballet of other national origins because of its singular innovations, which developed from classical ballet foundations. Although ballet stagnated for many years in the West, Russia and the rest of the Soviet Union cultivated its theatrical resources to develop unimpeachable superiority over all other national ballets. Only the pageantry of the Italian opera rivals the brilliance of the Russian ballet, and only the Spanish bullfight compares with its drama. The pursuit of perfection in Russian ballet has become an inspiration to thousands of audiences and a permanent part of Russian culture and pride.

Audiences feel the vitality of the corps de ballet during the most dramatic moments of the performance. Throughout the ballet, dancers seek audience approval by delivering increasingly lofty performances. In the final scene, they pour their remaining ounces of energy into the dance to make an unforgettably grand impression on every last spectator. Each member of the company strives to be remembered in the minds of the audience as a glorious image of movement. In response, the audience expresses approval in the form of applause, floral gifts, and ovations. The dancer offers his or her performance repeatedly in return for audience gratification.

Like the dancer who makes a personal attempt to appeal to people in the audience, the ordinary Russian citizen tries to make an impression on those who are in a position to help. The bureaucracy within Russia is so great that the most efficient way to accomplish anything is through personal favors. Rather than jeopardizing careers by assuming risk or showing initiative, most Russians will avoid taking responsibility or any other action that may be construed as controversial. Supervisors are accountable for the actions of their subordinates, and it is often easier to do nothing than to endure severe discipline for making any type of mistake.

For example, until the system changed a few years ago, citizens received ration coupons for scarce items such as coffee or vodka. To purchase a kilo of coffee, one stood in line until it was one's turn to order. If a person were to wait in line for three hours, get to the cashier's counter, and then discover that the coffee voucher was left on the kitchen table earlier that morning, he or she might explain his or her predicament to the clerk in hopes of a sympathetic listener. The clerk was likely to follow standard procedures by taking the easiest route— that is, deny the request. It was possible that the clerk would elevate the entire matter to his or her boss to remove his or her own liability by passing the responsibility onto someone else. Chances were, in this case, that the supervisor would deny the request so that he or she also could not be blamed if anyone found out. Passing the decision up the ladder posed the risk of annoying the supervisor and was therefore not done frequently. A third alternative, which obviously posed the greatest threat to the clerk, was to look the other way and honor the request. Although this choice presented the greatest consequences for the clerk should his or her actions be discovered, it also held out the very strong possibility of an opportunity or a reward if the clerk granted the favor. The customer usually would make some small offer in return for the clerk's kindness. Perhaps the customer had a small package of tobacco that he or she could offer as a gift, or he or she might offer to perform some service for the clerk in the future. Whatever arrangement was agreed on was, of course, mutually beneficial to both parties.

Similarly, the interchange between the dancer and the audience is symbolic of the basic exchange between total strangers in mundane matters. Whether the dancer gives pleasure to those who watch and is rewarded with faithful appreciation from the audience or the customer gets around a ration policy by sharing a treat with the clerk, each participant offers the other one something that he or she desires.

Just as Mexicans tend to use the fiesta to escape a mundane existence, so Russians place great value on the theatrical component of the performing arts. Films, plays, and ballet offer chances for diversion. The ultimate cultural fantasy comprises a melodramatic story line, extravagant scenery, and fancy costumes. The greater the pull of the heartstrings, the more Russians tend to love it; this sentimentality is part of the culture's rare self-indulgence. Like the ballet company that relies on theatrics to please the audience, the Russian shopper uses drama to persuade the clerk to lower the stated price. An indisputable part of Russian culture is the custom of bargaining and negotiation to beat the system. At an early age students learn to supply the "right" answer in the classroom. Sharing of answers is tolerated, and children become adept at skirting authority with minimal confrontation.

Favoritism and corruption have been used to get around the system in the past. The significance is not so much the specific behaviors, but rather the acceptance of and, in some cases, the glorification of beating the system. Disobeying laws is part of Russian culture, even if for mere trifles. In a society where order is forcefully imposed, citizens have been punished for minor infractions, often for symbolic purposes. For example, domestic air travel between Russian cities sometimes required special papers that included a curfew notice. Although explainable, a delay because of bad weather was serious for the individual caught in public during the curfew.

As explained earlier, financial wealth alone does not guarantee access to such things as roomy apartments, vital medicines, stylish clothes, or even decent meat and vegetables. In the aftermath of free market price liberalization, connections take on even greater value. Access to creature comforts still may be obtained *nalevo* (on the left) through friends and connections. To obtain ordinary consumer goods by Western standards, Russians must work strategically within intricate networks of contacts. A great deal of effort is required to create and maintain these relationships in the hopes that benefits will result. Russians are continual gift givers who hope to influence future generosity on the part of others. Such behavior is not likely to change, even with widespread privatization of the economy.

Russians initially tend to take extreme views and offer few concessions when negotiating. If a foreign opponent makes a concession, it is perceived as a weakness. Unlike American negotiators, Russians have little authority to make on-the-spot decisions and prefer not to make decisions spontaneously. Chess is a national pastime, and much of the relative strength of Russian players comes from their ability to think ahead. Players rely on strategic planning, whether offensive or defensive, to consider potential repercussions, which is similar to what Russians do when negotiating.

Further, many consider drinking vodka a national pastime. Drunkenness is accepted as a socially approved method of entertainment and escape that is helpful in coping with years of suffering and hardship. Russians respect the need to drink thoughtfully or sorrowfully. At the same time, they join together in triumphant discovery— singing, laughing, and forgetting time. Especially in rural areas, drinking is a part of any type of festivity. Despite severe shortages, Russians manage to make a feast out of nothing. Kitchen tables are the most likely setting for sharing conversation and vodka with friends. Throughout this culture there is a tenderness, and even an affection, shown by sober people to those who have overindulged. Everyone seems to understand the Russian need to consume vodka.

Another important difference is Russian patience in working out compromises. Although time is a precious resource for American negotiators, deadlines often go ignored in Russian negotiations. Budgets and production schedules have traditionally been difficult to meet, and the prevailing attitude has been "why bother?" Within the bureaucracy, it is apparent that citizens are used to tolerating long delays and complacency.

Compromise is not always necessary for achieving goals; compassionate appeals may be equally effective. Yale Richmond (1992) describes the time that he arrived at his hotel in Moscow hungry, after a long plane flight, only to learn from the woman in charge of guest services that the currency exchange office was closed for the day. He was traveling alone, did not have any rubles, and therefore would be unable to pay for dinner. When asked, she had no suggestions to offer. Instead of retreating, Richmond chatted with this complete stranger about his trip, the weather, his family, and her children, and eventually he returned to the subject of his hunger. This time she reached into her own purse and lent him some rubles until the next day. Although he did not expect to bargain with the woman, he approached her as another human being, and she responded with kindness.

Haskell (1963, 1968) makes several points about the role of realism in Russian ballet. First, Russian choreography tends to emphasize realistic interpretations through the expressions of characters, as noted in the part of Albrecht in *Giselle*. Whether Nureyev or Vikulov played the role, it was played with such vivacity that the transition from self-centeredness to remorsefulness over his lover's suffering was genuinely evident to the viewer. Besides individualistic realism, the spectacle is subordinated to the human values in the story. In Russian versions of *The Sleeping Beauty*, the scene in which Princess Aurora falls into her slumber is choreographed with more than 100 dancers on stage. Even in the midst of a Russian crowd, the audience can sense a genuine interaction among the principal dancers. Western productions of the same scene tend to be vacuous, usually employing only Princess Aurora and four suitors at most. Another Russian contribution to the world of ballet is the reliance on experts for accurate set and costume design. Leon Bakst, famous for creating lavish sets and costumes, was the first to tie his depictions to historical information relative to the era in which a ballet took place. Thus Russian costumes have always been able to boast a "thread" of truth, and sets on the Russian stage have likewise lent credibility to the ambience of the ballet.

It is well-known that idealism is very important to most Russians. Soviet idealism created a cultural myth specifically targeted to the young: that every life is full of personal choice, well marked and available; each providing comfort and material security; and each of equal value as noble contributions to the building of the new society. Ideological education was a cornerstone of the Soviet system, and institutions continue to shape young Russian lives today. Children have access to colorful, well-equipped schools, sports centers, swimming pools, theaters, and dance centers, although ideology plays a lesser role than it did previously. During Communist rule, atheism became the official policy on religious affiliation as party ideology replaced the church. Official pressures made it risky for most of society to openly participate in religion, which led to an underground system of hidden beliefs. Since the adoption of a 1990 law allowing religious freedom, many Russians have renewed their interest in the traditional values of the Orthodox church. In 1991, for the first time in more than 70 years, the Orthodox Christmas day (which is not December 25) was proclaimed a national holiday in Russia.

Realism also plays a role in everyday life in Russia as people attempt to survive daily obstacles. Connections, or personal contacts, are easily the most valued perquisite for the privileged. Knowing someone who is able to influence an outcome is an accepted way of life in Russia. Pulling strings is an effective way to arrange the swap of apartments between strangers and acquaintances. Procuring a single ticket to a ballet at the Bolshoi requires connections unless one is an extremely senior official, a member of the intellectual elite, or a foreign tourist.

Connections can also be serious business, as in the case of a doctor willing to recommend a surgeon to a patient who wishes to circumvent the bureaucratic health system. The ultimate accomplishment of a parent is to secure better educational opportunities for a child; special arrangements can be made outside of the formal admission system of a school. Regardless of the type of favor asked, it is understood that a return favor may be redeemed at a later date. In some cases, it can be very helpful to slip the contact a bribe of rubles, chocolates, or even a Western trinket such as a felt-tip pen or a wall calendar. Building personal recognition is the first step in securing a long-term connection. The point is not so much what is offered: "But you need klass enough to find the opportunity in the first place. It's not that easy" (Willis, 1985, p. 71).

Virtually everyone in Russia uses connections; top class members are differentiated from the lower classes by repeatedly being able to gain high-quality favors. Lower-class members also use connections; a typical Russian male might bargain to purchase a superior export vodka for a special occasion, and a Russian woman might seek information about the arrival of a new shipment of inexpensive cosmetics at a department store.

Another dramatic tool borrowed from a ballet performance is the use of *vranya*, or bluffing. Vranya is best characterized by the statement, "You know I'm lying, and I know that you know and you know that I know, but I go ahead with a straight face and you nod seriously." It is publicly distasteful for most Russians to admit that anything has gone wrong. Social ills have been repressed in an attempt to maintain the image of Russian superiority.

From a foreign perspective, Russians have been characterized as serious and unexpressive, betraying no emotion in public. They hold a reputation for hardiness and stoicism. Often this external toughness comes across as coarse indifference or pushy discourtesy to the visitor. In the brusque surliness of service people and glum faces of crowds full of impassive stares, foreigners find the gruff, cold impersonality we expect. Service people may feel as if they are privileged because they have a degree of access to goods. Some service people exhibit scorn because it makes them feel better, and others manifest exhaustion or aggravation from dealing with long lines. But this exterior is *maskirovannoye*, a false front. The stereotypical demeanor is part of the drama of Russian culture. Underneath the mask is a raw humanness that could not be more real.

Ballet is much more than a dance on stage; it is a marvel of choreography, music, costumes, and lighting that creates a distinct mood for each audience. Choreographers express ideas through every dancer's movements, whether presenting a precise theme or leaving an audience free to use its imagination. Composers write scores for accompaniment to the beautiful technique of ballet, and orchestral conductors lead musicians to perform scores at the proper tempo, rhythm, and volume for dancers. Wardrobe designers and lighting experts use special knowledge of their crafts for ballet productions, and visual artists also contribute to the mood by designing sets to provide the proper backdrop for each dance. Finally, trained athletic dancers combine flexibility, strength, and balance to perform a series of dances that often tell a story for spectators of all ages.

A final consideration of this characteristic of Russian culture is the seeming contradiction of drama and realism. On the surface, these principles appear to be opposites. Herein lies one of the major dichotomies within the culture. Theatrics project a contrived atmosphere, whereas realism is rejection of visionary ideals. One of the more puzzling aspects of Russian culture is the illusion of disparity. Russians are categorized as both lazy and hardworking; they want to have money, yet they despise it. Russians are depicted as uninterested in building relationships (Adler, 1991, p. 180) while simultaneously "warm and helpful" after new interpersonal relationships are formed (Richmond, 1992, p. 3). Russians seemingly want to get money rather than earn it. Russian people do not usually respect those who simply work hard, and yet they are willing to make sacrifices themselves. Denied religious freedom for more than 70 years, Russians still possess faith and hope. Russians tend to be dreamy and pragmatic; they place great value on the work of writers, artists, and dancers. Like members of other cultures, Russians are faced with choices about priorities.

Conflicting roles exist between public and private relationships. In their public roles, Russians are characterized as careful, cagey, and passive; in their private lives, they are depicted as honest and direct. Foreigners describe Russians as suffering, unruly, and stoic; they are also known as cheerful, generous, obedient, and hospitable. Like other nationalities, they can be publicly pompous and privately unpretentious, caring or unkind. Perhaps Fyodor Dostoyevsky described it best as "half saint and half savage." With friends, Russians feel free to pour out woes to one another and are not burdened by the need to disguise the realities of disappointment or pain.

The Russian Soul

Since the 13th century, Russians have been isolated from the rest of the world. Two events—the Tatar (Mongol) invasion and the Ottoman conquest of Constantinople—abruptly halted commercial, religious, and cultural exchanges with other nations and limited Russia's development for centuries. Russia had relatively little need for trade because it was self-sufficient in agriculture; most of its interaction with other nations related to land disputes. From the Russian perspective, territorial expansion resulted from victories over foreign invaders. At one time or another, Teutonic Knights, Lithuanians, Poles, Swedes, French, Germans, and Asian groups invaded Russia, which has no natural barrier defenses. On all sides, fear of invasion by neighboring adversaries led to a Russian preoccupation with state security. A tradition of serving the state, whether peasant or nobleman, evolved from the suspicion of the hostile powers that surrounded Russia. In subsequent centuries, Russian rulers purposely limited foreign influence on the empire; as a result, later attempts to introduce new methods and technologies were met with skepticism by the people.

The Russian soul reflects distance that has been preserved by the culture for hundreds of years. Reinforcement of the idea that distance is essential for survival remains a characteristic of the Russian citizen. As a people, Russians are considered self-reliant, strong-willed, and full of inner resources. Although it may seem that so many years of czarist regimes and the iron fist of communism had hindered the outward use of such resources, the argument is well supported that individual perseverance and creativity had actually thrived in spite of absolute rule.

Each member of a Russian ballet troupe must endure laborious training on a daily basis and possess unfailing discipline to perfect the art. Classes, rehearsals, and performances make up an exhausting routine for Russian dancers; this cycle amounts to a dancer's complete focus on the world of dancing with little time for much else. This distance or separation from everyday life allows the dancer to put all of his or her energy into the dance. Orthopedic surgeons, masseurs, and medicine have become part of the reality of contemporary ballet; physical demands often require dancing through bodily aches and pains. Relying on Russian self-determination, each dancer is able to achieve total concentration, fueled by the passionate intensity of the Russian soul. The result is unmatched excellence, both in technical performance and artistry.

The Russian soul is a mixture of intense feeling; it is emotion, sentiment, and sensitivity combined. It is triumph over seemingly insurmountable troubles or sadness arising from the discovery of stark truth. Over the years, much has been written about the magic and mystic nature of the Russian soul. What is known as something mysterious seems to boil down to this: At the very core of individual Russian expression is the enigmatic principle or soul that places absolute value on decency, respect, honesty, and moral goodness. Part heredity and part learned, the people of Russia seem to have a stony resolve unlike any other that can be interchanged with human compassion in the blink of an eye. Creative, electrifying, and daring, the Russian soul is the source of inspiration within the dancer.

Throughout the arts, the Russian soul is the unmistakable power that compels the writer, actor, painter, or dancer to aspire to greatness. A potent force, the Russian soul shaped the insightful expression of Dostoyevsky's writings. His literature revealed the extent of responsibility that Russians feel for the afflictions and pain of the rest of the world. Company and conversations begin to matter as soon as one steps into a Russian's personal life. Among friends and family, Russians become the wonderful, flowing, emotional people of Count Leo Tolstoy's novels, sharing humor and sorrows and confidences. They enter a simple intimacy in which individuals are less self-centered than in the West. Russians tend to pour out their hearts in total commitment to friendships and become easygoing, affectionate, and tender.

Further, intellectuals look for a spiritual compensation to escape the boredom of everyday life, whether in ballet, novels, or poems.

Russian culture reveres poetry for its wit, courage, and creativity. Poets such as Alexander Pushkin are regarded as heroes for daring to use metaphor to conceal meanings in light of censorship.

Intimacy appears to be more pronounced among Russian families than elsewhere in the world. Accommodations are typically crowded, with multigenerational families living in very small spaces. Although the situation is changing, extended families have resided together in cramped circumstances under relentless scrutiny for decades, usually within apartments. Beds serve as couches in sitting areas, and bathroom facilities are shared among many within the apartment. Privacy is an oddity; no Russian word exists to describe isolation in positive terms.

Many Russians like to think that they have a monopoly on virtue, whether it refers to family loyalty, a sense of duty, or love of nature. Emotionality is considered a positive attribute, and some of the most convincing arguments between Russians appeal to the irrational element of human existence. Guilt is also a factor in emotionality. Similarly, the presence of guilt helps the dancer feel more deeply. Russians feel that they can communicate emotions through their eyes, conveying love, hate, or passion. Whether emanating unbounded joy or expressing woeful melancholy, the Russian dancer performs with an inner dynamism that members of other cultures find very difficult to duplicate. The severe Russian climate is also responsible for both the resourcefulness and strength of Russian people. For centuries, peasants have endured long winters of bitterly cold temperatures, brutal winds, and frozen grounds while longing for spring. That new season inevitably brings the considerable work of quickly tilling soil and planting seeds so that crops may be harvested before the first frost less than five months later. Unpredictable weather and danger of crop failure are of great concern, yet Russians have proven able to endure hardship. Unable or, in many cases, unwilling to take risks with imported technologies, peasants rely on familiar, if primitive, tools and techniques. They are masters of patience and resolve, recognizing that they do not have control over everything in life. Yale Richmond (1992) explains: "In contrast to Americans, most Russians have lived, until recently, much as their ancestors did before them—in small villages, distant and isolated, their freedom of movement restricted, and without the comforts and labor-saving tools provided by modern society" (p. 9). The geography contributes to feelings of powerlessness; the mountainous terrain and desolate barren spaces outside of the cities are under perpetual permafrost.

Just as Russian workers in the city or country survive harsh winters and hot summers, children also learn to adapt to hardship.

Parental indulgence is a national cult, and toys teach meaningful lessons. Russian-made toys tend to break easily, and when children experience the disappointment or anger of a new or favorite toy falling apart, they learn that they have little control over their world. Russian children learn to accept the fact that their world is not perfect without too much bitterness. Perhaps this is why students of Russian ballet are able to adjust to grueling schedules of dance instruction, traditional classroom subjects, and physical workouts that build strength and flexibility without bitterness.

At all levels of society, the device of public shaming is central to the Russian system. There is a collective responsibility for children, exhibited through overprotectiveness. Russian babies are tradition-ally wrapped in *kosinkas*, a mummylike wrapping that allows little movement. Infants are so tightly bundled that they can barely move about. Russian culture reasons that swaddling is necessary for the first nine months of life to protect a baby from hurting him- or herself. The baby is unswaddled only for nursing and bathing at which time he or she is showered with love and affection. A baby learns to develop complete trust in his or her mother, who returns this trust with complete and uncritical love. Thus an infant is unable to fully explore his or her environment and must rely on only eyes or cries to express emotions. During the period of swaddling, the baby experiences repeated feelings of security and anger that are replaced with freedom and happiness when the kosinka is removed from time to time. Besides achieving total dependence on the part of parents, the Russian baby continually experiences polarized emo-tions in his or her infancy. As a result, the Russian child grows up with the dual beliefs of powerlessness and guilt for personal actions. Like the special relationship between Japanese mothers and their sons that results in the creation of *amae* or dependency (see Chapter 14), long-lasting psychological dependency is generally emphasized in Russian culture.

Without a doubt, Russian society has a pronounced collective emphasis. Young children are taught how to behave and relate to others at an early age. Respect and deference for authority figures is a norm in every classroom. Landon Pearson (1990) points out that "a respectful and, indeed, slightly fearful attitude to adult authority is inculcated into Soviet children from the moment they set foot into an educational establishment" (p. 111). From childhood on, Russians acquire an acute sense of place and propriety, of what is acceptable and what is not. They generally know what they can get away with and what should not be attempted. Student discussion is limited, and individual thought is not encouraged. Pupils learn that supplying "official" answers ensures good grades, which can lead to admission to higher education and a good job after graduation.

Educational institutions are designed to shape young minds using structured discipline and group dynamics. Much learning is based on memory drills and the modeling of rigid prescriptions. The greatest offense is to be different. Classes are divided into groups with overall performance the responsibility of each member. Enormous peer pressure is exerted over children to achieve stringent expectations. Russian children learn early the futility of challenging authority; parents are often chastised by teachers and other officials for the failure of offspring to meet social norms.

Formal ballet productions bring together dancing, music, design, and an audience. With the exception of solos by individual dancers, the ballet troupe dances together as one large body. Even these solos are precisely blocked or staged by choreographers to balance the entire performance. All company members are dependent on one another, and individual needs, rights, and desires are subordinated to the whole, to the company itself. It is the choreographer's job to integrate the dancer's body with the music score, the possibilities of the stage, and the mood to be conveyed. Choreographers must "explore and expand the dancer's capabilities" while ensuring that the components of the ballet production, as well as the dancers, are all in synch (Clarke & Crisp, 1976, p. 38). As a result, Russian dancers think of themselves as members of a company, and "People's Artists" of the former USSR, rather than as individual dancers.

The group ethic can be traced to the *mir*, or the small village cooperative that made all farming decisions for the community, even through the early 1900s. Not only did the mir choose which crops to plant and when, it also collected taxes and resolved conflicts. As Richmond (1992) notes, "Its authority, moreover, extended beyond land matters. It also disciplined members, intervened in family disputes, settled issues which affected the community as a whole, and otherwise regulated the affairs of its self-contained and isolated agricultural world" (p. 15). The mir consisted of household heads who discussed issues and reached group consensus about courses of action. Decisions based on the collective will were binding on every household. Even before the 1917 revolution, Russian czars approved of this type of informal local government because such units were capable of controlling the vast populace. The mir enforced tax collection and military conscription as well as other programs that influenced the lives of the peasants. In describing the mir, Richmond

(1992) aptly concludes, "Because the mir affected so many people, it played a major role in forming the Soviet character" (p. 15). It is interesting to note that popular usage of the word *mir* refers to the definition of peace.

A few examples of collective behavior include communal seating in restaurants and group participation in attending cultural and sports events. Physical contact such as jostling or pushing among total strangers is typical in crowds, as is holding hands among friends of the same sex. Older Russians generally are more than happy to offer unsolicited advice, even to foreigners, and it is seldom considered impolite to drop in on friends unannounced (Richmond, 1992, pp. 17-20).

In sum, like the ballet, Russian culture can be unpredictable and enigmatic. Russian culture today fuses together the earnest elements of emotion, spirituality, and survival once found in old Russia. Echelons within Russian society, drama and realism, and the Russian soul as expressed in Russian ballet are characteristics that have made the Russian people culturally unique. Although Russia may privatize its economy significantly and become more Western in its economic orientation, the characteristics of the Russian ballet described in this chapter should be of help in understanding its underlying culture for years to come.

8

Belgian Lace

It is clear that while the diversity of the cultures alive in Belgium may sometimes be a source of friction, this same diversity can and must also be above all a source of spiritual and material enrichment.

For this very reason, and because Belgium is the common ground where two great European cultures meet, we must continue to be what we have always been in the past: Pioneers in the construction of a united Europe.
—King Baudouin,
1986 Christmas radio and television message

Belgium is a small country slightly larger than the state of Maryland, with just more than 10 million people. The distance between its farthest points is 175 miles. Given its size and population, the casual observer should be careful not to underestimate its high degree of importance and interrelatedness in Europe and the world. Just as the gifted lacemaker takes fine threads from many spindles and weaves them into a fabric with a beautiful but strong pattern, so history, geographic position, and religion have woven the Belgian culture into a diverse but integrated people. To understand Belgium, it is helpful to describe it in terms of the metaphor of lace.

Before doing so, however, let us explore Belgium's turbulent and fascinating history. For hundreds of years its people, both the Flemings (of Dutch origin) in the north and the Walloons (of French ancestry) in the south, were ruled by several other nations. Over the past 500 years, Austria, Spain, France, and the Netherlands have each ruled the area of present-day Belgium. Although there were indigenous nationalistic movements that sought to create the nation of Belgium, it was the machinations of Lord Palmerston, arguably the most influential foreign affairs minister that Britain has ever produced, that led to its establishment in 1830. He wanted to create a buffer zone between the Germans and the French in the event of war between these two nations and in the process provide England with breathing space before she was forced to enter any conflict. Lord Palmerston's instincts were unerringly correct: Belgium was the site of some of the bloodiest battles of both world wars, and without this buffer zone it is conceivable and even probable that Germany would have overwhelmed both France and England (Tuchman, 1962).

The Flemish and Walloon cultures have existed side by side until they have developed a sense of "Belgian pride." At multinational or world-class competitions, a Belgian is a Belgian, and the entire country unites to watch the performance, regardless from which side of the language border the participant or team came.

Still, it cannot be denied that there are conflicts and tensions between Walloons and Flemings. Unlike many other cultural groups living in one nation or area who escalate these differences into bloody confrontations and war—for example, Catholics and Protestants in Northern Ireland or Croatians, Bosnians, and Serbians in the former Yugoslavia—Walloons and Flemings have patiently addressed their differences in a systematic way since 1968. In 1993, the country established three independent and separate parliaments within the three major regions of Wallonia, Flanders, and Brussels. The central government has relinquished much of its power except in such areas as finance, defense, and international relations. Although this solution may seem contrived and unduly complicated, it is far preferable than the alternative of war and destruction. In fact, Belgium serves as a very useful model that other nations with diverse cultural groups can follow to avoid such alternatives, and this model closely resembles our metaphor of Belgian lace.

Lace first appeared in the late 15th century in Flanders and Italy, where it was first used as a modest ornament for the linen of undergarments. By approximately 1600, lace had become a fabric of utmost luxury and a key article of trade and commerce. Nobles from all over Europe began to enhance their clothing with lappets and cuffs of lace. Dresses were soon adorned with lace overlays and shawls. Beyond clothing, lace began to drape tables, windows, and bed linens. Lace was a sign of social status and wealth. As a lacemaking center, Flanders established itself as a prominent industrial region within Europe.

Bobbin lace, first introduced in Flanders, requires the weaver to manage hundreds of bobbins in creating a single piece of lace. Systematically and rhythmically the threads from the 10 to 20 sets of bobbins are braided around brass pins skillfully affixed to a cardboard pattern to form a geometric or pictorial design. The design incorporates a delicate balance of lace and space that is best exhibited when the lace is placed on a dark background fabric such as deep-colored velvet or satin. During the Renaissance, lacemaking emerged as both an industry and an art form, as the following passage confirms:

> Form became more important than color; instead of intricate effects of limitless expansion, designers stressed clarity, symmetry, and stability. In the decorative arts, the new spirit was most noticeably expressed in sharp distinctions between pattern, background, and frame. No minor art form embodied Renaissance ideals more fully than lace. (Benton, 1970, p. 85)

Traditionally, the best lacemakers were cloistered nuns. To create a square foot of lace with an intricate design may require hundreds or even thousands of hours. Legend has it that some nuns would spend their entire lives producing lace for the Pope's robes. Although lace is no longer a predominant industry in Belgium, and machine-produced lace is the norm, the Belgians still take great pride in this traditional art form; most homes have at least one piece of handwoven lace on a table or displayed in a frame.

Many Belgians can hold up a piece of lace and tell if it was handwoven or machine-made, what its retail value should be, and from what region of the country it came. The texture and pattern of the lace have regional characteristics. For instance, in Brugge and Turnhout the texture is delicate and the patterns are ornate, whereas in St. Hubert the thread is coarse and the design more simple. Hence lace from Brugge might typically be used as a table runner between meals, and lace from St. Hubert might adorn the edge of the tablecloth used during a meal.

A Land of Contrasts

The beauty of lace can be fully appreciated only when the contrast of woven cloth and dark background are recognized within the overall form. Just as lace interweaves contrasting elements of a complex design into a single structure, so many contrasting elements are interwoven in Belgium, a small country that includes three recognized languages, two major cultures, three separate official regions, three flags, two major economic centers with separate industries, and three unique geographic landscapes. The starkest contrasts for Belgium are linguistic and political. In addition, there are other areas of contrast:

- the struggle between individualism and the need to belong to a group, conform to societal rules, and have strong family ties;
- the dichotomy between working and social welfare;
- the stark difference between urban and rural areas; and
- the desire not only for art and beauty but also for practicality.

Still, just as a lacemaker integrates contrasting designs in the masterpiece, the Belgian government attempts to integrate separate cultures into a unified republic, even when there are three separate parliaments. Linguistically, the Belgian government recognizes three native languages through regulations regarding the conduct of education and commerce within the areas populated primarily by native speakers. In Flanders, the northern portion of the country that borders the Netherlands, business and education are primarily conducted in Dutch, which is the native language of the Flemish people, who represent some 60% of the Belgian population. In Wallonia, the southern portion of the country that borders France, business and education are primarily conducted in French, the native language of the Walloons, who constitute approximately 34% of Belgians. In Limburg, a very small area bordering Germany with some 1% of the population, German is the native language. To be impartial and economically viable, in the capital city of Brussels, merchants, educators, government officials, and others conduct business in Dutch, French, or English at the mutual preference of the participants.

Brussels is at the crossroads of Europe and many multinational firms have established European offices there in recent years because of the proposed unification of the European Community (EC). At any given time, approximately 5% of the Belgian population is foreign.

In Belgian schools, for at least eight years children are required to study the native language of the region in which they live. They are also required to study a second language—which could be Dutch, French, English, or German—for at least four years. It is not uncommon to meet a Belgian, usually a Fleming, who is proficient in each of the four languages and others. However, Belgians are very proud of their native languages and cultures. If two headstrong Belgians, a Fleming and a Walloon, have to communicate, they will usually defer to English, because the Walloon will probably not be able to speak Dutch, and the Fleming will not condescend to speak French to a Walloon.

In everyday life, the impact of these linguistic differences varies significantly and may not be encountered at all by those who reside deep within Flanders or Wallonia. By contrast, Belgians living closer to the language border or in Brussels must deal with language differences daily. Belgians tend to appreciate the use of their languages and will generally warm to outsiders more quickly if an attempt is made to learn at least one language. Although many Belgians deal with the language differences everyday, it is in poor taste for a foreigner to point out the differences or to wonder aloud why the differences cannot be resolved through diplomacy.

The oldest Catholic university in the world, the University of Leuven, located 20 miles east of Brussels in Flanders, illustrates the consequences of the language conflict. For hundreds of years the university served both Flemish and Walloon students and scholars, using French as the official language on campus. After World War II, linguistic tensions began to mount, causing tensions between student groups and sporadic scuffles in cafés around the university. More than 20 years of hostility evolved to the point that the university was divided into two campuses: one in Leuven (Flanders) and one on the other side of the language border in Wallonia. This separation divided not only students and faculty but also resources such as the library collection. Books were literally divided by title, with those in the first half of the alphabet staying in Leuven and those in the second half going to the new campus. Conducting research now necessitates visiting two campuses, but this cumbersome and inefficient solution is preferable to a long-standing linguistic conflict.

As an extension of the dual languages and cultures of the Flemings and Walloons, the country has three prominent flags: the Flemish lion, the Walloon rooster, and the national Belgian tricolor of black, yellow, and red. Most Belgians identify more emotionally with the flags of their respective cultures than the national tricolor. The Flemish lion is the symbol of the Flemish resistance to French domination over hundreds of years.

As noted above, politically Belgium is a constitutional monarchy, divided into three republics: Flanders, Wallonia, and Brussels. Each republic has its own representatives in the central government or national parliament and its own divisions of the national political parties, which are also divided into subparties by language. Each subparty operates autonomously and yet generally follows the same political agenda as the parent party.

The two largest political parties are the Christian People's party, whose members are primarily Flemish and Catholic; and the Socialist party, whose members are less strict Catholics and non-Catholics and more heavily Walloon. These two parties are also responsible for publishing most of the major newspapers in Belgium (five of seven), and supervising social facilities for youth, sports confederations, care of the aged, hospitals, savings banks, and unions. Close to 70% of all workers are union members. The successful administration of the trade unions and other social programs depends heavily on social stability. Because of the extensive influence of these two political parties in the life of the average Belgian, other political parties have not gained a significant foothold. Although all Belgians are required to vote in every election, they are free to vote for candidates of any political group.

Turning to the contrast between individualism and the acceptance of group and societal rules, Hofstede's (1980a) cross-cultural study ranked Belgium 33rd out of 40 nations in its citizens' tendency toward individualism rather than group behavior. It is considered a major accomplishment for a young adult to become established in his or her own house apart from the family. Hard work is also valued, because it is seen as providing an incentive for individuals to branch away from the home. Still, even when the young leave the immediate family, they do not venture far geographically, usually living within 30 miles of their parents' home. This practice creates a strong family and community tie, essentially enhancing the Belgians' family orientation.

Belgian individualism is also displayed in the preference for owning their homes. Despite the great expense, nearly 65% of Belgians own the place where they live from condominiums to suburban-country homes. Peoples' homes are their castles, and Belgians tend to take great pride in the cleanliness of their homes. Early in the morning it is common to see people sweeping their porches and walkways. Although an American might use a garden hose to wash down a sidewalk, a Belgian would typically use a bucket and a scrub brush. This preference may be traceable to the historical shortage and high cost of fresh water. Belgians also tend to take very short baths; use soapy water to wash the dishes and then wipe the soap off with a towel, rather than rinse with water; and drink soda water, juice, beer, or wine rather than tap water or anything made with tap water.

Just as each region of Belgium has a distinctive style and texture to its lace, so condominiums and row houses are often organized and decorated very distinctively, reflecting the tastes of their owners. Unlike England's traditional houses (see Chapter 1), the interior layout of a Belgian row house cannot be assumed from its exterior appearance. In Flanders, it is common for extended families to gather together to construct the exterior brick walls of a new or remodeled home.

Although Belgians tend to be individualistic, their family orientation is strong. The family plays a central role in daily life. Family activities and meals are highly cherished. Most Belgian children go home after a long day at school, do their homework, eat dinner, help with chores, and spend time with their family. Family time often includes reading or watching television. On TV they can see programs broadcast in French, Dutch, German, and English, usually with subtitles in a second language. Because the state owns the Belgian television stations, there are few commercials.

On weekends, many Belgian children participate in scouting programs. Sunday lunch is usually the biggest meal of the week and will normally take place at the same relative's house every week, with family from the immediate area all attending. If a husband and wife live close to both in-laws, then they will frequently rotate Sundays between the two families.

Mothers often work. Out of a total workforce of 2.7 million, some 900,000 are women; however, they typically are found in traditionally nonmale occupations such as nursing and secretarial jobs. Few have completed a university education or occupy top-management positions. Day care is heavily subsidized by the state.

Families often spend weekends and vacations together, traveling to the Belgian coast for short stays and to Spain or the Riviera for longer stays. In the warm months, camping in the Ardennes (the mountains of southeast Belgium) is a frequent pastime.

When a couple marries, the woman takes the name of the man and connects it with her maiden name; for example, if she were a Smith and married a Jones, then her married name would be Mrs. Jones-Smith. Especially in Wallonia, it is not uncommon for a couple to live together until the woman becomes pregnant with their first child, at which time the couple will revert to Catholic tradition and marry in the church. Because of the Catholic influence, divorce is rare and only recognized after years of separation. However, the economy, more than the Catholic church, has influenced the size of families. The socially correct family size is two children, and a family has received a perfect gift from God if the two children are a boy and a girl.

In the family it is typical for the father and the eldest son to be the ultimate decision makers. Mothers usually administer discipline and rule household matters. Since around 1970, much has been done to emancipate women through legislation and political decision making. Although legal equality has been mostly achieved, it will take time to eradicate the convictions and prejudices that have been nurtured for so many years. Moreover, the gender-based segregation of half of the country's elementary classes (primarily in parochial schools) reinforces the traditional view of woman's role (Verleyen, 1987, pp. 189-192).

Aside from family, over his or her lifetime, the average Belgian will only have a few truly close friendships. Unlike the United States where people tend to be quick to establish friendships, Belgians generally require a great deal of time for relationships to mature. Most people with whom Belgians interact regularly will remain simply acquaintances, although they may have known each other for years (see also Chapter 4).

Belgians normally hold their right to privacy and their own opinions sacred. As lacemakers have a range of motions within which they pull from their bobbins and weave their threads around the brass pins, so Belgians seem to have similar ranges in their varied activities. Still, rarely does a Belgian stray far from the group by taking an extreme position. Belgium is generally a country of consensus, compromise, and cooperation. However, eccentric artists are revered as the embodiment of the eternal voice of protest, as long as they are not hostile or confrontational. For the individual, however, exclusion from the group can entail loneliness, pain, and, more often than not, material poverty (Verleyen, 1987, p. 119).

Overarching the individualism of each Belgian is a set of common political rules that have governed public policy and conduct for decades (Verleyen, 1987, pp. 147-150):

- The monarchy and Brussels are untouchable; in other words, all else could change, but there should still be a monarchy and Brussels should still be the capital.
- European unification and the EC are to be advocated without any reservation.
- The authority of NATO and the American ally may be the subject of frequent criticism, but they also enjoy the privilege of inviolability.
- Prosperity is to be shared and not to be used as a justification for confrontation or class struggle.

- Labor strikes should not be allowed to jeopardize the existing economic order.
- Privacy and personal liberty are not to be impeded in any serious ways.

The varied types of occupations and pastimes enjoyed by the Belgian population present yet another area of contrast. Belgium has a long tradition of agricultural activity. The central area around Brussels has rich soil and flat terrain that is conducive to farming, yet less than 10% of the GNP comes from farming, although the population is increasingly concentrated in the urban areas and engaged in industrial and service activities. Nonetheless, Belgians vigorously defend and subsidize their traditional agricultural base.

In the past few years a great debate has raged over national subsidies to the mining and steel industries located particularly in the Walloon region. Many believe there is no prospect of these industries ever regaining their former status or profitability. Many assert that governmental support should be rechanneled to help expanding industries where Belgium can compete in the EC and worldwide.

The contrasting fortunes of the north and south of Belgium have undergone a dramatic change over the last century. In 1830, French was the official language of the Belgian kingdom. The nobility spoke French, government proceedings and church services were conducted in French, and the wealthiest citizens, the Walloons, spoke French. French thus came to be perceived as the cultured language. Conversely, the Flemings were perceived as the uncultured and poorer members of Belgian society. As fortunes shifted from the coal and steel industries in Wallonia to the shipping and international trade industries of Flanders, the Flemimgs found themselves in a position to demand recognition of their language and cultural heritage. Over the last decade, Flanders has continued to prosper, whereas most of Wallonia has been devastated by depression and unemployment averaging more than 15%.

Belgians must attend school from age 6 to age 18. Programs are rigorous, and most children have at least two hours of homework every night after eight hours of school. To proceed from one level of education to the next, each student must pass an examination. The results of the exams determine what schools the student may attend and what vocation he or she may undertake. As in Germany, students begin studying for a vocation in their early teens. By the time they come out of secondary school, most begin internships in their chosen vocations or go straight into college. Belgians are highly educated and skilled craftsmen. Thus the high rates of unemployment are disconcerting and depressing for many of them.

In general, Belgians are hardworking, just like the lacemaker who may work nearly 1,000 hours on a intricate piece of lace that measures only one square foot, investing not only time but also pride in the quality of his or her work. Because of the great pride they take in their work and craftsmanship, regardless of how depressing the prospects of long-term unemployment might be, many Belgians would prefer to draw unemployment over doing menial work below their level of training or skill. Therefore immigrants from Third World countries are viewed as necessary to correct a temporary labor imbalance. Typically, immigrants are brought in from North Africa and Turkey to work in the mines and other menial jobs that Belgians reject. These immigrants are given access to many of the social programs such as medicine and government welfare, but they are ineligible to vote and are rarely allowed to become citizens. Although Belgians tend not to warmly welcome Third World foreigners, anti-racism legislation makes discriminatory public expressions against immigrants punishable by law. Further, although the Belgians feel that Third World immigrants are only temporarily needed, long-range forecasts show that the Belgian population is shrinking because of low birthrates and emigration, whereas the immigrant population is increasing. As mentioned earlier, social tradition has led most Belgian families to have two or fewer children despite the fact that the Catholic-influenced legal system prohibits abortion and most forms of birth control.

Overall, Belgians believe that people have a need and desire to work. To minimize unemployment, there has been an effort to reduce the work week from 40 to 38 hours, thus allowing a few more workers into industry. Retirement age is already set at 60 years, and all Belgians have at least 4 weeks of vacation paid by the government. The call for more reductions in working hours is related to a strong belief in trade union circles that the redistribution of available work will help force down unemployment rates (Verleyen, 1987, p. 231).

Today most Belgians are forward thinking in their economic activities and moving heavily into service and diplomatic industries in response to their native skills and worldwide economic demands.

Another sharp and abrupt contrast is between urban and rural settings. The Belgian countryside is green and lush because of the abundant rainfall and high humidity throughout the year. A drive through Belgium reveals long stretches of rolling green hills with little white farmhouses. The older farmhouses have their barns on the first floor and family quarters upstairs; the farmer with his large workhorse plowing his field is a frequent sight. At times like these, it is hard to imagine that Belgium ever entered the 20th century.

The cities typically appear as medieval fortresses, many with surrounding walls that prevent the gentle fall from urban to suburban to rural. There are no suburbs in Belgium. An aerial view at night would show roughly circular areas of dense lights surrounded by thin networks of lights along major highways and a few spots of light in rural areas. This view might resemble the contrasting lace made around Brussels that has densely woven patches delicately connected by threads to other densely woven patches.

Inside the cities are more contrasts between modern industrial facilities and the grandeur of older architecture. In Brussels, the Atomium, a large structure constructed on the occasion of the 1958 world's fair, resembles a giant silver atom. It has elevators that will take visitors up for a view around the city. The NATO buildings, among others, are modern and efficient. By contrast, the Brussels town square, the Grande Place, is surrounded by cobblestone streets and buildings with ornately carved facades, and it draws the visitor back to the city's 16th-century origins.

A final area of contrast in Belgian culture is that between their love for art and beauty and their sense of practicality. Obviously, most lace is beautiful and artistic, but it is also designed to adorn clothing and linens rather than to be simply admired. The artistic history of the country is evidenced by the prominence of museums, theaters, and artistic venues. Belgium seems to have a museum for everything. The largest is the open-air museum at Bokrijk. Rural buildings from various centuries have been excavated from all over the Belgian area and painstakingly rebuilt here. Many retirees dress up in the authentic costumes of the times and display the tools and crafts of the era from which the buildings come.

The Rijksmuseum in Antwerp has one of the finest collections of Flemish artists in the world. Flemish art was the world standard from the 16th through early 18th centuries. Exemplified by the Brueghels, the van Eycks, and Peter Paul Rubens, Flemish art started with the vivid colors and figures of the Italian Renaissance but made the people less elongated, plumper, and more realistic. Typical signs that a painting comes from the Flemish era are the presence of lace on the clothing in portraits or on the table in a still life and rosy red cheeks in portraits.

Inside many of the oldest churches in Belgium, one can find wonderful works of art, most with no apparent security systems. For example, it is not uncommon to locate a work by Rubens, van Eyck, or van Dyck hanging in an obscure village church where the doors are never locked. Some of these churches appear old and worn on the outside, but inside they have beautifully carved vestries and pedestals for the priests to stand on while preaching. Hung around the inside walls of the church are art works representing the 12 stations of the cross. Most churches were constructed so that lighting is primarily natural and from candles. The art here was created to inspire the worshipper rather than simply to be admired, so the concept that someone might steal these works from the churches is absurd to the average Belgian. The oldest churches are all Catholic, each having a statue of the Virgin Mary with blazing little white candles all around her. When Belgians, even nonpracticing Catholics, are troubled by work or family matters, one will frequently hear them tell how many candles they have lit for Mary.

The study of artistic history is strongly supported by the school system. Schoolchildren flood the museums throughout the school year for lectures and sightseeing. Early lessons stress the importance of Belgian artists, nearly to the exclusion of others. This emphasis on art is initiated at a very young age and is carried forward through most Belgians' lives. The people of Belgium do seem to have painting in their blood, and they like to hear themselves described as a nation of painters. Belgium is proud of its artistic past, and not without reason.

Another example of Belgian practicality is the site where the Battle of the Bulge was waged in World War II. This battle was a major victory for Allied forces, and the site has been a major tourist attraction for many years. It is marked by a large circular monument with pillars listing the names of the dead in that battle, suggesting a modern Stonehenge. The monument is surrounded by rolling hills that, during tourist season, are meticulously covered with rows of white crosses to mark the resting places of the dead. After tourist season (September through April), the crosses are removed and cows are pastured on the hills.

Control

Lace production requires strict and complex controls to avoid needless flaws. In addition, there must be balance between the spindles and the thread and between the patterns in the cloth. This emphasis on controls and balance is similarly found in the Belgian preference for controlling behavior, interacting with friends and colleagues in familiar situations and surroundings, and leading balanced lives. In Hofstede's (1980a) cross-cultural study of 40 nations, Belgium had the third highest score for uncertainty avoidance. There are several areas where Belgians tend to exhibit this high degree of control and uncertainty avoidance, including lifestyle, transportation, social conventions, rules and procedures, and stress management. Belgians are very regulated and suspicious of anyone who would change their adopted schedule or routine. Most Belgians have a deep-rooted attachment to what is called a "3 × 8" time schedule: 8 hours for work, 8 hours for play, and 8 hours for sleep. Modern management proposals to change the organization of work so as to increase industrial output are heavily opposed. Many who own their own small businesses work longer hours, but they also tend to live over their shops, so they are never far from home and family. Most shops and businesses are closed on Sunday, although since the Catholic church changed its policy to allow parishioners to attend high mass on Saturday evening, more Belgian businesses have Sunday hours.

To avoid uncertainty, the political and linguistic borders are well-defined and mapped. Savvy travelers usually can determine which regions they are in by the first reference on city street signs. However, this can all be very confusing to the unaware, because a sign may list two or more names for the same place—for example, Antwerpen (Dutch), Anvers (French), and Antwerp (English). In the city, most maps and signs will read "Antwerpen." However, if the consulted map came from Wallonia or France, then the city will be marked as "Anvers."

Belgium has several large ports, including Antwerp, which is the second largest port in Europe. To accommodate the huge amount of trade from its port cities, Belgium has designed the most immense transportation system in the world for a country its size. Like the threads in a piece of lace, the highways, railways, and canals in this system connect every city and village in the country, allowing goods to flow efficiently all over Belgium and into the rest of Europe.

Major roads are constructed in a hub-and-spoke fashion. There are usually roads encircling larger cities with spokes extending out toward other major cities. These highways have many signs and directions in various languages designed to accommodate industry and travelers. As one drives along the spokes from one city to another, the name of the road will change halfway between cities. Should one take the Mechelen road from Brussels to get to Mechelen, halfway to Mechelen the name of the road will change to the Brussels road, indicating that the traveler is now closer to Mechelen than Brussels. Changing road signs can severely complicate the trip of the inexperienced traveler, especially when the languages change. However, this practice is very orderly to the Belgian mind, just as the pattern and texture of a piece of lace is set by its origin.

As one drives over the cobblestone roads of the inner city and the occasional dirt roads in the country, there are no stop signs. It is assumed at every intersection that the driver to the right has the right of way, no matter what the circumstances. Therefore, technically at every intersection the driver need look only to the right before proceeding, and the Belgians will sometimes grow quite impatient with a traveler who stops to look in all directions before proceeding.

One of the most interesting jobs keeping some Belgians away from the unemployment office is that of road worker. Many city streets are paved with cobblestones. To maintain these streets, road crews can be seen working on a small area at the side of the road, digging up the cobblestones, placing them in a pile, cleaning them carefully, and then re-laying them. However, the stones are not simply replaced in a haphazard fashion: They are relaid in an orderly pattern similar to the manner in which lace is arranged, often with some artistic, geometric design. Hence this job, although superficially menial, appeals to the Belgian sense of industry, beauty, and practicality.

In social settings, Belgians are generally very formal in their interactions with others and use several explicit rules. For instance, when greeting others, the surname is the proper way to address all others except very close friends. The casual manner in which first names are used in many countries would probably offend most Belgians. This formality is common in business and social settings, even with neighbors and acquaintances.

Formal titles are used in many business and social settings in lieu of the full name; for example, "Monsieur" or "Mijnheer" for a man, "Madame" or "Mevrouw" for a married woman, and "Mademoiselle" or "Juffrovw" for a single woman. Titles are also used in many subordinate-superior relationships, such as student to professor and employee to boss. Both the French and Dutch languages incorporate formal and informal manners in which a person can be addressed. Informal address is used when addressing a child, but adults generally need to know one another well before communicating in this way. Among younger people and in business with English-speaking partners there is, however, less formality, and first names are commonly used.

Greetings are also an extremely important part of the social ritual. Handshakes are the norm unless the two parties are good friends. A person will typically shake hands with everyone during the greeting and again before leaving the meeting or event. Belgians will often lament if they do not have a chance to shake hands before parting. In addition, women greeting either men or women in an informal manner will generally kiss three times on alternating cheeks.

Belgians are quite conscious of social rituals such as gift giving. Gifts are given at any type of social visit and not to do so would be seen as rude. A typical gift when one is invited to dinner would be flowers, a small box of chocolates, or an unusual fruit such as a pineapple. If the visit were to extend to several days, it would be common practice to offer a gift for each day spent. Acknowledgments and thanks are made in writing for any gift received, even birthday and holiday cards. New Year's cards are sent in addition to Christmas cards.

Almost all social gatherings are somewhat formal. When alcoholic beverages are served, it is customary to wait until everyone is served and then, with some ceremony, to raise one's glass to each person in turn, catching his or her eyes and wishing "Gezondheid," "Santé," or the like. Likewise, it is customary to wait for everyone at the table to be served before eating. Just before taking the first bite of food, everyone says "Smakelÿk" or "Bon appétit"—in other words, wishes everyone else a tasty meal. Invitations are frequently sent to dinner guests, even to close friends, and a formal four-course meal is normally prepared. Afternoon tea also can be a formal event. People, including close friends and family members, seldom drop by another's house without first telephoning. Neighbors also observe this protocol, maintaining a high level of formality when interacting. All this formality, however, does not keep Belgians from visiting one another. They normally love to socialize; they just like to plan ahead when someone is coming. Their plans often include going to the bakery on the corner to get a special dessert to serve with tea, which may be either a traditional or an herb tea.

When one enters a Belgian home, there is generally an unheated entry way with stone or linoleum flooring where coats are hung and wet shoes kept. By contrast, the living area of the house is generally warm and cozy. Thoughts of putting on a cold coat and wet shoes may explain why guests stay so long on winter nights.

Belgians tend to require certainty and privacy in social settings as well as in everyday life. In some Belgian residences almost every door has a lock. In a home or a business this means that even cabinets and closets can be locked. A homeowner may need 50 keys to guarantee privacy and security. In the older buildings of the University of Leuven, there is even a light above the professor's closed office door. When a student wants to see the professor, he must ring a bell, in response to which the professor activates the light's color to indicate whether the student should come in (green), wait a few minutes (yellow), or go away (red). Although this may seem extreme, it appeals to the Belgian sense of practicality.

Certainty is also highly desirable in social agreements. A Belgian's word is his or her bond, and promises must be kept. However, beneath all of the formal rituals and procedures, Belgians tend to be quite friendly, low-key, and good-natured. To see this side of their personality, one can go to a local pub and observe the closeness of the relationships and abundant consumption of beer. Beer is not only a cherished drink but also a source of pride for Belgians. Most Belgian cities have at least one brewery, and the smell of hops hangs in the damp winter air. Belgians will make beer out of most any grain and wine out of most any fruit.

Another place where Belgians are sure to congregate is at the local *frituur* or french fries stand. In most neighborhoods it is a place of escape from the cold weather and where Belgians can learn all of the latest gossip. Belgian french fries, *frites* (pronounced "freets"), are thickly sliced and fried once at low heat enough to soften them. Then they are allowed to cool completely before being fried again in very hot lard. The result is a crispy outside, with a soft inside, much like the bread in the bakeries. Frites are served in a paper cone with a choice of 20 or more toppings, including stew meat (usually horse meat with a beer gravy), curry sauce, and "sauce American," or ketchup. They are as popular in Belgium as hamburgers are in the United States.

Before lacemakers arrange the spindles and threads to begin weaving pieces of lace, they design the patterns on cardboard and very carefully punch brass pins in the cardboard patterns to guide the threads during weaving. Similarly, one manifestation of high uncertainty avoidance is that Belgians have regulations and customs that act as brass pins to guide behavior in most situations. They tend to dislike the government and police officers; but, loving order, they tolerate the intrusion. Dealing with government offices is tedious. There are specific papers and experts for everything. First one must figure out what paper to fill out for the needed service, and then the trick is to figure out what building and what window has the expert who can process the paperwork.

A foreigner moving to Belgium has 30 days to register and get a resident visa from the city that governs the area where the foreigner will be living. Then the visa must be renewed every three months and a new one must be issued whenever the foreigner changes addresses. Citizens of the EC are not required to carry visas, but most Belgians carry personal cards or business cards, with their family name, home address, and telephone number, which they can exchange or leave with a note on the back if they missed someone on whom they came to call.

Hofstede correlated high uncertainty avoidance with high anxiety and stress. This characteristic is manifested in Belgians in several ways. One is that they are a "doing" society: busy all day long, typically rising very early. Many Belgian sayings refer to the judicious use of time, such as "Time is money," "Make hay while the sun shines," and "Time heals all, so get back to business" (Verleyen, 1987, p. 55). They try to prepare for everything so that nothing can go wrong. Much of this feeling must be attributed to their geographical location and historical lack of control over invading armies. As noted earlier, modern Belgium has only been a country since 1830. The North Sea on the west is Belgium's only natural boundary. Therefore, any emperor conquering the continent generally started in Belgium (one of the so-called Low Countries) and moved on from there, as did Hitler in the 20th century.

The religious orientation of the Belgians also contributes to their need to be constantly busy. Catholic doctrine places high importance on good works and personal industry in this life to ensure a comfortable station in the next. Approximately 75% of Belgians are Catholic. Historically, Belgium produced more nuns and priests per capita than any other nation in the world. Although religious intensity has declined since World War II and most Belgians do not attend church regularly, more than 60% are still educated in Catholic schools.

As the official religion of Belgium, Catholicism has its parishes, priests, and schools heavily subsidized by the state. Freedom of religion is guaranteed in the Belgian constitution, and most major religions can be found somewhere in Brussels. But for most Belgians, religions other than Catholic are for foreigners.

One result of the great effort that Belgians make to follow tradition and avoid uncertainty is that they frequently have little breakdowns. It is not uncommon to call on them for an appointment and be put off because today they are having a *zenuw inspanning*, a Dutch phrase translated as a "nervous strain." Typically, this means they have overslept, overexerted themselves, or generally are not prepared to face the world for a while.

When they feel a breakdown coming on, the average Belgian will call a doctor who will routinely prescribe tranquilizers and bed rest. Belgian medicine is socialized and easily obtainable. The health care infrastructure is immense, given the population size. The number of hospital beds and doctors per 1,000 inhabitants is an unchallenged world record. Home visits by doctors and nurses are common, and paramedic support is widespread.

Cooperation and Harmony

The lacemaker's primary thoughts while weaving a strand of lace must always focus on the balance and symmetry of the design. A careful balance is maintained to ensure that neither the lace nor the linen overpowers the other. The overall effect should be one of harmony, with no stray ends or spaces to mar the unity of the structure. Each movement of the lacemaker may be quick and concise but is always within a small range of motion. There are no extreme movements.

Further, lace itself is a subtle and unobtrusive material. All white or ivory, traditional lace is used to neutralize the bold colors of background material, to soften the hardness of wooden tables, or to balance an object visually. The carefully balanced nature of lace with its neutralizing and nonextreme tone is reflected in the Belgian approach to the world, especially in continuity, statesmanship, and modesty.

Belgians exert a great deal of energy maintaining continuity, the status quo, balance, and a set standard of living for all. They normally work to ensure that their internal cultural and linguistic differences do not disrupt daily life, squelching conflicts by remaining neutral or by reaching mutual consensus among the involved parties. Throughout its existence, Belgium has had linguistic tensions of varying intensity. Yet these tensions have never mounted to violence or bloodshed. When necessary, concessions were made and tempers were defused so that tensions would be carefully balanced. In lacemaking, this means the threads are held tightly to reduce slack and the potential for unnecessary gaps and holes that might weaken the durability and quality of the cloth.

Although Belgians can do little to control the weather in their country, the moderate climate seems to reflect their approach to life:

the middle road between extremes. Because of the gulf streams off the coast, the climate is very mild, ranging only from the mid-30s in winter to the mid-70s in summer. The weather is frequently cloudy or rainy, with little snow and few fully sunny days. However, a winter day with clouds is preferable to a cloudless day, because the cloud cover tends to insulate the land.

The middle road between extremes is also where the Belgian manager can usually be found. Subordinates will refer to managers using formal titles and last names; however, a manager will seldom stand out because of appearance, conspicuous consumption, or attitudes that might separate management from line workers, as frequently happens in the United States. Again, to Belgians wealth is to be shared rather than flaunted.

Further, the Belgian balancing and peacemaking approach to life is replicated in their competitive (or not-so-competitive) nature. Belgians tend to be cooperative to a greater extent than they are competitive. Their social and economic structure was designed in a fashion that actually lessens the competitive drive. For instance, the socialized system for health and welfare provides full health care and monetary subsistence for all citizens. Because all those who are unemployed are eligible for welfare, receiving more than 70% of what they would have obtained if they were working, there is no problem of homelessness. Further, there is no time limit on eligibility for unemployment, as long as the person appears at the appointed time each week at the unemployment (labor bureau) office and regularly applies for openings in her or his stated occupation. The appointed time changes each week to prevent working around the appointment.

Recently there has been discussion of limiting the unemployment allowance to five years, but as long as the government can afford it, Belgians will probably not limit this subsidy. Most citizens feel it is a social right to have a certain standard of living regardless of a person's ability to find a job for which he or she is suited. Needless to say, the unemployment subsidy, social security and health care system, and other socialized services in Belgium are largely responsible for one of the highest tax rates in Western Europe. Although Belgian workers tend to be highly skilled and hardworking, thus creating a situation in which there is high productivity per worker, the tax rates are so high that the cost of labor almost offsets productivity.

Another factor of Belgian society that induces a less-competitive nature is that the salary earned in many jobs does not vary to reflect effort and performance. For instance, a professor who instructs classes, devotes an inordinate amount of time to research, and publishes regularly will not be paid any more than a professor who maintains a much more relaxed lifestyle. Other than personal achievement, which is not necessarily highly valued, there is little reward for working harder than the average professor or co-worker. There is a greater emphasis on cooperation between colleagues rather than climbing over one another to get to the top.

Further, Belgians share a great tradition of statesmanship and the ability to negotiate on behalf of others. Peter Paul Rubens, the Flemish painter, was a legendary statesman. Although he could paint, his greatest efforts were in fostering international cooperation. He was hired by royalty and wealthy merchants to paint portraits of others. Since he had the subject seated for long periods of time, he was paid to put forth the philosophy or argument of his benefactor. For example, he was sent by Spanish King Philip IV to paint English King Charles I, all the while negotiating a trade agreement between the two nations. This is one reason why Rubens painted approximately 1,600 royal portraits.

Modern Belgians have carried forward this tradition. The cooperative nature of the Belgians is again apparent in their approach to the EC and the world. Belgium's linguistic and cultural diversity has made it an ideal model for such negotiations. Partly because of this unique status, Brussels was selected as the headquarters for the Common Market. In 1967, for many of the same reasons, NATO moved its headquarters from Paris to Brussels. Today, of the approximately 12,800 international associations in existence, nearly 1,300 are headquartered in and around Brussels. Because of Belgium's unqualified acceptance of these organizations, its balanced nature, and its central location, Brussels has become one of the most important international areas in the world.

In addition, international corporations seeking expansion into European markets have flooded the Belgian borders over the past 30 years. Approximately 40% of Belgian industries are foreign-owned. The Belgian government offers international groups major tax incentives to bring central offices or high-tech activities into the country. Despite generous wages, high manufacturing costs, and exorbitant personal tax rates, companies have sought out manufacturing facilities in Belgium to take advantage of the transportation infrastructure and friendly economic climate. Thus another element that the Belgians seemingly balance effortlessly is the internationalization of their small country while maintaining their own identity.

Finally, although there are obviously many reasons for Belgians to be proud and boastful, people outside the country are rarely aware of Belgian accomplishments. For instance, many readers may not have been aware of the importance of Belgium to lace and vice versa before reading this chapter. Also, it is not generally known that Belgians produce some of the best beer and chocolates in the world. Belgium has the highest per capita output of any European nation. Approximately 10% of the EC's external and internal trade volume is produced in Belgium with only 2% of the EC's population.

Despite Belgian prominence in the international circle, many people are still unfamiliar with the country. The reason behind this lack of international recognition seems to be primarily the result of the Belgian approach to life. Belgians are not generally boastful, tending not to expound about their capabilities and accomplishments. In contrast, they act much like a small piece of lace on the collar of a garment; they bring out the best qualities of those with whom they work without being flashy or calling attention to themselves. Some view this approach as an "inferiority complex" of sorts, but this idea is contradicted by the definite pride that Belgians feel toward different characteristics of their country. Belgians do not typically feel they are less important or worthy of praise, as an inferiority complex would suggest; in fact, quite the opposite. Belgians tend to believe that the country can and will be an integral player in the EC and the world. The typical Belgian emphasizes the role of coordinator and peacemaker among international markets, sometimes sacrificing publicity and worldwide recognition.

In short, Belgium is as complex as its renowned lace, and its citizens have learned to meet the challenges posed by the interactions that must occur among its cultural and linguistic groups. Although this country has been unified for only some 160 years, its past has been rich and its future is bright, especially as an integrated European Community becomes a reality and Belgium replicates its former prominence, at least partly because of its industry in weaving exquisite lace. Belgium adds character and richness to the EC, just as a small piece of lace adds beauty and depth to a well-crafted garment.

9

The Spanish Bullfight

The characteristic that on the surface best portrays Spaniards is their contagious vitality, that is, their love of life. Therefore, it may seem paradoxical that the metaphor used in this chapter to describe Spanish culture is the bullfight, a confrontation with death. Yet this feature touches on other less-obvious qualities pervasive among Spaniards: Underlying their *alegría* or outer joy, Spaniards tend to host a deeply ingrained sensitivity to the tragic and an equally strong emotional pull toward the heroic. Perhaps these sentiments, more than their love of life, are what have made the bullfight so popular among Spaniards for hundreds of years.

The bullfight combines a passionate celebration of life with an elaborate system of rituals, a grandiose and artistic spectacle with blood, violence, and a genuine danger to the valiant performers. It exemplifies Spanish pride, individualism, emotionalism, and many other characteristics of Spanish people and culture. The following discussion will relate different aspects of Spain's culture to the many facets of the bullfight. But first, the sequence of the event itself is provided to establish the language and image of the bullfight.

The bullfight, or *corrida de toros*, meaning "running of the bulls" (also *la corrida* or *los toros* for short) takes place on Sunday afternoons or on holidays, timed precisely against the setting of the sun. It is the only event in Spain that traditionally starts on time. The corrida begins with the white handkerchief signal of the officiating president and the sounding of a trumpet. The commencement of the bullfight is celebrated with the colorful opening *paseillo* or parade of participants who march in hierarchical order to the upbeat tune of the *paso doble*. Once the parade is over, the president again uses his white handkerchief to signal the entrance of the first bull, as he does to signal the beginning of each stage of the event.

The corrida has three separate groups (*cuadrillas*) of principal participants, each comprising a *matador* and his assistants. The cuadrillas fight and kill two bulls each, for a total of six bullfights during the event. When the first bull is released into the ring, it is confronted by three of the matador's assistants, the *banderilleros*. These men maneuver the bull with their magenta and gold capes, revealing to the matador the bull's peculiarities of movement; sometimes the matador also participates in this stage.

A few minutes later, the matador enters the ring and demonstrates his bravery with his more artistic cape passes, including the classic *verónica*. The matador's valor or lack thereof often evokes emotional responses among the spectators. They applaud, cheer, and shout "Olé!" when impressed by the matador's bravery, or they boo and whistle when displeased with his performance. In this way the public interacts with the matador, prompting him to perform more and more dangerous moves. These in turn further arouse the audience.

After the initial demonstrations with the bull, the two *picadores* enter the ring on horseback. One stands by as a reserve, whereas the other provokes the bull into charging his own horse. This allows him to get close enough to the bull to jab it with his long, spiked pole. The picador's task is to weaken the bull's neck muscles sufficiently that its head will hang low enough for the matador to make the kill.

The second stage of the bullfight allows the bull to perk up from its difficult ordeal with the picador. In this more exciting part of the fight, the banderilleros on foot each place two *banderillas* (colorfully decorated wooden sticks with barbed tips) into the bull's neck, where they remain. At this point the bull is rested and more ferocious than ever and is ready to challenge the matador in the final stage of the fight.

In the last phase, the matador has 15 minutes to display his skill and build up the drama of the "moment of truth," performing dangerous passes with the much smaller *muleta* (red cape), which is draped over his sword. Before beginning, he salutes the president, asks permission to kill the bull if it is his first bull of the afternoon, and may dedicate the kill to a friend, a dignitary, or the public. Once the kill is complete, the response of members of the audience determines to a large extent the level of the reward the matador is to receive. A brave bull also is applauded as it is dragged from the arena.

The same three stages are repeated for each of the five remaining bulls in the corrida, alternating cuadrillas with each new bull. The bullfight officially ends when the president leaves his seat.

Ancient Origins of the Bullfight

The bullfight has long been a popular feature of Spanish culture. Its appearance in Spain has been attributed to several possible sources, including festivities of the ancient Minoan culture on the island of Crete 2,000 years before Christ, Roman circus combats, and the Moors. Whichever explanation may be true, the roots of the Spanish bullfight lay buried under layers of different peoples who invaded the Iberian Peninsula (modern Spain and Portugal), bringing their respective cultures with them.

The same waves of invasions that somewhere along the way gave birth to the bullfight also bred the uniquely Spanish blend of races. People have inhabited what is now Spain for more than 100,000 years. Traces of the peninsula's prehistoric inhabitants include the famous cave paintings of Altamira, which are at least 13,000 years old. Recorded history picks up with the migration of the Iberian people from northern Africa into the southern two thirds of the peninsula, around 3000 B.C. A series of other peoples subsequently entered Spain to conquer, trade, or settle. The Phoenicians (a Semitic race) went first, followed by Celts (a Nordic race), Greeks, Carthaginians (from Carthage in northern Africa), Romans, Jews, Germanic tribes, and Moors. Gypsies are the most recent racial group to have taken their place in Spanish society, arriving from Egypt in the Middle Ages.

The physical characteristics resulting from the coming together of these various racial groups on the Iberian Peninsula are a mixture of short, dark, Semitic types (predominant in the South) and taller, fair descendants of Celtic and Germanic ancestors (most common in the North). Combinations of these traits are also frequently seen, such as the large number of people with dark hair and blue eyes. Another prevalent trait among Spaniards is the classic Roman nose. In sum, there is no single image that would accurately portray a "typical" Spaniard, although certain combinations of features are notably Spanish, especially if one looks separately at the different regions of Spain. In addition, certain personality traits cross tribal boundaries. Wheaton (1990) reports, "The Greek philosopher Stabo found common traits among all the isolated bands living on the peninsula: hospitality, grand manners, arrogance; indifference to privation, and hatred of outside interference in community affairs" (p. 21). These are characteristics that are still frequently used to describe the Spanish temperament.

The various invading peoples are also responsible for importing several prominent cultural attributes into Spain. The Romans (who ruled Spain for 400 years beginning circa 200 B.C.) brought their "vulgar Latin" language with them, which was to evolve into today's Castilian Spanish. The Spanish word for their country—*España*—is only a slightly modified version of the Latin name *Hispania* that the Romans gave to the country (Spain had previously been called *Iberia* by its Iberian inhabitants and *Hesperia* by the Greeks). The Romans also constructed aqueducts, bridges, roads, and walls. The famous two-level aqueduct of Segovia stands as an impressive relic of the Roman rule. Finally, the Romans were responsible for the spread of Christianity into Spain.

Attributable to the more than 700-year presence of the Moors, or Muslim Arabs, are more than 4,000 words in modern Spanish. Words for many agricultural products the Moors brought with them derive from this source, such as the Spanish word *arroz* from the Arabic *al ruzz* (rice), *aceite* from *al zait* (olive oil), and *naranja* from *naranj* (orange), foods that are now an intricate part of the Spanish diet (Graham, 1984). Also included are many words beginning with "al." The Arabic influence in Spain is also responsible for advances in the fields of irrigation, mathematics, medicine, and, most notably, architecture, among others. The light, airy, and colorful *Mezquita* (mosque) in Córdoba and the impressive palaces of the Alhambra and the Generalife in Granada are present-day monuments of Moorish architectural feats.

Cuadrillas

The successive waves of invasion and immigration can be likened to the repeated attacks of the fighting bull and, even more appropriately, to the series of six bulls that are released into the ring during the course of the event. In terms of this metaphor, foreign invasions were so common throughout Spain's early history that it would take two consecutive corridas for the defending toreros to experience as many attacking bulls as there were invading peoples! Furthermore, to defeat the attacking bull in the bullfight, several men must band together. This is the reason for the formation of the three cuadrillas. Translated, *cuadrilla* does not mean "team"; the men in the cuadrilla do not work closely together. Rather, it means "group, band, or gang," reflecting the fact of safety in numbers and that the toreros combine their distinct, individual efforts to achieve the death of the bull.

Like the attacking bull, the repeated invasions of the Iberian Peninsula by foreigners produced a tendency for the inhabitants to cluster together for a sense of security and control over the environment. This effect is reflected in the fact that Spanish peasants on the steppes of central Spain chose to build their houses near one another, forming many small hamlets, villages, and towns. Their fear of loneliness and desire for security were so strong that they were, and still are, willing to travel great distances to work their fields just so that they may live in the vicinity of others (Crow, 1985).

The tendency for Spaniards to live close together has generalized to urban housing arrangements, which take the form of apartment living rather than isolated home owning. In Spain, as in much of Europe, it is desirable to live as close to the center of the city as possible—that is, where the "action" is. Marvin (1988) writes, "It is felt that as one moves further from the centre, so the quality of life gradually diminishes, because at the far limits of the town there are few bars, shops and *plazas* [squares] where people gather" (p. 129). The effect of this sentiment can be compared to housing patterns in the United States, where the ideal middle-class home is considered to be a house in the suburbs with a nice-sized yard or, for the wealthy, a mansion in the midst of many acres of land. In Spain, however, the wealthiest Spaniards choose to make their urban apartments their permanent dwellings. They may, however, enjoy a country home as a secondary, weekend getaway.

Finally, the widespread insecurity among Spaniards that historically made city life so appealing may well be the reason why Spain had an above-average score on uncertainty avoidance in Hofstede's (1980a) study of cultural values in 40 nations; that is, Spaniards prefer to interact with long-term friends and acquaintances rather than with outsiders. As a result, Spaniards tend to work in the same organization for many years or even their entire lifetime. Relating the need for control over one's environment and nature to the bull-fight in southern Spain, where the event first appeared, Marvin (1988) writes:

> Nowhere is this subordination and "culturizing" of nature, in Andalus-ian terms, more dramatically demonstrated than in the *corrida*. It is an urban event intimately linked with the country, which brings together, in the centre of human habitation, an uncontrolled wild bull, an item from the realm of nature, and a man who represents the epitome of culture in that, more than any ordinary man, he is able to exercise control over his "natural" fear (the fear felt by the human animal), an essential prerequisite if he is to control the wild animal. . . . The *corrida* is constructed in such a way that the imposition of human will is extremely uncertain because of the difficult circumstances; a situation which in turn generates tension, emotion, and dramatic interest. (pp. 130-131)

In other words, the Spaniard's struggle against the uncertainty of nature and isolation is dramatized and celebrated through the me-dium of the bullfight. Similarly, the bullfight illustrates how, having grown accustomed to close physical proximity in the act of self-defense, Spanish people feel comfortable in crowds and often seek communal festivities. The bullfight itself attracts a large crowd and traditionally took place in the main plaza, the most central area of each town.

However, Spaniards' true loyalty does not extend to the larger collective; it is generally directed only toward a smaller unit: family, friends, town, or region. Like the cuadrilla, the family is a large and affectionate clan whose members ferociously defend one another's honor, rights, jobs, and so on. The worst insult one can give a man is to derogate his mother, and the worst thing one can say to a woman is to insult her child (Wheaton, 1990). The protective spirit of the family also extends to the upbringing of the children. Parents dress their children well and pamper them. They bring them along wherever they go and allow them to stay up until all hours of the night. This produces children who are good-natured and outgoing and who have a strong sense of self and of their own importance (Wheaton, 1990).

The backbone of the tribal system during Spain's history of battles and invasions was the women. Tough and resourceful, they held the group together and catered to the needs of family members (Crow, 1985). However, the woman's role is more of a nurturing than an authoritative one. Thus it is the husband, not the wife, whose role can be compared to that of the matador—that is, as the person who has the last word. Like the matador who adoringly dedicates the kill to his wife or sweetheart, the Spanish husband accords his wife her due respect as stronghold of the family; he thinks of her as if she were a saint. And he expects her to behave like one. Until very recently, the laws supported this expectation.

General Franco's 36-year dictatorship, from the Spanish Civil War until his death in 1975, had policies that were more backward for women than any other European country. A wife had to have her husband's written permission to do many things outside the home, such as opening a bank account, obtaining a passport, or traveling abroad. Civil divorce was illegal until 1981. Abortion, homosexuality, and adultery also were punishable by law. Abortion is still highly restricted and difficult to obtain. Extramarital affairs were considered unconditionally criminal for women; men were only at fault if they tainted the family's honor by failing to keep their affairs clandestine (Wheaton, 1990). The macho "Don Juanism" is so ingrained in Spanish culture that it was considered perfectly acceptable for a husband to keep a mistress on the side.

All of this has been rapidly changing in the past 15 years. Now an estimated 400,000 mothers are unmarried, and 60% of married women use contraceptives (Wheaton, 1990). Kissing and embracing in public are common. University attendance is split equally between the sexes. However, few women in Spanish society attain high-level jobs, and Spanish heritage is, of course, still patrilineal. Although a child goes by both his or her father's and mother's last names, within three generations the mother's name is lost. In addition, when a woman gets married, she adds her husband's name to her own, linking the two by the possessive word *de* ("of"). For example, if a woman named Maria Alberti married a man named Miguel Sanchez, her name would officially become Maria Alberti de Sanchez. If her husband then died, she would become Maria Alberti Viuda de Sanchez—literally, "Maria Alberti Widow of Sanchez." In short, although Spanish customs are changing, they are steeped in traditions such as those surrounding one's surname that perpetuate Spain's patrilineal orientation.

The family is only one side of the Spanish tendency to cluster into tight-knit groups such as the cuadrilla. The larger unit is the geographical region. Historically, when the people of Spain started grouping together, they did not unite under a national flag; the geographical boundaries that sliced up the country topographically and climatically also retained invaders and inhabitants within isolated regions of the peninsula. Foreign influences and native loyalties were therefore determined by region, resulting in vastly differing cultures and distinct personal appearances.

The greatest geographical barriers in Spain are its mountain ranges. Although foreigners normally think of Spain's sunny beaches and flat, coastal plains, it is actually one of the most mountainous countries in Europe, second only to Switzerland. It is also one of the largest countries in Europe, third in size after Russia and France (and larger than California but smaller than Texas). Thus distance also separates people and allows for great variation in the land.

In depicting the importance of the family unit in Spanish culture, it was said earlier that bullfighters work in three distinct groups, or cuadrillas. In a similar vein, the sectioning off of the seating in the bullfight arena can be said to parallel Spain's geographical, climatic, and cultural divisions.

Sol y Sombra

Seating at the bullfight is divided into three sections: sun (*sol*), shade (*sombra*), and a combination of sun and shade (*sol y sombra*). This is made possible by the previously mentioned fact that the hour at which the bullfight takes place is timed against the setting sun. Tickets for seats in the shade are the most expensive. They cost approximately double the price of seats in the sun, which are the cheapest. Because bullfight tickets are relatively expensive to begin with, the price differential in seating separates the members of the audience into wealthier and poorer groups.

With few exceptions, Spain itself can be divided into the cooler, wet, more prosperous North and the hot, dry, lethargic South. It also has a large, central plateau area (the *meseta*, or tableland) that undergoes extremes of both heat and cold, and poverty and wealth, making it comparable to the sol y sombra sections. A more detailed description of some of the better known Spanish regions will help illustrate the depth of regional differences in geography, climate, people, and culture.

In the northwestern corner of Spain just above Portugal lies Galicia. Its frequent rain and drizzle, lush vegetation, and wide *rías* (fjords) simulate the northern European landscape of the natives' Nordic ancestors who settled in the region. The Galicians also share their fair skin, light eyes, and bagpipe music with their Celtic cousins, the Scots. Working as fishermen, shepherds, and farmers, the people in rural areas of Galicia speak a soft dialect of Portuguese. Their folk songs and stories tell of their deeply sentimental love of their homeland.

Moving eastward along the northern coastline of Spain, one eventually encounters the Basque provinces. The region is one of Spain's most prosperous. Bilbao, the nation's industrial capital, is situated on the Basque coastline. The Basque countryside is adorned with beautiful Alpine vistas of rolling hills and Swiss-style farmhouses and is home to the hardworking, rugged descendants of the Iberian Peninsula's earliest settlers, the Iberians. The Basque language, Euskara, bears no demonstrable relation to any known language in the world. It is thought to date back to the prehistoric Bronze Age thousands of years before Christ. The Basques have one of the strongest separatist movements of all Spanish regions. Their notorious radical separatist organization, the ETA (an acronym for the Euskaran phrase "Basque Nation and Liberty") is responsible for widespread terrorist activities against the Spanish Civil Guard and Spanish civilians.

In Spain's northeastern corner, sandwiched between the Pyrenean mountains and the Mediterranean Sea, is the other region that harbors resentment against the control of Madrid. Supported primarily by its large textile and tourist industries, Catalonia shares the prosperity of the Basque region. Its culture is more European than the rest of Spain, having soaked up the refined flavor of Paris during its centuries under French control. The Catalan language is highly related to the southern French Provençal. It is a Mediterranean development of Latin and is taught in school and spoken by most Catalans. Barcelona, the capital of Catalonia, rivals Madrid in population and is playing an increasingly central role in European life and international affairs, for example, hosting the summer Olympic games in 1992. Catalans, although often characterized by their *seny*, or "canny common sense," also demonstrate artistic capability. The region has produced several master Spanish artists, including Salvador Dalí, Joan Miró, and architect Antoni Gaudí, and contributed to the artistic development of Málaga-born Pablo Picasso.

In the center of Spain, on its sparsely populated meseta, at an altitude of 2,000 to 3,000 feet, lies Castile, which exerts a dominant influence on Spanish culture. It is the birthplace of Spain's official national language known outside of Spain as Spanish and within it as Castilian. Castile also is politically dominant, with Spain's capital Madrid at its center. The landscape of this region consists of vast expanses of arid steppe on which 10,000 castles were built during the battles of the Middle Ages (hence the name *Castilla*). The dryness of the Castilian air allows for extremes of temperature, making the region akin to the sol y sombra seating at the bullfight. A Spanish proverb says, "Nueve meses de invierno y tres de infierno" ("Nine months of winter and three of hell"), and this accurately describes the Castilian climate. In Madrid, for example, even on the most treacherously hot days of August, the temperature can be deliciously cool in the shade, and one quite often needs a sweater in the evening.

Finally, Andalusia in southern Spain is home of the bullfight, Gypsies, and stereotypically dark Spaniards. The climate is relentlessly hot and dry. The peasants' parched faces mirror the parched face of the land, teaching the Andalusians both the cruelty and beauty of life (Wheaton, 1990). Strongly influenced by the long Moorish presence in Andalusia, the natives express their intense feelings of joy and tragedy through their flamenco dancing and lamenting *cante jondo*, or "deep song." Andalusia's scattered towns of whitewashed houses and red-tiled roofs reveal its Mediterranean essence. The majority of Andalusian land, however, belongs to a small number of large estates where acres and acres of irrigated rolling hills and valleys are used to cultivate olive groves and other agricultural products.

The above descriptions only hint at the incredible variety of Spain's regions and at the harshness of life in the heat of the Spanish sun. Although Spain lies roughly between the same parallels as Cape Cod, Massachusetts, and Cape Hatteras, North Carolina, and Madrid is at the same latitude as New York City, the mountains around Spain's periphery keep the Atlantic and Mediterranean moisture out. The central plateau bakes like an oven. The resulting austere living conditions throughout much of Spain are what engendered that underlying Spanish sense of sadness and tragedy that seems to relate more closely to the Spanish love of the bullfight than does the Spaniards' outward gaiety. Crow (1985) explains the sadness of Spain as follows:

> Spain is a tragic land, its songs are sad songs, and its dances are tragic dances. They are all suffused with a sense of loss and separation, a sense of tragedy and of imminent doom. One moment man is alive, the next he is several scattered fragments of the universe. His being is but a temporary union of these fragments. It is the flight of a bird through a room. (p. 367)

The Pompous Entrance Parade

A more joyful side of Spanish culture is represented by the paseillo at the beginning of the bullfight. The corrida opens with the proud march of all those individuals who appear in the arena during the course of the afternoon. Lavishly costumed, everyone from the matador to the *areneros*, who tidy up the sand, struts into the ring in descending participatory importance. Every last one proudly shows himself off to the public eye. The aristocratic opening stems from the bullfight's aristocratic past; until the late 1600s, only *hidalgos* (nobles) fought bulls to prove their manhood to their ladies, peers, and underlings (Crow, 1985).

The values permeating both the paseillo and Spanish culture are honor, dignity, and pride, as well as a contempt for manual labor. These aristocratic values seeped into Spanish culture during its centuries of battles and heroes. The swelling of the noble class in Spain at this time was so great that even today it has been estimated that approximately 50% of the Spanish population has some claim to a title (Wheaton, 1990). Together, these are the values that make up the most important of all overriding Spanish characteristics: individualism.

Spanish individualism is a proud variety. It is based on the Spaniard's utter internal self-sufficiency in knowing that he or she is his or her own ideal person. Crow (1985) eloquently describes this aspect of the Spanish mindset in the following passage about Spanish pride:

> The Spaniard, thus, does not feel that he is born to realize any social end, but that he is born primarily to realize himself. His sense of personal dignity is admirable at times, exasperating at others; selfhood is the center of his gravity. His individual person has a value that is sacred and irreplaceable. In the universe he may be nothing, but to himself he is everything. (p. 11)

Proud Spanish individualism produces many outcomes for Spanish culture. It helps to explain the people's lack of effective collective efforts (for example, their frail nationalism, poor governments, and inefficient administrative bureaucracy). Because Spaniards refuse to subordinate their personal beliefs to a collective goal, and because everyone has to have a say in everything, there is a tendency for nothing ever to get done. As a result, simple procedures such as obtaining a train ticket from a ticket office in Spain can become long, drawn-out ordeals. Many Spaniards who can afford it opt to hire a *gestor,* or person who will wait in the necessary lines and wade through the bureaucracy in their place (Wheaton, 1990). Crow (1985) observes:

> Spanish individualism is still anarchic and inorganic. The race is not cohesive except when it is unified "against someone or something." If Spaniards could only work as hard for as they do against things, their country would be one of the most dynamic and most progressive in Western Europe, perhaps in the world. (p. 361)

On top of their difficulties in cooperating, part of the problem Spaniards have had in being productive is that their culture does not teach them to view work in the same positive light in which Americans see it. Work is seen as a means to an end—survival—not an end in itself. For example, although American teenagers are often encouraged or forced by their parents to take summer jobs or part-time jobs during the school year even though the parents could easily support them, Spanish families prefer to give their children educational and cultural experiences, such as sending them to France or England for the summer. The independence gained through work experience is not considered as important.

Further complicating the situation, jobs in Spain are often difficult to obtain and not very lucrative. As a result, Spaniards may be extremely hardworking when necessary to make ends meet (moonlighting is common in Spain), but in many regions the economic constraints on getting ahead curb their ambition. In fact, the only Spanish word for success in business is *triunfo,* a word borrowed from the battlefield and theater (Graham, 1984). The Spanish word for business also reveals the culture's disdain for commercial and administrative activities. The term they use is *negocio,* which translates literally as "the negation of leisure" (Graham, 1984).

Finally, many Spaniards do not terribly mind if they accomplish little, because they value self-expression more than material success. This is why the Spaniard has to be neither a Picasso nor a successful businessperson to be self-satisfied; recall that even participants in the mundane aspects of the bullfight parade proudly around the ring. Crow (1985) quotes an Englishman he met in Spain as having said, "In this country every blessed beggar acts like a king!" (p. 362). Rather than through material goods, Spanish individuals tend to be content to express their self-sufficiency through "wit, grandiloquent phrases, appearances, courtesy, generosity, and pride" (Wheaton, 1990, p. 68). Extremely articulate and enjoying the sound of their own voices, Spaniards will often spend hours conversing in the street cafés or bars where they meet. The odd result of this manifestation of Spanish individualism is that "often the most arrogant person in a group is the most charming" (Wheaton, 1990, p. 68). It is no coincidence that pride emerged as a dominant value in Spain; in a land of poverty and insecurity, it is the only thing that a person cannot lose.

As proud individualists, the idea of a good time for many Spaniards involves being in a large, noisy crowd and having an audience for whom to practice "the art of self-adoration" (Wheaton, 1990, p. 68). This is in essence what the bullfight participants have achieved during the opening parade, in the midst of just such a large, noisy crowd. And, like the bullfighters with their elaborate costumes, Spaniards tend to spend a large chunk of their monthly salary on fashionable clothes to enhance the effect of their performance. The expense is not wasted, however, because they spend much of their time under the scrutiny of the public eye, getting together in public places rather than in their homes, a situation that partly results from their rather cramped living space. This also is like the bullfight participants' parade around the public arena. Thus the Spanish enjoyment of showing off is well represented by the bullfight's entrance paseillo.

The proud marchers of the paseillo adhere to a rigid hierarchical order as they file around the ring. Their subordination to authority, like their pride, is a remnant of the warrior class efforts to survive in a hostile environment (Graham, 1984). As a result, Spaniards readily accept a certain amount of inequality in the power structure of their society. Yet they still feel proud. In Hofstede's (1980a) study of 40 different countries' cultural values, Spain scored just above the average on power distance, or the degree to which an unequal distribution of power and status is accepted, as we might expect. On Hofstede's dimension of individualism versus collectivism, Spaniards' individualism balanced their group-based defense system, making Spain rank just above the mean in favor of individualism.

Finally, the pride and acceptance Spaniards feel about everyday life has contributed to the current of realism in Spanish art. Wheaton (1990) writes, "An invitation to contemplation, careful observation of life as it is, and directness of expression are qualities that come to mind when one asks what it is that has remained consistently 'Spanish' about Spanish art" (p. 290). From ordinary scenes such as a shepherd feeding his dog to images of Christ with streams of blood pouring from under his crown of thorns and Picasso's horrifying cubist depiction of the bombing of Guernica, Spanish artists concerned themselves with documenting the world around them. The same tradition has allowed Spaniards over the years to face violence and death with dignity. It has also fueled the flame of their burning sense of tragedy.

Audience Involvement

The excited cheers and shouts of "Olé!" as the bull's horns whisk past the matador's gracefully leaning body highlight the strong Spanish emotionalism. The shouts and cheers are not only a form of self-expression but also a form of audience participation, affecting the matador's behavior and further performance. Furthermore, once the matador makes his kill, the public displays its judgment of his performance. The audience's judgmental response in turn indicates the appropriate salute for the matador to make. If the members of the audience are displeased, they boo and whistle, and the matador does not reenter the ring. If they are pleased, they cheer, and the matador will step back into the ring to acknowledge the applause. If the positive public response is prolonged, the matador will take a lap of honor around the ring with his banderilleros. If the matador's performance was very good, the members of the public wave handkerchiefs to request that he be honored with an ear of the bull. The president must comply if the majority of the audience wave their handkerchiefs. It is then up to the president to decide whether to award two ears for an exceptional performance or, in rare cases, even the tail. After any of these rewards, the matador takes a lap of honor around the ring while the audience throws objects (wineskins, hats, articles of clothing, and so on) to the matador that are then thrown back, much like autographs. Other objects are meant as gifts to the matador, such as flowers and cigars.

Likewise, the emotional nature of Spanish expression is not only a one-sided outpouring but also an interactive form of communication. Therefore, although Spaniards' emotionalism might on the one hand reflect their proud individualism, on the other hand its participative and empathetic qualities surpass this notion. They convey the Spanish culture's emphasis on relationships, generosity, hospitality, and recognition of social needs.

These attributes relate back to the social behavior introduced in the previous section. The Spaniards' gregarious and fun-loving nature is magnified by their uninhibited emotionalism. Spanish men are not too shy to compliment women, whether acquaintances or strangers. There is even a special name for these pleasant remarks: *piropos*. Spaniards also are not afraid to allow the conversation to move to a personal level, which helps avoid the small talk of the American cocktail party and so-called shop talk between business acquaintances. Thus Spaniards come across as genuine, interesting individuals rather than as superficial socialites or narrow-minded career people.

In allowing themselves to act on their emotions, Spaniards are incredibly generous and hospitable. Just as they enthusiastically wave their handkerchiefs in the air if they are moved by a matador's performance in order to reward him with a trophy from the bull, the Spaniards are moved by their relationships with other people to want to give them whatever they can. This takes the form of sharing food, cigarettes, or general kindness, which contributes to the upbeat social atmosphere.

The Spanish social life, for example, is often accompanied by the communal enjoyment of food and drink. To accommodate this taste, Spanish bars serve a wide variety of appetizer-sized portions of food called *tapas*, which groups of friends order to share. On a side note, the exotic nature of the food echoes the somewhat grotesque and exotic nature of the bullfight, as exemplified by tapas such as *pulpo* (octopus), *calamares* (squid), *morcilla* (blood sausage), *oreja de cerdo* (pig's ear), or, on the more ordinary side, *tortilla* (potato omelette), *empanadillas* (meat or seafood patties), goat cheese, olives, and ham. Overall, the loud talking, odor of food, and joviality produced by beer and wine create a sense of vitality and life that further intensify the emotional nature and gaiety of Spanish social interactions, much like the interactive involvement of an excited audience with a bullfighter.

Spaniards also share in their day-to-day lives outside of social gatherings. If a Spaniard brings a package of food to eat on the train, the first thing he or she does after opening the packet is to offer its contents to everyone nearby. The traveler in Spain should not feel reluctant to accept a cookie or a piece of *chorizo* (sausage) in such a situation and should avoid hoarding his or her own food.

Spanish hospitality is primarily an outgrowth of Arabic culture. Phrases and customs expressing courtesy such as "Esta es su casa" ("This is your home") and "Buen provecho" ("Enjoy your meal") are traces of Moorish domination (Wheaton, 1990). Spanish hospitality is not to be mistaken, however, for the American custom of inviting virtual strangers into one's home. In Spain (as in other Latin countries), one can know people for years without being invited into their home for a meal; if a dinner invitation is called for, it is much more likely to take place in a restaurant.

In addition, like Arabs, Spaniards are generally relationship-oriented. So, as with their propensity toward material sharing, Spaniards' concept of time focuses on interpersonal interactions. Thus, for example, completing the natural cycle of a conversation or other human interaction takes on more importance for the Spaniards than punctuality. In Hall and Hall's (1990) terms, Spaniards have a polychronic orientation toward time, doing several activities simultaneously while being highly involved in interactions.

Spanish emotionalism and generosity are also related to Spain's national social policies. A strong social security program, trade unions, almost totally subsidized universities, and a mandatory month's paid vacation for all workers reflect Spaniards' responsiveness to people's needs. Being less materialistic and aggressive than many other cultures such as Japan and the United States, Spain fell onto the so-called feminine side of Hofstede's (1980a) masculinity-femininity dimension.

One attribute of Spain's feminine orientation is an emphasis on the quality of life. For example, the workday in Spain is traditionally broken into morning (approximately 9 a.m. to 1 p.m.) and afternoon (roughly 4 p.m. to 8 p.m.) by a leisurely pause for the day's main meal. The meal may be followed by a little nap, the famous *siesta*. In summer when the midday sun is very hot, shops and businesses conserve human energy by closing for an hour or so longer than usual and staying open later in the evening. Many offices may even have a summer schedule (*horario de verano*), which entails longer morning hours (perhaps from 8 a.m. to 2 p.m.) and the afternoon off altogether.

Another purpose of the midday siesta is that it gives parents a chance to see their children, who return from school for the meal. It also pushes the whole day's schedule back so that the lighter evening meal is not served until 9 p.m. or 10 p.m. in most households. People then tend to stay up later than in most other countries, spending time with their families or going out with their friends. The importance of enjoying life and the company of others is punctuated by the fact reported in the Spanish newspaper *País* that Spaniards sleep less than any of their European neighbors (Wheaton, 1990). The ceaseless movement of pedestrians out for a stroll in the streets of Spanish cities also reflects the Spanish taste for leisure. Thus the centrality of relationships, emotional expression, and living well, as represented by audience responsiveness in the bullfight, is a distinguishing feature of Spanish culture.

The Ritual of the Bullfight

The logical outcome of all of the overarching features of Spanish culture described above—regionalism, a sense of tragedy, proud individualism, and emotional interaction—is an attraction to the ritual, which provides an arena for all of these characteristics. The ultimate ritual in Spanish society is the bullfight. From its ritualistic handkerchief signals to its precisely regulated sequence and strictly defined roles of matador, banderilleros, and picadores, and from the official role of the president to the sacrifice of the wild bull in the moment of truth, the corrida is permeated with rituals. Rituals define the bullfight; they make it what it is. This point is often missed by foreigners, who mistake it for some sort of cruel sport. It is not a sport. The ritual is a way of combining festivity with solemnity and life with death. These are some of the features that draw Spaniards to the bullfight, and these are the same features that draw Spaniards to a more encompassing ritual in Spanish society: religion.

Christianity entered Spain during the Roman rule in the first century after Christ. Although the Romans resisted it, Christianity was taken up by Spaniards with an unparalleled fervor. The tales of torture, martyrdom, and sainthood of the early Spanish Christians appealed highly to their sense of tragedy; the Spaniards' many hardships made them appreciate the ascetic Catholic values. At certain times in history, the Spanish zeal for Christianity went out of control, to the detriment (and death) of many. In particular, at the end of the 15th century under the reign of the Catholic monarchs Ferdinand and Isabella, religion sowed the seeds for the persecution and expulsion of hundreds of thousands of Jews under the auspices of the Holy Inquisition. At the same time, a large missionary effort was launched to convert the "heathen" native peoples of the recently dis-covered New World. Whole cultures were consequently disrupted.

In addition to its fervor, Spanish Catholicism differed from that of most other Catholic countries in another way. The Spanish people preserved their pagan traditions right alongside their new Christian beliefs. Therefore, to the Spaniard, God is not an intangible, elusive concept but an almost human, concrete presence. The Spaniard's relationship with God is thus very personal. Spaniards see God as patient and forgiving of human weaknesses and are not afraid to have "conversations" with Him, asking for personal favors. As if they were visiting a friend, Spanish people are also very informal at Mass. They arrive late, greet acquaintances out loud, drag chairs, and, at coastal resorts, attend in their beachwear. Then, even though the service is only 20 minutes long, people are rushing for the exit before it is even over (Wheaton, 1990).

The personal aspect of Spanish religion was enhanced by the Moors as well as by Spain's pagan past. The Moors also enjoyed an all-encompassing relationship with God (Allah) and left evidence of this fact in the Spanish language. The expression "Si Dios quiere" ("If God wills it") is widely used, as is the phrase "Ojalá" ("I hope so"), which derives from the Arabic "Wa shá' a-l-lah" ("May God will it") (Wheaton, 1990). Even the exclamation "Olé!" (meaning something like "Right on!" and shouted throughout the bullfight) derives from the word *Allah* (Wheaton, 1990).

However, Spanish people do not always deal directly with God. Because they like religion to have a personal flavor, it is just as common if not more so for Spaniards to pray to the Virgin Mary and the saints. Thus one often finds small candles lit in front of images of these figureheads in churches, with a charitable contribution box nearby to compensate for the requested favor. However, favors are not asked randomly of any saint. Someone who loses something prays to St. Anthony; a traveler wears a protective medallion with the image of St. Christopher. Many Spaniards also make pilgrimages to places where the Holy Virgin appeared. Finally, these religious references surface in everyday life, such as the common female name of Maria del Pilar, usually Pilar for short, after the Virgin of the Pilar in Zaragoza; and the equally common name Conchita, a nickname for Maria de la Concepción (Mary of the Immaculate Conception).

A wilder aspect of paganism that is wound into Spanish religion is the popular celebration, or *fiesta*. The fiesta is a ritual like the bullfight (which is actually part of many fiestas, exemplifying their pagan nature). Each region of Spain has its most famous fiesta, such as the fiesta of San Fermín in Pamplona, Las Fallas in Valencia, El Roco in Andalusia, and Holy Week celebrations throughout the country. These celebrations involve extravagant costuming, floats, processions, and drinking that stray far from piety. As a case in point, does the scene of dozens of men running in front of rushing bulls sound more Christian or more pagan? The answer is obvious, yet this ritual is observed as part of the celebration of a Christian saint in Pamplona. To the Spaniard, religion simply does not occupy a separate compartment in life; it can be incorporated into life's most mundane and most dramatic moments.

The pervasiveness of religion in Spanish daily life would seem to work in favor of the Church, but in recent years it has actually contributed to the institution's decline. In part a reaction to the

Church's oppressiveness under Franco's dictatorship, and partly because of the people's personal relationship with religion that does not necessitate the involvement of an intermediary institution, church attendance is relatively low. In 1985, according to one survey, only 50% of the Spanish population were practicing Catholics, and of those, only 18% attended Mass regularly (Wheaton, 1990).

The ritual of the bullfight also is losing its appeal in contemporary Spanish society. It is being replaced little by little by soccer matches and other forms of Sunday afternoon entertainment. However, soccer simply does not capture the essence of Spanish culture in the way that the bullfight does. Although soccer draws the same kinds of excited crowds as the bullfight, soccer fans have no role in the game comparable to audience participation in the bullfight such as judging the matador. And where soccer players form highly cooperative teams, bullfighters' groups are much looser. The latter more accurately reflect Spanish collective behavior. Finally, in contrast to the fact that the bullfight is an elaborate ritual, soccer is a sport, albeit a popular one. Therefore, there is little chance that soccer will ever completely replace the bullfight in Spanish culture.

In summary, Crow (1985) concisely recapitulates some of the points of this chapter:

> Spain today is a composite of all that has gone before. Her taproot reaches into the bottomless past. On several successive occasions in history she has flowered in beauty, shedding her glory over the civilization of Europe. On many other occasions she has grimly closed her door on the outside world, and retired into the gloom of fixed memories. In spite of her perenially [sic] poor government, her vitality is ever present, and appears inexhaustible. The Spanish people are among the most generous, the most noble human beings on earth. Their spontaneous art places them in a unique category among the nations of Europe, both for its quantity and for its incomparable beauty. With one foot in the present and the other in the past, Spain today stands straddling the unfathomable abyss. (p. 356)

As the people of Spain pursue an accelerated course of modernization, they are evolving into the more cosmopolitan embodiment of a united Europe. It is hoped that Spaniards will not lose their special love of life that makes Spain so unique and wonderful. Whatever the eventual outcome, the bullfight will remain as a major, if not the major, metaphor for understanding deep-seated cultural values and attitudes among the Spanish people.

10

Irish Conversations

It is a truism that the use of language is essential for the development of culture, and most, if not all, cultural groups take great pride in their native languages. Thus it is not surprising that voice is one of the four essential elements of opera, the metaphor for Italy (see Chapter 3). In the case of Ireland, it was the brutal English rule over the nation extending over several centuries that essentially made the Irish an aural people whose love of language and conversation was essential for the preservation of their heritage. More specifically, the intersection between the original Irish language, Irish Gaelic, and English has made the Irish famous for their eloquence, scintillating conversations, and unparalleled success in fields where the use of the English language is critical, such as writing, law, and teaching.

The Celts or Gaels conquered Ireland and its native inhabitants, the Firbolgs, several centuries before Christ. They split Ireland into various kingdoms whose petty kings usually ruled over a local group of clans. During this period, the belief in magical powers was the guiding force of the civilization, and even today many of the landmarks and traditions in Ireland can be traced back to this time of magical creatures.

Ireland escaped the rule of the Roman Empire because of its far distance from Rome. St. Patrick, who had previously been captured and enslaved, returned to Ireland in A.D. 432 and had great success in christianizing it. When the Roman Empire fell in A.D. 756, Europe plunged into its Dark Ages, but Ireland's golden age of learning and scholarship began and lasted until the 11th century. In A.D. 795 the Vikings from northern Scandinavia started to invade Ireland, founding settlements along the coasts and establishing Dublin as their capital. Eventually the Irish united under the high king, Brian Boru, and defeated the Vikings at Clondorf in A.D. 1014. The Vikings were allowed to remain in their seaport towns, intermarried with the Irish; in time, they were absorbed by Irish culture.

Starting about A.D. 1160, the English, sometimes at the invitation of the petty kings or rulers, became increasingly involved in Ireland's affairs. However, the English who settled in Ireland were quickly absorbed by the culture through joint business ventures, intermarriage, and a perception that England was too distant from Ireland to have the ability to control it. In 1366 the English passed the infamous Statutes of Kilkenny as a defensive reaction against this absorption, and they outlawed intermarriage and concubinage between the English and Irish and the use of Gaelic by both the English and "the Irish living among the English" (Beckett, 1986). The English were even forbidden the use of Irish names and dress, and laws excluding the Irish from positions of authority were passed. Although many of these statutes were strictly enforced in later centuries, they tended to be disregarded in Ireland when first passed.

In 1534, Henry VIII began to exert strong English control over Ireland. His successors initiated a "plantation policy" by seizing Irish lands and encouraging Protestants to settle in the country in an attempt to make the nation Protestant. There were several Irish revolts, but they were beaten down. The 10-year revolt starting in 1641 was particularly important, with 600,000 people dying, and eventually Oliver Cromwell, the Puritan leader, put the revolt down mercilessly and brutally. Cromwell kept a diary describing the joy that he experienced at inflicting so much pain on the Irish for the greater glory of God. Although many of the Irish still resent the English, they hate Cromwell.

The Irish eventually sided with James II, a Roman Catholic who became king of England but was forced from the throne in A.D. 1685, at least in part because he had abolished many anti-Catholic laws. Although he tried to regain his throne, he and his Irish supporters were defeated in the Battle of the Boyne in A.D. 1690. For the next two centuries, deplorable conditions among Irish Catholics worsened. Additional land was seized by the English, and by 1704 the Irish held only about one seventh of the land in Ireland. A series of penal laws were passed so that Catholics could not purchase, inherit, or even rent land; they were also excluded from the Irish Parliament and the army, and they were restricted in their rights to practice Catholicism. Also, Catholics were barred not only from the one university, Trinity, but even from most of the schools in which English was the language of instruction.

To counteract the assault on their culture, the Irish used illegal schoolmasters who taught in Irish Gaelic in "hedge schools" or those hidden from sight behind hedges; sometimes the classes convened in the homes of the students. Because the schoolmasters did not have access to many school materials and not even classrooms, almost all of this education was oral in nature, involving memorization, oral presentations, and debates.

Between 1782 and 1798, the all-Protestant Irish Parliament ruled the country, and it did restore to Catholics their rights to hold land and lifted the restrictions on the practice of Catholicism. However, Catholics still did not have political rights and the wretched lot of most Irish did not change. In 1798, the English put down another rebellion. In 1829, the English loosened the penal laws governing the Irish, largely through the efforts of Daniel O'Connell, the Irish representative to the English Parliament.

In 1831, the English established a national school system in Ireland in which only English could be used. An Irish child had to wear a wooden baton around his or her neck. If these children were heard talking in Gaelic, the teacher would mark the baton, and the children's parents usually beat them at home, because the parents' opportunities to work and thus even to live were completely in the hands of the English. Many of the Irish began to discard Gaelic, at least openly.

Patrick Pearse, an Irish patriot who was later executed because of his leadership of the 1916 uprising, characterized the educational system as a "murder machine" designed to stamp out Irish language and culture. Today only some 75,000 people out of a population of 3.7 million use Gaelic, even though it is now a required language in the school system and many claim some knowledge and use of it. Unlike most nations, Ireland has two official languages, Irish Gaelic and English.

Further, Britain had set up an agricultural system that made the Irish dependent on one crop, potatoes. When that crop failed, the Great Potato Famine of 1845-1849 occurred. The English refused to provide any major assistance to the Irish because of their belief in the workings of a free market economy and allowed approximately 1 million out of 8 million people to starve to death, an event often compared with the Holocaust of World War II. Even before the famine, the conditions among the Irish had become so deplorable that English satirist Jonathan Swift argued eerily in "A Modest Proposal" that the Irish babies would be better off if they were killed and eaten, and some of his modest proposals closely resembled what actually happened in the Holocaust.

Ireland as we know it today began to emerge in 1916 when a small group of Irish patriots commandeered the old post office building in Dublin on Easter Sunday. The English executed the rebellion's 15 leaders, which sparked a war against the English that led to the modern division of Ireland into two parts: the Protestant north with a minority Catholic population and the Catholic south. The focus of this chapter is the Catholic south, which occupies five sixths of the land.

Supposedly, everybody knows everybody else's business in a country village. Ireland largely comprises such small country villages and its culture reflects this fact. Whenever the Irish meet, one of the first things they generally do is determine one another's place of origin. The conversation usually helps to identify common relatives and friends. Given the wide circle of friends and acquaintances that the Irish tend to make in their lives, it is usually not difficult to find a link.

Ireland's size is little more than 1% of that of the continental United States. It lies to the west of Great Britain, to which it is economically tied. Ireland has four major cities: Dublin, Cork, Limerick, and Galway. In the early 1970s, more than 60% of the workforce was employed in agriculture, but today only 16% can be found in that line of work because of the transition to a more industrialized society. Although the country has modernized significantly in the past 20 years, it is still far behind many of its European neighbors. Also, many of its young people emigrate, largely because of a lack of jobs, an expensive welfare system, and a correspondingly high tax rate. Most Irish families have sons, daughters, or close relatives who have emigrated.

Because of the high level of education in modern Ireland, Irish immigrants do well in other countries, but many would like to return to Ireland simply because it is a "being" society in which the quality of life is valued more than the pursuit of monetary gain. Ireland did become part of the EC in 1973, which should help the country economically in the long run.

The importance of conversation to the Irish makes it a fitting metaphor for the nation. However, to understand the metaphor fully, we need to explore the intersection of Irish Gaelic and English, after which we can focus on an essential Irish conversation, praying to God and the saints. The free-flowing nature of Irish conversation is also one of its essential characteristics, as are the places where conversations are held.

Intersection of Gaelic and English

The Irish are a people who tend to enjoy simple pleasures, but the complexity of their thought patterns and culture can be baffling to outsiders. They generally have an intense love of conversation and storytelling and have been accused often of talking just to hear the sound of their own voices. The Irish use the English language in ways that are not found in any other culture. They do not just give a verbal answer, they construct a vivid mental picture that is pleasing to the mind as well as the ear. With the transition from Gaelic to English, the Irish created vivid images in Gaelic and expressed them in English; the vivid imagery of many Irish writers originated in the imaginative storytelling that was historically a critical part of social conversation. To the Irish, Gaelic was a graphic, living language that was appropriate for expressing the wildest of ideas in a distinctive and pleasing manner.

Because of the slow arrival of electronic technology in Ireland and the country's long suppression and isolation, the talent for conversation is an art form that has not yet been lost. Among the Irish, food tends to be secondary to conversation, and a visitor will often observe that the Irish seem to forget about their food until it is almost cold. If, however, an Irishman admonishes a countryman for eating too much or too quickly, the witty reply is frequently to the effect that one never knows when the next famine will occur. This emphasis on the primacy of conversation is in contrast to the practice found in other cultures, such as the Italian and French, where not only conversation but also food is prized.

If the size of the population is taken into account, it seems that Ireland has produced many more prominent essayists, novelists, and poets than any other country since approximately 1870. This prominence reflects the intersection of the Gaelic and English languages and the aural bias of the Irish. They also have produced great musicians who combine music and words in a unique way. Conversely, the Irish have not produced a major visual artist equal to those of other European countries, and their achievements in science are modest.

There are countless examples that could be used to illustrate this intersection, but the opening words of James Joyce's (1964) *Portrait of the Artist as a Young Man,* in which he first introduced the technique of stream of consciousness, aptly serve the purpose:

> "Once upon a time and a very good time it was there was a moocow coming down along the road and this moocow that was coming down along the road met a nicens little boy named baby tuckoo."
>
> His father told him that story; his father looked at him through a glass; he had a hairy face.
>
> "He was a baby tuckoo. The moocow came down the road where Betty Byrne lived: She sold lemon platt.
>
> "O, the wild rose blossoms
>
> "On the little green place.
>
> "He sang that song. That was his song.
>
> "O, the green wothe botheth." (p. 1)

There are several points about this brief but pertinent passage that deserve mention. It expresses a rural bias that befits Ireland, and it reflects the vivid Gaelic language in which Joyce was proficient. Also, it immediately captures the imagination but leaves the reader wondering what is going to happen: He must read further if he wants to capture the meaning, and it seems that the meaning will become clear only in the most circuitous way. Further, although the essence of the passage is mundane, it is expressed in a captivating manner. The reader is pleasantly surprised by the passage and eagerly awaits additional pleasant surprises. In many ways this passage is an ideal example of the manner in which Gaelic Irish and English intersect. And, although some of the modern Irish and Irish-Americans may not be aware of these historical antecedents, their patterns of speech and thought tend to reflect this intersection.

Perhaps the most imaginatively wild of the modern Irish writers to incorporate the intersection of the Gaelic and English languages in his work is Myles na gCopaleen, who also used the pseudonym Flann O'Brien. He wrote some of his novels and stories in Gaelic and others in English. Even the titles of his books are indicative of this imaginative focus: for example, *The Poor Mouth: A Bad Story About The Hard Life* (O'Brien, 1974). "Putting on the poor mouth" means making a pretense of being poor or in bad circumstances to gain advantage for oneself from creditors or prospective creditors, and the book is a satire on the rural life of western Ireland. His masterpiece, *At Swim-Two-Birds* (O'Brien, 1961), sets the scene for a confrontation between "Mad Sweeny" and "Jem Casey" in the following way:

> *Synopsis, being a summary of what has gone before,* FOR THE BENEFIT OF NEW READERS: *Dermit Trellis,* an eccentric author, conceives the project of writing a salutary book on the consequences which follow wrongdoing and creates for the purpose
> The Pooka Fergus MacPhellimey, a species of human Irish devil endowed with magical power. He then creates John Furriskey, a depraved character, whose task is to attack women and behave at all times in an indecent manner. By magic he is instructed by Trellis to go one night to Donnybrook where he will by arrangement meet and betray. . . . (p. 563)

The remaining characters are sequentially introduced in the same imaginative way.

In the area of music, the Chieftains, who have performed together for more than 25 years, represent the distinctive approach of the Irish to music. Their songs, played on traditional instruments, are interspersed with classic Irish dances and long dialogues that sometimes involve the audience. Similarly, Thomas Moore, who lived in the 19th century, is sometimes cited as the composer who captured the essence of the intersection of the Gaelic and English languages in such poetic songs as "Believe Me If All Those Endearing Young Charms," which he wrote for a close friend and beautiful woman whose face was badly scarred in a fire (Moore, 1959):

> Believe me, if all those endearing young charms
> Which I gaze on so fondly today
> Were to fade by tomorrow and fleet in my arms
> Like fairy gifts fading away.
> Thou woust still be ador'd
> As this moment thou art
> Let thy loveliness fade as it will.
> And upon the dear ruin
> Each wish of my heart
> Would intwine itself verdantly still. (p. 214)

A constant reminder that the Irish are radically different from the English and Americans is their brogue. When the conversion from speaking Gaelic to speaking English was occurring, this brogue was an embarrassment for many Irish. The English looked down on these "inferior" people who were unable to speak "proper" English (Waters,

1984). Today, the brogue is prized by the Irish and appreciated throughout the world.

Given that Ireland is a rural society in which unhurried conversation is prized, it should be no surprise that it is more of a "being" than a "doing" society in which there is a balanced approach to life. In fact, many of the Irish are astonished at the "doing" entrepreneurial activities of their 44 million Irish-American counterparts who have made St. Patrick's Day, which remains a holy day in Ireland, into a fun-loving time for partying that embraces all people (Milbank, 1993). The Irish generally take life much more slowly than Americans, who tend to watch the clock constantly and rush from one activity to another. No matter how rushed the Irish may be, they normally have time to stop and talk.

The Irish also tend to place more importance on strong friendships and extended family ties than do Americans. Nothing illustrates this emphasis more than the behavior of many early Irish immigrants when they first arrived in the United States. They settled near other friends or relatives who had preceded them to the United States and developed a reputation for being very clannish. But slowly the Irish love of conversation and curiosity about all things led to their interaction with others and their Americanization.

Prayer as Conversation

Prayer or a conversation with God is one of the most important parts of an Irish life. More than 95% of the population is Roman Catholic, and regular attendance at Sunday Mass is estimated at 87% of the population, the highest percentage of any country in the world. Almost every Catholic household contains crucifixes and religious pictures. These serve as outward reminders of the people's religious beliefs and duties.

Further, this prayer is accompanied by acts of good works that stem directly from the strong ethical and moral system of the Irish. They are recognized as having made the highest per capita donation to relief efforts in countries such as Ethiopia, and they are quick to donate their time, energy, and even lives to help those living in execrable conditions. The extent of the crisis in Somalia, for instance, was first reported to the United Nations by Mary Robinson, president of Ireland, and an Irish nurse was killed after arriving in Somalia to help out.

The separation between church and state found in most countries does not exist in Ireland. Until 1972 when Ireland joined the EC, a constitutional amendment guaranteed a special status to the Roman Catholic church. The Church did not oppose the removal of this amendment because it was secure in its majority (Bell, 1991). Such a secure outlook was well justified because little has changed except for the wording of the constitution, and the Church plays an important role throughout the life of the Irish.

The state relies on the works of the Catholic church to support most of its social service programs. For example, most of the hospitals are run by the Catholic church rather than by the state. These hospitals are partially funded with state money and are staffed with nuns, when possible. The state has little control over how the money is spent, especially because it lacks the buildings and the power to replace the Church-run system that was in place when the state was formed.

The national school (state) system is also under the control of the various religious dominations in Ireland. It is the primary source of education for primary schoolchildren. The state funds the system, but the schools are run by local boards, which are almost always controlled by the clergy. There is a separate national school for each major religion. The local Catholic national school is managed by the local parish priest, whereas the Protestant vicar has his own separate school. Many instructors in these schools are nuns or brothers who work very inexpensively and keep the costs much lower than the state could. Conversely, in the United States it is no longer lawful even to pray in public schools. In exchange for these lower costs, the state has relinquished control. This is really the Church's last line of defense, because it has the ability to instill Catholic morality and beliefs in almost every young Irish child in the country.

In many ways the Catholic church does not actually influence the state's actions. Rather, it relies on Catholic lay groups to uphold the Church's teachings and to pressure the state. These watchdog groups can be quite vocal and often wield considerable power in their communities. Many times they are more conservative than the local parish priest. As the Irish become better educated and gain greater exposure to the rest of Europe, the preeminent position of the Church is slowly being eroded. However, as long as the Catholic church continues to control the primary school system, it will have a significant influence on the people's attitudes.

The Church also influences society by censoring books and artistic material, which has caused many Irish artists such as James Joyce and Sean O'Casey to leave Ireland to enjoy greater freedom in their work. The Irish have to travel to Britain or to Northern Ireland to purchase outlawed books or to see movies written by their Irish countrymen.

Sunday Mass is a special occasion in Ireland, and the entire family attends. On this occasion everyone wears his or her Sunday best. One Irish woman tells the story of returning home for a visit from the United States and, on Sunday morning, being asked by her mother if she did not have a better dress to wear to church; she had become lax in her church dress after spending several years in the United States. During Mass it is not unusual to see all the women and children sitting in the front of the church and the men standing or sitting in the back. This dichotomy does not mean that the Irish believe religion should be left to women and children; it only reflects the specific gender roles in Ireland, which are gradually changing, but at a rate that is slower than in other Western countries.

The Irish tend to begin and end their day with prayer. This is their opportunity to tell God their troubles and their joys. One of the more common prayers is that Ireland may one day be reunited. This act of talking to God helps to form a personal relationship between the Irish and their God. It is difficult to ignore the dictates of God, because He is such a personal and integral part of the daily Irish life. God is also present in daily life in the living personification of the numerous priests, brothers, and sisters found in Ireland. They are not shut away in cloisters, but interact with the laity throughout the day.

Entering the religious life is seen as a special calling for the Irish. In the past when families were very large, it was common for every family to give at least one son or daughter to the religious life. It was the greatest joy for an Irish mother to know that her son or daughter was in God's service, which was prized more highly than a bevy of grandchildren. Vocations to religious life have decreased in recent years, but Ireland still has many more priests per capita than most other Catholic countries.

In the Republic of Ireland there are few problems between Catholics and other religious groups, unlike the situation that exists in Northern Ireland. In fact, Catholics enjoy having Protestants in their communities, and they treat them with great respect. In one rural area where the Protestant congregation had dwindled, the Catholic parish helped Protestants with fund raising to make repairs to their church. This act of charity illustrates the great capacity for giving that the Irish possess, because generally they are not greatly attached to material possessions and are quite willing to share what they have with the world.

A Free-Flowing Conversation:
Irish Hospitality

Conversations with the Irish are known to take many strange turns, and one may end up discussing a subject and not knowing how it arose. Also, it is not only what is said that is important, but also the manner in which it is expressed. The Irish tend to be monochronic, completing one activity before going on to another, yet they cannot resist divergences and tangents in their conversations or their lives. They often feel that they are inspired by an idea that must be shared with the rest of the world regardless of what the other person may be saying. The Irish tend to respect this pattern of behavior and are quite willing to change the subject, which can account for the breadth of their conversations as well as their length.

Like their conversations, the Irish tend to be curious about all things foreign or unfamiliar, and they are quick to extend a hand in greeting and to start a conversation, usually a long one.

It is not unusual for the Irish to begin a conversation with a perfect stranger, but for most of the Irish there are no strangers—only people they have not had the pleasure of conversing with. The Irish do not usually hug in public, but this in no way reduces the warmth of their greeting. They often view Americans as too demonstrative and are uncomfortable with public displays of affection. They tend to be a very hospitable, trusting, and friendly people. Nothing illustrates this outlook more than their national greeting, "Cead mile failte" ("One hundred thousand welcomes"), which is usually accompanied by a handshake.

In addition, the Irish are famous for their hospitality toward both friends and strangers. As Delany (1974) points out: "In the olden days, anyone who had partaken of food in an Irishman's home was considered to be secure against harm or hurt from any member of the family, and no one was ever turned away" (p. 103). This spirit of hospitality still exists in Ireland. In the country, the Irish tend to keep their doors not only unlocked but also open. Whenever someone is passing by or asking for directions, it is difficult for them to leave without being asked into the house to have something to eat or drink. It is not unusual for the Irish to meet someone in the afternoon and invite him or her to their home for supper that evening, and this happens not only in the country but also in the cities. They welcome people into their family and bring out their best china, linen, and the finest foods. Meals are accompanied by great conversation by both young and old.

Many of the Irish do not believe in secrets and, even if they did, it would be hard to imagine them being able to keep one. They seem quite willing to tell the world their business and expect their visitors to do the same.

However, the Irish are often unwilling to carry on superficial conversations. They enjoy a conversation that deals with something of substance, and they are well-known for breaking the often-quoted American social rule that one should not discuss politics or religion in public. The Irish enjoy nothing more than to discuss these subjects and to spark a deep philosophical conversation.

Places of Conversations:
Irish Friends and Families

There really is no place where the Irish would find it difficult to carry on a conversation. They are generally quite willing to talk about any subject at any time, but there are several places that have a special meaning for the Irish. Conversation in the home is very important for an Irish family. It is also one of the major social activities of an Irish public house or pub.

The typical Irish family is closely knit, and its members describe their activities to one another in great detail. Meal time is an event in the Irish household that should not be missed by a family member, not so much because of the food but the conversation. In fact, as noted previously, the food is really secondary to the conversation, and sometimes the Irish even forget to eat or delay doing so until the food is cold. Supper is the time of day when family members gather together to pray, eat, and update one another on their daily activities. The parents usually ask the children about their day in school and share the events of their own day.

Education and learning have always been held in high regard by the Irish. Teachers are treated with great respect in the community, and their relatively high salaries reflect their worth to the community. Ireland has a literacy rate of 99% because of compulsory national education. College education is available to all through government grants for those who cannot afford university fees. Given the dearth of employment opportunities, college students often complete a postgraduate degree before entering the job market. The Irish who emigrate normally bring with them a well-rounded education that is valued by employers abroad. Still, even when the Irish have advanced formal training, they generally do not flaunt it.

A frequent topic of conversation at family dinners is news of extended family, friends, or neighbors. The Irish have an intense interest in the activities of their extended family and friends, but this interest is not for the pure sake of gossip. They generally are quick to congratulate on good news and even quicker to rally around in times of trouble or need. When someone is sick, it is not unusual for all of the person's friends and family to spend almost all of their time at the hospital. They help the family with necessary tasks and entertain one another with stories and remembrances. Many of the Irish have a difficult time understanding the American pattern in which the nuclear family handles emergencies and problems by itself.

This practice also holds true whenever there is a death in the community. Everyone gathers together to hold an Irish wake, which combines the viewing of the body with a party that may last for two or three days. There is plenty of food, drinking, laughing, conversation, music, games, and storytelling. Presumably the practice of a wake originated because people had difficulty traveling in Ireland over poor roads and by nonmechanized means of transportation, and the wake afforded an opportunity not only to pay respect to the deceased but also to renew old friendships and reminisce. Although the problems of travel have been solved, the Irish still cling to this ancient way of saying goodbye to the decreased and uplifting the spirits of those left behind.

An event that is as important as the wake is a wedding; it is a time of celebration for the entire family and neighborhood. There is customarily a big church wedding followed by a sit-down dinner and an evening of dancing and merriment. Registry office weddings are very rare in Ireland, as might be expected in this conservative and Catholic-dominated nation. Young people usually continue to live with their parents until they are married, and then they frequently buy a home close to them.

Irish parents are generally quite strict with their children. They set down definite rules that must be followed. Irish children are given much less freedom than American children, and they usually spend all day with their parents on Sunday and may accompany them to a dance or to the pub in the evening. Parents are usually well acquainted with the families of their children's friends and believe in group activities. The tight social community in which the Irish live makes it difficult for children to do anything without their parents' knowledge. There is always a third cousin or kindly neighbor who is willing to keep tabs on the behavior of children and report back to parents, some of whom have even managed to stretch their watchful eyes across the Atlantic to keep tabs on their children living in the United States. This close control can sometimes be difficult for young people, but it creates a strong support network that is useful in times of trouble.

A frequent gathering place for men, women, and children is the local pub, because the drinking age is not enforced throughout most of Ireland. There are two sections in most pubs: The plain workingman's part and the decorated part where the cost of a pint of beer is slightly higher. In the not-too-distant past, it was seen as unbecoming for a woman to enter a pub; there are still some pubs in which women are comfortable only in the decorated part, and they typically order half-pints of beer, whereas the men order pints. Normally, the pubs do not serve food, which may reflect the Irish de-emphasis of food noted previously.

Pubs tend to be very informal, often without waiters or waitresses and with plenty of bar and table space. Young and old mingle in the pub, often conversing with one another and trading opinions. The Irish are raised with a great respect for their elders and are quite comfortable carrying on a conversation with a person of any age or background. They tend to be a democratic people by nature and, although they may not agree with a person's opinion, they will usually respect him or her for having formed one.

Irish pubs are probably the site of the most lively conversations held in Ireland. The Irish tend to be a very sociable people who generally do not believe in drinking alone. This pattern of behavior has often resulted in their reputation for being alcoholics. Many Irish drink more than they should, but the problem often appears worse than it is because almost all of their drinking takes place in public. Further, co-workers and their superiors frequently socialize in pubs, and they tend to evaluate one another in terms of not only on-the-job performance but also their ability to converse skillfully in such a setting. The favorite drink of the Irish is Guinness, a strong black stout. It is far more popular than the well-known Irish whiskey.

Even more important than a good drink in a pub is good conversation. The Irish are famous for their storytelling, and it is not unusual to find an entire pub silent while one man tells an ancient folktale or what happened to him that afternoon. It is also not unusual for someone to recite a Shakespearean play from memory in its entirety.

Besides stories, many a heated argument can erupt in a pub. The Irish seem to have a natural love of confrontation in all things, and the conversation does not even have to be about something that affects their lives. They are fond of exchanging opinions on many abstract issues and world events. It is during these sessions at the pub that the Irish sharpen their conversational skills. However, although these conversations can become heated, they rarely become violent.

Irish friends, neighbors, and families visit one another on a regular basis. As indicated above, rarely if ever is one turned away from the door. In fact, the door is usually kept open, and visitors are expected to walk right in. Family and friends know that they are always welcome and that they will be given something to eat and drink. It is not unusual for visitors to arrive late in the evening and stay until almost morning. Such visits are usually not made for any special purpose other than conversation, which is the mainstay of the Irish life no matter where it is held.

Ending a Conversation

A conversation with an Irishman can be such a long and exciting adventure that a person thinks it will never end. It will be hard to bring the conversation to a close because the Irish always seem to have the last word. Ireland is a country that welcomes its visitors and makes them feel so comfortable and accepted that it is hard to break free and return home after an afternoon or evening of conversation.

Geert Hofstede's (1980a) research profiling the value orientation of 40 nations includes Ireland, and his analysis confirms many of our observations. Ireland is a masculine-oriented society in which sex roles are clearly differentiated, but the status of women clearly has improved during the past 20 years. However, it is not an acquisition-oriented society, as Hofstede's classification might suggest, but a "being-oriented" society in which the quality of life is given precedence over material rewards.

Further, Ireland clusters with those countries emphasizing individualism, as we might expect of a people who are willing and eager to explore and talk about serious and conflict-laden topics. Individualism is expressed through conversation and views on issues that affect society; major tasks are unlikely to be performed by the individual, and entrepreneurship is not a strong trait among the Irish. Individualism is also expressed in other talents such as writing, art, and music. As suggested previously, music offers its own means of conversation, and Ireland reportedly has one of the highest number of musicians per capita of all countries. Still, the Irish tend to be collectivist in their emphasis on the family, religion, a very generous welfare system, and the acceptance of strong labor unions.

Ireland also falls into the category of countries emphasizing a strong desire to meet new people and challenges (low uncertainty avoidance). And, with the possible exception of the high status accorded to the clergy, the Irish cluster with those countries that attempt to diminish social class and power differences as much as possible.

In short, the Irish tend to be an optimistic people who are ready to accept the challenges that life presents, although there is a melancholy strain in many of the Irish that is frequently attributed to the long years of English rule and the rainy weather. They usually confront things head-on and are ready to take on the world if necessary. They can be quite creative in their solutions, but also quite stubborn when asked to compromise, and they tend to be truly happy in the middle of a heated but stimulating conversation. Given their history and predilections, it is not surprising that the Irish prefer personal situations and professional fields of work where their aural-focused approach to reality can be given wide reign, even after they have spent several generations living in countries such as the United States and Australia.

11

The Turkish Coffeehouse

Turkey is a remarkable land of contrasts that joins the continents of Asia and Europe. It has elements of old and new, Islam and Christianity, mountains and plains, modern cities and rural villages. Often referred to as the "cradle of civilization," Turkey is filled with archeological remnants of the ancient Greeks and Romans, along with treasures of the sultans and caliphs of the Ottoman dynasty. Perhaps most interesting of all are the people of Turkey, who are rich in emotions, traditions, and hospitality. Turkish origins can be traced to the Mongols, Slavs, Greeks, Kurds, Armenians, and Arabs. Like Thais, Turks have never been conquered or colonized by other peoples. This distinction, along with a geographic boundary that straddles two continents, makes Turkey unique. Turkish culture today is a marriage of Turkish traditions and Western ideologies.

Turkey is a mountainous peninsula slightly larger than Texas that shares borders with Bulgaria, Greece, Iran, Iraq, and Syria. Considered a strategic location because of its control of the straits linking the Black and Aegean Seas, Turkey is the only NATO country other than Norway to border the states of the former Soviet Union. The western portion of Turkey, Thrace, is in Eastern Europe, whereas the larger eastern section, Anatolia, is part of Asia. Of 58 million people, 85% are Turkish and 12% Kurdish, and roughly one third of the population is part of the labor force. More than 10 million agricultural workers endure hot summers and cold Turkish winters. Literacy estimates at more than 80% are higher than ever, and the average life expectancy is 70 years of age. Unlike other Islamic societies, the Republic of Turkey was established in 1923 as a secular democratic nation. There is, however, a small but growing minority that would like to see Turkey become a theocratic nation again. The Turks are proud of both their achievements as a modern state and their rich heritage.

An appropriate metaphor for understanding Turkish culture is the coffeehouse, a part of everyday life in Turkey. What the coffeehouse represents is quite different from its counterparts in other countries. An emphasis on both Islam and secularity is the first of four characteristics of the coffeehouse that mirror Turkish culture. Coffeehouses also provide an important forum for recreation, communication, and community integration. Moreover, the customers who frequent coffeehouses reflect a male-dominated culture. Finally, the Turkish coffeehouse found in villages and towns is modest in comparison to the exotic *tavernas*, distinguished pubs, and chic cafés found in the larger cities.

Before we can understand how these four characteristics of the coffeehouse reflect Turkish culture, we must know something about Turkey's unique history. Ancient Anatolian civilization dates back to 6500 B.C.E. As early as 1900 B.C.E., the Hittites occupied Turkey. Seven hundred years later, the Phrygians and Lydians invaded the land. These early Anatolian groups ruled until the Persian Empire took hold in the 6th century B.C.E. Then the Greek-Hellenistic rule emerged, followed by the Romans in 100 B.C.E. Each succeeding group left its mark on the people by contributing customs, language, and trade practices.

In the year A.D. 330, Constantine the Great named Constantinople the capital of the Byzantine Empire. Arabs relocated westward, and by 700 the empire included Anatolia, Greece, Syria, Egypt, Sicily, the Balkans, most of Italy, and some areas of North Africa. Turkish tribes began to migrate from central Asia to Anatolia in the 11th century A.D. The Oguz Turks, who embraced the new religion of Islam, then occupied a vast part of Anatolia during that century. After their setback in the Crusades, Turkish *gazis*, or Islamic warriors, fought against the Byzantine Empire and began to build the Ottoman dynasty. The Ottomans conquered the region and expanded their reign to the Christian Balkans. In 1453, the Ottomans conquered Constantinople, which was virtually the last stronghold under Byzantine rule. Constantinople, which is known today as Istanbul, was then rebuilt as the capital of the Ottoman Empire and the center of Sunni Islam.

The Ottoman Empire reached its peak of wealth and power under the rule of Süleyman the Magnificent in the 1500s. He controlled all or part of states including present-day Turkey, Iran, Iraq, Egypt, Israel, Syria, Kuwait, Jordan, Saudi Arabia, Russia, Bulgaria, Romania, Hungary, Czechoslovakia, Yugoslavia, Albania, Greece, Algeria, Libya, Tunisia, Ethiopia, Somalia, and Sudan. His vast empire covered three continents and was noted for its system of justice and expansion of the arts, literature, architecture, and craftwork. For almost six centuries the Turks lived in or near Europe and interacted with Europeans, assimilating parts of European culture over time. Süleyman's death in 1556 marked the end of a wonderfully creative era. The empire began its decline with the loss of Hungary and the Crimea in the 1700s. In the next century the Ottomans lost control of Egypt and most of the Balkans, and this was followed by the loss of Serbia, Romania, Cyprus, Algeria, and Tunisia.

In 1908, a group known as the Young Turks attempted to restore power to the empire. Instability in the region brought about drastic territorial changes and reduced the Ottoman holdings even further. The shrunken empire entered World War I on the side of the Central Powers in 1914. By the end of the war, the Arab provinces were lost and a nationalist movement began. These events led to both the proclamation of a new nation and additional contributions to Turkish culture.

In 1923, the Treaty of Lausanne established the Republic of Turkey as we recognize it today. Mustafa Kemal, also known as Atatürk (literally, "Father of the Turks"), renounced all earlier conquests and introduced widespread reforms to guide the country. His deliberate reforms transformed the diverse empire into a nation while shaping daily life for every Turkish citizen. Along with the internal modernization of the country, the republic turned toward Western principles and conventions. Turkey became a NATO member in 1952 and an associate member of the European Common Market in 1963.

Turkish coffee was first introduced during the Ottoman Empire. In the 15th century merchants from the Far East traveled along the Silk Road to trade their exotic spices and other wares in European markets. In an effort to encourage trade and offer hospitality, hostels for travelers called *caravansaries* were built. As they passed through ancient Turkey, the merchants bartered along the way and offered their products in exchange for hospitality. According to the strictest rule of the Koran, the sultans forbade the drinking of coffee because it is a drug. In spite of the restriction, coffee drinking became so popular that the palace rescinded the rule and allowed its consumption. Today, Turkish coffee is as popular as ever.

Islam and Secularity

One of Atatürk's most important reforms was the adoption of a constitution that encouraged secularism. Although an overwhelming number of Turkish citizens are Muslims (approximately 96%), other religions such as Greek Orthodoxy and Judaism are tolerated in Turkish society. During the rule of the Ottoman Empire, both religion and culture were totally integrated with government, and Islamic world power was concentrated in Turkey. Atatürk and his followers felt strongly that adherence to the caliphate was an obstacle to the country's attempts to Westernize. Major changes resulting from secularism included a shift from Islamic to European legal codes, closing of religious schools and lodges, and recognition of the Western calendar rather than a religious one. Despite these sweeping changes, Islam still thrived and in the 1950s religious education was reintroduced. The Turkish government now oversees a system in which children are exposed to a measure of religion in schools, and clergy members receive salaries from the government.

The distinction between Turkey and other Islamic nations is noteworthy. Unlike them, Turkey is a secular nation. Governments, schools, and businesses operate independently of religious beliefs. Even traditional clothing, such as veils for women and fezzes for men, were abandoned in the shift from Islam to secularity. Consequently, Islam does not affect daily Turkish life as much as it would in an Arab nation. Religious power over Turkish institutions is nonexistent, and this fact reflects a preference for association with other Western cultures. However, as noted above, a small but growing political movement has evolved around the issue of making Turkey a theocracy like those found in Iran and other Arab nations.

Like Catholicism in Ireland, which was constitutionally divorced from the government in 1937, Islam is separate from state matters, but is ever present in the daily lives of citizens. In contrast with Ireland, however, religious groups in Turkey do not wield significant power to influence government. Turkish Muslims do not necessarily converge on the mosque when the call to prayer is sounded the way Catholics in Ireland flock to church for Sunday Mass. Islam is a religion for individuals to communicate directly to God without an intermediary spokesman. Consequently, those who pray at mosques do not need to coordinate their visits. Afterward, Turks may head to the coffeehouse for refreshments and socializing.

Five well-known pillars embody the essence of Islam. The first is acceptance of the creed, "There is no God but Allah, and Muhammed is his prophet." The second pillar comes from the Koran, or Holy Book, and involves keeping life in its proper perspective. This can be done through prayer, five times a day, to submit one's self to God's will. Third is the observance of the holiday of Ramadan by fasting during daylight hours for one month as determined by the lunar calendar, and fourth is giving to charity. Fasting underscores humans' dependence on God, teaches self-discipline, sensitizes compassion, and forces one to think. The final pillar is a once-in-a-lifetime pilgrimage to Mecca for those who are able. It is understood that those who reach the holy city where God revealed himself have demonstrated their devotion to Him.

In Turkish towns, the two most important places for social gathering—the mosque and the coffeehouse—are in the town square. The coffeehouse is often adjacent to the village mosque and may even provide a small operating fund or rent for the general upkeep of the mosque. Throughout the world, inhabitants of small towns tend to be more conservative than city residents, and Turkey is no exception. As a result, Turkish townspeople tend to follow their faith more strictly than their urban counterparts. Also, Eastern and Central Turkey are more religious than Western Turkey, in part because of the diversity of the people living in the Western parts. Although there has been a resurgence of religious practices since the 1950s, Islamic fanaticism remains a minor influence today, and even moderate Muslims have tried to revive some traditions that were eliminated with the arrival of a secular nation.

In addition to rent, many of these coffeehouses occasionally collect donations from patrons to pay for the mosque's water and cleaning. Traditionally, Muslims are called to prayer five times each day, although the frequency of prayer for contemporary Muslims is a function of both the level of piety and the availability of time. Thus a visit to the coffeehouse also can be considered a ritual, ironically linked with the daily ritual of prayer. Further, cleanliness is an important related Islamic value, and the owner of a coffeehouse typically squirts a bottle of water on the dirt floor from time to time to keep the dust from rising. Even some of the original popularity of coffeehouses was because of the Islamic prohibition of alcohol and the use of coffee as a substitute and acceptable beverage.

Many other Turkish cultural values and beliefs derive from the Islamic faith, some of which are not directly related to the operations of the coffeehouse. In particular, Muslims believe that the future will be better than the past. The village parents who struggle to support their children may rely on this optimism for decades. Also, the ideas that the soul lives forever and that every person is responsible for his or her actions are also important considerations for Muslims in accepting their lot in life.

The Ottoman Empire governed the people by *seriat,* or Islamic law. Turks also adhered to moral and social rules, such as respect for one's father, on a daily basis. These ideas persist in modern Turkey. Unlike purely theocratic Islamic nations, Turkish legal decisions are not judged by one code alone. Likewise, civil marriage ceremonies must be conducted, irrespective of religious ones, to obtain recognition under Turkish law. Civil code based on European models was intro-duced in 1926. Still, basic customs from the Ottoman days, just like the survival of the coffeehouse, have been carried over into modern Turkish society. Some Turks still refuse to accept interest accrued from savings accounts because such profits are prohibited in the Koran. Widely used Turkish phrases derived from Islam include "Salaam," a friendly greeting that literally means "Peace be upon you," and "Masallah," which means "God protect you from harm." Both phrases are used in everyday language in much the same way that Americans respond with "God bless you" when someone sneezes. Other examples include abstinence from or moderation in drinking alcohol, fulfilling oral promises, and using the catchall phrase "Bismillahir-rahman-irrahim," or "I am starting this in the name of merciful Allah," which is said when starting a task, whether a journey, a test, a wedding, or a meal.

Among Turkish traditions, the household extends beyond the nu-clear family, and individuals are loyal to the entire family or kinship group. Women especially are expected to offer hospitality to all guests. If a visitor knocks on the door before or during mealtime, he is almost always invited to join the family in the dining room or at the kitchen table. It is considered common decency to offer the visitor food and drink, and a hearty appetite is a compliment for a Turkish host or hostess. Sitting with crossed legs can be disrespectful to Turkish elders. As in mosques, Turkish guests offer to remove their shoes as a gesture of cleanliness on entering someone's home. Marriage decisions are influenced by families in rural areas, and in some instances dating is not permitted. One should keep in mind that these are merely generalizations about Turkish customs and do not apply to all Turkish citizens. Turkish compassion and hospitality come from the ethical aspects of the Islamic faith, as do racial equality and religious tolerance. Islam acknowledges the legitimacy of other semitic religions that preceded it, but it holds that both Judaism and Christianity are incomplete. Finally, part of the greatness of the Ottoman dynasty is attributable to Islam, which brought together different peoples and united them through spiritual means.

The concept that every event in an individual's life is predetermined has its roots in the religion of Islam. Like many other religions, Islam attributes circumstances beyond one's control to a supreme being. Muslims believe that a person will act according to his or her own decisions under a given set of circumstances. For example, much of the younger population is migrating to the cities to obtain jobs and better schooling. This trend does not reflect anyone's fate in particular, but individuals who decide to change their lifestyles by leaving their villages subject themselves to *kismet*, or fate. In other words, God meant for those people to move on and start a new way of life. If these people eventually relocate back to their own villages, then that also is kismet. This belief allows an individual's shortcomings to be more easily accepted.

The Turkish orientation toward time goes hand in hand with the belief in destiny. It is easy to say that most Turks are not especially conscious of time, and one of the attractions of the coffeehouse is that customers can linger there if they so choose. Hosts and hostesses are concerned if their guests do not arrive promptly at the time given for an invitation to a social event, but they are very understanding. Delays at airports and train stations are not a cause for alarm. *Polychronistic* best describes the Turkish ability to concentrate on different things simultaneously, whether at work, at home, or in the coffeehouse. Although schedules and appointments are important, people and relationships are also valued. To the polychronic Turks, time is intangible and supports the development and maintenance of long-term relationships. Elements of the past, present, and future tend to merge, and they permeate Turkish values and norms.

If a Turk were asked to ponder the ideal position of his or her country in international dealings, he or she would probably refer to the halcyon days of the Ottoman Empire. The historic aspect of the country is crucial to understanding the Turkish mindset, and a comparison of today and yesterday is absolute. Conversely, Turks place much emphasis on what future generations will accomplish. This explains why it is important that children are given optimal educational opportunities irrespective of costs and degree of parental sacrifice. Personal savings take the form of real estate or gold-reserve investments. Kismet and time orientation are inextricably linked together in Turkish culture.

Understanding the idea of destiny helps us comprehend why time is relatively unimportant. In the United States, if a business project falls behind schedule, a firm risks embarrassment and scrutiny by consumers, investors, shareholders, and the government. In Turkey, the same type of delay is attributed to God's will and is more easily forgiven. Thus the phrase "Inshallah" ("If it is God's will") is heard quite often. A famous Turkish joke about a fellow named Hodja illustrates the degree of time and urgency in daily business.

One day, a fellow named Hodja brought some material to a tailor and requested that he measure him and make a shirt from the material as soon as possible. The tailor measured him and said, "I am very busy but your shirt will be ready on Friday, Inshallah." Hodja returned on Friday, but the tailor apologized that the shirt was not ready and said, "Come back Monday and, Inshallah, it will be ready." On Monday, Hodja went back to the tailor only to find out that the shirt was still not finished, and was told, "Try again Thursday, Inshallah, and I promise it will be ready." This time Hodja wisely answered, "How long will it take if we leave Inshallah out of it?!"

Recreation, Communication, and Community Integration

Coffeehouses became popular during the 16th century. They have always been sources of information, especially when illiteracy rates were high. In those days, one person would read the newspaper to an eager audience. Throughout the reign of the Ottoman Empire, defense strategies were discussed and developed in the coffeehouses. These establishments had battery-operated radios before they were introduced in homes, and the same was true when television arrived. Today a patron enjoys camaraderie when viewing a soccer match at the coffeehouse instead of watching it on his television set by himself at home, and this pattern fits the group-oriented Turkish lifestyle.

Turkish men go to the modern coffeehouse to become part of a group. They feel very comfortable when surrounded by friends and family, and they prefer the stability of belonging to an organization to individualism. And, as an old Turkish proverb states, one cup of coffee is worth 40 years of friendship. According to Bisbee (1951):

> The prime ingredients of the Turks' idea of fun and amusement seem to be relaxation, imagination, sociability and humor. Sitting is almost, if not quite, the most popular recreation of all. Turks sit at windows, in gardens, at coffeehouses . . . anywhere and everywhere they can see a pleasing view and relax in conversation. (p. 145)

In Turkey there is a relationship between collectivism and accomplishing the goals of the group. In small villages, the coffeehouse is often the setting in which important village debate, discussions, and decisions are made. One custom, *imece*, describes a Turkish social gathering at which everyone pitches in to help a neighbor undertake a large task, such as building a new home. In many instances of imece, the initial request for assistance and plans for the event are proposed at the coffeehouse. Turks prefer to approach problems in a logical but personalized manner, and they will discuss practical solutions at length in the coffeehouse. In small Turkish towns, the mayor can frequently be found at his second, more unofficial office— the coffeehouse. It is not uncommon to find community notices tacked onto a coffeehouse bulletin board. For example, the government might post an announcement that crops will be sprayed with pesticides on a particular date or that a public hearing to discuss a new water project will be held. Messages are left for others who will eventually show up; it is the information center in which most communication takes place, including political discussions and gossip. Being a member of the coffeehouse is considered important, regardless of the topic under discussion.

Likewise, women have a need for affiliation; they get together at weekly coffees or teas at the homes of friends. The weekly coffee presents an opportunity to show hospitality and become involved with others. Traditional Turkish hospitality extends to strangers, particularly in rural areas. The group itself is highly valued, and individual identity is determined on the basis of group membership. Conformity to group norms and traditions is expected; trust and reliance within the group are important (Dindi & Gazur, 1989, p. 17). In Geert Hofstede's (1980a) 40-nation study of cultural values, Turkey clusters with those nations that emphasize collectivism rather than individualism.

Family gatherings are very important, as are deep friendships. Turks are nostalgic when it comes to family traditions and special occasions. Just as a man can stop by the coffeehouse whenever he wants, so too it is not considered impolite to drop in at a friend's home without an invitation. This is true regardless of one's economic, social, or educational status. Fostering good relationships requires time, and Turks feel that such time is always well spent.

Coffeehouses open early in the day and for many Turks are the place to stop before beginning the day's work. In late afternoon, workers stop in before going home to their families. After dinner, some men visit the coffeehouse to catch up on the latest news. In summer, customers sit outside on sidewalks or patios to escape the oppressive Turkish heat and catch an occasional cool breeze. In winter, everyone gathers around the warmth of a stove or furnace in the coffeehouse. Just as the Italian piazza is the place in which to stroll to see others and be seen, the village coffeehouse provides a place for social gathering. As in bygone eras, the village coffeehouse remains a center for everyone, regardless of income, education, or social status.

A traffic accident illustrates what Hofstede's study described as the Turks' feminine nature. According to Hofstede, femininity expresses the extent to which societies value caring for others, quality of life, and people. Within moments of the accident, everyone who witnessed the collision, along with those who did not, is on the scene. No one present would dream of minding his or her own business. Each stranger then offers help, comments, and interpretations of the accident—and chaos results! If a vehicle breaks down at night, Turkish passersby generally do not hesitate to stop and offer assistance to the driver. To ignore someone in distress would be considered indecent. By contrast, many Americans would not dare to stop for fear of their own personal safety. In Turkish culture, involvement and interdependence are the ideal. Turks care about others and show their concern by stopping to help perfect strangers. People are important in Turkish culture, and most Turks will sympathize with those who are less fortunate. Above all, Turks pride themselves on hospitality and being helpful to strangers.

Feministic values are also exhibited in the way Turks show interest in others through conversation. Whether sharing small talk at the coffeehouse or within the hospitality of one's home, the Turkish people tend to be curious by nature. Consequently, very little in one's life is a real secret. Communication is the essence of Turkish existence. When one Turkish stranger meets another, he typically asks where the first is from. What he is more interested in is who his parents are and where they are from. The next few minutes are spent quizzing the other person with questions such as "Oh, my brother-in-law's uncle is from there; do you know Ahmet?" or "Surely you must know Ali." Such so-called Turkish geography is really a game played to discover to which clan the stranger belongs, just as in other countries such as Israel and Ireland. Thus identifying relationships displays the Turks' collectivist orientation, and the interest in others demonstrates the bias toward femininity.

A Male Domain

A Turkish coffeehouse is a place where men assemble throughout the day and throughout the year. Regardless of age, men gather at the coffeehouse to play backgammon, share gossip, or just enjoy company. Young boys accompany their fathers and play alongside the tables until they are old enough to join discussions. Old men sit on wooden chairs and sip coffee while reminiscing, offering words of wisdom, and solving the world's problems.

A visit to the Turkish coffeehouse is a favorite pastime for male Turks of all ages. In recent years, the city coffeehouse has decreased in popularity when compared to its counterpart in smaller towns and villages. One can draw a correlation between the prominence of coffeehouses and cultural values in cities versus rural areas. In the larger cities of Istanbul, Ankara, and Izmir, life is hectic and people have little time to sit and chat. But Turkey is still primarily an agrarian society; people working outside industrialized areas are often limited by weather conditions and daylight. With extra time on his hands, a farmer may visit the coffeehouse, and it is a welcome diversion for a man out of work. Coffeehouses remain popular in rural areas where Turkish traditions and male roles are strong. The popularity of the city coffeehouse has declined as a new generation places less emphasis on traditional values and a greater emphasis on earning a living. Within the city, older citizens tend to be more devout and frequent the coffeehouse more than the young, who often spend their free time on self-improvement. Turkish city dwellers today spend most of their leisure time on alternative activities such as cinema, theater, and concerts. As cities become more cosmopolitan, urban coffeehouses are less likely to attract clientele in comparison with coffeehouses in less populated locales. The coffeehouse remains a cherished institution outside of the cities where lower- and middle-class customers enjoy good coffee and good conversation, and city dwellers recognize its historical importance and speak of it fondly even when they do not frequent it.

There is no question that Turkey has a male-dominated culture and the nature of such domination is constant at the coffeehouse. Although women are welcome, the coffeehouse has always been considered a male domain. This is true of other public places in Turkey, even today. The Islamic origins of the population still influence the role of women. For example, most women pray at home rather than at the mosque.

A long tradition of men as breadwinners, leaders of the family unit, and decision makers in local politics and matters of national concern exists in Turkey. As heads of families, men in rural areas decide which crops will be planted and at which market crops will be sold. Village coffeehouses often become markets where brokers trade farm commodities. Within the clan structure, it is understood that sons will be in charge of the family and daughters will marry into their husband's family. As in other Western cultures, sons carry on the family name. Within the traditional family, a father's request is always obeyed, and Turkish fathers are especially protective of their daughters.

A Modest Environment

The simplicity of the coffeehouse itself is noteworthy. The furniture is basic and the chairs uncomfortable. A typical coffeehouse in a small village may consist of one small room, a kitchen, and several small wooden or aluminum tables and chairs. A smoky atmosphere from cigarettes or the *nargile*, the traditional waterpipe, is unmistakable. Although each coffeehouse differs, the sounds are always familiar: Steady chatter, heated discussion, and hearty laughter can be heard above the clatter of cups and saucers, and Turkish music comes from a radio.

Turks are concerned more with substance than form. The true draw of the coffeehouse is the opportunity for release and self-indulgence. The release is only temporary, allowing escape from the stress or monotony of the moment, and the indulgence reflects the element of Turkish culture that says, "Experience life."

As noted earlier, Turkish life in the city is quite different from that in the village. In the cities, neighborhood coffeehouses abound. However, the middle and upper classes tend to spend time at various elite establishments, such as bars or cafés, instead of being loyal to a particular coffeehouse. Apartment living is popular in Turkish cities. Turks are less transient than are Americans and tend to live in the same building for years, where they are surrounded by family and friends. Simply put, people are valued in Turkey. Respect for others is important. Like other Mediterranean peoples, however, Turks have little fear of consequences for failing to respect laws. Along with liberal interpretations of traffic signals, patience is not a Turkish strong suit. A prime example is the early morning scene when workers try to catch a bus: It is every man for himself as people struggle on the downtown streets of Ankara to get on the crowded buses. In most other situations, however, Turks have considerable respect for the rights of others.

Coffeehouses are family-run establishments. It is often the owner's son who takes orders and delivers teas and coffees to the table. One should not expect to be served a meal there; however, patrons are more than welcome to bring food in. Many hungry patrons will first stop at a local carryout for a freshly baked snack. *Simit*, a round flat bread topped with sesame seeds, is a familiar sight at coffeehouses. As expected, a coffeehouse owner does not mind food being brought into the coffeehouse because he knows that more food eaten means more drinks ordered. Unlike at Turkish restaurants, a customer is welcome to remain at the coffeehouse as long as he wishes. The coffeehouse is not a high-profit enterprise. By the same token, it is rare that coffeehouses fold because they provide incredible services to their communities as meeting places and information centers.

Turkish coffee is always made in a special way; first the grains are ground into a fine powder, then water and sugar are blended with the powder, and finally the mixture is boiled over a flame. The three possible versions of Turkish coffee are *sade* (no sugar), *orta* (some sugar), and *sekerli* (more sugar). At the coffeehouse, the waiter will call out the orders to the kitchen so fresh pots can be made. When he returns, the waiter never seems to remember who ordered what. A running joke is that one day Atatürk, who is greatly respected by the Turks, went to a village coffeehouse with his entourage. The waiter took everyone's order and brought the coffees to the table. Atatürk was amazed that the waiter had gotten the order correct and told him so. When asked by Atatürk how he remembered, the waiter responded, "Yours is the only order that counts!"

Life Outside the Coffeehouse

Many activities occur outside of the coffeehouse, and we need to understand them and the manner in which they reflect cultural values. For example, observance of Islam in Turkey today has led to popular misconceptions about the role of women. Since the adoption of this religion more than 1,000 years ago, conservative ideas evolved, including the seclusion and submission of women to men as a form of protection. At one time it was expected that women retreat to the harem out of deference to men. However, even in the harem, women had some degree of power in terms of training daughters and young sons in household management, arts and crafts, and religion. The harem was highly political; concubines were selected for sultans by their mothers, and royal marriages were arranged there in those days. In 1925 the wearing of veils by Turkish women was officially discouraged. In the following year, Atatürk, the founder and first president of modern Turkey, introduced civil marriage codes that abolished polygamy and established divorce and child custody rights for both men and women.

As in earlier times, Turkish women have always been subtly capable of influencing their husbands' way of thinking. In Turkey, women are brought up to show respect for their husbands, and they do not openly flaunt any power they may hold over their men. Turkish women rarely make firm denials of a husband's decision, yet they may quietly oppose decisions with which they are unhappy. In either case, the wife recognizes the needs of her husband's ego and is typically shrewd enough to offer small suggestions rather than demand compliance with her wishes.

Many Turkish women possess an emotional inner strength and maturity that developed from the burdens of maintaining a stable family life under harsh economic conditions. This is particularly true for those who live in remote areas. In rural villages, women are responsible for meals, housework, and child care. Turkish kitchens are busy all day long as women prepare delicious meals of roasted lamb, rice pilaf, or other specialties. Throughout Turkey, women take pride in a cooking style that intermingles Arabic, Greek, and European influences.

One important development for women in the villages is that they have become responsible for working outside the home, too. The unemployment rate tends to be high—10% or higher—and many men have difficulty finding work. Inflation as high as 60% also strains the availability of jobs. Lack of employment opportunities for men in small towns and villages has sustained the appeal of the coffeehouse. External employment is often a necessity for women, who will work outside of their homes on local farms and in factories or sell handmade items to support their families. Beautiful woven carpets, ceramic pottery, mosaics, and other items handcrafted by Turkish women are appreciated throughout the world. The women's determination in taking care of daily life affords them some measure of power over their husbands' behavior. Women who work in the fields cook, eat, clean, and even sing together. Urban wives who may be on a more equal educational footing with their husbands may also affect their behavior and decisions that can be as trivial as recommending what clothes a husband should wear or as monumental as deciding to risk a new business venture. Finally, career-oriented women reflect modern Turkish societal norms, which recognize joint decision making and cooperative patterns of husband-wife authority, along with traditional respect for the husband. Note that families still closely supervise the activities of unmarried women, and strong attitudes prevail about the proper conduct for women.

Further, respect for one's parents is absolute. In turn, a parent is expected to be concerned about his or her child's future. The extended Turkish family is proof of the respect afforded to elders. Grandparents, aunts, uncles, and cousins often live in or near the same dwellings as core family units. The notion of an old-age home is nonexistent. Likewise, hired baby-sitters are unusual because family members care for children. Parents are willing to stretch the family budget to provide a tutor or send a child to better schools. Most parents also feel obligated to give their children a moral education. Children are a continuation of a family's reputation, and famous children are an even greater source of pride for doting parents.

Boys and girls are brought up similarly with a few exceptions. Before 7 years of age, a boy is circumcised in a religious ceremony that symbolizes his ascent to manhood. On graduation from high school, there is a mandatory 18-month period of military service. Men who attend a university have the option of deferring their service until they reach 32 years of age. There is no compulsory service for women, although they are allowed to enlist for noncombatant positions if desired.

Traditionally, the new bride became part of her husband's family only after she had produced an heir. Except in rare circumstances, this is no longer true. Today, Turkish daughters-in-law are immediately accepted into the family household. The family structure is important, and the divorce rate is relatively low. In Turkey, it is unusual for people to live on their own, unless they are dormitory students.

Another significant reform, the right to education for the masses, was effected in 1924. Atatürk believed that education was an essential element of Westernization. Today education is seen as the legitimate discriminator for the social classes in Turkey. Elementary school is mandatory for all children. Like the United States, the school year begins in September and ends in June. In keeping with national policy, secularity is practiced. Although *laik*, or separation of church and state, is understood, school vacations coincide with the Islamic holidays of Ramadan and Kurban. In addition to monitoring regular schools, the Turkish Ministry of Education also controls religious schools to limit their influence. For those schools that have limited resources, the school day is taught in half-day shifts. Wearing of uniforms is required for the young children. A dress code also requires neat grooming such as conservative haircuts for boys and hair ties for girls with long hair. Children learn respect for teachers at an early age. In the classroom, students normally stand whenever a teacher enters the room. It is considered disrespectful to disagree with the teacher.

The curriculum includes math, science, history, Turkish language, art, music, physical education, and morals. After fifth grade, similar to what happens in Germany, children study for a placement examination that determines their future path of study. In larger towns and cities, tutors are often hired to complement formal school instruction. For those who score well, the next year is spent at a private secondary school to learn a second language, most often English, French, or German. The language study is followed by two years of preparation for high school. These students attend high school for three years; on graduation, those who wish to continue their studies at a university take a difficult entrance examination. Students who do not score as well on the placement exam attend a general secondary school followed by entry into a vocational or technical school to learn a trade. Those students interested in entering a university are also invited to take the entrance exam.

The competition for attending universities is keen because of the limited number of universities in the country. Approximately 20% of the 900,000 students who test are accepted into the universities annually. There is an obvious inequity in this system. Those who are privileged enough to have access to better-quality academic resources have a better opportunity for admission to a university.

In Hofstede's comparative study of values in 40 nations, Turkey clustered with those nations emphasizing the acceptance of larger *power distances* between groups; the measurement indicates the extent to which unequal power distribution in institutions and organizations is automatically accepted by a society. A prime example of

the large power distance in Turkish society is the inequity of access
to higher education, which is free. At the university level, students
must be accepted into respective fields of study, such as law, medicine, or engineering before attending the university. Students rank
their preferences of fields of study and, based on individual proficiency, are matched to their choices. The selection process is highly
competitive; within the 29 universities in Turkey, many disciplines
have a limited number of student spaces available. Thus a university
student may aspire to a profession for which he or she is effectively
barred, unless he or she can study that profession abroad. Although
selection to an institution is competitive, interaction among students
is cooperative. It is common practice for students to work together
on homework and study. Students tend to take studying seriously
and to appreciate their learning opportunities.

Further, humor is an important mechanism in Turkish culture and
is a good way to make friends and maintain friendships, both inside
and outside the coffeehouse. Turkish humor is distinctive; Turks do
not mind making fun of themselves. When things become too serious, a joke is welcomed to strike a balance and provide relief. The
coffeehouse itself provides a similar relief from life's predicaments.
Whether in political satire, television shows, or within the coffeehouse, humor is used frequently. For example, Turkish coffee is
served in a small cup and has a thick, almost muddy, consistency; it
is usually served with a glass of water. A popular joke involves
differentiating between a Turk and a foreigner. The difference? A
Turk drinks the water first, to clean his palate; the foreigner takes the
water after the coffee, to wash it down!

In Turkey, humor takes on many forms. Weekly comedy magazines
have a wide readership, particularly among university students.
Stories that center around a former prime minister named Akbulut
are popular; it seems that this gentleman was underqualified for the
job, and he is used as the butt of many good-natured jokes unrelated
to politics. The *Laz* of northern Turkey are also figures in jokes
throughout the country. Anecdotes about this minority from the
coastal region by the Black Sea evoke laughs even in that area.
Laughter provides recreation and reminds Turkish citizens that they
should stay humble.

Humor is taught early on, and folk heroes such as Nasreddin
Hodja are loved by children and grown-ups alike. As a boy, Hodja
always had something clever and humorous to say in every situation. Hodja stories are well-known and relate to everyday life in
Turkey. A favorite story goes as follows:

Hodja was walking down the street when he noticed something glittering in the gutter. He ran over to pick it up and noticed it was a small metal mirror. He looked in it and said to himself, "No wonder they threw this thing away. I wouldn't keep something as ugly as this either!"

What makes Hodja special is that he always expresses a note of encouragement and tries to live a happy life of honesty and simplicity. His jokes run the gamut from religion to mothers-in-law to sultans and even his own hearty appetite! His jokes not only are retold at the coffeehouse but also often begin, "One day when Hodja was at the coffeehouse. . . ." The proof of this character's popularity is that most, if not all, people in Turkey like to claim that Hodja was born in his or her village!

Humor is an effective communication technique and can even serve as a way to avoid confrontation and conflict. Turks are generally quite modest about their accomplishments. This makes sense because besides being impolite, self-boasting would tend to separate an individual from his group. Instead, it is perfectly acceptable for good friends or family members to brag about others. Modesty complements the Turkish values of tactfulness and diplomacy. Turks prefer to avoid confrontation and to handle disputes indirectly whenever possible. Being direct is considered rude and insulting; directness goes against the respect Turks feel for other people (Dindi & Gazur, 1989, p. 19). Respect for authority is very highly regarded and unconditional in many instances. In his 40-nation study, Geert Hofstede (1980a) showed that uncertainty avoidance statements epitomize Turkish culture. For example, the strong need for consensus, the undesirability of conflict and competition, and the strong belief in experts and their expertise are understandable when examining the face-saving nature of Turkish culture.

Turkey faces considerable challenges in the very near future. High unemployment and inflation have left the economy unstable, and past government corruption and military coups cast doubt over true Turkish democracy. The question of Kurdish independence still must be addressed for the 7 million Kurds who live in Turkey. Although Turks prefer further integration with Western Europe, Turkey has not yet been offered full membership in the EC. At the same time, Islamic fundamentalists point to a growing economic gap between rich and poor in their attempt to discourage Westernization. Disputes over Cyprus continue to strain Greek-Turkish relations, terrorism exists within Turkish borders, and Turkish minorities in the Balkan states are persecuted.

On the other hand, the future holds promise for Turkey. The end of the cold war, support for the destruction of Saddam Hussein's regime during the Persian Gulf War, and important Turkish energy resources provide hope for increased stability in the region. Water projects on the Tigris and Euphrates Rivers will help provide better irrigation of Turkish farmland when completed. Trade with the republics of the former Soviet Union now totals several billion dollars each year. Despite inflationary problems, economic reforms of the 1980s have caused a steady growth of 6% per year in the gross domestic product of Turkey. Collectively, these events demonstrate that Turkey possesses a good amount of strength and resilience.

This is our portrait of Turkey, a traditional agrarian nation that is seeking rapid modernization. The coffeehouse reflects many of the important values and behaviors of the Turks, particularly the relationship between Islam and secularity, recreation, communication, and community integration, male dominance, and the importance of substance over form within such a modest environment. And, although Turkey is changing, its citizens still recognize the historical and cultural importance of the coffeehouse, even when they only frequent it periodically. Thus there will always be a place for the coffeehouse in Turkey, especially in the rural areas and small towns that still dominate life in this country.

12

The Israeli Kibbutzim
and Moshavim

Probably no other institution is as uniquely Israeli as the kibbutz, the collective farm that played a critical role in the Jewish settlement of Palestine and later establishment and development of the Jewish state. As Lawrence Meyer (1982) describes it, "The Kibbutz is the ultimate symbol of pioneering Labor Zionism, the institutional embodiment of the dream of returning to the land, working it, receiving sustenance from it, and reviving an ancient culture in the process" (p. 327).

The first kibbutz was founded in 1909; today there are more than 260. Although many of them still engage in farming, others are involved in several different industrial activities. Although they account for less than 3% of a population of 4.4 million, the influence of the kibbutzim (plural form of kibbutz) and their democratic and egalitarian character have had on Israeli society is vastly disproportionate to their modest numbers. For example, 15% of the representatives in the Israeli Parliament are members of the kibbutzim.

The basic principles of kibbutz life are community ownership of all property, absolute equality of members, democratic decision making, the value of work as both end and means, communal responsibility for child care, and primacy of the group over individuals. However, there are many pressures on the kibbutzim, and a variant of it, the moshav (moshavim, plural) allows for private ownership of some property by its members and for more individual freedom for its members; moshavim now account for 30% of all kibbutzim. In this chapter we will describe kibbutzim and include some final remarks about moshavim.

Members of the kibbutz receive no pay for their work. All of their essential needs—food, shelter, clothing, medical care, and education—are provided by the community. Children are raised with their peers, meals are usually eaten in the kibbutz dining hall, and members convene regularly to discuss and vote on issues. Many jobs rotate among members. All positions of authority—such as those of kibbutz chief executive, plant managers, and supervisors—change every two or three years. Power is not permitted to accumulate in the hands of individuals. The kibbutzim range in size from 100 to 2,000 members and are small enough so that the individual's role in the community is visible and tangible.

Because of the kibbutz's relative success as a social, innovative, political, and economic enterprise, it has attracted worldwide attention. Also, the kibbutz is a vehicle for obtaining insight into the Israeli character and the mythology from which the Israelis draw their self-identity. The perception of the kibbutz as an ideal existence stems from the initial goal of the founders: that the kibbutzim would be the core of society rather than be only an alternative.

To understand the kibbutz, we need historical background. Israel's place in history is directly related to its geography. It is a very small country on the coast of the Eastern Mediterranean. Only 260 miles in length from north to south, it averages 60 miles from east to west and shares borders with the Arab nations of Lebanon, Syria, Jordan, and Egypt. Still, the country's landscape is marked by abrupt changes from mountains to plains, and from fertile green areas to harsh deserts. The diversity of the scenery is immense: There are more than 15 distinct geographical regions.

The history of Israel has been one largely characterized by uniqueness and oppression, and at various times it has been ruled by Christians and Muslims. In their early history, the Israelites, in opposition to the tribes surrounding them and their belief in polytheism, worshipped only one God. For this belief they suffered persecution and enslavement, thus creating the condition for their flight from Egypt under Moses' leadership. Christianity and Islam trace their origins to Judaism and this belief, and Muslims hold that Muhammad ascended to heaven from Jerusalem, while Christians maintain the same belief about Jesus, thus making the city sacred for all three religions. What sets Judaism apart from other major religions is its search for meaning in all aspects of life, and the kibbutz is a reflection of such uniqueness (Smith, 1958, 1991).

The opening of the Suez Canal in 1869 significantly increased the geopolitical and economic importance of the Middle East, and Jewish immigration began to grow significantly. Most newcomers emigrated to Israel not for religious reasons but because of Zionism, a unique modern national and ideological movement.

Born in the last half of the 19th century, Zionism was the movement for the redemption of the Jewish people in the land of Israel. It derives its name from the word *Zion*, the traditional synonym for Jerusalem and Israel. The movement gained strength because of the continued oppression and persecution of Jews in Eastern Europe and increasing disillusionment with their formal emancipation in Western Europe. Emancipation had neither put an end to discrimination nor led to the integration of Jews into their local societies. The Zionist movement aimed at attaining an internationally recognized, legally secured home for the Jewish people in their historic homeland. Inspired by Zionist ideology, increasing numbers of Jews emigrated to Palestine at the end of the 19th century. These early pioneers drained swamps, reclaimed wastelands, founded agricultural settlements, and revived the Hebrew language for everyday use. It was at this stage that kibbutzim became intertwined with the history of Israel as they were founded by Zionists seeking to create a new society for the Jewish people.

After the Ottoman Turks were defeated in World War I, Britain took control of Palestine. Until World War II, consecutive waves of Jewish immigrants arrived, and an infrastructure of towns and villages, industry, culture, and health, educational, and social systems was developed. Meanwhile, immediately before and during World War II, Jews in Europe suffered immensely, and the Holocaust was among the most brutal genocides ever practiced by any culture. Renewed calls for an independent state were raised.

In 1947, the United Nations' General Assembly adopted a resolution calling for the partition of the land into two states, one Jewish and one Arab. On May 14, 1948, the state of Israel was declared. The next day, a combined Arab force attacked the new state and, although it was badly outnumbered and suffered the loss of 1% of its entire population, Israel won its war of independence 6 months later.

In 1948 and immediately thereafter, the new state of Israel faced the daunting task of turning Zionist ideological dreams into reality. Immigrant absorption was an immediate priority. In its first three years, Israel welcomed 678,000 immigrants, many from the Arab countries, and in the process doubled its population. The nation's economic growth over the next decade was truly remarkable, especially in light of the fact that Israel has few natural resources and does not even have water in some major areas of the country. With the development of modern and sophisticated farming and irrigation techniques, orchards and groves were blooming even in the most arid regions of the country. Tens and hundreds of new towns and agricultural settlements came to life, modern industrial plants were built, roads throughout the country were paved, and a modern army was equipped virtually from scratch.

This success could not have occurred without outside help, which has continued to this day. By 1991 Israel had become the single largest recipient of charity, grants, and assistance per capita in the world, the bulk of it from the United States.

In 1956 and again in 1967, Egypt moved aggressively against Israel, which won both wars. The 1967 "Six Day War" brought a devastating defeat for Egypt, Syria, and Jordan as Israel gained possession of the Sinai Peninsula, the Gaza Strip, the Golan Heights, the West Bank of Jordan, and East Jerusalem. For the first time in 2,000 years, Jerusalem was again under Jewish sovereignty. However, the country relaxed its military posture, and the Egyptians and Syrians attacked again in 1973, this time on Yom Kippur, the holiest day on the Jewish calendar. Israel was caught by surprise, and although it won the war, the losses were significant.

Today Israelis are in the awkward position of living in a cramped geographical area within which Palestinians also live, although separately. There are great tensions between these two groups, and Israel has been cited frequently by Amnesty International for violating the Palestinians' basic rights. Even Israelis are divided on the issue of the poor treatment accorded these Palestinians, and there is a movement for Palestinian self-rule that some Israelis also champion. In this chapter, the focus is on the Israelis, although clearly their troubled relationship with the Palestinians at least needs to be mentioned.

With the understanding of both Israel and the kibbutz's origins in mind, it is possible to see how the kibbutz reflects many of the essential features of Israeli society and the Israeli character. First, the explicit social and ideological values to which the kibbutzim adhere are also manifested in the Israeli society, although to a lesser degree. Also, the small size of both Israel and the kibbutz are related to specific behavioral outcomes, and the traumas that the Israelis have experienced have led to the evolution of a distinctive worldview and personality profile both in the kibbutzim and Israeli society. It is these points of comparison between the kibbutz and Israeli society that we will highlight.

Explicit Values

Most, if not all, societies possess explicit values that its members share, at least to some degree. In Israel these values are explicit in the kibbutz and, correspondingly, in Israeli society. They include democracy, egalitarianism, a group-oriented mixture of socialism and individualism, and a deep connection to the land.

One main feature of the kibbutz is the direct and total democracy it practices. Almost every decision and rule are voted on by all kibbutz members, and no major decision can be made by only one or a few individuals. Analogously, democracy is a deep-rooted Jewish value. Having to confront many perilous situations as a group rather than as atomistic individuals, Jews developed a self-deprecating sense of humor that deflated pretentiousness and heightened a feeling of social democracy, from which evolved political democracy. Both social and political democracy were brought to Israel by immigrants from Western countries, but mainly by East European immigrants who founded many kibbutzim before the establishment of the state. The successful preservation of political democracy occurred in part because of the disproportionate influence of kibbutz members in Israeli politics.

Formally, Israel is a parliamentary democracy consisting of three branches. The executive branch (the government) is subject to the confidence of the legislative branch (the *Knesset*, Israel's parliament), and the judiciary branch, whose absolute independence is guaranteed by law. The 120-member Knesset is elected every four years. The entire country is a single electoral constituency, and Knesset members are assigned in proportion to each party's percentage of the total national vote. In this way even tiny parties that succeed in gaining only 1% of the votes can be represented. This system of voting was a result of a preference for a government that would not reflect only one party, but the consensus of at least half a dozen; a preference not to follow the policy of having one party but to accept the lowest common denominator of many. The system thus lends greater leverage to small and even minuscule factions and interest groups, and a good amount of bargaining occurs among the parties, some of it quite dishonorable. As discussed in Chapter 3, Italy has moved away from this form of government and toward a genuine two-party system simply because of the amount of dishonorable bargaining and corruption that occur when one or a few individuals are able to stymie action.

Bargained deals often result in "undemocratic" concessions to religious splinter groups, who hold the balance of power between the main political blocks. Such concessions have led to strict Sabbath laws and laws such as those that prohibit the raising and selling of pork. Many of these laws are unacceptable to a large portion of Israelis. Electoral reform is often discussed, and recently hundreds of thousands of people took to the streets to demand the introduction of such reform. Specifically, such reforms aim to reduce the number and power of splinter groups and to make individual candidates responsible to the voters, not simply to the party machine.

A prominent example of how important democracy is to Israel is the status of the army within the society. Although necessity has turned the army into an essential part of Israeli life, Israel is far from being a military society. The average Israeli spends a large portion of his or her adult life in the army, both during three compulsory years and then during at least 30 days a year as a reserve, but he or she remains very much a civilian. The Israeli army is highly professional, with a basic discipline similar to that of many other armies, but it is always the first preference to train the soldier by example, not by order and punishment. As Israeli author Amos Elon (1971) points out:

> The army is not an aristocratic institution, as it continues to be in some democratic countries. There is no deliberate attempt to break the will of recruits. It is a citizen army, and the gap between officers and men is minimal. There are few privileges of rank. The Israeli military code bluntly states that officers have no privileges whatsoever, only duties. Officers are usually addressed by their first names. There are no fancy uniforms . . . military titles are used in writing, but rarely in verbal address. The use of such titles in civilian life, after retirement is frowned upon. . . . [J]ob turnover among officers is unusually rapid and the army is almost never a lifelong occupation. Most officers are weeded out soon after they reach forty. This practice has helped to prevent the establishment of a military class. (p. 252)

Hence it is an army that exists out of necessity, not out of choice. It combines the needs that evolve out of Israel's memories of its tragic past of persecution, the state of war, and its small size with the wish to maintain a democratic society, which will not be controlled by any elite. Thus far Israel has been successful in maintaining that combination.

The kibbutz is close to the ideal of an egalitarian society. The equality of all people within the small, enclosed society of the kibbutz is one of its most fundamental principles, and the periodic rotation of critical and powerful roles is one very effective way of preserving egalitarianism.

Likewise, the egalitarian principle is basic to Israeli society. In Hofstede's (1980a) study of cultural values across 40 nations, Israel had the second lowest score on the dimension of power distance or the belief that inequality among members of a society should be emphasized. The roots of the idea of the equality of all people are historical as well as ideological.

Twenty centuries of oppression have made Jews skeptical of the indiscriminate use of power. Many Israelis find the mere striving for power to be objectionable. This has caused a basic disrespect for authority, which is a main characteristic of Israeli society. Also, the anarchist strain that is found in Israel has its origins in the Marxist and Socialist ideas that the first pioneers espoused: Some envisioned the entire society as a network of collective agricultural and industrial associations involving a minimum degree of coercion and a high degree of voluntary, reciprocal agreements. Although this vision did not materialize, belief in egalitarianism continues to this day. Volunteerism, rather than formal authority, is highly regarded throughout Israeli society, and especially so in kibbutzim and cooperative movements. Members spend a relatively large amount of time on voluntary activities, such as serving on different committees and working extra hours. Another form of volunteerism is the high percentage of kibbutz members who serve in the elite units in the army and as officers. It is almost a social norm to volunteer for these assignments.

Further, the ideological basis of the kibbutz is socialism, whose basic tenet is that the major means of production and distribution are managed and controlled by the community as a whole; this is actively practiced in the kibbutz. Members live according to a system whereby each person works as he or she can and receives what he or she needs. Almost all needs are met by the kibbutz, including food, shelter, clothing, medical care, the raising of children, and education.

A similar type of socialism exists in Israeli society at large. The concept of national responsibility for basic health, housing, and social welfare is a given. Even the recent influx of hundreds of thousands of Ethiopian and Russian Jews has not led to a fundamental requestioning of priorities, although the costs are enormous. There were only a few homeless people until this recent immigration, which has led to an extreme shortage of housing, a problem that already has been solved. And, although 25% of the population lives below the poverty line, not one Israeli has died of hunger or malnutrition. If not the immediate family, then the extended family or the community at large will try to handle such a problem. Education is free, and health insurance is set at a price all people can afford.

Another key value in the kibbutz and Israeli society is the primacy of the group over the individual. From the outset of the Zionist movement until the proclamation of the state, the emphasis was consistent: The purpose of the Zionist movement was the redemption of the Jewish people. The movement, and later the state, focused on the group rather than the individual. Moreover, the early pioneers arriving in Palestine firmly believed in this socialistic approach, and they quickly realized the value of group cooperation as they attempted to make the land habitable.

Many of these pioneers were not accustomed to manual labor, were weakened by malaria and other diseases, and suffered from hostility from the Arabs. Making the group more important than the individual to overcome such obstacles was not only desirable but also necessary. This experience had the same effect on Israeli society as a whole, although to a lesser extent.

The current demands on the individual in Israel are great because of the continuing tenuous security that the nation faces, which implies that survival rests on group cohesiveness. Therefore, each Israeli must sacrifice some individuality to meet these demands. Mandatory military service is required for both sexes, taxes are among the highest in the world, and Israelis can take only a small sum of money out of the country for investment elsewhere. The ultimate betrayal in the eyes of Israelis is to leave the country permanently. Rarely will an Israeli living abroad admit that he is doing so permanently. Still, as many as 800,000 Israelis have emigrated (Kotkin, 1993).

A similar attitude toward people who left the kibbutz to live elsewhere formerly existed. People who grew up in the kibbutz and decided to pursue a different way of life found they were rejected by the group, although this rejection was not always conscious (Bettleheim, 1969). Such reaction is much less intense than before, partly because a relatively large number of young people choose to leave: between one third and one half of each age group, sometimes even more.

The relative unimportance of the individual is most apparent in an encounter with the bureaucracy, which is bothersome in most nations. However, the Israeli system presents itself to the Israeli citizen not as a guardian and servant, but as a warder. The stories about the indifference and callousness of the Israeli bureaucracy are legion. Almost every dealing with a government or public agency involves standing in line for a long time, and it is quite common to have to wait in several queues to arrange one matter. The combination of constant demands on the individual and the unpleasant bureaucracy leads to a resistance to authority that manifests itself with disregard to whatever seems unessential for the general safety or survival. For example, cheating on taxes is a common practice.

Thus, even though the instinct for self-preservation has given rise to social discipline, there is still a widespread, almost compulsive resentment of any regimentation. The result is a peculiarly Israeli mixture of self-reliant individualism and socialistic readiness to cooperate. This interplay between individualism and collectivism is also portrayed in Hofstede's (1980a) study of 40 nations, in which Israelis scored near the middle on the individualism-collectivism dimension.

Deep connection to the land is another value held both by the kibbutz and Israeli society. It partly stems from the knowledge that land is necessary for survival and protection, and it is partly the consequence of a rebellion against generations of Jews who had no real connection to any land. The land the Israelis inherited was poor in many ways, but the vigor of the response has been overwhelming. People of the kibbutzim have shown their love and connection to the land through working it and making it fertile and blooming. In Israel at large, the connection was shown through the attempts to settle as much of the land as possible, even the most remote areas.

Size and Behavioral Outcomes

The kibbutz and Israel are small, both physically and in members. Israel's population is only 4.4 million, and the distances between cities are very short. Driving from the Mediterranean to the border with Jordan takes 90 minutes. Both Haifa and Jerusalem are only an hour's ride from Tel-Aviv. More than 80% of the population is concentrated in this small triangle. Much of the country is uninhabited desert, and it is consequently even smaller than it appears on most maps, where it is a tiny speck roughly the size of New Jersey.

As a result, both in the kibbutz and Israel, specific behavioral outcomes occur that are not common in larger organizations and societies. Relations of all kinds are much more intimate in both the kibbutz and Israel than in larger entities. In the kibbutz a child spends almost all of his or her time with the same group of children throughout childhood. Because there are typically only a few hundred people in the kibbutz, an adult member interacts with the same people almost everyday. Similarly in the larger Israeli society, people tend to maintain a relatively steady and intimate group of friends, but with a relatively large number of acquaintances and contacts on the periphery. This results in the near certainty that when two Israelis who have never seen each other meet, they will find friends in common within a matter of minutes. Spending time with friends is probably the favorite pastime in Israel. People very often meet at one another's houses, without a need for an external entertainment or purpose such as watching a video.

Families also have close ties. Small geographical distances lead to easy access and relatively frequent visits and gatherings. This sense of closeness also manifests itself in the responsibility many parents feel toward their children even when they have become adults. When parents can afford it, buying an apartment for a son or daughter when they marry is a common practice, and financial help frequently continues even after that stage.

Children tend to expect this help because of the high cost of living. Israel is as much socialist as capitalist, and 40% of the industrial economy is controlled by the state or the Histadrut, the national labor cooperative. In 1989, Israel's trade deficit was 10% of GNP, more than five times higher on a percentage basis than the United States', and among the highest in the world (Kotkin, 1993). Foreign investment in Israel also has declined significantly, reaching a level that is just 20% of Singapore's, a nation-state of 2.5 million.

Given the country's small size, maintaining anonymity and privacy requires hard work. It is extremely difficult for individuals to achieve anonymity, and intimate details about someone's past and present are common knowledge, even in the larger urban centers. This intimacy and smallness help to establish a strong sense of community.

Further, this sense of closeness leads to a heightened intensity of experience. Tragedy rarely remains isolated within the narrow confines of family intimacy; it spreads to wider social circles. In the kibbutz, with its communal dining room and similar collective arrangements for hundreds of members, this is obvious. But it is often just as true in the towns, where news travels fast and immediately affects even apparent strangers. Each death in war electrifies the country as though it were the first time, drawing strangers closer to one another. It is at such moments that a sense of cohesion is so strong it makes the country seem more like a large village than a state.

Finally, mass media powerfully dramatize this state of affairs. Israelis are obsessive listeners to radio news. No people in the world tune in to the news as often, as regularly, and with such fervor.

Traumas, Worldview, and Personality

The Jews have experienced proportionately more traumas than most, if not all, major cultural groups. Two modern traumas that have had an enormous influence on the Israeli worldview and personality, both in the kibbutz and outside of it, are the Holocaust and the continuing struggle with the nation's Arab neighbors.

More than 6 million Jews, approximately one third of all Jews, perished in the Holocaust during World War II, and the memory of this remains vivid in Israel. Further, it had an enormous impact on the process of creating the state of Israel. As Elon (1971) points out, the Holocaust:

> caused the destruction of that very same Eastern European world against which the early pioneers had staged their original rebellion, but to which, nevertheless, Israel became both an outpost and heir. Because of the Holocaust there is a latent hysteria in Israeli life that . . . accounts for the prevailing sense of loneliness, a main characteristic of the Israeli personality. (p. 199)

It helps to explain the obsessive suspicions, especially of outsiders in both the kibbutz and society at large, and the urge for self-reliance at all cost in a world that never again can be viewed as safe and secure. Clearly, the Holocaust left a permanent scar on:

> the national psychology, the tenor and content of public life, the conduct of foreign affairs, on politics, education, literature and the arts . . . the notoriously lively bustle . . . and seemingly endless vivacity of Israeli life merely serve as compensatory devices for a morbid melancholy and a vast, permeating sadness. . . . It crops up unexpectedly in conversation; it is noticeable in the press, in literature, in the private rituals of people. (Elon, 1971, p. 199)

There are countless public and private monuments to the Holocaust. Israelis do not let themselves forget. One day a year is devoted to the mourning for the victims. The public commemoration serves a compulsive need to reassert the group and demonstrate its continuing vitality. However, as older members of society die, they are replaced by others who, although remembering the Holocaust, place more emphasis on other issues and the future.

Most Israelis believe wholeheartedly that the Holocaust was possible simply because Jews had no country of their own and consequently lacked the means of resistance. To them, it is a proof that the earlier Zionist theme of a need for a land was absolutely correct. The Holocaust also explains in part why Israelis are willing to endure any hardship imposed by their government with hardly any protest.

Arab hostility has only helped to sharpen the outlines of the picture of utter loneliness drawn by the Holocaust. Since independence in 1948, Israelis have lived in a state of geographical and political isolation unusual in the modern world. Most countries today share common markets or at least open borders, a common language, or the same religion; Israel does not. It also has no military, political, or economic alliance. This claustrophobic isolation has given rise to a pessimism that is a main feature of the Israeli personality. It is a root cause for Israeli stubbornness and largely explains why pious reprimands from other nations have little effect.

The kibbutz, although in a completely different way and for very different reasons, is also isolated in many ways from Israeli society as a whole, choosing to keep to itself. Although egalitarian in their own society, kibbutzniks tend to view themselves as an elite, and this view about the kibbutz is also held by other Israelis. Their social systems, such as education, are almost completely separate. They also are not much influenced by criticism that comes from the outside, feeling that others who have not shared their experiences cannot judge them.

Because memories of the Holocaust are so alive, Arab threats of annihilation achieve just the opposite of their original intention. Such threats have kept Israelis wary and ready for combat long after the initial period of pioneering enthusiasm waned, and they have increased Israeli resolve, inventiveness, cohesion, vigor, and a nervous but fertile anxiety. It has also helped foster the sense of shared social purpose. This kind of cohesion and unity is also strong in the kibbutz, although like the rest of the Israeli society, kibbutz members are the harshest critics of their own communities.

Ironically, Zionism in its early period was predicated on faith in peaceful change. The discovery that it was nearly impossible to achieve has profoundly affected the Israeli worldview. Redemption has become intertwined with violence on a continual basis, and the resulting dissonance is now a part of this worldview, creating an outlook that is a combination of the hopeful and the tragic.

The never-ending state of war has brought about an awareness of Ein Brera: There is no choice. This viewpoint reflects a fatalistic attitude. Zionists, the former rebels against their fate, have come to accept the assumption of fatalism and continual warfare. This fortress mentality was certainly not part of the original Zionist dream.

Although men are subject to military service until the age of 55:

> it is the younger Israeli who must bear on . . . his shoulders the main burden of the seemingly endless emergency. One result has been a growing cult of toughness among younger people. . . . Frequent and prolonged periods of service in the army breed a stark, intensely introverted, icy matter-of-factness in the young that contrasts sharply with the externalized, rather verbose emotionalism of their elders (Elon, 1971, p. 231)

Still, they accept their responsibility, substituting an unreflective elemental urge for self-preservation for the Zionist vision of their elders. This tendency to shy away from feelings is a basic trait in the character of the new generation of Israelis, and it was also observed by Bettleheim (1969) in his classic psychological description of the children of the kibbutz. The second generation, those born in the kibbutz, are committed to "a literalness, a matter of fact objectivity which has no place for emotions." It seems, though, that in the past few years people are once again more comfortable with expressing their emotions more openly.

Still, as might be expected in such a small land and organizational entity living under a constant state of siege, claustrophobia has emerged as a major problem. When combined with a sense of adventurism, this claustrophobia drives many Israelis, including kibbutz members, to trips outside Israel, ranging from the conventional two-week tours in Europe to exotic trips that last for months and years. Kibbutzim members, given the small size of the relatively confined society in which they exist, can experience this sense of claustrophobia even more intensely than other members of Israeli society. Many of the young people go off and explore the life outside, working and living for a year or two in the city. The sense of claustrophobia is in part the reason why some of them choose not to return to the kibbutz, just as it leads some Israelis to live outside Israel.

There are, naturally, additional factors that help to form the Israeli worldview other than traumas; two of the most important are immigration and religion. Israel is rife with contradictions, such as pessimism and optimism, fatalism and determination, and so forth. One of the most salient of Israel's contradictions is the composition of its population. More than half of the citizens are native-born, but the rest are immigrants from around the world: Europe, Asia, Africa, North America, South America, and Australia. Even most native-born Israelis are only one or two generations removed from their immigrant past. Most immigration societies face problems resulting from serving as a melting pot for widely divergent backgrounds, but in Israel there is a noticeable distinction between Ashkenazic Jews and Sephardic or Oriental Jews. The Ashkenazim are Jews from Eastern and Western Europe, the United States, and Australia. The early Zionists and founders of the state were almost all Ashkenazim. Sephardic Jews are those who immigrated from Islamic countries in the Middle East and North Africa and who came to Israel only after the establishment of the state. Sephardic Jews had to enter a modern Western society when many of them had significantly lower literacy rates and education, were short on professional skills, and had little money. The largely Ashkenazic establishment, unlike the newer immigrants, was socialist and secular, and it tried to transform the mostly traditional Sephardim into models of themselves. Although a large number prospered in their new country, many did not. By the 1960s it became clear that a "second Israel" had emerged with a real gap between the two groups. This has resulted in a campaign aimed at improving the conditions and opportunities of Sephardic Jews. Although disparities still exist, it seems that the gap has been narrowed.

In a definite manner, the kibbutzim represent part of this status problem. Almost all kibbutzniks are from European descendants, and in many ways they represent an Ashkenazic elite that was unofficially reluctant to have Oriental immigrants join its ranks. However, this is slowly changing, and there is a much higher degree of acceptance of these immigrants and their offspring in kibbutzim.

The other major issue affecting the Israeli worldview is religion. Serious conflict exists between religious and secular Israelis, and it is an explosive issue that has not been resolved, only shelved temporarily. In fact, it has been impossible even to reach an agreement in Israel over the most basic question, Who is a Jew?

Jews in Israel are not differentiated by synagogue affiliations as much as by the manner in which they relate to the Israeli land and state. Because of the Jews' reconnection with their land and building of a modern state, there are now four main options for defining oneself as a Jew (Friedman, 1989). First, 50% of the population is secular; they are the ones most responsible for building the new state of Israel. For secular Zionists, being back in the land of Israel, erecting a modern society and army, and observing Jewish holidays as national holidays all became a substitute for religious observance and faith. The second group consists of religious Zionists, who make up 30% of the population. These are traditional or modern Orthodox Jews who fully support the secular Zionist state but insist that it is not a substitute for the synagogue. The third group has approximately 5% of the population; it also includes religious Zionists of a more messianic bent. The members of this group believe that the rebirth of the Jewish state is only the first stage in a process that will culminate with the coming of the Messias. They form the backbone of the Gush Emunim settler movement, which acts on the belief that every inch of the land of Israel should be settled by Jews. Finally, there are ultra-Orthodox, non-Zionist Jews who constitute approximately 15% of the Jewish population. They believe that a Jewish state will be worth celebrating only after the Messias comes and the rule of Jewish law is total, and that the pinnacle of Jewish life and learning was that achieved by the great 18th-, 19th-, and 20th-century yeshivas (Jewish schools for higher education) and rabbinic dynasties in Eastern Europe. They have attempted to recreate that life in Israel and still dress in traditional dark coats and fur hats, naming their yeshivas after towns in Eastern Europe and preferring to speak Yiddish rather than Hebrew. They also refuse to serve in the army or celebrate Independence Day.

Given such strong opinions and points of view, it is not surprising that these groups clash fiercely over the relationship of religion to the state. Although secular Jews want the state to be completely separate from religion, religious Jews want them intertwined. Another serious clash is over the issue of the young men from the fourth group not serving in the army, which is bitterly criticized by Zionist Jews.

Most kibbutzim are decidedly secular, and their founders actively rebelled against everything represented by Judaism in their native Eastern Europe. In this sense, the worldview of kibbutzim is similar to that held by the largest group in the population.

Thus far we have emphasized the internal character or personality of Israelis, but this should be related to overt behavior that they manifest. The common perception is that Israelis are impolite, arrogant, and brash. A classic example of this behavior is the high-risk, macho manner in which Israelis drive. They do not keep the proper driving distance between cars because of the fear that someone will cut ahead of them. Drivers honk at each other if the car in front of them does not move within a nanosecond of the traffic light turning green. Further, this arrogant behavior is exhibited in the way people cut corners in their business and personal dealings, and in the impolite manner in which customers are frequently treated. This roughness of Israeli culture is a reflection of the way Israeli society works, and it is not deliberately directed at the outside but is a spillover from anxiety and internal frictions. Many American Jews visiting Israel experience great difficulty relating to Israelis because of this roughness.

In part this behavior stems from the constant feeling of insecurity, the simultaneous need to suppress it, and the need and desire to go on about normal daily life and behavior. Such contradictory needs build great repressed tensions between the desire to admit fears and worries and the belief that it is not appropriate, helpful, or masculine to do so.

Also, this behavior is partly the result of a Mediterranean influence; Italians will behave in a similar manner. Still, this is only surface behavior. Israelis are quick to react, scold, and act impolitely, but also quick to calm down. This harshness on the outside combined with a soft inside is the reason why the image of native-born Israelis is portrayed by the sabra, a cactus plant with thorns on the outside but a delicate inner part. Correspondingly, there is relatively little violence in terms of rape, murder, or extortion, and the streets are safe at night.

Israelis are generally direct people. According to Joyce Starr (1991):

> They are eager to get down to business, to get right to the heart of things. The little extra graces that give the Middle East its charm and style are seen by Israelis as useless decorations, impediments that only waste time. Everything is up front, without pretense, and matters are stripped down to bare essentials. Israelis almost never phrase things with "I think" or "It seems to me," the classical American way of avoiding hurting the other. They will simply attack with "you are wrong." (p. 45)

In addition, informality is the norm in Israel. People introduce themselves to strangers using only first names. This behavior is repeated almost everywhere: First names are used between employees and employers, schoolchildren and teachers, and soldiers and commanders. As noted previously, Israelis seek to de-emphasize status and power distance between individuals, and they have little

patience for formality or protocol, for complicated ritual and procedure. Israeli men rarely wear suits and ties. This informality is
associated with a display of openness and frankness that encourages
people to speak their mind and offer their opinion freely to another
without feeling that they are being presumptuous for doing so. It is
also associated with the way people socialize with one another: It is
very common to simply drop by a friend's house without calling in
advance. When someone asks, "Why don't you drop by?" they
actually mean it.

Both the directness and the informality are essential ingredients of
the kibbutz way of life. Because status differences are greatly, if not
totally, de-emphasized and all matters are subject to debate and
participative decision making, weekly meetings create a platform
where opinions are usually expressed freely, including opinions
about the members themselves. Informal social relationships are
easy to maintain, because the physical size of the kibbutz is so small.
Informal clothing can actually be a source of pride.

Finally, Israel is a classic "doing" society in which action is taken
proactively to control situations and overcome environmental problems (see Chapter 1). Although Americans like to think of themselves
in a similar fashion, Israelis outshine them: They have an uncanny
ability to improvise, and they are at their best when doing so. Israelis
pride themselves on their ability to fashion solutions to both mundane and desperate problems as they occur. In part, this ability comes
from their historical experience when Jews had no rights and the
only way to survive was to look for a shortcut. The more recent
experience—when the new Israeli state had to overcome many difficult and complex problems in a short time—has strengthened this
ability.

Starr (1991) gives an amusing but insightful example of this ability
when she explains why an American salad bar would not work in
Israel: "Israelis would bring two or three friends, all of their children,
pay for one person, and send the kids to take more salad because it's
'free.' If that restaurant was in Israel, the owner would have gone
bankrupt" (p. 21).

Within the kibbutz, the ability to improvise was developed to its
highest form. Many kibbutzim possessed only scant resources, so
their members learned to use all of them in inventive ways. Without
such improvisations, they might well have failed. Part of the fame
that modern and inventive Israeli agriculture has acquired worldwide can be related to the experiences kibbutzim had to face.

Besides being an action-oriented society, Israel is also an intellectual society. A high percentage of people hold university degrees, and the number of books bought per capita is one of the highest in the world. This trend also exists in the kibbutz, and one way that kibbutzim try to maintain a high cultural level is through special cultural events, either internally produced or brought from the outside.

As organizations change, so does the culture in which they exist. The most popular model for looking at organizational change and growth is biological or evolutionary—that is, organizations go through distinct stages. Edgar Schein (1985) has described a three-stage model; the first stage is birth and early growth, during which the main ideas and sources of inspiration come from the founders and their beliefs. These ideas serve as the glue holding the organization together. During the second stage, organizational midlife, there is a decline in the commitment that members make to the organization and the loss of key goals and values, which results in a crisis of identity. If an organization is to achieve the third stage, organizational maturity, and become even stronger, it needs to redefine its goals and values to meet the expectations of a changing world. In effect, the kibbutz is experiencing an organizational midlife crisis and, correspondingly, so is Israel.

In particular, most Israelis are not willing to work the required hours that each type of kibbutz requires, although they frequently feel that their children should spend at least three months working on one to reconnect with the country's past. Moshavim have become a popular alternative simply because of the rigidity of life that most kibbutzniks lead, and they are characterized by a lower degree of ideological fervor, the ownership of private property, and the espousal of some rights for individuals, even to the extent of benevolently accepting that some members want to leave permanently.

Fortunately, the ideological rigidity of the founders of both Israel and the kibbutz has eased considerably, and the new generation is responding to a changing world. In the kibbutz, the rigid rules of living with only the bare essentials has changed dramatically. Life has become more prosperous, members now have all or most modern appliances in their own rooms, are able to take more vacations abroad, and so on. These changes parallel those in the larger Israeli society, which has become much more materialistic.

Another dramatic shift in kibbutzim is industrialization. Israeli agriculture has reached its upper limit, mainly because of the lack of water. By 1980, Israel was using all of its replenishable water supply

(Meyer, 1982). Today, almost all kibbutzim have at least one factory. This transition occurred because of the belief that the future lies in industry rather than agriculture. Still, it has been accompanied by other changes and problems. Economic decisions in the kibbutz have become more complex as a result of industrialization, and it is harder for all members to participate in all decisions because they lack the knowledge to understand the issues.

There is also a definite shift in the kibbutzim, particularly the moshavim, from an emphasis only on group effort and collective well-being to a combination of group effort and the recognition of individual needs, privacy, and family. Many kibbutz members, and correspondingly many Israelis, demand more freedom for self-expression and individual preferences. One result in the kibbutz has been the decline in the practice of collective child rearing, which was once synonymous with kibbutz life and an essential part of its ideology. Another manifestation of this trend is the larger flexibility that kibbutzim show people who want to pursue freely chosen careers.

Although kibbutzim are still well represented in the Knesset, their influence has declined over the past decade, at least in part because the Labor party has suffered major political losses since 1977. It also probably results from the emphasis on the group, which often resulted in creating people who want to adhere to group norms rather than lead. Today kibbutzim leadership is mainly in setting an example, not in being involved in politics.

Still, kibbutzim have been an absolutely essential part of Israel's struggle to survive, and their values have been a bellwether for the country. If the kibbutzim and Israeli society are to achieve and maintain the third stage of maturity, it would probably be wise to rekindle the spiritual and moral heritage of kibbutzim throughout Israel in some form, because their basic values were and probably are indispensable for continued growth and success.

13

The Nigerian Marketplace

Nigeria is the most economically advanced and most populous black African nation, with a population of some 90 million. It came into existence as a modern political entity in 1914 when the British amalgamated three of their West African colonial territories: the colony of Lagos and the southern and northern Nigerian protectorates. Each territory was previously consolidated by the British out of a diverse collection of indigenous kingdoms, city-states, and loosely organized ethnic groups through treaties or outright conquest. Thus Nigeria as a geopolitical entity was essentially a creation of British imperialism. Nigeria remained a colony of Britain before it gained independence in 1960.

Archaeological evidence attests to several millennia of continuous habitation of parts of present-day Nigeria. One of the earliest identifiable inhabitants were the Nok people, who inhabited the northeastern part of the country between 500 B.C. and A.D. 200. The Nok were skilled artisans and ironworkers whose abstractly stylized terracotta sculptures are admired for their artistic expression and high technical standards (Burns, 1963, p. 25). High-quality bronze art at

Ife and Benin City in the southwestern parts of the country also predated the arrival of Europeans in the region. Over the centuries, successive waves of migration along trade routes into Nigeria from the north and northeastern part of the African continent swelled the population, which eventually became organized along tribal lines into kingdoms, emirates, city-states, and loosely organized ethnic groups. This was the setting the early European adventurers, notably Portuguese navigators, found when they first made contact with the people of the coastal regions in the 14th century A.D.

The marketplace is an appropriate metaphor for understanding the culture of the people of modern Nigeria. In this context, *marketplace* refers to the physical areas of a city, town, or rural village where the indigenous commercial activities are concentrated. This metaphor has a special significance because the bulk of the history of the region up to modern times can be summed up in one word: trade. Many of the ancestors of modern Nigerians first migrated to the region along trade routes; the slave trade was primarily responsible for the arrival of Europeans in large numbers; and, after the abolition of the slave trade by the British in 1808, the need to enforce the abolition and to replace the trade with legitimate commerce was a primary motivation for the British to maintain a presence.

For centuries, before the arrival of the Europeans, the marketplace was the community center for a town and the surrounding settlements. It was the center of commerce, the local town hall, and the main social center all rolled into one. This characterization is still true in the rural areas, where some 70% of the Nigerian population still lives. Market networks link many towns and villages together. The networks consist of major markets that meet on specific days and attract traders for miles around. In the past such networks were the conduits through which new commodities, outside influences, and immigrants reach local communities.

The characteristics of the Nigerian marketplace that stand out include its diversity, dynamism, and the balance between tradition and change. Each characteristic strongly reflects modern Nigerian society.

Diversity

The typical Nigerian marketplace, especially that in a larger town, is a sprawling, usually bustling place where virtually every commodity is available. As a general rule, the market is divided into rows of covered stalls, with a narrow aisle separating each row, which are assigned specific commodities, ranging from perishable foods to household electrical appliances. The marketplace is where the vast majority of people shop for their daily needs. This is the case even in urban centers with modern department stores. Commodities in plentiful supply include fresh meat and fish, vegetables, household goods, electrical appliances, jewelry, building materials, clothing, and traditional medicinal herbs.

Sellers of similar commodities often unite to form market associations to look after common interests. Nearly everything is available either wholesale or retail. The major marketplaces are usually centrally located, with a network of roads linking most parts of the town to the market. In addition to commodities, the marketplace offers services, including privately operated taxi and bus services to any part of town, heavy hauling, appliance repair, custom tailoring, and secretarial services. Intercity transportation hubs also are usually located close to the main markets. Diversity refers not only to the wide range of goods and services available but also to the size, relative importance, and modernness of the market compared to others in the area.

The diversity of the Nigerian culture is one of its hallmarks. The country is comparable in size to Texas and New Mexico combined and has approximately 300 ethnic and subethnic groups, with as many distinct languages and dialects. Often a dialect is clearly understandable only to the inhabitants of a town and its immediate environs. Just as the marketplace is clearly divided into sections by commodity and into subgroups by market associations, so the Nigerian society is clearly delineated by ethnic and language differences. But just as the separate commodity sections form an integral whole to serve a common clientele, so Nigerian society tries to forge a national identity out of the widely diverse ethnic groups artificially joined together into a nation by the British.

The heterogeneity of Nigerian society is physical, social, religious, and linguistic. Each ethnic group is concentrated in clearly defined geographical areas that it has occupied for centuries. The same is true of subethnic groups. Two large rivers—the Niger (from which the country's name was derived) and the Benue—form a Y shape that divides the country into three parts. Each part is dominated by one of three main ethnic groups: the Yoruba, the Hausa-Fulani, and the Ibos. The Yoruba are the only major ethnic group with a traditional aristocracy. Although the power and influence of the aristocrat class has diminished over the years, they remain a major social force in

Yoruban society. Yoruba-speaking ethnic groups also extend beyond the Nigerian border into the Benin Republic.

The Ibos are primarily located east of the Niger. Although they are more densely concentrated in their primary geographical area, they are more fragmented politically than are the Yoruba or the Hausa-Fulani. The Ibos are notable for their business acumen and strong work ethic. The Hausa-Fulani occupy most of the area north of the Niger and the Benue, which is more than twice as large as the southern regions combined. In most cases, differences in physical features among ethnic groups are not significant enough to reliably distinguish a member of one ethnic group from another.

In the past, permanent facial markings were used to distinguish ethnic groups from one another. Their primary purpose was to identify friend or foe in warfare rather than to serve as bodily decoration. The practice of facial markings has been largely abandoned in modern times. Today, names and attire are more reliable indicators of ethnic belonging than physical attributes.

With so many different ethnic groups and languages, it would seem that defining the contours and structures of this highly heterogeneous society is impractical. Admittedly it is difficult, but it is not impossible for several reasons. First, despite the great number of ethnic groups, four—Yoruba (20%), Hausa (21%), Fulani (9%), and Ibo (17%)—make up more than 65% of the Nigerian population (1991 census). In addition, the Hausa and the Fulani have so intermixed over the centuries that they are now commonly regarded as a homogenous group.

Second, the correspondence between language and ethnic group varies. Several groups may speak essentially the same language and have similar cultural characteristics but prefer to identify themselves as separate entities in terms of differences that span centuries. For instance, the Yoruba have at least 20 subethnic groups, each of which vigorously protects its separate identity.

However, modernization and the federal government's adoption of policies that promote a sense of national identity have gradually resulted in the emergence of common national characteristics. Examples of such government intervention include the establishment of English as the official language of government and commerce throughout the country, the practice of posting some federal employees to states other than their own, and the requirement of an immediate one-year national youth service of all graduates of postsecondary institutions. In recent years, the influence of the mass media, especially television, also has helped to break down cultural barriers among ethnic groups.

But Nigeria has a long way to go to achieve interethnic harmony. Interethnic mistrust is deep and a primary reason for the repeated failure to establish a viable Western-style democracy in Nigeria since independence, giving the military an excuse to establish authoritarian regimes for 24 of the past 32 years. Although most Nigerians are patriotic and genuinely want their country to work, deep-rooted ethnic allegiance often takes precedence over national allegiance. For example, the Egba are among the 20-odd subethnic groups of the Yoruba, but when the chips are down, an Egba considers himself an Egba first, a Yoruba second, and a Nigerian last. In the distant past, members of the subethnic groups have fought bitter fratricidal wars among themselves. Territorial expansionism, control of trade routes, and the desire to cash in on the lucrative slave trade were among the reasons for these wars.

In his landmark study of the cultural differences across 40 countries, Geert Hofstede (1980a) did not analyze a single black African nation. This was not because the multinational corporation in which the analysis was completed (IBM) had no subsidiary in any of them, because there was one in Nigeria during the study period. But IBM, along with several other multinational corporations, later chose to leave the country rather than comply with a new federal decree requiring 40% Nigerian equity in certain classes of foreign business investments in Nigeria. This is cited to illustrate an important aspect of the Nigerian psyche: a strong sense of national honor and self-worth. Although Nigerians in general admire and actively attempt to emulate Western economic and social development, they are quick to take offense at real or perceived condescension on the part of Western expatriates.

Even though Hofstede's study did not include a black African nation, it is not difficult to estimate where many of them, including Nigeria, would fit in his four major dimensions. Traditionally, there is a large power distance between social classes and between superiors and subordinates in most Nigerian ethnic groups except the Ibo. If the four major ethnic groups were ranked for power distance, the Hausa-Fulani probably would score the highest, followed closely by the Yoruba and trailed by the Ibo. The Hausa-Fulani are predominantly Sunni Muslims who have adopted much of the Islamic world's rigid social order and way of life. The Yoruba's high power distance is tempered considerably by opportunity for upward mobility based on individual achievement. The Ibo were noted for their egalitarian society for centuries, and have largely remained so.

Collectivism and high uncertainty avoidance are more evenly applicable to the bulk of Nigerian society regardless of tribal affiliation. Virtually all of the disparate ethnic groups believe in the extended family system. Hometown associations are formed with the express purpose of improving the infrastructure and facilities in the community. For example, during the early years of national development, it was not unusual for a community to sponsor the overseas studies of a promising local student in the hope that he or she would return to serve the community. Nigerians also score high on uncertainty avoidance, preferring to deal with people and situations with which they are familiar.

Also, masculinity or aggressive masculine behavior in the pursuit of dominance over others can most probably be attributed to the Nigerian society as a whole. However, with regard to the role of women, there are notable differences among the three major ethnic groups. The Hausa-Fulani, true to their Muslim religion, tend to consider women as quite subordinate to men in virtually every respect. This is not the case among the Ibo and the Yoruba, where women have traditionally faced little opposition to their entrepreneurial spirit.

Social Dynamism

Nigerians often have been characterized as resourceful, pragmatic, entrepreneurial, and energetic (Aronson, 1978, p. 137). In this context, *social dynamism* refers to the energy, vigor, and adaptability of Nigerian society. These qualities are readily observable at the marketplace, which bustles with activity, especially on Saturdays when most families do their weekly grocery shopping. Traders hawk their wares in singsongs particular to their commodity. The bargaining is energetic, with the burden on the customer to negotiate a fair price. Although many items have fixed prices, most do not. This means that the smart shopper must come to the market fully armed with a knowledge of the latest fair prices for the commodities of interest. The shopper also must be savvy about the various shady characters who are attracted to the marketplace. The typical seller, in turn, has perfected the art of keeping a poker face in order to extract as much profit from the sale as possible without antagonizing the customer.

Many shoppers have favorite stalls that they repeatedly patronize. Such repeat buyers are often taken care of quickly, with the minimum of negotiating necessary to arrive at a mutually acceptable price. In recent years, sellers seem to have concluded that the time and effort spent on haggling are not worth the extra profits and have started to place a fixed price on as many items as possible. Prices are usually set by market or trade associations, and changes in them are frequently communicated by word of mouth several times a day.

Doing things quietly is not the Nigerian way, whether it be an argument, a political discussion, a celebration, or a sad occasion. Just as the market bustles with a cacophony of sights and sounds, so Nigerians complete most activities with gusto. The dynamism of Nigerian society is reflected in the business and political landscape, the attitude toward education, the manner in which the people celebrate holidays and family events, and their favorite leisure pursuits.

At independence, Nigeria's economy was engaged almost exclusively in the production of food for home consumption and commodities (e.g., cocoa, groundnut, and palm oil) for export. The vast deposits of oil and natural gas were not yet discovered. Since then, successive governments, including military regimes, have made the development of the economy a priority. Today, despite recent setbacks caused primarily by worldwide oil price reductions, the Nigerian economy is the most vibrant in black Africa.

Just as the local marketplace bustles from dawn to dusk with activity, so Nigeria's more formal economic scene bustles with complicated deals and contracts. Nigeria has considerable crude oil and natural gas resources and has been a member of the Organization of Petroleum Exporting Countries (OPEC) since the 1960s. This natural wealth has provided the resources to modernize the economy, especially during the boom years of the 1970s, when vast amounts of new crude oil deposits were being discovered in the coastal areas at the same time that crude oil prices were steadily rising in the world market. In the 1970s the federal government took steps to ensure greater Nigerian participation in such key economic activities as banking, insurance, manufacturing, and oil production that were then dominated by foreign companies or their local subsidiaries. The policies have been quite successful. Nigerian interests in key aspects of economic activities now exceed 70% (Schatz, 1987) and continue to grow.

Unfortunately, only a small fraction (less than 10%) of the population controls much of this wealth. The wide gap between rich and poor is a major concern for Nigeria's economic planners. For many years, the federal government dominated and closely controlled the economy, but in recent years it has recognized the detrimental effects of meddling too much in the economy and has moved toward establishing a freer market.

The Nigerian political arena is not for amateurs or the fainthearted, just as the marketplace is not for amateurs who are not versed in the fine art of haggling. Politics in Nigeria is a rough and tumble game, and only the fittest survive. For example, military leaders promised free elections for January 1993 but delayed them until June because of allegedly widespread corruption; they also proclaimed that the 23 presidential candidates, many of whom had spent a great amount of their own money on the presidential campaign, were not eligible to run in that June election.

However, unlike the situation in many African countries, no Nigerian political leader has ever tried to impose a single-party state. The electorate is too sophisticated for that. Modern Nigeria is a federation of 23 states and a new federal capital, Abuja, which is located near the geographical center of the country. The political framework is similar by design to the federal system of the United States, but the institutions and requirements reflect the needs and experience of the country. The federal government has an executive branch, a legislative branch, and a judicial branch. All 23 states are similarly organized.

Officially, Nigeria is a Western-style democracy, but the threat of authoritarian rule is never far away, and there have been several military coups. Nigerians are accustomed to waking up to a brand-new government that has suddenly taken shape overnight. They have learned not to let the political instability interfere too much in their daily lives and business activities.

Many of the traders and craftspeople in the marketplace are graduates of apprenticeships in their specific areas. In the same manner, Nigerian society believes that a sound educational system will provide the energy that would propel the country into the industrialized age. Parents who have the means hire private tutors, send their children to prestigious schools that may be far from home, and give up their own comforts so that their children can do better than themselves. Like the political system, the education system is patterned after that of the United States. One reason for this is that many of the policy makers in government were educated in the United States.

Education is free and compulsory to the sixth grade, but most Nigerians choose to go on if they have the means. English is the official language of instruction. It is introduced at the primary school level and used exclusively at the secondary and postsecondary levels. The government, recognizing the value of a high level of literacy to rapid development, has tried to take advantage of the oil wealth to implement free education at all levels. It has not been able to achieve this objective because of the sheer size and cost of the educational system, which is government-controlled at all levels. Admission to postsecondary institutions is limited and extremely competitive. Although these institutions continue to expand steadily, currently they are not capable of admitting all of the students who qualify for admission.

Nigerians are not shy about making a public scene when the need arises, just as haggling in the marketplace is sometimes done with rancor whenever either party steps over the line of decorum. Arguments are typically carried on in a loud and animated manner, but they rarely lead to physical combat. Bystanders eagerly offer their own loud opinions about the ongoing dispute. The urban centers, especially in the south, are overcrowded, and there is a constant influx of students and job seekers from the rural areas. Competition is intense for nearly everything. Jobs, housing, transportation, and other daily necessities of life are in scarce supply in the cities, even though they receive a disproportionate share of federal development budgets.

Thus believing "it's a jungle out there," the smart urbanite steps out each morning prepared to survive another hectic day. Western expatriates usually are untouched by all this hustle and bustle of daily life because they tend to live in the quieter, wealthier neighborhoods that had their origins in colonial times when the government and the larger foreign companies built residential reservations for their expatriate staff. These exclusive neighborhoods are now predominately Nigerian.

However, not everyone goes to the market with the intention of shopping. Some go to take in the scene, window shop, or meet friends. Nigerians take their leisure seriously and try to find the time to indulge in their favorite leisure activities. They are keenly interested in sports, and their preferred sporting activities reflect their dynamism. Wrestling was a popular sport in many parts of the country before the arrival of the Europeans. It is still popular, as is boxing. But neither come close to the interest in soccer as both participatory and spectator sport. Nigerians are generally not interested in nonphysical sports.

Checkers is popular among the lower working class, and the game is typically accompanied by friendly banter and nonmonetary bets. The favorite way to relax is to be in the company of friends who can trade war stories about the vagaries of daily life, pass on the latest social gossip, and solve the country's problems. Nigerians in general do not seek isolation and solitude; they avoid them as much as possible.

Holidays and ceremonies are an important aspect of Nigerian culture. Both Christian and Islamic holidays are nationally observed, as are local community festivals, some of which have been observed for centuries. Some of these local festivals were of a pagan nature but are now largely stripped of religious significance. Common ceremonies include weddings, the naming of a new child, and funerals. Such ceremonies often are lavish affairs, depending on the celebrants' wealth. Ostentatious display of wealth is the norm, and the rich often welcome the opportunity to do so. Such display is often overdone. It is a brash, bold, in-your-face statement to the world that the celebrant is rich and is not ashamed to show it. Everyone knows what the status symbols are: big wedding or funeral, chauffeured car, expensively tailored suits, and big houses complete with servant quarters. There was even a time, during the oil boom years, when owning a jet was added to the list.

Holidays provide a respite from what many in the populace regard as the rat race of daily life. Even the marketplaces are silent and empty on the major holidays. The favorite way to spend a holiday is to hold a feast or to attend one. Either way, it is an opportunity to congregate and socialize with good friends.

Recreation and leisure in the Western sense is practiced only by a small percentage of the population, mainly the wealthy elite. They may play tennis or golf or go for a swim. There are exclusive country clubs where admission is usually based on wealth, connections, and social status. The vast majority do not have the means or the time to indulge in Western-style leisure, and the average Nigerian does not go on a road trip just to see the country or for a hike in the woods just to commune with nature. In the cities there are plenty of nightclubs, movie houses, restaurants, and private clubs that Nigerians tend to frequent. As noted above, watching sports is also a favorite pastime.

Balancing Tradition and Change

Modern Nigeria society is markedly different from the ones that existed before outside influences began to take hold in the early 19th century. Nowhere is this more noticeable than in the way the center of political and economic power has shifted from local traditional rulers and their council of senior chiefs to the educated elite, business magnates, politicians, and military. No country wants to be an island, isolated from all outside influences. But if outside influences threaten to engulf aspects of the society that are cherished by its members, then it is necessary to take actions to preserve them. This is true for modern Nigeria, where the trick is to modernize without sacrificing cherished traditional values.

Among the daily facets of life that were tightly controlled by the traditional rulers in precolonial times were the local marketplaces, especially the most important ones. Among the Yoruba, for instance, the largest and most influential markets were situated in front of, or in close proximity to, the king's official residence; these were called *Oja Oba* (the king's market). In some areas, the official title of the local head chief was *Loja* (owner of the market). Virtually all markets are now administered by local government councils, which are popularly elected bodies. Although control of the markets has shifted from the traditional rulers to the people, they are still regarded in many places as the titular heads of the markets, especially in the rural areas. The changes in market administration are indicative of the changes that have occurred in Nigerian society as a result of modernization.

Other notable aspects of culture and tradition that have changed considerably over the years include religious preferences, the traditional family compound, dating behavior, language, sports, and leisure pursuits. However, the changes are not universal. As a general rule, the rate of change in the urban centers has far outpaced that in the rural areas.

In precolonial days, power was heavily concentrated in the hands of local kings and their chiefs. Palace intrigues and territorial expansionism through intertribal warfare were common features of life. Again, noted exceptions to this situation were the Ibo, whose egalitarian social structure did not allow for the concentration of power in any one individual or small group of rulers.

Although their power and influence have been largely curtailed by the establishment of more democratic political systems, traditional rulers still play an important role in their communities. They are regarded as the custodians of their people's legacy and identity, and they are usually at the forefront of the fight to defend traditional values against the unrelenting onslaughts of Western values. In addition, some senior local traditional rulers, especially in the north, have learned to exert influence behind the scenes. Moreover, northern Islamic traditional rulers also tend to be their community's religious leaders. This pragmatic approach has resulted in some senior traditional rulers becoming even more powerful than they would have been if they still had direct political power. But they are no longer referred to in English as "king." The most common English term used is *traditional ruler.*

When a traditional ruler dies, eligible candidates still campaign vigorously to win ascendancy to the throne, because there is almost never an automatic line of succession. Candidates are drawn from traditional ruling families, and only the adult male members are eligible. In some areas, the chieftaincy rotates by tradition from one ruling family to another.

Traditional rulers are selected by a council, whose members are invariably called "kingmakers," that consists of the community's senior chiefs. The selection process varies from community to community. Note that, although the selection process has largely remained unchanged, the criteria for selection have changed markedly over the years. In modern times, candidates with adequate formal education who have distinguished themselves in some fields are favored.

An important area where major changes have occurred is religion. The first religious incursions came from the north, when the Fulani, under Usman Dan Fodio, overran the Hausa and other northern states in the 18th century. The conquerors forcibly established Islam in the city-states that dotted the region. Usman Dan Fodio would have carried out his vow to expand his *jihad* (holy war) all the way down to the sea if the British, who were then establishing a presence in the south, had not put a stop to his ambition (Burns, 1963, pp. 50-51). The early European explorers and traders entering the country from the south were quickly followed by Christian missionaries. Today, only a small percentage of Nigerians still adhere exclusively to indigenous animist religions. Approximately 47% classify themselves as Muslims, nearly 38% as Christian, and the remaining 15% as other.

Nigerians are generally a spiritual and religious people. Before Christianity and Islam were imported into the region some two centuries ago, most ethnic groups had developed a set of common spiritual beliefs ranging from mindless superstition to the concept of a supreme being (Burns, 1963, p. 264). Before the arrival of Europeans, some religious priests had acquired extraordinary social powers that rivaled those of the local king through the manipulation of the peoples' fears about the supernatural. It took years to convert the majority of the populace to the imported religions. Even then, many did not find the spirituality they needed in what they considered the sterile forms of worship of European Christianity. Some also were turned off by the perceived condescension of Christian missionaries.

Indigenous Christian sects, however, founded and led by Nigerians soon began to proliferate, especially in the Yoruba-dominated western region. Notable sects include the cherubim and seraphim sect, the Apostolic church, and the African church. What these indigenous sects have in common is a form of worship that is more reflective of Nigerian society: less formality in worship, singing and dancing to lively indigenous Christian music, spontaneous audience participation during worship services, and a deeper personal relationship with God. Today some of these sects are increasing their memberships at a rapid rate.

Although many of the inevitable changes that have come with modernization have been welcomed by the general population, others have been perceived as socially regressive. An example of this is the way the traditional family compound has changed. In the past, as the male children in a family became adults, they were given plots of land adjacent to the family home on which to build their own houses in preparation for starting their own families; female members of the family were expected to get married and become members of their husbands' families (also see Chapter 16). Today, young adults are more likely to move to the cities, first to further their education and then to work or engage in business. In the cities, the relative scarcity of land and the high cost of building construction makes the idea of family compounds impractical. The end result has been a decline in the allegiance to larger kinship groups. Urban centers continue to grow in size and population, whereas the rural areas stagnate or shrink.

Courting behavior has changed in some ways and remained the same in others. Traditionally, there was no such thing as dating in a Western sense. Once a couple was seen together in public, they were expected to marry eventually. Few Nigerian ethnic groups use go-betweens to get young couples together; most couples choose each other independent of parental or other interventions, even in the rural areas. The vast majority still prefer to marry within their own ethnic group, but that is changing among young, college-educated professionals. Today, Western dating behavior has become prevalent in the cities, where anonymity has helped to throw off some of the taboos of courting that continue to be observed in the rural areas. As a result, having experienced freedom of choice in the cities, a young bachelor often returns to his rural hometown to look for a bride.

Weddings are usually major events, with members of the extended family on both sides in attendance. Alternatives for weddings include the local magistrate court, a church or mosque, or a traditional wedding. Many couples choose a combination of the traditional wedding with one of the other alternatives. Most brides take their husband's surname immediately after marriage. Divorce was at one time rare but is becoming a common occurrence, partly because of the pressures of modern life and the decline of the family compound.

Like courting behavior, linguistic patterns have changed considerably. Because of the waves of migration of the young from the rural areas to the urban centers, many of the 300-odd ethnic languages are sometimes now spoken by as few as 10,000 people. The three main languages—Hausa, Yoruba, and Ibo—are spoken by more than 65% of the population. It is telling that after nearly 80 years of nationhood, few Nigerians are interested in learning to speak another ethnic group's language.

Also, urban versions of the major languages have developed. For instance, *Lagosian* is the term given to the style of Yoruba spoken in Lagos, the former capital, which is in Yorubaland. Lagosian is a stylized version of spoken Yoruba that is peppered with English words and considered by young Yorubans to be the most sophisticated version of the language. Another urban language is pidgin English, which is spoken chiefly within the lower working class. It cuts across ethnic lines, providing a means of communication among the disparate ethnic groups that live and work side by side in the large urban centers.

Just as some markets have remained in the same location for centuries, selling many of the traditional foodstuffs that the ancestors of modern Nigerians ate, so some beliefs, practices, and social norms have endured the onslaught of centuries of outside influence. Aspects of the Nigerian culture that have survived colonialism and modern influences largely intact include seniority and authority relationships, social roles and status, a rigid class structure (where it existed), orientation to time, view of work, early socialization, the extended family system, and traditional festivals.

A strict system of seniority governs normal interpersonal relations. Children, for instance, are not expected to look their parents or elders directly in the eye while being scolded. This expected deference applies to any interaction in which one party is significantly senior to the other. The prerogative to use first names is granted only to close friends and superiors. It is considered an insult for a younger sibling to address an older sibling casually by the first name unless they are close in age. An age difference of only one year is enough for an older individual to expect respectful address.

A common way to address a superior respectfully is to precede the first name with a respectful salutation. Among the Yoruba, one way to do this is to precede the first name of the older sibling with *buroda* (derived from "brother") or *anti* (derived from "auntie"). Both terms have English origins, but it is not clear how they began to be used by the Yoruba as a means of conveying deference. Parents are invariably addressed using the local equivalents of the Western "Dad" or "Mom."

This seemingly stratified ordering by age group and seniority reflects the high power distance discussed previously. But there is only a weak stratified class structure per se except among the Hausa-Fulani in the northern states. The larger the age difference or seniority, the greater the amount of deference expected. Methods of greeting seniors, parents, and other adults vary among ethnic groups, but they generally involve some head bowing if the greeter is male or knee bending if the greeter is female.

In return for deference, seniors are expected to guide, lead by example, and generally support their subordinates. Although the major criterion for determining seniority in social situations is age, there are instances where the senior in a situation is the younger person. In the workplace, for instance, a supervisor may be senior to much older workers from whom he or she may expect the deference accorded to seniors.

In business situations and among the educated, Western greeting behavior is more prevalent than traditional greeting behavior, but traditional greetings are still expected where the age or seniority gap is significant. This requirement does not extend to subordinate expatriates, who are routinely excused from traditional greeting requirements in favor of Western ones. Superior expatriates also are not accorded traditional greetings, not because they are not considered worthy, but perhaps because they know it is not expected.

The Nigerian's attitude toward work is a study in contrasts and points to a deep-seated social problem that retards economic progress. On the one hand, the entrepreneurs operating firms of various sizes work prodigious hours to build and maintain their businesses. On the other hand, the average salary or wage earner wants to put in as little effort as possible. Because the first group often must hire the second, a conflict of goals results. This attitude is not a manifestation of an inherent laziness; it seems to be a manifestation of a lack of faith in the system. Many workers simply do not believe that advancement on the job is based on job performance. They have been conditioned to believe that favoritism, nepotism, and other unfair methods are the usual means of advancement. This attitude is reinforced by the fact that seniority (length of service) rather than performance is a common criterion for advancement, especially in the civil service.

The effect of this attitude on national productivity is not difficult to fathom. The same deep distrust of the establishment is why Nigerians of all stripes dislike paying taxes. Salary and wage earners cannot avoid having their taxes withheld, but entrepreneurs can and do work around the tax system without feeling the least bit guilty. The widespread incidence of official corruption and mismanagement is often cited as justification for cheating the government out of taxes. Many entrepreneurs convince themselves that they can best use the money for the public good rather than let bureaucrats decide how to spend it.

The role of women also has not changed significantly over the years. They continue to bear the brunt of child care and household responsibilities in addition to holding down jobs or running their own businesses. The typical Nigerian husband considers it beneath his dignity to perform household chores. There is often a clear delineation between the kinds of tasks, commercial activities, and jobs that a man and woman normally do. This delineation of tasks and activities is much in evidence in the Nigerian marketplace, where women far outnumber men both as traders and customers. The casual observer might infer from this that the marketplace is a female domain, but this perception is inaccurate. Although women have always outnumbered men in the marketplace, the men have wielded the real power behind the scenes.

In this regard it was noted above that the marketplace was administered formerly by the local head chief and more recently by elected local government councils. Both the head chieftaincy and the councils are male-dominated institutions. The true picture is that although women dominate at the retail level men dominate at the production, wholesale, and administrative levels of the market structure. In addition, some commercial activities are perceived to be either male oriented or female oriented. Sometimes there appears to be no logical reason for the distinction other than the mere fact that the activity has been a male or female preserve for as far back as anyone can remember. For instance, butchers are almost exclusively male, whereas fishmongers are almost exclusively female. Female-oriented activities are purposely avoided by men, and male-oriented activities are often closed either overtly or covertly to women.

This distinction between what activities are proper for males and females is much sharper in rural areas than in cities, where the educated younger generation has learned to compromise. A woman raised in a city is far more likely to be assertive with men than a woman raised in a rural area. The city woman is also more likely to dismiss with derision the male view that a man's home is his castle. She is also more likely to abandon an untenable marriage, especially if she is among the thousands of enterprising women who have achieved financial independence in their own right. Education and personal achievement tend to be social levelers when it comes to sex roles.

Women have been active in local and national politics for years, dating from the early colonial periods when market women rioted to protest the imposition of taxes on women. Politics in Nigeria is still largely male dominated, but women are making steady progress.

The one area where women have distinguished themselves is in commerce. This is also just about the only area where society has given them wide latitude. The homes, streets, and the markets of Nigeria are alive with women trading, and many have built large-scale trading enterprises with little outside aid. In the workplace, Nigerian women have as much opportunity for advancement as their counterparts in any Western country, including the United States.

Overt or covert discrimination against women persists, however, because the typical Nigerian man, in the final analysis, was not raised to regard women as equals. Polygamy is legal, but it is neither encouraged by authorities nor tolerated by women. It is no longer fashionable among the educated class and has been steadily declining in recent years, except in the Muslim north.

Further, the decline of the family compound has not resulted in a parallel decline in the extended family system. The extended family system is a cherished aspect of African societies. Simply put, this concept means the embracement of near and distant relatives as full members of the nuclear family. The extended family is the African parallel of Western social welfare systems. Members of extended families take care of one another, find jobs for young members, band together to help members in times of sorrow or hardship, intervene to solve marital problems, and come together to celebrate one another's successes. When a member marries or otherwise has reason to celebrate, there is no need to send out formal invitations to extended family members: Everyone knows they are invited and expected to attend.

In addition, Nigerians have always tended to be conscious of status differences. In the Nigerian marketplace, some retailers achieve prominence and become unofficial deans of the market or leaders of the market associations. Social status is important to Nigerians, but status consciousness is not the same as supporting a rigid social-stratification system. In the past, the highest status was accorded to the king, followed by his chiefs. Other persons conferred with high status may include war heroes, successful traders, or great farmers. Today, as in the past, Nigerians, especially men, aspire to be recognized by their community as persons of "timber and caliber," which is a popular term connoting high status and integrity. Status can be earned through education, business success, philanthropy, exemplary character, leadership qualities, or some combination of these. However, wealth by itself does not automatically confer status. A wealthy man of dubious character and negligible philanthropy may be shunned by the community.

In modern Nigeria, one of the most sought-after status symbols is a chieftaincy title, which is considered higher in status than an earned doctoral degree. When an individual with an earned doctorate becomes the chief of his hometown, he may use the title "Chief," followed by the title "Dr." in parentheses—for example, "Chief (Dr.) XYZ." A chieftaincy is highly valued because it is an affirmation by the community that the conferee has been recognized as a community leader.

Although chieftaincies are of various ranks and importance, all conferees are eligible to use the title "Chief." There are separate title lines for men and women, who also can be chiefs. Traditional rulers see two clear advantages in the modern chieftaincy system. It encourages successful citizens to be philanthropic, because that is an important criterion for becoming a chief. Further, it promotes the preservation of traditional culture and values because it co-opts the conferee into the community's traditional structures.

Ironically, the increasing popularity of chieftaincy titles has threatened the institution's integrity. Many successful Nigerians feel incomplete without being recognized by their hometown with a chieftaincy. As a result, rumors of payoffs, favoritism, and award of chieftaincies to ineligible individuals sometimes surface.

The desire for status also carries over into the workplace. Prestigious job titles and impressive offices are prized. People are often defined by what they do for a living and how high they have risen in their profession. However, most people work simply as a means of earning a livelihood; the concept of work for its own sake is not widely valued. And, as suggested previously, evidence of large power distance is prevalent throughout the workplace. Subordinates are expected to show deference, but it is not uncommon for superiors to have strong informal relationships with some immediate subordinates. The size of the power distance is roughly proportional to the vertical distance between the two parties on the organizational chart.

Another area that highlights the balance between change and stability is that of time. Westerners hold a common misconception that Nigerians, like many Africans, do not pay much attention to the clock. Nigerians are quite capable of going by the clock and are pragmatic enough to recognize when they should do so. In superior-subordinate relationships, the subordinate is expected to be prompt and thus usually shows up at the appointed time. Workers, despite their attitudes toward work, usually report to work on time. School-children are routinely punished for arriving late to school. Nearly everyone who can afford a watch has one. Westerners apparently came up with the practice of being fashionably late; Nigerians merely raised it to an art form.

However, certain economic and social aspects have contributed to the relaxed approach to time. In rural areas, there is usually no need to watch the clock because the pace of life is slow. In cities, severe traffic congestion and an unreliable public transportation system make it difficult to foresee how long a trip across town will take. Although city dwellers readily start off early to arrive at their jobs or schools on time, they do not feel pressed to do the same for casual social engagements. Everyone understands the difficulties of being on time, so they are not offended when appointments are missed. Just as the trader at the market patiently waits for the next customer when business is slow, so the Nigerian host waits patiently for guests to arrive. Thus Western hosts should not be surprised if their Nigerian guests show up hours after the appointed time without apologizing profusely for the delay. However, when the issue is business, Nigerians will try their best to be prompt and apologize for being late.

There is a significant contrast in culture and values between the younger, college-educated generation and the the older generations that, as a rule, are less educated. The older generations are more conservative in their views and are alarmed that traditional values are rapidly eroding among the younger generations. They fully support economic and social progress, but not at the expense of cherished traditional values.

In trying to strike a balance between tradition and change, perhaps the greatest difference is between the Muslim north and the largely Christian south. Most of the values, culture, and traditional institutions in the Muslim north have survived intact; it is ultraconservative compared to the Christian south. Typical northern Muslims, regardless of age, are not impressed by Western manners, culture, and values. They are more likely to identify with the culture and values of the Islamic world. Thus a Muslim community leader in the north is more likely to address a community meeting in either Hausa or Arabic than in English even if both he and his audience speak English fluently.

Some observers sometimes characterize the southern educated elite as trying to be more Western than Westerners. There is an element of truth in this characterization. It is not unusual, for instance, for English to be the first language of the child of an educated southern elite rather than the parents' ethnic language.

Throughout this chapter we have attempted to offer an accurate portrayal of the people and culture of Nigeria. Like a portrait, it is a snapshot of the nation and does not include all of the detailed nuances of this highly diverse society. Still, the image of the marketplace is critical to understanding traditional and modern Nigeria. It is an appropriate metaphor for many African nations that face the gigantic task of integrating diverse ethnic groups while modernizing—all without losing the cherished aspects of their traditional cultures.

14

The Japanese Garden

Americans seem to be mystified by the Japanese. In the early 1980s, almost all American writings on Japan praised the country wholeheartedly and tended to highlight only its positive features; for an example, see William Ouchi's (1981) best-selling book, *Theory Z*. By 1990, many American writers and citizens had radically altered their view of Japan from one of uncritical acceptance to what one *Fortune* article called "fear and loathing" (Smith, 1990). Such mystification is understandable if one examines the basic metaphors or mindsets through which Americans and Japanese see the world. Whereas American football reflects the American perspective, most, if not all, Japanese would immediately identify the Japanese landscape or wet garden as an appropriate, if not the most appropriate, metaphor for understanding Japanese culture.

There are two general types of Japanese gardens: (a) the wet or landscape garden and (b) the dry Zen Buddhist or religious garden. The major difference between them is that instead of water or a pond, the dry garden has raked pebbles that simulate water. Hence the wet and dry Japanese garden are functionally equivalent to one another, and both are designed to create a sense of integration between the observer and nature and an atmosphere in which meditation can take place. The focus in this chapter is on a wet Japanese garden.

Like the water flowing through a Japanese garden, Japanese society is fluid and changing while retaining its essential character. Alone each droplet has little force, but when combined with many others, it has enough force to form a waterfall, which cascades into a small pond filled with carp. The pond appears calm, yet beneath the surface a pump constantly recirculates water back to the top of the waterfall. A rock tossed into the pond causes a ripple and then sinks to the bottom, ever to remain separate. Undoubtedly, the scene is designed to replicate nature and to capture its true essence, and the sound of the gently flowing water amid this small re-creation of beauty evokes a feeling of harmony, oneness with nature, and perhaps even timelessness.

The garden itself serves as a reminder of the centrality of nature to the development of Japanese society, religion, art, and aesthetics: not just nature but the way in which the Japanese perceive nature. Just as the garden is part of nature, the Japanese tend to view themselves as integral with it. In contrast to the Western view of nature as something to be confronted and subdued, the Japanese generally see it as something to be accepted.

An agricultural people, the Japanese developed a passionate love of nature and keen awareness of its inherent beauties. No part of Japan is more than 70 miles from the sea, and the mountains, which cover 80% of the land, are in view from any vantage point. Japan's temperate climate and abundant rainfall contribute to a view of nature as a friendly blessing and source of growth and fertility. Thus it is not surprising that the earliest Japanese literature manifests a deep appreciation of the beauties of the sea, mountains, and wooded glens.

The three basic elements of the Japanese garden are stone, plants, and water. Usually these are combined to form larger elements common to Japanese landscape gardens such as flowing water, ponds, and groupings of stones, trees, and shrubs, each in as natural an appearance as possible to evoke the feeling of artlessness.

Like the water in a Japanese garden, Japan is seldom still. It is a complex, dynamic society that has undergone enormous change in the past 125 years, transforming itself from a feudal state into a modern industrialized nation that has fought two world wars, the second of which brought utter defeat. Since then, the country has risen to become a major economic power. In the process, the Japanese have absorbed Western technology, science, education, and politics while retaining their unique cultural identity.

Still, underlying this profound change is the perspective that is mirrored in the Japanese garden. To see how the elements of such a garden are manifested in Japanese society, we focus on four topics: harmony (*wa*) and *shikata*, or the proper way of doing things, with emphasis on the form and order of the process; combining droplets or the energies of individuals into group activities; *seishen*, or "spirit" training; and aesthetics.

Wa and Shikata

To understand Japan, it is important to know its history, which can be viewed as a continual search for wa or, in the Japanese garden, harmonious relations among elements so as to create a feeling of effective interaction between human beings and nature. The Japanese are a remarkably homogeneous people who have lived in relative isolation for centuries. Before the end of the last ice age some 11,000 years ago, Japan was connected by land to the rest of Asia. Because those groups that wandered in the region could go no farther, they remained and mixed with those who came later. Historical records show that a considerable number of people flowed into Japan from the Korean peninsula until the eighth century A.D. By that time, the mixing was nearly complete, and for the past 1,000 years immigration has been infinitesimal.

Virtually devoid of natural resources such as iron and oil, the Japanese borrowed the technique of rice farming from the Chinese sometime around 1000 B.C. Each village became self-sufficient, but the complexity and interrelatedness of the tasks associated with rice farming led the Japanese to emphasize the importance of group activities and group harmony—without which there would be starvation.

In the seventh century B.C., this emphasis on harmony was expressed in the country's first constitution, which was written by Prince Shotoku. The first of its 17 articles made harmony the foundation for all of the others. This is in marked contrast to the Western conception of the importance of life, liberty, and the pursuit of individual happiness.

The Japanese have always been distinctly aware of the difference between things foreign and native, and early on they recognized the value of borrowing from others while maintaining their Japaneseness.

After A.D. 552, when Buddhism was formally introduced to the Yamato court from China, the Japanese increasingly became conscious of the superior continental civilization of the Chinese. From the seventh to the ninth centuries, they made a conscious effort to borrow with vigor Chinese technology and institutions; they studied the philosophy, science, literature, arts, and music of China in depth; these in turn deeply influenced Japanese thought, culture, and habits. The Japanese even adopted the Chinese writing system, which had a unique character for each of the thousands of Chinese words. However, even though the Japanese wrote in Chinese, they spoke only Japanese, which is as different from Chinese as it is from English. Japan's island location was far enough from China to escape invasion but close enough to benefit from interacting with this nation which, at that time, was the most technologically advanced and powerful in the world. From the 9th to the 12th centuries, the Japanese blended these new elements with their own culture to form a new synthesis.

In the 12th century, Yoritomo Minamoto first used the title of Shogun (generalissimo) of Japan and established his headquarters in Kamakura, now an hour's drive from Tokyo, or Edo as it was then called. Although the imperial family living in Edo was still allowed to perform ceremonial activities, the real power rested with the shogun, and clan lords reported directly to him. This shogun era lasted until 1868, at which time the imperial family's power was restored (the Meiji Restoration).

During the shogun era, the emphasis on harmony continued, although in a distinctly different manner. Surprisingly, the shogun system was similar to European feudalism. Some 10% of the population consisted of samurai (warriors) who pledged absolute loyalty to the shogun. Thus this system is quite different from that of the Chinese Confucian system in which loyalty to the family is the overriding value, and the subjugation of the samurai to the shogun paved the way for the transference of loyalty to the ultimate family, the nation. Also, unlike Europe, the Japanese did not have a cult of chivalry. The samurai were also men of learning, and they prided themselves on their fine calligraphy and poetry skills.

Most of the population, however, had only limited rights, and a samurai could kill any commoner on the spot if he failed to abide by the many rules and practices pervasive throughout the society. Under such conditions it is little wonder that the Japanese sought to achieve harmony and to protect "face," which is an unwritten set of rules by which people in society cooperate to avoid unduly damaging one another's prestige and self-respect. Even today the Japanese tend to apologize in advance before making a critical comment on another person's project so as to avoid the loss of face for either party; many begin formal speeches the same way. In a similar vein, Japanese baseball games are scheduled to end after 3 hours and 20 minutes, and ties are common, which is fine with face-saving Japanese who are interested in preserving wa.

Japan's sense of isolation was heightened during the reign of Shogun Ieyasu in the 16th century when he banished Jesuit missionaries, cut off the ears of Christians, and mandated the building only of coastal vessels that were not fit for ocean travel. With the exception of a small Dutch trading area in the Kyushu port of Nagasaki, relations with the outside world were cut off.

In 1853, Japan was forced to end its self-imposed seclusion when Commodore Perry and ships of the U.S. Navy arrived off the shores of Edo. The country had no choice but to sign unequal trade treaties with the United States and principal European powers. These developments led to a weakening of the shogun system and its replacement by the imperial family in 1868.

It is extremely difficult, if not impossible, for a gaijin (foreigner) to be fully accepted in Japan; to do so would upset harmonious relations between and among groups that have taken years to develop. A foreigner is like the rock tossed into the garden's pond that momentarily disturbs the harmony but quickly disappears from sight. However, many visiting Americans misperceive the extreme care and attention given to them as genuine friendship or at least genuine acceptance. Why this occurs leads us naturally to shikata, which is necessary if wa is to be maintained.

Because of the subsistence-level economy that developed in the rice-growing villages and the emphasis on nature, the Japanese came to believe that an inner order (the individual heart) and a natural order (the cosmos) are linked together by form (see DeMente, 1990). Shikata is the way of doing things, with special emphasis on the form and order of the process; in compound forms, the term is *kata*. Thus there is a kata or katas for eating properly, for using the telephone, for treating foreigners, and so on. To the Japanese, the process or form for completing an activity is just as important as completing the activity successfully, whereas Americans have historically been concerned with the final result rather than the process for achieving it. The Japanese emphasis on total quality management (TQM) and *kaizen* (continual improvement) is consistent with shikata: They tend to feel that doing something in the proper manner will ultimately lead to doing it in the most successful manner.

Katas were developed within this hierarchical society because it was assumed that everyone has specifically categorized and defined *bun* (life roles) in which obligations are spelled out in detail. Edwin Reischauer (1988, p. 146) has termed the Japanese the most punctilious people on earth because of such explication, if not the most polite. At two in the morning, one may see several older Japanese standing at a street corner patiently waiting for the light to change before crossing the street, even if no cars may be in sight for miles. A person's outward conduct, as manifested in the obeyance of rules, is a reflection of one's inner character. There are even katas associated with Japanese baseball, and visiting American baseball players frequently find it difficult to adjust because they must hold the bat in a particular way and observe other rules that they consider irrelevant.

The importance of katas cannot be overemphasized, and there are specific katas for activities that Americans tend to handle in many different ways, such as greeting visitors and exchanging business cards. When a kata for a new activity does not exist, the Japanese may have difficulty completing it. Thus some Japanese officers who wanted to discontinue fighting in World War II bemoaned the fact that no kata for surrender had been developed simply because it was so unthinkable: "We don't know how to surrender" (DeMente, 1990, p. 68).

When a Japanese violates a kata, the reaction may be harsh. In one instance, five 14-year-old girls bullied a classmate into committing suicide because she failed to show enough sincerity when attending a funeral ceremony for the mother of one of the five girls.

Seishin Training

To live comfortably in such a rule-ordered society, an individual needs a great deal of self-control; in Japan, he or she is socialized from birth to acquire it. In the Japanese garden, the carp symbolizes masculinity, valor, endurance, and tenacity. Analogously, the concept of *seishin* (spirit), which is an integral part of the Japanese philosophy of life, stresses the importance of self-discipline and devotion to duty. Through discipline and adversity, a person achieves self-development and, most important, self-mastery. Seishin training has been most commonly applied to the study of martial arts, flower arranging, and the tea ceremony. In the case of the martial arts, physical training is seen as a means to a spiritual end of attaining inner balance and harmony. Mastery of skill requires self-control and self-discipline; this leads to the development of inner strength.

Perhaps the best way to understand Japanese behavior is to take part in such martial arts as karate and swordplay. Karate (empty hands) was introduced to Japan by Buddhist monks as both a form of self-defense against marauders and spiritual training. Once again, forms or katas constitute much of the training that karate students receive, and they will practice these forms by themselves for hours before engaging in any kind of combat. Eventually, karate students are taught to "think through" obstacles; one of the most difficult challenges facing a parent is to see a 9-year-old son or daughter trying to think through or break a 1-inch-thick plywood board with an openhanded blow. Sometimes the karate instructor will have the unsuccessful student repeat the exercise three or four times to exhibit self-control and learn to handle adversity, and some young students have broken their hands while engaged in this activity.

Although theoretically the ultimate result of seishin is an improved state of personal spiritual growth and freedom, many Japanese use it to attain practical ends such as a better performance in school or work. Large Japanese firms appeal to this element of Japanese thought in their training programs that have been called "hell camp" because the trainees are allowed to sleep only a few hours per day and undertake physically demanding activities designed to instill a sense of self-discipline and devotion to the company. In many modern transformations of the philosophy, the central emphasis is on the development of a positive inner attitude by means of which external constraints can be overcome and difficulties resolved. Japanese tend to believe that any obstacle can be overcome provided one tries hard enough.

Seishin helps an individual not only stand on his or her own and endure personal hardship but also to live in a group-oriented society. Serving the group's interests often involves self-sacrifice. To the Japanese, social conformity is not a sign of weakness but of strong inner self-control that has helped the individual to overcome his or her more antisocial instincts. Endurance for this conformity is made easier through character training and self-discipline.

Manifestations of seishin abound in Japanese society. One often sees Japanese elementary schoolchildren dressed in shorts, the school uniform, in the middle of winter. Junior high school students are not allowed to wear jackets, sweaters, or any other garment over their school uniforms in winter, although Japanese classrooms are rarely heated. During the first few weeks of January, junior high school students are required to begin the day with a 30-minute jog around the school grounds. Most junior high schools also hold weekly schoolwide meetings outside. If it is sweltering hot, then Japanese students do not ask to be excused; they stand at attention as long as they can before fainting. This practice helps to develop a toughness of character and an ability to endure hardship at a young age.

Seishen training tends to be associated with Zen Buddhism, which is a unique form of Buddhism that has enjoyed a resurgence of interest in Japan since the 1970s. Although Hinduism incorporates the belief in many personal gods, Buddhism rejects them. It does, however, accept the Hindu emphasis on meditation as a major vehicle for achieving nirvana or salvation. Buddha emphasized four noble truths: Suffering is inevitable, suffering occurs because of selfish or self-centered desires, such desires can be overcome, and the method of overcoming such desires is by following the Eightfold Path, which is the Buddhist version of the Ten Commandments.

Zen Buddhism continues the emphasis on meditation, and most Zen training occurs in a large meditation hall. Trainees and monks frequently meditate in the lotus position for hours on a cold, stone floor in a room in which the temperature is 40 degrees, and one monk will prod and hit the trainees or students with a bamboo stick if their attention wanders. About twice a day all students meet with monks who ask them to respond to koans (riddles) that are designed to help them attain open minds or see things as fresh and new. Zen Buddhism proposes that one can free oneself from his self-centered world by perceiving the timelessness and oneness of the universe. Likewise, in a Japanese garden the whole of nature can be seen despite the individual parts. Also, each part of the garden can capture the essence of nature in its own way. The garden depicts a freed world that has been physically reduced and spiritually enlarged to suggest the size and grandeur of nature. Japanese who recognize that they are part of nature and hence mortal essentially stop time by allowing it to have its own way. In the same manner, although the seasons may change the appearance of the Japanese garden, the stones, trees, and water in it are always visible and unchanged.

Combining Droplets or Energies

Achieving harmony through kata and seishen training leads naturally to the topic of combining energies of individuals in groups or, analogously, combining droplets of water in the garden to form a waterfall. This emphasis on the group begins at birth, for the mother tends to shower an excessive amount of love and attention on the child, especially a boy. In Japan, infants and children are constantly in contact with their mothers, are treated permissively, are seldom left alone, and often sleep with their parents until age seven or eight. For the first two years of life, the child is swaddled and carried by the mother in a special device attached to her body. All of these practices result in a high degree of dependence on the mother and an attitude of *amae*, which means to look to others for affection. As the child grows up, this dependence on the mother as the source of gratification is transferred to the group, particularly the person's *senpai* (mentor).

During the first few years at a business firm, an employee may be assigned to an older individual or senpai, who will show him or her how to perform a job and adjust to a new environment. More commonly, relationships between a senpai and a *kohai* (student) develop informally. The senpai offers advice and encouragement and may play an important role in the socialization of the youngest employees.

The Japanese emphasis on the group is quite apparent and permeates practically every aspect of Japanese life. It can be seen in the educational system, the structure of business organization and work, and the political system, to name only a few.

At school, children are identified by their class. For example, in junior high school, a student might say, "I belong to ichinen ni kumi," or Year 1, Class 2 (each grade is composed of approximately six classes). For the next three years, that student will spend every day with the other 40 to 50 students in the class and identify him- or herself with that group. A well-known Japanese proverb—"The protruding nail will be hammered"—aptly explains the behavior of individual students. Adhering to this proverb does not pose a problem for most students, who have learned that security, acceptance, and love flow from the group. In fact, most students display a sense of belonging that would be envied by many of their counterparts in the West, who often feel alienated and alone.

On the other hand, life can be intolerable for the rare student who does not fit comfortably in a group. Fellow students relentlessly bully, pick on, tease, and persecute this individual. This phenomenon, known as *ijime* (usually translated as "bullying") leads to several deaths every year. If the student has any friends, they quickly desert him or her for fear of being excluded from the group, which is the worst fate that can befall a Japanese child or adult. According to Ministry of Education figures, 155,000 instances of bullying took place between April and October 1985 (Tasker, 1987).

Students achieve group identification not only with their class but also with their school, particularly at the college level. The university one attends frequently determines one's future career prospects, because the top businesses hire primarily, if not exclusively, from the top universities. Ties made in college days are important in Japanese life, and throughout their life Japanese workers will identify themselves with the university they attended.

In Japan, a job means identification with a larger entity through which one gains pride and feeling of being part of something significant. An individual's prestige is tied directly to the prestige of his or her employer. The company is not typically viewed as an entity trying to take advantage of its employees in order to make profits, but as a provider of individual security and welfare. When Japanese are asked what they do, they usually respond with the name of the companies for which they work, not the jobs they perform. By contrast, Americans will normally respond to the question of what they do by mentioning the occupation or job first, often without even divulging the name of the employer. Japanese workers or managers usually perceive their companies and other institutions with a strong sense of "we" versus "they." Approximately 30% of Japanese managers and workers, primarily those who work for larger firms, actually are guaranteed lifetime employment until the age of 55, after which they can work for a larger firm's subcontractors until age 70, although at reduced salary. This guarantee strengthens the feeling of identification with a firm. And even when a firm is not financially able to make such a guarantee, which is more frequent now, its owners tend to feel far more obliged to their employees than do their American counterparts. Some owners who have liquidated their firms have spent several months and even years ensuring that their terminated employees are able to obtain jobs elsewhere. Even in the United States, Japanese firms will frequently retrain their American employees during an economic downturn rather than lay them off or fire them, as is the norm among American-owned firms.

Also, the distinctive structure of the business firm that is found in Japan supposedly fosters group identification. Before World War II, much of Japanese industry was organized into six huge *zaibatsus*, or family-owned companies, each of which consisted of approximately 300 companies and their suppliers. Each zaibatsu combined the activities of many subcontractors with whom it had long-term contracts, a manufacturing organization, a major financial institution, and an export-import organization. Such a form of organization is outlawed in the United States and other developed countries and was actually forbidden by law in Japan after World War II. However, a nonfamily variant of the zaibatsu, the *keiretsu*, has emerged and become prominent.

American and European managers frequently complain bitterly about the operations of the keiretsus, because they have a great deal of power over many activities in the marketplace and can persuade Japanese distributors not to carry foreign products. Ironically, however, the most dynamic and prosperous companies in the Japanese economy tend to be those that are not members of keiretsus (Tasker, 1987). Similarly, although foreign executives have charged that the Japanese Ministry of Trade and Industry (MITI) has unfairly supported rising industries such as personal computers and high-definition television through its various policies and regulations, some of Japan's most profitable corporations such as Honda and Sony have become successful without its help; MITI actually advised Mr. Honda, its founder, to go into another line of business.

Further, the organizational structure and work allocation in Japanese firms also emphasize the group. Work is often assigned to various office groups and is viewed essentially as a group effort. Frequently there are no formal job descriptions existing separately from work groups. A company will often reward the office group, not the individual, for work well done. Even the physical arrangement of the office emphasizes the group: The manager will sit in front of the workers in a classroom-style setting, and they will work in subgroups with their own supervisors. If the work group is small, everyone will sit around a table, with the most senior members closer to the manager. As a general rule, the Japanese do not allow managers to have their own offices and, even if the work requires that they be given offices, tend not to prefer this arrangement.

Japanese groups abound in society: women's associations, youth groups, parent-teacher groups, and hobby groups, to name just a few. Political parties and ministerial bureaucracies often divide into opposing factions. The new charismatic religions, such as Soka Gakkai, are composed of small meeting groups. In sightseeing, the Japanese tendency to perform activities in a group is particularly evident: They often wear the same types of clothes and behave as if they were one.

Decision making in Japan also reflects this emphasis on the group. For example, in a Japanese company a business proposal is usually initiated at the middle or lower levels of management. The written proposal, *ringi-sho*, is distributed laterally and then upward. Everyone who reviews it must impress his or her personal seal of approval. Making decisions requires a great deal of time, largely because a good amount of informal discussion has preceded the drawing up of the ringi-sho. In spite of its time-consuming nature, the consensus approach to decision making does have important merits. Once the decision is made, it can be implemented quickly and with force because it has the backing of everyone in the department. By contrast, American managers frequently make decisions quickly, but a great amount of time and effort is required for implementation, often because only a few key people have actually been involved in the decision-making process itself.

Just like the water droplet, the individual is significant only in so far as he or she represents the group. If individuals disagree with one another, then the overall interest of the group comes before their needs. Cooperativeness, reasonableness, and understanding of others are the virtues most admired in an individual. Harmony is sought, and conflict is avoided if at all possible.

The extent to which the individual is responsible to the group and the group responsible for the actions of the individual is illustrated in the following incident. An American teacher was accompanying an eighth-grade Japanese class on its annual field trip to Kyoto when one of the Japanese teachers kindly informed the American that the students would be required to sit in the school auditorium for one hour after returning from Kyoto. When the American teacher asked why, the Japanese teacher responded that one of the students had been 10 minutes late to the school meeting earlier that morning and thus all would be punished.

Like the water that flows in the garden, the Japanese prefer to flow with the tide. In contrast to the West, observers have noted the relative absence among the Japanese of abstract principles, moral absolutes, and definitive judgments based on universal standards. The Japanese think more in terms of concrete situations and complex human relations. Although the Japanese may seem to lack principle to the Westerner, to the Japanese the Westerner may seem harsh and self-righteous in judgment and lacking in human feeling.

As Ellen Frost (1987) points out, many Japanese refer to this difference by saying that the Japanese are "wet" people, whereas Westerners are "dry":

> By "dry" they mean that Westerners attach more importance to abstract principles, logic, and rationality than to human feeling. Thus, Westerners are said to view all social relations, including marriage, as formal contracts which, once they no longer satisfy individual needs, can be terminated. Their ideas of morality are generalized and absolute, with little regard for the particular human context. . . . By contrast, the "wet"

Japanese are said to attach great importance to the emotional realities of the particular human circumstances. They avoid absolutes, rely on subtlety and intuition, and consider sensitivity to human feelings all-important. They notice small signs of insult or disfavor and take them deeply to heart. They harbor feelings of loyalty for years, perhaps for life, and for that reason are believed to be more trustworthy. (p. 85)

The term *naniwa bushi* exemplifies this wet quality. In modern use, the term is applied to persons who are open-minded, generous, and capable of appreciating another person's position, even when that position is neither logical nor rational. A negotiator who adopts a rigid position, recites a familiar catalog of grievances, and appears to have no understanding of Japanese concerns is said to lack naniwa bushi. Such a person is judged to be neither effective nor trustworthy. Some Japanese feel that many Westerners adopt such a negotiating style, which seems to be one of the reasons why difficulties occur between them. Thus it seems logical that Japan does not have clearly identifiable political parties, as in the case in the United States, but a loose arrangement of powerful interest groups that negotiate their differences by naniwa bushi.

Some observers see the Japanese identification with nature as the explanation for the origin of the relativism of Japanese attitudes. Others point to the influence of Chinese thought with its situational approach to applying principles. Whereas the division was between good and evil in the West, the division was between yin and yang, two complementary life forces, in China. Thus the Japanese tend to see situations more in terms of gray tones, whereas Americans see them as black and white. However, others suggest that this relativism stems from the child-rearing techniques discussed above. Most probably all of these explanations are interrelated and have some validity.

The emphasis on situational ethics is illustrated in the Japanese legal system. If the convicted shows that he or she is genuinely repentant for what he or she has done, then it is highly likely that a more lenient sentence will be given. Further, laws passed by the Japanese Diet or central government are loosely structured so that the courts can interpret them differently by situation. In contrast, the U.S. Congress attempts to write laws in such a way that all possible issues are spelled out carefully and, as a result, judges must operate within relatively strict limits. Further, the Japanese orientation toward harmony and group loyalty means that conflict resolution is valued, not the individualistic assertion of legal rights. For example, in the hamlet of Kurusu, conflict over the building of a factory received national attention from new media; two years later, shame still pervaded the community. Consequently, the legal system and Japanese values reinforce the emphasis on group consensus or solutions before coming to court. The opposite situation exists in the United States, because individuals involved in legal disputes are aware that judges must interpret laws that are already finely delineated.

This practice does not mean that the Japanese do not have a sense of right and wrong. They simply place greater emphasis on the particular situation and human intentions than do Westerners. Lacking a Judeo-Christian heritage, Japanese do not possess a feeling that certain areas of life are obviously sinful. The major issue is whether an action harms others and has a disruptive effect on the group and community. Many experts assert that the Japanese are motivated primarily by a sense of shame to correct a problem when such disruption occurs, whereas individualistic Westerners are motivated mostly by a sense of guilt at their failure to fulfill responsibilities. The Japanese orientation is particularly evident in their attitudes toward sex and drinking.

As Diana Rowland (1985, p. 115) explains, sex is not viewed as sinful but as just one of the more pleasurable necessities of life. In Japan, sex is not as strongly associated with love as it is in Western culture but is seen as being more related to desire. Traditionally, marriages were arranged (many still are today) and were not designed to be the sole means of satisfying sexual needs. Therefore, extramarital affairs were not censored. In practice, however, a double standard existed; men were free to keep a mistress (or mistresses) and seek sexual pleasure in any way they chose, whereas women were supposed to toe the line of marriage. One Japanese wife explained to an American friend:

> Why should the wife care if her husband goes off to "play"? It doesn't mean anything. She knows he will never leave her. In fact, I think the bond in a Japanese marriage is much stronger than that in the West. A Japanese woman would not consider divorcing her husband over such a trivial matter.

This attitude may be changing because of the rise of AIDS. Still, it confirms the fact that situational ethics is important to the Japanese.

Drinking and even drunkenness are good-naturedly tolerated and even encouraged. In fact, almost anything one does while drunk except driving is considered forgivable. Intoxication allows the Japanese to express themselves freely without fear of repercussion, and it is normal for members of a Japanese work group to spend several hours after work drinking and eating as a group before catching a late bus home. However, Western women sometimes find this behavior difficult to accept, even when a Japanese man is very polite when not drinking. In one celebrated instance, a British female high school teacher finally lost patience with a Japanese co-worker who had repeatedly harassed her while he was drinking and "decked" him at an office party. However, even though Japanese may indulge in unruly behavior while drinking, they rarely display hostility or violence.

Like the natural order of the Japanese garden, the Japanese believe in a natural order in society. Therefore, as reflected in the history of hereditary power and aristocratic rule in feudal Japan and in modern Japanese organizations, different ranks and statuses are considered natural. Within an organization, peoples' ranks are usually more important than their names. For example, the principal of a school is often addressed simply as *kocho sensei,* the Japanese term for principal. This emphasis on title establishes an individual's rank within an organization while serving to reinforce group identity.

The Japanese are great believers in establishing a person's status as quickly as possible so that the proper interaction and communication can take place. When meeting for the first time, Japanese businesspeople follow the kata of *meishi,* or immediately exchanging business cards, largely to establish each person's specific position and group affiliation. This exchange is not to be taken lightly, and the recipient of such a card is expected to read the card carefully and even repeat the person's name and title before putting the card away. To immediately put the card away, as many Americans do, would be insulting to the giver.

Language is also used to reinforce the natural order of ranks and statuses. Various endings are added to words of introduction that subtly indicate the status of a person, particularly in the case of a gaijin. The Japanese language is famous for such subtlety. Even at work, honorifics are used to address higher-status managers, although they are frequently dropped during the later stages of a working day when these managers indicate by their language and behavior that everything is going smoothly.

Even slight differences in seniority establish rigid status differences. Although two individuals may be merely one year apart in age, this fact determines who will be senior and junior for the rest of their lives.

A good part of personal self-identification derives from status. Furthermore, one is expected to act according to that status. To do otherwise would be unbecoming. Because they serve as role models and are addressed by the honorable title *sensei*, teachers in Japan must pay particular attention to their behavior outside of school. For example, if caught driving while under the influence of alcohol, a teacher would lose face and probably have to resign his or her position.

A hierarchy exists not just within the group but also between different groups. Most Japanese have a clear idea of the informal rank among universities, business firms, and even countries. This latter ranking helps to explain Japanese attitudes toward people from different countries. For example, those from "developed" countries such as the United States, England, France, and Canada are considered to possess higher status than those from developing Asian countries. Even within Japan, certain groups suffer discrimination, particularly the 600,000 Koreans. At one time in history, the Japanese had a caste system similar to that of India and, although it is outlawed, those who work on slaughtered animal products in any way are considered inferior by many Japanese, and private detectives are hired before most marriages to ensure that one's child does not marry into one of these families. Reportedly, some Japanese firms go to excessive lengths to ensure that only "pure" Japanese will be offered positions with them.

One of the great dangers of overemphasizing the uniqueness of being Japanese and group harmony is that a destructive groupthink may occur. Some prominent Japanese have openly criticized minority groups in the United States in ways that many Americans consider racist, and Dr. Tsunoda of Tokyo Medical and Dental University has even argued that the Japanese are unique because they have an unusual brain structure. According to Tsunoda, the Japanese brain mixes rational and emotional responses in the left hemisphere, whereas the Western brain is divided into the rational left side and emotional right side.

As already indicated, Japanese political parties are not parties per se but representative of powerful interest groups, and political scandals that would not be countenanced in other developed countries have occurred in Japan at least in part because of their existence. These examples should suffice to demonstrate that there are some downside risks associated with the emphasis on Japanese uniqueness and group conformity.

Contrary to expectation, this emphasis on status and rank coincides with a lack of class consciousness. Ninety percent of Japanese consider themselves as belonging to the middle class. In Japanese society, ties are vertical; loyalties overwhelmingly tend to lie with the immediate group. For example, a Japanese factory worker for Toyota identifies himself as a Toyota man and has little solidarity or identification with a factory worker for Honda.

Promotion is based largely on seniority in Japan, although this is not the only consideration. An individual may not jump a rank and must serve a prerequisite number of years in the previous rank to be eligible for promotion. However, only a limited number of positions are available for a much larger number of eligible employees. Therefore, the company promotes a certain percentage of eligible employees from each group until individuals reach a specific age, at which time it is unlikely one will be promoted any further.

It is important to note that hierarchy in Japan is not directly associated with clear authority and clearly delineated roles as in the West. For example, senior but less competent employees may be given relatively high titles that entail minimal responsibility, and an extremely able young individual may be given more responsibility than his or her title indicates. Also, although the Japanese emphasize group consensus and harmony, managers actually tend to share information with their subordinates and delegate decision-making authority to them less than do American managers. In one large-scale study involving 911 Japanese managers and 450 American managers, only 1.4% of the Japanese managers indicated that they shared much information with subordinates as compared with 31.6% of the American managers; only 3.1% of the Japanese managers stated that they delegated complete authority to their subordinates compared with 15.6% of the American managers (see Japanese Productivity Center Study, 1984).

As these examples suggest, appearance does not always reflect reality in Japan, just as the water in the garden's pond appears to be quite calm, even still. Yet the architect of this garden knows that beneath the surface the water is continually being sucked into a horizontal pipe and pumped back to the top of the waterfall.

Like the pond, from the outside the Japanese appear to be extremely harmonious. However, this appearance does not consider the intense competition that exists in Japanese society. Firms compete fiercely for market share, rival political parties compete for power, and individuals compete ferociously to enter the top universities. For example, in the Japanese automotive industry, nine Japanese firms vie for power versus only three American firms in the United States. On the individual level, conflict occurs between family members, between friends, and between co-workers. However, individuals often suppress their true feelings; if open conflict erupts, it is kept within the confines of the group.

In general, Japanese usually express *tatemae*, the group opinion, although it may differ from *honne*, what he or she really thinks. The Japanese associate this duality with the legitimate needs of the group and the reinforcing role of each person within it. Ellen Frost (1987) explains this dichotomy:

> *Tatemae* . . . is used in connection with a view made from an accepted or objective standpoint. *Honne* has the meaning of one's true feelings or intentions. . . . This doesn't mean anyone is lying. There is a delicate but important difference between tatemae and honne which comes up in any situation where a person must consider more than one's own feelings on the matter. (p. 92)

To Westerners this lack of frankness smacks of insincerity. However, to many Japanese the failure to observe honne and tatemae shows insensitivity and selfishness. Japanese tend to appreciate foreigners who outwardly conform to certain rules of behavior. Whether they actually respect these rules is not relevant; observance of them is a sign of appropriate and hence sincere conduct on their part.

However, this suppression of the self may have some negative effects. Dean Barnlund (1989) conducted a comparative study of Americans and Japanese on the issue of the private and public self that was well received by both Japanese and American experts. He basically argues that, because Americans tend to expose their private selves much more than the Japanese, they have a much better understanding of their private selves and are able to cope in an active manner to threatening interpersonal experiences. Barnlund (1989) concludes:

> The Japanese appear to be more socially vulnerable and to cultivate greater reserve, are more formal and cautious in expressing themselves, and communicate less openly and freely. Americans, in contrast, appear more self-assertive and less responsive to social context, are more informal and spontaneous in expressing themselves, and reveal relatively more of their inner experience. (p. 64)

Some Japanese respond that Americans say and do things that they later regret. To the Japanese, one aphorism speaks directly to the issue: "He who speaks does not know; he who knows does not speak." Frequently the most powerful member of a group is the last to speak—if he or she deigns to speak at all. What matters, however, is that the Japanese emphasis on the group is protected by the use of honne when they interact among themselves and with foreigners.

Aesthetics

The Japanese aesthetic sense is well developed, distinctive, and perhaps their most important contribution to the world. As with most of the activities discussed previously, this aesthetic sense is heavily based on the natural interaction between human beings and nature.

Japan has only one indigenous religion, Shintoism, which is nature based and animistic; even the Japanese term for God is translated as "up the mountain." Joseph Campbell (1962) captures the aesthetic sense of this religion in the following passage:

> Such a place of worship is without images, simple in form, wonderfully roofed, and often painted a nice clear red. The priests, immaculate in white vesture, black headdress, and large black wooden shoes, move about in files with stately mien. An eerie music rises, reedy, curiously spiritlike, punctuated by controlled heavy and light drumbeats and great gongs; threaded with the plucked, harplike sounds of a spirit-summoning kot. And then noble, imposing, heavily garbed dancers silently appear, either masked or unmasked, male or female. These move in slow, somewhat dreamlike or trancelike, shamanizing measure; stay for a time before the eyes, and retire, while utterances are intoned. One is thrown back two thousand years. The pines, rocks, forests, mountains, air and sea of Japan awake and send out spirits on those sounds. They can be heard and felt all about. And when the dancers have retired and the music has stopped the ritual is done. One turns and looks again at the rocks, the pines, the air, and the sea, and they are as silent as before. Only now they are inhabited, and one is aware anew of the wonder of the universe. (p. 475)

The importance of nature can be seen not only in Shintoism but also in Japanese painting, literature, and language. Long before it was considered acceptable in the West, landscape painting was a major theme of the *sansui-ga* painting introduced from China at the end of the Kamakura period (A.D. 1185-1333).

Nature is often the subject of the seasonal references in waka and haiku poetry and in the seasonal introductions that the Japanese customarily use in correspondence. The Japanese language is full of references to nature; it even has a special word to describe the sound of cherry blossoms falling.

Aesthetically, both the water in the Japanese garden and the garden itself try to represent nature as it is, not to order and impose a visible form on it as a Western garden may, but to capture its intrinsic being. The gardener does not create the beauty but merely allows it to express itself in louder and plainer terms. In doing so, he not only considers the placement of rocks and trees but the effect that time, namely, the change of seasons, will have on the garden. He observes the laws of *mujo* (mutability) and *sisei ruten* (perpetual change of the universe). For example, the garden may be designed in such a way that in winter the bare branches will have their own particular appeal. Given this emphasis on the natural impermanence of things, it is not surprising that the three great nature-watching rituals in Japan are snow gazing in approximately February, cherry blossom viewing, and viewing the ninth moon of the year or the harvest moon; all of these activities preferably occur in a Japanese garden.

The gardener also observes another Japanese aesthetic theory that developed from the Japanese acceptance of nature—that of uniqueness. No two trees are alike. The gardener thus does not search for the perfect rock, for such a rock cannot exist in a world characterized by uniqueness; instead, he looks for a tree or rock that expresses its own individuality. The gardener also does not seek to order perfectly a garden that is made of imperfect and unique objects. To insist on a harmony other than the underlying one naturally revealed would be unnatural.

Zen Buddhism's influence on the development of Japan and the Japanese garden—not just the religious garden but the landscape garden—has been enormous. As suggested previously, Zen Buddhism proposes that one can free oneself from this world by perceiving the timelessness and oneness of the universe. Likewise, in a Japanese garden the whole of nature can be seen despite the individual parts. Also, each part of the garden can capture the essence of nature in its own way. The garden depicts a freed world that has been physically reduced and spiritually enlarged to suggest the size and grandeur of nature. Japanese, who recognize that they are part of nature and hence mortal, essentially stop time by allowing it to have its own way. In the same manner, although the seasons may change the appearance of the garden, stones, trees, and water are always visible and unchanged in the Japanese garden.

In Japan, the Buddhist concept of transience has been integrated into the indigenous concept of nature as an extension of self. This integration can be seen in the oneness with nature and the Buddhist feeling that worldly display counts for nothing. For example, Zen teachings gave rise to the principles of *wabi* and *sabi* that are inherent in the tea ceremony, Japanese garden, and flower arrangements. Wabi is the aesthetic feeling of discovering richness and serenity in simplicity; it is an emotional appreciation of the essence of things, including the ephemeral quality of life. Sabi bespeaks a feeling of quiet grandeur enjoyed in solitude, and it normally involves the beauty that comes from the natural aging of things. To the Japanese, something old is to be respected, even its imperfections. Clearly, the Japanese garden is an ideal setting for experiencing wabi and sabi.

In *The Global Business*, Ronnie Lessem (1987) discusses two principles that explain the Japanese aesthetic: *shibui* and *mono-no-aware*. Shibui refers to a quality of beauty that has a tranquil effect on the viewer; the object, whether natural or made by humans, clearly reveals its essence through perfection of form, naturalness, simplicity, and subdued tone. Mono-no-aware refers to merging of one's identity with that of object or mood, especially one tinged with recognition of the impermanence of things. Lessem suggests that this aesthetic awareness leads to a sensitivity to man and nature that is rare in Europe and the United States.

A Japanese citizen may stroll in the garden or perhaps just sit at its edge, listening to the water and soaking in its beauty. The garden provides a place of escape from society both physically and spiritually, just as many Japanese seek refuge through their hobbies.

This refuge usually takes the form of some kind of identification with nature, as in the case of cultivating one's own tiny landscape garden or arranging flowers. Millions of Japanese express themselves through the traditional arts, dancing, music, and literature. In developing their individual skills they practice self-control and self-discipline. In Japan, pursuit of a hobby, called *shumi* (literally, "tastes"), is important to one's self-identity and even self-respect.

Except for the sound of the flowing water, all is quiet near the Japanese garden. Silence is an important value to the Japanese. As mentioned previously, a common Japanese proverb is "Those who know do not speak; those who speak do not know." Conversation is often punctuated by long stretches of silence. The Japanese say that it is during these silent intervals that real communication takes place, and that they can sense others' feelings and thoughts. Westerners should not feel compelled to fill in the gaps with conversation, which may only annoy Japanese who already perceive Westerners as talking too much.

To return to Geert Hofstede's (1980a) research on the four dimensions of cultures, Japan is in the cluster of countries that values the group more than the individual, as we might expect, although it ranked only 19th out of 40 countries on this dimension. Further, Hofstede's research indicates that the Japanese tend to avoid uncertainty and seek comfort in familiar situations and groups, and both the emphasis on the group and status tend to strengthen this sense of familiarity. In addition, Japan ranked first on the masculinity scale among the 40 countries, thus indicating that its people are aggressive in the pursuit of worldly success and material possessions. As indicated previously, the carp in the Japanese garden symbolically represents this aggressiveness or masculinity. Unlike the Chinese, who are hampered by their excessive devotion to the past and ancestor worship, the Japanese have historically been great borrowers from other cultures and are quick to change when conditions warrant such action. In this sense, the Japanese are similar to the individualistic Americans.

But the Japanese are clearly different from Americans, as our metaphor of the Japanese garden indicates. Still, worried Japanese elders are concerned that the water in the garden will not continue to flow smoothly because the "new humans" may have lost their appreciation of things Japanese. Iwao (1990) proposes that the results of recent Japanese opinion polls illustrate three major changes in Japanese character over the last decade: a tendency toward diversity and individuality, a need for swift results and instant gratification, and a desire for stability and maintenance of the status quo. Indeed, young Japanese seek more leisure time and are more likely to devote themselves to personal goals than in the past. As Iwao suggests, consumer behavior reflects a movement toward diversity and individuality. Female roles, attitudes toward marriage, and work also are changing.

The water in the Japanese garden is flowing quickly and with force. It may even cause the shape of the pond to alter somewhat. The change of the seasons also will bring changes to the garden. Yet the basic design and elements of the garden will always remain, for this island nation of homogenous people relies heavily on its groups to maintain stability and ensure change and progress within the framework of a high-context culture that emphasizes the natural ordering of individuals, groups, and activities.

15

India: The Dance of Shiva

India is a country bursting with diversity: Virtually every writer describes it as one of the most culturally and geographically diverse nations in existence. It is the seventh largest country in the world, approximately one third the size of the United States. With a population of 849 million, India has more people than all of Africa and more than North and South America together. The Indian cities of Bombay, Ahmadabad, and Bangalore are among the most densely populated places on earth. Sometimes troubled and divided, India is the world's most populous democracy. One of the world's largest and poorest nations, India has sought to modernize itself without sacrificing its commitment to individual freedom.

Religious diversity is a major feature of India, and it is fitting that our image of and cultural metaphor for this country should be based on religion. As Swami Vivekananda (Nikhilananda, 1953) so succinctly stated, "Each nation has a theme in life. In India religious life forms the central theme, the keynote of the whole music of the nation" (p. 118).

For 2,000 years of its history, India was almost completely Hindu. But for the last millennium or more, Indian culture has been a synthesis of different racial, religious, and linguistic influences; Hinduism itself has undergone many changes because of the impact of other faiths. It is therefore incorrect to contend that Indian culture is solely Hindu culture. However, to begin to understand India, we must start with Hindu traditions. The overwhelming majority of Indians—70% as a minimum (Lannoy, 1971, p. 3)—are still tradition oriented, and changes in their culture and society cannot be understood without reference to that tradition.

There are numerous deities or gods in the Hindu religion, each a different manifestation of the same supreme being. The most important gods are Brahma (the Creator), Vishnu (the Preserver), and Shiva (the Destroyer). Among the greatest names and appearances of Shiva is Nataraja, Lord of the Dancers. The Dance of Shiva has been described as the "clearest image of the activity of God [that] any art or religion can boast of" (Coomaraswamy, 1924/1969, p. 56), and it also reflects the cyclical nature of Hindu philosophy. Through this metaphor we will begin to explore Indian culture and society.

Among Hindus, dancing is regarded as the most ancient and important of the arts. Legend attributes to it even the creation of the world: Brahma's three steps created earth, space, and sky. Every aspect of nature—man, bird, beast, insect, trees, wind, waves, stars—displays a dance pattern; collectively these are called the *dainic nrtya* (daily dance). But nature is inert and cannot dance until Shiva wills it; he holds the *damaru* (sacred drum), whose soundings set the rhythms that beat throughout the universe. Shiva is like a master conductor, and the dainic nrtya is the response of all creation to his rhythmic force.

Shiva is seen as the first dancer, a deity who dances simply as an expression of his exuberant personality (Banerji, 1983, p. 43). His dance cannot be performed by anyone else: Shiva dances out the creation and existence of the world. But just as the mortal dancer gets tired, so Shiva periodically relapses into inactivity. The cosmos becomes chaos, and destruction follows the period of creation. This concept of the Dance of Shiva is innate in Eastern ideas of movement and history: It is continuous and simultaneously constructive and destructive (Gopal & Dadachanji, 1951).

The Dance of Shiva represents both the conception of the world processes as a supreme being's *lila* (pastime or amusement) and the very nature of that blessed one, which is beyond the realm of purpose or understanding (Coomaraswamy, 1924/1969). The dance symbolizes the five main activities of the supreme being: *srishti* (creation and development), *sthiti* (preservation and support), *samhara* (change and destruction), *tirobhava* (shrouding, symbolism, illusion, and giving rest), and *anugraha* (release, salvation, and grace). Considered separately, these are the activities of the deities Brahma, Vishnu, Rudra, Mahesvara, and Sadavisa, respectively. Taken together, the cycle of activity illustrated by the Dance of Shiva encapsulates Hinduism as the main driving force of Indian society. The idea of cycles is a common thread in traditional Indian philosophy and is the theme that will run through our discussion of its culture.

Two distinct variants of basic Indian culture spring from the people's Dravidian and Aryan ethnic origins. The Dravidians probably came to India from the eastern Mediterranean coasts, forming the highly developed Indus Valley civilization 3,000 years before Christ. Approximately 1500 B.C., this civilization fell into decline, and the people migrated to the southern part of the Indian subcontinent. At approximately the same time, Aryans arrived in India from Persia to settle almost all of the Indo-Gangetic Plain. Today 72% of the population is of Aryan origin; Dravidians account for 25%. The remaining 3% is made up of a myriad of other groups including Mongoloids. India's most populous cities—all ranking among the 40 largest in the world—are Bombay (11.8 million inhabitants) in the west, Calcutta (10.7 million) in the east, Delhi (8.5 million) in the north, and Madras (5.7 million) and Bangalore (4.6 million) in the south.

Religion and language separate the people far more than ethnic background or geography. Although more than 80% of Indians are Hindu, sizable numbers belong to other religious groups: Muslim (11%), Christian (3%), Sikh (2%), Buddhist, Jain, and aboriginal animists (Hoffman, 1991). Hindus are spread all over the country, with smaller concentrations at the southern, northeastern, and northwestern extremities. The minority populations (the term is relative, because Muslims alone number 100 million) actively resist being dissolved in a Hindu melting pot. Muslims are in the majority in Kashmir, and Sikhs are concentrated in Punjab. Buddhism claims some 5 million adherents in its homeland (and more than half a billion worldwide), including more than 50% of the population in western Kashmir and in Sikkim. Mixed religious groups are found in the northeastern and southwestern parts of the country.

The four major religions—Hinduism, Islam, Christianity, and Sikhism—are all associated with specific languages in which their original scripts were written: Sanskrit, Arabic, Latin, and Gurumukhi, respectively. The first three are not spoken languages in India, and, in a modernized form, the last is a state language of Punjab. In addition to Arabic, Muslims in India evolved a language of their own, Urdu, and several other regional languages. There are at least 300 known languages in India, 24 of which have at least 1 million speakers each.

After India's independence from Britain in 1947, Hindi, a north Indian language, was proclaimed the national language. Hindi was then spoken by only some 25% of the people, but it was the single most prevalent language in the country. The South had virtually no Hindi speakers, and southern people opposed starting the process of learning an "alien" language. As a result of these objections, the original constitution recognized no fewer than 15 "official languages" (3 more were added in 1992), and English was designated as an "additional official language" as a compromise. Even today, Hindi is the native tongue of fewer than half of all Indians, and English is often the language of national communication. English is spoken throughout the country, an enduring legacy of colonial days that is increasingly important for India as the globalization of markets and communications continues.

India's history reflects the cycles of chaos and harmony epitomized by the Dance of Shiva. Time after time, India has recovered from episodes that would have ended the existence of any other nation. In fact, Shiva's son, Ganesh, is the symbol of good arising from adversity. According to the legend, Parvati, the consort of Shiva, would spend hours bathing, dressing, and adorning herself. This often meant that Shiva was kept waiting, so Parvati set their son Ganesh on guard to prevent Shiva from bursting in on her unannounced and catching her in a state of unreadiness. One day Shiva was so frustrated by Ganesh's actions that he cut off the child's head. Distraught, Parvati completely withdrew from her lord, and Shiva realized he would have to restore the child to her if he was to win her back. He resolved to use the first available head he could find, which happened to be that of a baby elephant. The boy regained his life and now had the added advantage of the elephant's wisdom. Similarly, India's past and present contributions to art, science, and the spiritual world of the unknown are immense, despite periods of turmoil and apparent anarchy.

The estrangement of North and South India, illustrated by the debate over language, has historical roots that reach far back into the past. The South has enjoyed calm and relative tranquillity throughout most of its history, whereas the North has been subjected to a series of foreign invasions, often on a grand scale. Consequently, the northern culture is more a product of a mixed heritage. Among the most significant modifying influences in the North were the various Muslim invasions beginning circa A.D. 1000. As a result of these, the administrative structure of northern India was repeatedly destroyed, society often deprived of leadership, and religious faith shaken.

Muslim rule of North India began early in the 13th century and lasted until the middle of the 19th century. Muslim rulers were harsh on Hindus. It is against Muslim belief to worship any idol or image of God, so the invaders destroyed many thousands of Hindu temples and replaced them with mosques. A discriminatory tax was imposed on non-Islamic subjects, and Hindus were given low-level positions if employed at all. Forceful conversion of Hindus to the Islamic faith was widely carried out. Hindus in their own land were turned into second-class citizens and never shown the beautiful side of Islam. The confrontation between two virtually incompatible religious systems led to implacable mutual hatred between their respective followers. The echoes of this conflict resound even today. For instance, in 1992 more than 200,000 Hindus stormed and destroyed a 450-year-old Muslim mosque erected by the Moguls to replace a Hindu temple on the site that marks the birthplace of the Hindu god Rama. Hundreds of people were killed in the ensuing bedlam. Such instances are relatively common.

Unlike the North, southern India enjoyed a stable, almost uninterrupted regime of Hindu kingdoms until 1646 when Muslims succeeded in conquering and unifying all of India. The Muslim Mogul empire began to disintegrate during the 18th century, with independent regional kingdoms springing up all over. The influence of the British East India Company rose as Britain ousted rival Western colonial powers in the South. During those days of weakness, plundering invaders came from Persia and Afghanistan. North India entered a state of anarchy from which it did not emerge until the British gradually extended their control, leading to the establishment of the British Raj (rule) in the 19th century.

The British government instituted direct rule over India in 1858 following the Sepoy (Indian) Mutiny. Many Indians think of this event as the first war of independence. The sepoys—Indian soldiers in British employ—mutinied over a rumor that animal fat was being used in the cartridges they had to bite in order to load their rifles. Hindus heard that it was beef fat, Muslims heard pig fat, thus violating the taboos of both. British troops barely put down the insurrection: The British garrison at Kanpur, with its women and children, was slaughtered, and Kanpur became a rallying cry for British vengeance (Arden, 1990).

Early expressions of nationalism first crystallized in the Indian National Congress in 1885 and the All-India Muslim League in 1906.

Following the infamous massacre of more than 400 unarmed demonstrators at Amritsar by General Dyer's troops in 1919, Indian leaders put aside their previous faith and hope in the good intentions of the British Empire. Inspired by Mahatma (literally, "great soul") Gandhi, the Indian National Congress began a program of *satyagraha* (peaceful noncooperation) with British rule. Tragically, just months after India's independence was finally granted, Gandhi was killed by a Hindu extremist who had denounced him as an appeaser of the Muslims.

The British granted independence in 1947, but the country was partitioned into a largely Hindu India and a Muslim Pakistan. Overnight, partition created great communal strife, and 12 million refugees moved across the new India-Pakistan border during 1946-1947—Hindus into India, and Muslims into Pakistan. More than 200,000 people were killed in the accompanying riots, giving the world a lasting image of a modern India seemingly at war with itself. In fact, except for times of crisis, India has managed to accommodate and contain the destructive forces latent in group differences. But it is also true that today the political and social compromises that have permitted the country to deal with its diversity are under extreme pressure.

Faced with threats of succession, caste warfare, and sectarian violence, stern measures have sometimes been adopted by India's central authorities. The army has been called on more frequently to restore order to the country's troubled provinces than to defend the country from external threats.

Jawaharlal Nehru, the head of the Congress party, became the first prime minister of India in 1947. He was unwaveringly loyal to the basic concepts of freedom, democracy, socialism, world peace, and international cooperation and emerged as an eloquent statesman for the world's nonaligned and less-developed nations. Two years after Nehru's death in 1964, his daughter, Indira Gandhi (no relation to Mahatma Gandhi), succeeded to her father's office. Mrs. Gandhi struggled to modernize India and make it an economic power, but perhaps she lacked her father's devotion to "the spirit of man." She invoked the emergency provisions of the constitution in 1975 and suspended civil liberties, citing the need to address some of the nation's persistent problems "on a war footing." When elections were called in 1977, the Indian people expressed their resentment against the methods of the "emergency" and voted her out of office. After full democracy was restored, an apparently chastened Gandhi returned to power in 1979, where she remained until she was assassinated five years later.

Rajiv Gandhi, Indira's son, became prime minister on her death but claims of widespread corruption in the government probably cost his Congress party a general election. The succeeding government was short-lived, unable to sustain a parliamentary majority for its policies. During the next campaign, Rajiv Gandhi also was assassinated, and the Congress party was swept back to power on a huge sympathy vote.

It appears that the Nehru-Gandhi dynasty that has dominated India's modern political system is now at an end or at least suspended; Rajiv's son and daughter may be strong contenders in the future. The family's journey and its sequence of evolution, power, death, return, creation, destruction, and, perhaps, ultimate salvation epitomize the actions of the Dance of Shiva and the cyclical nature of Hindu philosophy.

Cyclical Hindu Philosophy

The Indian perspective on life tends to differ most sharply from that of Europe and the United States in the value that it accords to the discipline of philosophy (Coomaraswamy, 1924/1969, p. 2). In Europe and the United States, the study of philosophy tends to be regarded as an end in itself—a kind of mental gymnastic—and as such it seems of little importance to the ordinary man or woman. In India, philosophy tends to overlap with religion and is regarded as the key to life itself, clarifying its essential meaning and the way to attain spiritual goals. Elsewhere, philosophy and religion pursued distinct and different paths, which may have crossed but never merged (Munshi, 1965, p. 133). In India, it is not always possible to differentiate between the two.

In Hindu philosophy, the world is considered as illusory, like a dream, the result of God's lila. According to one interpretation, India's ancient name of "Bharata Varsha" literally means "land of the actors" (Lannoy, 1971, p. 286). In an illusionary world, people cannot achieve true happiness through the mere physical enjoyment of wealth or material possessions. The only happiness worth seeking is permanent spiritual happiness as distinguished from these fleeting pleasures. Absolute happiness can result only from liberation from worldly involvement through spiritual enlightenment. Life is a journey in search of *mukti* (salvation), and the seeker, if he or she withstands all of the perils of the road, is rewarded by *moksha*—exultation beyond human experience or perception. In the same way that the

Dance of Shiva leads the cosmos through a journey, Hindu philosophy directs each individual along a path.

Four basic paths or ways lead to the ideal state: *bhakti yoga* (intense devotion or love of God), *karma yoga* (selfless work or service), *jnana yoga* (philosophy or knowledge of self), and *raja yoga* (meditation or psychological exercise). The four ways are not exclusive, and an individual may choose or combine them according to the dictates of temperament and circumstance. Whatever path is followed, every Hindu is aware of the difficulty of reaching the ideal state in a single lifetime. This is the point at which the concept of *reincarnation*, or the cycle of lives, becomes important.

Individual *jivas* (souls) enter the world mysteriously: by God's power, certainly, but how and for what purpose is not fully explainable (Smith, 1991, p. 100). They begin as the souls of the simplest forms of life, but they do not vanish with the death of their original bodies: They simply move to a new body or form. The transmigration of souls takes an individual jiva through a series of complex bodies until a human one is achieved. At this point, the ascent of physical forms ends and the soul begins its path to mukti. This gives an abiding sense of purpose to the Hindu life: a God to be actively sought and patiently awaited through the cycles of many lives.

The doctrine of reincarnation corresponds to a fact that everyone should have noticed: The varying age of the souls of people, regardless of the age of the body (e.g., "An old head on young shoulders"). Some people remain irresponsible, self-assertive, uncontrolled, and inept to their last days; others are serious, friendly, self-controlled, and talented from their youth onward. According to Hindu philosophy, each person comes equipped with a highly personalized unconsciousness that is characterized by a particular mix of three fundamental qualities: *sattva* (clarity, light), *rajas* (passion, desire), and *tamas* (dullness, darkness). Their relative strength differs from one person to another, but the Hindu idea of destiny holds that the unconscious has an innate tendency to strive toward clarity and light (Kakar, 1978).

The birth of a person into a particular niche in life and the relative mix of the three fundamental qualities in an individual are determined by the balance of the right and wrong actions of his or her soul through its previous cycles. The rate of progress of the soul through this endless cycle of birth, life, and death—the soul's karma—depends on the deeds and decisions made in each lifetime. One way of mapping the probable karma of an individual is to consult astrological charts at the time of his or her birth, and this is an important tradition in Indian society.

The Dance of Shiva portrays the world's endless cycle of creation, existence, destruction, and recreation, and Hindu philosophy depicts the endless cycle of the soul through birth, life, death, and reincarnation. We will now turn to examining the cycle of individual life within that greater series of lifetimes.

The Cycle of Life

According to Hindu philosophy, a person passes through four stages of life, the first of which is that of a student. The prime responsibility in life during this stage is to learn. Besides knowledge, the student is supposed to develop a strong character and good habits and emerge equipped to produce a good and effective life.

The second stage, beginning with marriage, is that of a householder. Here human energy turns outward and is expressed in three realms: family, vocation, and community. The wants of pleasure are satisfied through the family, the wants of duty through exercising the social responsibilities of citizenship, and the wants of success through employment.

The third stage of life is retirement, signifying withdrawal from social obligations. This is the time for a person to begin his or her true education—to discover who one is and what life is all about. It is a time to read, think, ponder life's meaning, and discover and live by a philosophy. At this stage, a person needs to transcend the senses and dwell in harmony with the timeless reality that underlies the dream of life in this natural world.

The Hindu concept of retirement is exemplified in a story told by a traveler in India (Arden, 1990, reprinted with permission). The traveler saw a white-bearded man seated on a blanket, writing in a notebook. The man looked up and smiled as the traveler walked past. "Are you a Buddhist?" asked the traveler. The man shook his head. "A Hindu? A Muslim?" Again the man shook his head. He then replied, "Does it matter? I am a man." The traveler asked what the man was writing. "The truth," he said, "only the truth."

The final stage is one of *sannyasin*, defined by the *Bhagavad-Gita* ("Song of the Blessed One") as "one who neither hates nor loves anything." In this stage, the person achieves mukti and is living only because the time to make the final ascent has not come. When he or she finally departs from this world, freedom from the cycle of life and death is attained.

A person can pass through the four stages of life in a single lifetime or stay at each stage for many lifetimes. Even Buddha is reputed to have passed through several hundred lives. Progress is determined in the light of the activities and inclination of the person at each stage of life. For example, Indian religion is replete with rituals, the primary purpose of which is to receive the blessings of God. Each ceremony involves the singing of *bhajans* (religious songs) and discourses by *satsang* (priests and other religious persons). The sincerity with which people indulge in these activities and apply the tenets of the philosophy in their practical lives determines their progress through the cycle of life and death. A person may expound philosophy at great length, go to the temple every day, and offer alms to saints and the poor, and yet indulge in all sorts of vices. These contradictions in life are resolved on death by karma, which dictates that on reincarnation each person will receive rewards or punishment for his or her accumulated good and bad deeds.

The Hindu desire for positive outcomes of daily activities, resulting in positive karma, leads to a brief discussion of the importance of astrology. With so much at stake, almost everyone in India consults the stars, if not on a daily basis, then at least on important occasions. Matching the horoscopes of a bride and groom is as much a part of planning a marriage as choosing the flower arrangements. It is routine for Indians to consult the stars about the best day to close on a house or sign an important contract. When it was revealed that an astrologer helped Nancy Reagan set her schedule, Americans hooted with derision. In contrast, no one in India batted an eyelid when former Prime Minister Narasimha Rao delayed naming his cabinet because an astrologer warned that the intended day was not auspicious enough.

Like Hindu philosophy, the Indian concept of time is cyclical, characterized by origination, duration, and disappearance ad infinitum. This is reflected in the dramatic structure of traditional Sanskrit plays. These are typically based on the themes of separation and reunion and tend to end as they begin. Various devices are used—the dream, the trance, the premonition, and the flashback—to disrupt the linearity of time and make the action recoil on itself (Lannoy, 1971, p. 54). Similarly, the Dance of Shiva is a repetitive cycle of creation, existence, and destruction: constant change within a period of time, although ultimately time itself is irrelevant.

In an attempt to neutralize the anguish of impermanence and change, the carved religious images that every village home possesses are made of permanent materials such as clay or metal. This also reveals the functional role of the image in a materially restricted environment. The practice of religion at home is one of the main reasons Hinduism was able to survive the invasion of foreign powers over the centuries. And just as religion is important to the family, so the family plays a dominant factor in Indian society.

The Family Cycle

Most Indians grow up in an extended family, a form of family organization in which brothers remain together after marriage and bring their wives into their parental household or compound of homes. Recent migration to cities and towns in search of economic opportunities has contributed to the weakening of many traditions, including that of extended families. In this section, we describe family traditions that exist most strongly in the India of some 400 million people that continues to be marginally affected by industrialization. Although weakened in some parts of society, many aspects of the family cycle are still important to all.

The preference for a son when a child is born is as old as Indian society. A son guarantees the continuation of the generations, and he will perform the last rites after his parents' death. This ensures a peaceful departure of the soul to its next existence in the ongoing cycle of life. The word for son, *putra*, literally means "He who protects from going to hell." In contrast, a daughter has negligible ritual significance. She is normally an unmitigated expense, someone who will never contribute to the family income, and who will take away a considerable part of her family's fortune as her marriage dowry. Although formally abolished, the institution of dowry is still widespread in India, but it is becoming increasingly fashionable among educated Indians not to indulge in the practice.

A striking reflection of this gender preference is the continued "masculinization" of the Indian population, particularly in the north. In 1961, there were more than 1 million fewer girls than boys under 10 years of age. By 1971, this difference had risen to approximately 2 million; the 1981 census indicated that the deficit of females was roughly 4 million (Narayana & Kantner, 1992, p. 28). The main reasons for this outcome are the higher mortality rate of female children and the tendency to limit family size once there is a sufficient number of sons. Also, the recent availability of sex-determination tests has allowed women to ensure that their firstborn is a boy, because they can abort unwanted female children.

Just as the Dance of Shiva represents preservation, oversight, and support, parents tend to nurture their children with great care. A

Hindu child grows up in the security of the extended family and has few contacts with other groups until school. Although the mother is chiefly responsible for the care of the child, there is also close contact with other females and mother surrogates, and this continues for much longer than in many other cultures. A child is usually breast-fed for at least two years (although significantly less in the case of a female child) and any time that it cries. Consequently, most infants are virtually never left alone.

The strong ties of home life do not conflict with the Hindu belief in the liberty of the soul removed from worldly concerns. Love of family is not merely a purpose in itself, it is a way to the final goal of life. Love will not yield the rewards of mukti when it remains self-centered, which is why the Hindu try to diffuse their love over sons, daughters, guests, and neighbors (Munshi, 1965, p. 115).

Children in India are considered sacred, a manifestation of God, but if the Hindu ideal is an extreme degree of infant indulgence, reality is somewhat different in India's poorer areas. There typically many young children are under one roof, and 1 in 10 will die in infancy, so babies are not regarded as extraordinary creatures. Except for the firstborn son, they tend to be taken for granted. This is reinforced by the belief in rebirth; as an individual is not born only once, his or her birth cannot be regarded as a unique event. The mother has probably witnessed the birth of several babies and may have seen them die. When her child cries, falls sick, or is accidentally injured, she is not beset with feelings of intense guilt. A mother's work may be long and hard, both in the home and in the fields, so she is unable to give her child undivided attention.

Even as the Dance of Shiva leads the world through the joys of existence, an element of chaos is inherent in the world's daily dance. Similarly, nature in India has been full of threats to a child's safety—famine, disease, and chronic civil disorder. As a rule, until modern times more than half of all deaths befell children in their first year of life. But as the nation got a grip on its affairs and as campaigns against diseases such as malaria and smallpox took hold, mortality rates fell. By 1981 nearly three of four newborns could expect to survive to age 20 (Narayana & Kantner, 1992, p. 26). However, research completed in the Punjab region suggests that young females tend to receive less favorable treatment. Fewer than half of deceased female children received any kind of medical care in the first 24 hours of the illness to which they finally succumbed; two thirds of male children did (Kielman, 1983).

The cultural importance of children is derived from the need to carry on the cycle of life. This continued importance is reflected in statistics that show that, although death rates since 1921 have fallen from 47.2 per 1,000 to 11.8 in 1986, birthrates have declined much more slowly: from 48.1 per 1,000 to 35.0 over the same period (Narayana & Kantner, 1992, p. 21).

Government attempts to regulate the birthrate have become synonymous with its sterilization programs. In 1986-1987, slightly more than 40% of couples were using some form of contraception, 70% of which is provided by sterilization. For developing countries generally, sterilization accounts for 40% or less of contraceptive use (Nortman, 1985). Resentment against coerced sterilization in India helped defeat Indira Gandhi's government in 1977. As a result of the political fallout, birth control was set back as a popular cause; the government avoided open discussion of family planning, and there is still scarce mention of the subject in party manifestos or political speeches (Narayana & Kantner, 1992, p. 71). Today there is no organized political opposition to family planning, but the voluntary family-planning programs that do exist are generally badly run. Middle-class Indians, influenced by education and the desire for an improved standard of living, are increasingly adopting family-planning methods. But when the formidable psychic barrier of traditional Hindu beliefs in the life cycle are considered, it seems clear that rapid population growth will continue in the poorer, rural areas.

An Indian father is frequently remote, aloof, and a much feared disciplinary figure, just as Shiva is distant from the world he nurtures. But there are also special bonds between father and son, and the relationship is one of mutual dependence. A son must obey his father unquestioningly, pay him respect, and offer complete support in every need both in life and after death. The father owes his son support, a good education, the best possible marital arrangement, and inheritance of property. One Indian proverb reads, "A son should be treated as a prince for five years; as a slave for ten years; but from his sixteenth birthday, as a friend."

Early in his life, the son learns that women are lower in status than are men. The position of all women in this hierarchical society means that they must constantly make demands and plead with superiors for one thing or another. The son soon develops an attitude of superiority. A female's authority can seldom be absolute, except for the unchallengeable position that the senior grandmother may inherit. A son finds out that anger may be productive; violent outbursts of anger are often effective if directed against someone of uncertain status. Similarly, the destructive powers of the Dance of Shiva are effective in creating new opportunities and patterns.

The relative position of men and women is clear in Indian society, and the question of competitive equality is not customarily considered. The Hindu marriage emphasizes identity, not equality. Generally, women are thought to have younger souls, and therefore they are nearer to the world than men and inferior to them. Girls are trained to be submissive and docile and to fulfill culturally designated feminine roles. The ideal of womanhood in Indian tradition is one of chastity, purity, gentle tenderness, self-effacement, self-sacrifice, and singular faithfulness. Throughout history, Indian women have had dual status: As a wife, she seduces her husband away from his work and spiritual duties, but she is revered as a mother.

Among the burdens Indian women have are female infanticide, child marriage, *purdah* (feminine modesty and seclusion), marital mistreatment, and the low status of widows. Until the mid-19th century, *sati*—a widow's voluntary self-immolation on her husband's funeral pyre—was not uncommon; the widow believed her act would cleanse her family of the sins of the three generations. Poor families are more likely to be fearful of not being able to scrape together enough money to find their daughters husbands and may resort to killing infant girls. Generally speaking, however, the lower down the economic hierarchy, the more equal are the relations between the sexes. Of course, many factors can bring about or alleviate hostile feelings toward women, but the various forms of mistreatment suffered by them are often viewed as part of their destiny or karma as women. The Dance of Shiva is not destined to lead to joy throughout the world, and if the corresponding experience of humanity includes unhappiness for women in society, that is simply the way things are.

A man's worth and recognition of his identity are intimately bound up in his family's reputation. Lifestyle and actions are rarely seen as the product of individual effort but are interpreted in the light of family circumstance and reputation in the wider society. Individual identity and merit are enhanced if the person has the good fortune to belong to a large, harmonious, and close-knit family, which helps to safeguard a child's upbringing and advance a person in life. Training in self-reliance is conspicuous by its absence, and children are typically not encouraged to be independent. The family contributes to decisions that affect an individual's future, maximizes the number of connections necessary to secure a job or other favors, comes to aid in times of crisis, and generally mediates an individual's experience with the outside world. For these reasons, the character of the respective families weighs heavily in the consideration of marriage proposals.

Arranged marriage is still the norm in India. Advertisements regularly appear in European and American newspapers for the purpose of identifying potential candidates. The Western concept of romantic love arises from the Western concept of personality and ultimately from the un-Indian concept of equality of the sexes. Still, the concept of life as an illusion makes the idea of loveless marriage easier to understand.

Marriages are usually for a lifetime; divorce is considered socially disgraceful. The average age for Indian women to marry is 18 or 19, whereas only 13% of U.S. women of this age are married. The percentage of Indian women aged 15 to 19 who are married ranges from 14% in states where a high value is put on female education to more than 60% in less-developed states (Narayana & Kantner, 1992, p. 31). In the case of child marriage, the girl lives at her parents' place until she is 15 or 16 years of age, after which she moves to the home of her husband's family. A newly arrived daughter-in-law is sometimes subject to varying forms of humiliation until she becomes pregnant. This treatment originated historically from the urgent need to ensure the early birth of a son in times of low life expectancy, although life expectancy in India has improved considerably to 58 or 59 years. Also, the size of the dowry that a girl brings with her also can determine how she is treated or mistreated in her husband's home. The husband's family may keep making demands on her for additional support from her family; if it is not forthcoming, she may be tortured or even burned alive, although the outcry against such treatment seemingly has diminished such illegal practices.

The restricted life of women in the conservative atmosphere of India does not prevent them from developing a strong sense of self-respect. Their ultimate role is to preserve unity and continuity in the chain of life, and there is pride and dignity in their sense of identity with the family and their role as wives and mothers. Indian society seems to have given women, rather than men, resilience and vitality under the difficult circumstances of life in that country. But all ultimately respond to the Dance of Shiva, and whether that brings great joy or unhappiness to the current life is irrelevant compared to the ongoing search for mukti.

Since the beginning of time, dancing has been a rite performed by both man and woman; Shiva and his wife, Parvati, are often depicted in ancient sculptures as one composite figure, half male and half female. Typical figurines of Shiva have four arms, broad masculine shoulders, and curving womanly hips. Similarly, there is a place for both genders to contribute to modern Indian society. In this century, Indian women have undergone a social revolution more far-reaching and radical than that of men. While this process has been going on, women have attained positions of distinction in public and professional life. The political dominance of Indira Gandhi is one example of how women can be held in high esteem by all Indians.

In summary, it can be seen that the extended family unit is still a strong feature of Indian society. Just as the Dance of Shiva wills all nature to respond to its rhythm, so each member of the family fulfills a role dictated by family tradition.

The Cycle of Social Interaction

A sense of *dharma* (duty) is the social cement in India; it holds the individual and society together. This is typical of a collectivist society in which all members are interdependent and their roles complementary. Dharma is conceptually broader than the Western idea of duty: It includes the totality of social, ethical, and spiritual harmony (Lannoy, 1971, p. 217). Dharma consists of three categories: *sanatana dharma* (universal principles of harmony), *varnashrama dharma* (relative ethical systems varying by social class), and *svadharma* (personal moral conduct). Among the prime traditional virtues are leading a generous and selfless life, truthfulness, restraint from greed, and respect for one's elders. These are principles that are consistent with a virtual global idea of righteousness.

Hinduism has progressed through India's moments of crisis by repeatedly lifting the banner of the highest ideals. The image of the Dance of Shiva is strongly evoked by the following passage from the *Bhagavad-Gita*: "Whenever the dharma decays, and when that which is not dharma prevails, then I manifest myself. For the protection of the good, for the destruction of the evil, for the firm establishment of the national righteousness, I am born again and again" (Deutsch, 1968, p. 31).

The oldest source of ethical ideas is the Mahabharata, or Great Epic of Bharata, the first version of which appeared between the seventh and sixth centuries B.C. This extensive composite poem of 90,000 couplets in 18 books traces the rivalry between two families involved in an unrelenting war. The story is interrupted by numerous episodes, fables, moral tales, and long political and ethical discourses, all of which serve to illustrate the illusory nature of the world and encourage the reader to strive for God. This sacred book, a repository of Hindu beliefs and customs, is based on the assumption that dharma is paramount in the affairs of society. The epic took at least 1,000 years to compose and is still the most widely read and respected religious Hindu work. Its most popular and influential part is the *Bhagavad-Gita*, a book Gandhi once said "described the duel that perpetually went on in the hearts of mankind."

A recent European traveler in India gave this illustration of the power of dharma. Sitting precariously among local people on top of a bus during a long journey, the traveler was astounded when a sudden shower of money fell into the dusty road behind them. An Indian alongside the traveler began shouting and pounding on the roof of the bus for the driver to stop. Some ways down the road, the bus pulled over and the man rushed away. All the passengers disembarked and waited for the Indian to return, laughing at his comic misfortune and manic disappearance. Eventually, the man reappeared, clutching a big handful of notes, including Western money. It was then that the traveler realized his own wallet was gone from his back pocket; it had come loose and blown away from the top of the bus, scattering the equivalent of a year's income for the average native (some $350). The Indian, a total stranger, had run back and convinced the poverty-stricken locals to hand over the money they were ecstatically gathering from their fields. The traveler began to thank his new friend for his troubles, but with the comment "It was my duty" the Indian declined to take any reward.

It is generally believed that social conflict, oppression, and unrest do not stem from social organizations but originate in nonadherence to dharma by those in positions of power. It is their actions that have created the cycle of disharmony. Hindus see a quarrel as a drama with three actors—two contestants and a peacemaker—and it is not the protagonists but the peacemaker who is seen as the victor in the dispute, because it is he or she who has restored harmony (Lannoy, 1971, p. 198).

Individuals who head institutions are believed to be the sole repositories of the virtues and vices of the institution. Traditionally, social-reform movements focused not so much on abolishing the hierarchical organizations or rejecting the values on which they are based, but on removing or changing the individuals holding positions of authority in them (Kakar, 1978). For example, during the declining years of both the Mogul and British Indian Empires, the ruling classes enjoyed lives of luxury and extravagance in India. Conspicuous consumption by the aristocratic elites at the expense of the productive classes remains in the India of the late 20th century. The identity may have changed, but the attitude remains.

The issues behind social and political ferment in India today are not rooted primarily in economic deprivation and frustration, although these make the mix more volatile (Narayana & Kantner, 1992, p. 2). Instead, it is the widespread feeling that the institutions on which the society was founded no longer work. In a reflective piece written shortly after Rajiv Gandhi's assassination, the New Delhi correspondent of *The Economist* wrote:

> The state is seen as corrupt and callous, incapable of delivering justice or prosperity to the people. . . . The police and civil servants are seen as oppressors and terrorists. The law courts are venal and can take decades to decide a case. The rule of law does not seem to be working in settling people's grievances. What seems to work is violence and money, and all political parties are engaged in a mad race to maximize the use of both. . . . Amid this moral decay, religious, ethnic and caste crusades have a growing appeal. People find a purity in them which they do not find in secular, national parties. And an increasing number of people are willing to kill in the name of causes which they find holier than the discredited law of the land. ("Death Among," 1991, p. 39, © 1991 The Economist Newspaper Group, Inc. Reprinted with permission. Further reproduction prohibited.)

The tragic recourse to mob violence by religious followers at different times in the country's history is a contradiction that astounds casual observers of India. How can such terrible things happen in a country where everyone believes in harmony and awaits the ultimate consequences of good and bad deeds in reincarnation? Hindus believe that *sila* (character or behavior) has its roots in the depths of the mind rather than in the heat of the action (Lannoy, 1971, p. 295). Because all worldly acts are transient, part of the illusion of life, they can have no decisive moral significance. Within the Dance of Shiva, destruction exists as strongly as creation and preservation; so it is with India.

This is not to say violence is condoned by Hindu faith; just the opposite. But Hindus avoid the theological use of the terms *good* and *evil*, preferring to speak of *vidya* (knowledge) and *avidya* (ignorance). Destructive acts by people who are ignorant are not regarded as sins, but those acts committed by people aware of their responsibilities are counted against them in their seeking of mukti.

Bathing in the holy water of the Ganges is believed to wash away all of a person's sins and is required of every Hindu at least once in his or her life. Indians tend to synthesize or integrate with nature because they assume this to be the natural relationship of human beings with the world, unlike Westerners who tend to exploit the physical environment for their own purposes. But the belief in the spiritual purity of the Ganges is so strong that government attempts to clean the badly polluted waters have little chance of being effective. Many people simply do not accept that anything can spoil the Ganges' perfection. As a consequence, rotting carcasses of both animals and partially cremated people are a common sight along the river banks. The image of death among life, decomposition next to creation, and pollution mixed with purity is evocative of the Dance of Shiva.

Another pervasive social dimension in India is *verna*, or the caste system, which is now officially outlawed but remains a source of constant tension. Following the assumed natural law that an individual soul is born into its own befitting environment, Hindus assume that an individual belongs to a caste by birth. Four main castes each contribute to society in specific ways:

1. Brahmans, as seers or religious people;
2. administrators;
3. producers, such as skilled craftspeople and farmers; and
4. followers or unskilled laborers.

Each natural class has its appropriate honor and duties, but as privilege has entered the scale, with top castes profiting at the expense of those lower down, the whole system has begun to disintegrate. Below the system is a fifth group, the untouchables, who lie outside the major activities of society. Its members are engaged in work that is considered socially undesirable and unclean. Untouchability, as it exists today, is often described as a perversion of the original caste system.

Within each caste or group there are numerous *jati* (subcastes) that influence the immediacy of all daily social relations, including work. Approximately 3,000 jati exist, and they are further divisible into another 30,000 sub-jati with unwritten codes governing the relationships between jatis. Friendships with members of the same jati tend to be closer and more informal than those with members of other jatis. As a general rule, a person's name provides information not only about his or her jati but also about the region of the country from which the person's family originated. For example, Gupta is a family name from the trading class, although many have gone into the professions, especially teaching. Most Guptas come from the north Indian states of Haryana, Uttar Pradesh, and West Bengal.

The jati's values, beliefs, and prejudices become part of each individual's psyche or conscience. The internalized jati norms define the right actions or dharma for an individual: He or she feels good or loved when living up to these rules and guilty when transgressing them.

When society was divided strictly by caste, there was no attempt to realize a competitive equality, and within each caste all interests were regarded as identical. But that also meant that equality of opportunity existed for all within the caste: Every individual was allowed to develop the experience and skills that he or she needed to succeed at the caste's defined role. The castes were self-governing, which ensured that each person was tried and judged by his or her peers. Central authorities viewed crimes committed by upper-caste members more severely than those of the lower caste. Because it was simply not possible to move outside of the caste, all possibility of social ambition, with its accompanying tension, was avoided. This suits the Hindu belief in harmony. The comprehensiveness of the caste system, together with holistic dharma, contributed to the stability that prevailed among the vast mass of people for much of India's history. Preservation of order interspaced with disorder is a characteristic of the Dance of Shiva.

The worst facet of the caste system falls on the untouchables. This caste has come to symbolize India's own brand of human injustice, victims of a system that kept people alive in squalor. Of course, social hierarchy is universal, found not only among Hindus but also among Muslims, Christians, Sikhs, Jains, and Jews (Srinivas, 1980). There is also a prevalence of pollution taboos in all civilizations, including the most advanced and modern; eliminating dirt is an attempt to introduce order into the environment (Lannoy, 1971, p. 146). But Hindu society pays exceptional attention to the idea of purity and pollution, and historically this has resulted in the virtual ostracism of the untouchables from the rest of society.

By way of historical explanation, Hindus believed that proximity to the contaminating factor constitutes a permanent pollution, which is both collective and hereditary. Therefore, they had a dread of being polluted by members of society who were specialists in the elimination of impurity. Hindu society was more conscious of grading social groups according to their degree of purity than of a precise division of castes into occupations. The untouchables—traditionally society's cleaners, butchers, and the like—were at the bottom of the Hindu hierarchy because they were considered irrevocably unclean. A similar caste system was developed in Japan, and it also has been outlawed, although its effects remain.

Although India's traditional social structure was based on institutionalized inequality, today the government, and supposedly the nation, is committed to social equality. Beginning with Mahatma Gandhi, public figures have tried to reform the attitudes of Indian society toward the untouchables. Gandhi named them *Harijan*—literally, "Children of God." The entire caste system was declared illegal by the Indian constitution, and today untouchables are guaranteed 22.5% of government jobs as compensation for traditional disfavor. These policies have met with some success, but such deep-rooted prejudice cannot be eliminated by a mere pen stroke.

The ambiguity of caste in occupational terms is another wedge by which the lower castes push their way up the scale. However, ambiguity is not so great as to render the system inoperative. Violations of caste norms, such as intercaste marriage, still evoke responses of barbaric ferocity. Educated Indians look on such incidents as throwbacks to the inhumanity of feudal times that must be dealt with sternly by the authorities. But efforts to create greater equality of opportunity for members of the traditionally disadvantaged castes meet stiff resistance from these same ranks (Narayana & Kantner, 1992, p. 5).

Additional reforms remain problematical, as recent history suggests: The intermediate castes, typically peasants and laborers, account for 52% of the population, yet a commission in 1980 found they held only 12.5% of central government jobs and only 4.7% of jobs at officer level. In 1990, the government introduced policies reserving 27% of jobs in central and state jobs for these castes and Christian and Muslim groups that were socially backward. In protest, dozens of upper-caste students burned themselves to death. The upper-caste Brahmans, a mere 5.5% of the population, have traditionally run government departments, but the struggle for jobs in India is so intense that the students saw themselves as victims of injustice, not historical oppressors. The then Prime Minister V. P. Singh was forced to resign when the government's coalition partner withdrew its support of the government, mainly over caste-reform issues. But no party dares oppose job reservation, given the voting power of the intermediate castes ("Castes Adrift," 1992).

The Harijan quickly realized their ability to assert their democratic rights as equal citizens through organized political activity. The effect of politicization of caste in modern times has made it clear that power is becoming ascendant over status. Modern education also acts as a solvent of caste barriers. These factors hold out the best hope for the disappearance of castes over the longer term.

The hierarchical principle of social organization has been central to the conservatism of Indian tradition. Among the criteria for ordering is age and gender. Elders have more formal authority than younger people, and, as we have already related, men have greater authority than women. Many times women are not involved in social functions or conversations and are required to cover their heads in front of elders or mature guests. Most relationships are hierarchical in structure, characterized by almost paternal nurturing on the part of the superior and by filial respect and compliance on the part of the subordinate. The ordering of social behavior extends to every institution in Indian life, including the workplace, which we will examine shortly.

It is clear that the traditional social structure of India is undergoing change and reform. This is consistent with the evolutionary aspects of the Dance of Shiva. But any change requires the destruction of old ways, and pressure is beginning to build within the old system. It may be that before those changes are complete, Shiva will rest and chaos will rule for a time. Or perhaps a new rhythm is beginning for the dance of the 21st century, and the daily dance of Indian society will quietly adjust in response.

The Work and Recreation (Rejuvenation) Cycle

There are several different perspectives on the importance of work: to earn a living; satisfy the worldly interests of accomplishments, power, and status; and fulfill the desire to create and care for the family. An aspect considered more important in India is that work enables, prepares, and progresses the individual through the cycle of life toward the ultimate aim of achieving mukti. The Indian approach to work is best defined by the *Bhagavad-Gita*: "Renunciation [of works] and the unselfish performance of work both lead to the highest happiness. But of these two the unselfish performance of works is better than the renunciation of works" (Deutsch, 1968, p. 60).

Work was originally prescribed as dharma without any concern for material outcomes. Castes were occupational clusters, each discharging its role and being maintained in turn by the overall system. But meeting the obligations to one's relatives, friends, and even strangers and maintaining relationships constituted the ethos of the system. Even with the rapid expansion of industrial activity in the 20th century, requiring large-scale importation of Western technology and work forms, Western work values have been only partially internalized by Indians. Today, with government-mandated affirmative action, it is not unlikely that someone from a higher caste may work for someone from a lower class. Many Indians have developed a state of mind that allows them to put aside caste prejudice in the workplace but, on returning home, conduct all of their social activities strictly according to caste norms.

We have already seen how family life develops an acute sense of dependence in the individual that serves to fortify the participative and collective nature of society. Similarly, most Indian organizations have numerous overlapping in-groups, with highly personalized relationships between group members. They cooperate, make sacrifices for the common good, and generally protect each other's interests. But in-groups often interfere with the functioning of formally designated sections, departments, and divisions and can lead to factionalism and intense power plays within an organization. Just as disorder within order is a characteristic of the Dance of Shiva, so incompetence is often overlooked because work performance is more relationship oriented than contractual in nature. A competent person may be respected but not included in a group unless he or she possesses the group characteristics.

Family, relatives, caste members, and persons speaking the same language or belonging to the same religion may form in-groups. There are typically regionally oriented subgroups formed on the basis of states, districts, towns, and villages from which people's families originated. Within the group, Indians are quite informal and friendly. People frequently drop in without prior appointments and stay for meals without formal invitation.

Given this emphasis on the in-group, it is not surprising that foreign firms have a difficult time establishing subsidiaries in India. It takes approximately 30 days for an Indian to finalize the paperwork that allows his or her firm to operate in India; until very recently, it took a foreign firm 12 to 18 months to complete the task of establishing an Indian subsidiary and perhaps another 12 months to get permission to export. Given the infamous necessity of bribing government and business managers in India to pave the way for a more timely completion of this task, some Western firms have decided that the result is not worth the effort. Other foreign firms that had operated subsidiaries in India found the experience so frustrating that they closed them down and left the country. Still others had their businesses nationalized during Mrs. Gandhi's reforms of the 1970s. However, as the pace of national economic development quickened during the 1980s, the business environment gradually changed for the better.

Even some relatively small foreign firms have decided that the opportunity for profitable operations in India now outweighs the traditional disadvantages, and the Indian government is attempting to privatize the economy and attract foreign firms.

Geert Hofstede's (1980a) attitudinal survey of the cultural differences between some 40 countries is especially helpful in the case of India, which tends to cluster with those countries having a high degree of uncertainty avoidance. Indians tend to work with lifelong friends and colleagues and minimize risk-taking behavior. This orientation is consistent with the Hindu philosophy of life as an illusion, Indians' preoccupation with astrology, and their resignation to karma. India also falls with those countries characterized by large power distances and a collectivist or group orientation, as we would expect. India nearly clusters with the countries emphasizing individualism (21st out of 40 countries), an intermediate position that may reflect the nation's movement toward national and economic development. Finally, India has a high score on masculinity, which is consistent with the emphasis on male domination in Hinduism. Generally, the values described by Hofstede reflect a historical continuity and resilience of the Indian social system, despite the onslaught of foreign invasions, colonial rulers, and economic dislocations.

The hierarchical principle continues to be a source of stagnation in modern Indian institutions. Younger people have limited or no say in decision making. Persistent critical questioning or confrontations on issues necessary to effect change simply do not occur. Any conflict between intellectual conviction and developmental fate manifests itself in a vague sense of helplessness and impotent rage. Younger workers gradually resign themselves to waiting until they become seniors in their own right, free to enjoy the delayed gratification that age brings with it in Indian society. The apparent lack of control and ambition displayed by the participants at work is similar to the resignation of the world to the will of Shiva. The world responds to Shiva's rhythm, captive of its pace and unable to influence it.

The importance of honoring family and jati bonds leads to nepotism, dishonesty, and corruption in the commercial world. These are irrelevant abstract concepts; guilt and anxiety are aroused only when individual actions go against the principle of primacy of relationships, not when foreign standards of ethics and efficiency are breached. This gives rise to legendary tales of corrupt officials that are widely shared among travelers and businesspeople who have spent time in India.

Indian organizations have been shaped by colonial experiences that have bureaucratized them and polarized the positions of the rulers (managers) and the ruled (workers). As a consequence, the role of the manager tends to be viewed as that of an order giver or autocrat. In "Communicating Across Cultures," a popular management-training videotape produced by Copeland Griggs Productions (San Francisco), there is a telling vignette involving an American manager and one of his Indian subordinate managers. As a general rule, American managers perceive their role to be that of a problem solver or facilitator and attempt to involve subordinates in routine decisions (Adler, 1991). The American manager in this videotape attempted to use this style with his Indian subordinate, who wondered about his superior's competence and held him in some contempt for not being autocratic. The clear implication is that American managers must act more authoritatively in India than in the United States.

Some Indian managers who have seen this videotape immediately relate to the feelings of their compatriots: As many as 85% of Indian subordinates believe they work better under supervision (Kakar, 1971). This desire appears to lead to more layers of hierarchy in Indian-owned than American plants in India: 8 to 10 as against 5 to 7 (Negandhi & Prasad, 1975, p. 60). Further, there is a tendency for managers at the lower levels to make conservative decisions or deny responsibility. Disagreements are only infrequently solved by negotiations; one must go to authority above to seek solutions.

One source of rejuvenation and recreation for Indians is the many religious festivals held throughout the year. These festivals are usually associated with agricultural cycles or the rich mythology of India's past. In some regions, community festivals involve the active participation of not only Hindus but also members of other religions. Family bonds are reemphasized and strengthened through the joint celebration of religious festivals. The Indian sense of fun and play is given free rein during the festivities, which often include riddles, contests of strength, role reversals, and rebellious acts. Just as the Dance of Shiva is an expression of this joy and exuberance, festivals give Hindus an opportunity to express their feelings of devotion and happiness.

Religious raptures, possessions, and trances are common during Indian seasonal festivals. This is a structured and sometimes highly formalized phenomenon that enriches the consciousness of the individual and the group. There are also the attendant dangers of degeneration into hysterical mob psychology that Indian history has witnessed many times. Festivals allow the discharge of intense emotion that is otherwise submerged in a network of reciprocity and caste relations, but they also can be used to reestablish order. In this sense, festivals mirror the activity, relapse, and reordering of the cosmos that is the result of the Dance of Shiva. But just as the dancer cannot help dancing, the celebrant is not always capable of restraining his or her religious fervor.

Memorials to the grand line of India's "modern gods"—Mahatma Gandhi, Jawaharlal Nehru, and now Indira Gandhi—are as much the objects of pilgrimages as any temple or festival. Indira Gandhi was killed by her own trusted Sikh bodyguards just five months after she ordered the storming of the Golden Temple at Amritsar by the Indian army to dislodge Sikh rebels. Her home in New Delhi is now a museum and shrine visited by thousands daily. The spot in her garden where she was gunned down is bracketed by two soldiers; her bullet-ridden *sari* (dress) is on display inside. Crowds gather before these, and many people weep. Another Indian example is that of N. T. Rama Rao, a former movie star and chief minister of the state of Andhra Pradesh from 1983 to 1989. Rama Rao acted in leading roles in more than 320 films with mythical, historical, and folkloric themes. Among the masses, Rama Rao was associated with the qualities of the gods he played, and when he gave up his movie career to establish a new political party, he was immediately voted into office. The fact that his party's radical Hindu fundamentalist policies sometimes caused strife within society is not inconsistent with the concurrently constructive and destructive nature of the Dance of Shiva.

The favorite pastime of Indians is watching movies, either at movie theaters or by renting videos from the shops that have sprung up all over the country, and today India is the second largest producer of films in the world. Movies that draw on images and symbols from traditional themes are dominant in popular Indian culture. They incorporate but go beyond the familiar repertoire of plots from traditional theater. Films appeal to an audience so diverse that they transcend social and spatial categories. The language and values from popular movies have begun to influence Indian ideas of the good life and the ideology of social, family, and romantic relationships. Robert Stoller's (1975) definition of fantasy—"[the] protector from reality, concealer of truth, restorer of tranquility, enemy of fear and sadness, and cleanser of the soul" (p. 55)—includes terms that are equally attributable to the illusory nature of the Dance of Shiva, and it is easy to understand why films play such a major role in Indian recreation and rejuvenation.

Summing Up

India is the heart of Asia, and Hinduism is a convenient name for the nexus of Indian thought. It has taken 1,000 to 1,500 years to describe a single rhythm of its great pulsation as described by the Mahabharata. By invoking the image and meaning of the Dance of Shiva and drawing parallels between this legendary act of a Hindu deity and many of the main influences of traditional Indian life, we have attempted to communicate the essence of India's society in this chapter.

It is not always possible to identify a nicely logical or easily understandable basis for many of the contradictions that exist in Indian society, just as it is difficult to explain the existence of racism, sexism, and other forms of intolerance and injustice in Western countries. In India, the philosophy of life and the mental structure of its people come not from a study of books but from tradition (Munshi, 1965, p. 148). However much foreign civilization and new aspirations might have affected the people of India, the spiritual nutrient of Hindu philosophy has not dried up or decayed (Munshi, 1965, p. 148); within this tradition, the role of the Dance of Shiva, described below, is accepted by all Hindus:

> Shiva rises from his rapture and, dancing, sends through inert matter pulsing waves of awakening sound. Suddenly, matter also dances, appearing as a brilliance around him. Dancing, Shiva sustains the world's diverse phenomena, its creation and existence. And, in the fullness of time, still dancing, he destroys all forms—everything disintegrates, apparently into nothingness, and is given new rest. Then, out of the thin vapor, matter and life are created again. Shiva's dance scatters the darkness of illusion (*lila*), burns the thread of causality (*karma*), stamps out evil (*avidya*), showers grace, and lovingly plunges the soul into the ocean of bliss (*ananda*). (Coomaraswamy, 1924/1969, p. 66)

India will continue to experience the range of good and bad, happiness and despair, creation and destruction. Through it all, its people will continue their journey toward moksha, or salvation from humans' worldly concerns. Hindu philosophy is the key to understanding India and how a nation of such diversity manages to bear its immense burdens while its people seem undeterred and filled with inner peace and religious devotion.

And through it all, Shiva dances on.

16

American Football

This is spectacular! There must be at least 300 performers on the field, each with a flag and a lavish smile, all synchronized to the slightest move. The sun is glittering on the dancers' shiny clothes, and the wind is dancing with the flags to the beat of the drums and the sounds of the horns. The sky is clear except for a Good Year blimp circling high above the stadium where the Washington Redskins play their home football games. The fans are so responsive that they react spontaneously to anything and everything that occurs. They cheer the cheerleaders! They cheer the announcer! They cheer other fans! They even cheer the beer man! These fans are seriously committed to having a good time at the football game this Sunday afternoon. The crowd seems to be homogeneous; fans are wearing the same colors, supporting the same team, and hoping for the same outcome. Yet every fan has added his or her own personal touch to this weekly extravaganza. That man over there has painted his face with the team's colors. This younger guy in front has a huge banner with a witty message that indicates his frustration with the coach. A couple on the left are dressed as an Indian chief and his squaw, manifesting their appreciation and relish for the team's name. Everybody is eating, yet no one is particularly rapt in this food feast. They are just continuously munching and crunching while essentially doing something else.

The cheerleaders gather on one side of the field and intensify their dance routines. The music is suddenly blasted, shaking one's body. A bomb—yes, a bomb—explodes on the field, igniting a thunderous roar from the crowd. Smoke fills the air, and the middle part of the field is virtually concealed. As the smoke clears, one seems to detect a car on a podium right on the 50-yard line. Yes, it is a car. Now that the view is clear, one can see a Honda standing gallantly on a wide podium surrounded by dancers and models. The Honda jingle is played on the stadium's loudspeakers, the crowd is singing along, and then the announcer proudly proclaims Honda as a sponsor of this week's game. Just as the announcer ordains, the reliable Honda Civic is driven away followed by the dancers who are still persistently frolicking and prancing in a marketing celebration.

After the sponsor of this game is announced (and never before), the stage is set for the actual game of football. A sport that captures many of the central values of American society, football has steadily become an integral component of the community: Friday night high school football games played throughout the United States, Saturday afternoon college games, and professional games watched avidly in person or on television are all part of the American landscape. Even becoming a cheerleader is highly valued, and the actions taken to influence such an outcome are legendary, including those of one Texas mother who planned the assassination of the mother of her daughter's rival for a coveted position on the junior high cheerleading squad.

In the United States, football is not only a sport but also an assortment of common beliefs and ideals; indeed, football is a set of collective rituals and values shared by one dynamic society. The outlandish speed, the constant movement, the high degree of specialization, the consistent aggressiveness, and the intense competition in football, particularly professional football, all typify American culture.

Football is a team sport, yet the individual is glorified and celebrated. The extent of individualism in football seems to be unsurpassed in any other team sport. All of the major trophies in football are named after individuals who have contributed to the sport: The Heisman Award, the Vince Lombardi Bowl, and many other trophies extol the individual. In professional football, every player has a particular role to play. The play's success depends on how well all of the players perform, yet there is frequently one player who exerts extra and unusual effort. This distinguished player is seen as making the play happen and receives most of the accolades for doing so.

Professional football teams are actually multimillion-dollar corporations subdivided into departments and divisions, each with a large, highly specialized staff. Each member of this football "organization" has one highly specialized task. Each squad has its own coach or coaches, and there are also medics, trainers, psychiatrists, statisticians, technicians, outfit designers, marketing consultants, and social workers with specific duties and assignments. There is even a person assigned to carry the coach's headphone wire throughout the game so that he will not trip on it! Professional football epitomizes perfection for many Americans. The plays in football are complex and precisely executed athletic routines; the players' movements and maneuvers are designed to achieve a high level of physical perfection; and the National Football League (NFL), in general, embodies all that is impeccable and optimal in the American mind: profits, fame, and glory.

There is a certain mystical appeal to professional athletes that frequently compels Americans to fantasize about becoming football players, who are judged to have it all by the community. Some Americans view football players as icons possessing superhuman traits. Sportswriter Thomas Boswell (1990) has made the following comments about the centrality of sports to American life; these are particularly appropriate for football:

> These days, sports may be what Americans talk about best. With the most knowledge. The most passion. . . . Not so long ago, such discussions . . . were couched in specifically religious terms. . . . Today, where would we reach first for material or metaphor to make such points to our children? Probably to sports. . . . In fact, sports has become central to what remains of our American sense of community. . . .
>
> In sum, great athletes in late 20th-century America have—without knowing it or wanting it—been put in something akin to the position mythic or religious figures occupied in other cultures and times. . . . They play the role of surrogates in our thinly veiled ethical conversations. (pp. 24, 26, 28, © 1990 The Washington Post, reprinted with permission)

Success or failure in football is a direct result of a team's efforts. In other words, failure can be avoided; it is up to the individual team to acquire success. Fans do not usually feel sorry for losing teams. Losers are generally forgotten and ridiculed, whereas winners are glorified and praised. Such reactions are in sharp contrast to those found in other countries (see, for example, Chapter 14).

Football is a ceremonial celebration of perfect movement. The finesse of the wide receiver who dances through space in a dramatic way to catch the ball, and the delicacy of the running back's movement when avoiding tackles suggest that the football player is also a dancer and not merely an athlete. In fact, dancing is the ceremonial countenance of football: Cheerleaders joyfully dance on the sidelines; players dance gracefully on the field, particularly after scoring a touchdown; and fans dance to the music played over the loudspeakers during halftime.

Professional football also embodies deep religious sentiments and a profound belief in the family. In the NFL, teams sometimes bring priests to conduct prayers before each game and after each victory; religious functions are frequently encouraged and planned by the teams' management; and coaches such as Joe Gibbs talk frequently about religion, how it has affected their lives, and how it relates to football.

The "families" within a single football team are the different groups of players forming a "squad," each of which is one family that includes a group of players with similar attitudes and traits. Each player relates primarily to his squad. There are three squads on every football team, each with its own distinguishable characteristics and values. The defensive squad is usually the most aggressive and violent. The offensive squad includes the higher-profile, higher-paid players. The special-teams squad is characterized by big plays and high intensity. It is amazing how players try to fit into each particular squad's culture, even to the extent of using outlandish nicknames such as the "Hogs" to describe themselves.

Professional football thus is a metaphor that describes and explains various critical aspects of American culture. In this chapter, the focus is on three fundamental aspects of football that form the basic components of the metaphor, namely, individualism and competitive specialization, huddling, and the ceremonial celebration of perfection.

Individualism and Competitive Specialization

Even though football's rules and regulations are constantly changing from one season to the other, the basic values and ideals of the sport have changed very slowly over the years. In American society, innovation and modification are encouraged and sought, but usually not when it comes to values and ideals. American values, like those of football, have developed rather slowly and few radical shifts in ideals have taken place over the past two centuries. Equality of opportunity, independence, initiative, and self-reliance are some of the values that have remained as basic American ideals throughout history. All are expressive of a high degree of individualism. In fact, in Hofstede's (1980a) 40-nation study of cultural values, the United States ranked first on individualism. Those same ideals are elementary in professional football and have been so over the years.

In addition, competitive specialization, both for individuals and the groups in which they participate, appears to be the most evident feature of American life. Generally speaking, the notion of "specializing to compete" is the principal ideological ideal that Americans adhere to, practice, safeguard, and promote worldwide. Competitive specialization is the tool with which Americans tend to tackle life's main challenges. This tool is often serviced and maintained with high levels of emotional intensity and aggressiveness. From this perspective, it is not surprising that most Americans, when asked what they do, immediately describe their occupation or profession, unlike the Japanese, who tend to respond with the name of the company in which they work (see Chapter 14).

Similarities between real life in the United States and a professional football game are astounding, especially within the warlike atmosphere that pervades this sport. Football closely parallels the actions that take place in extroverted and sometimes even belligerent American society. According to the Myers-Briggs Personal Interest Inventory, which is the most widely used personality scale in the United States, 75% of Americans are extroverted and aggressive in personal relations (see Keirsey & Bates, 1978). Although such extroversion is in large measure a positive feature of American life (Barnlund, 1989), the United States leads most, if not all, countries in terms of indicators that profile the negative aspects of extroversion and aggressiveness. For example, the rate of incarceration in the United States is far higher than that of any other nation: 426 per 100,000. The next highest rate is 333 for South Africa, and for Japan it is only 45 (LaFraniere, 1991).

Americans recognize instinctively the link between life in the United States and what happens on the football field. Violence and aggressiveness are part of football's appeal to American society, and they both relate football to actual life. Aggressiveness, which is often interpreted as energy and intense motivation, is encouraged in the United States. Analogously, aggressiveness is a celebrated characteristic in football. The teams compete with one another, players on the same team compete for starting positions, and even fans compete for better tickets.

This type of individual competition and aggressiveness seems to be particularly suited to the United States. Richard Hofstadter (1955) graphically describes why social Darwinism—or the so-called philosophy of the survival of the fittest individual—appealed to Americans at the turn of the 20th century:

> With its rapid expansion, its exploitative methods, its desperate competition, and its peremptory rejection of failure, post-bellum America was like a vast human caricature of the Darwinian struggle for existence and survival of the fittest. Successful business entrepreneurs apparently accepted almost by instinct the Darwinian terminology which seemed to portray the conditions of their existence. (p. 44)

This viewpoint was cogently and persuasively championed by Russell H. Conwell, the first president of Temple University and a minister of the Methodist church. Starting in 1861, he delivered his famous "Acres of Diamonds" speech that linked social Darwinism to religion more than 4,000 times:

> I say you ought to be rich; you have no right to be poor.... I must say that you ought to spend some time getting rich. You and I know that there are some things more valuable than money; of course, we do. Ah, yes.... Well does the man know who has suffered that there are some things sweeter and holier and more sacred than gold. Nevertheless, the man of common sense also knows that there is not any one of those things that is not greatly enhanced by the use of money. Money is power; money has powers; and for a man to say, "I do not want money," is to say, "I do not wish to do any good to my fellowmen." It is absurd thus to talk. It is absurd to disconnect them. This is a wonderfully great life, and you ought to spend your time getting money, because of the power there is in money.
>   Greatness consists not in holding some office; greatness really consists in doing some great deed with little means, in the accomplishment of vast purposes from the private ranks of life; this is true greatness. (in Burr, 1917, pp. 414-415)

Perhaps the best contemporary indication of this emphasis on individualism and competition can be found in the area of the compensation for chief executive officers (CEOs) of U.S. corporations. Between 1991 and 1992, there was a 56% jump in such compensation, and to be in 1992's "Top 10," a CEO had to make more than $22.8 million. Moreover, the gap between the CEO and others in the U.S. corporation is widening significantly: In 1960, CEOs averaged $190,000 in total compensation, which was 41 times what a factory worker made. By 1992, the comparable figure was 157. No other nation comes close to such disparities. This was too much competitive individualism even for the editorial writers at *Business Week*, ordinarily a strong advocate of business positions, especially because the link between CEO total compensation and firm performance is weak ("Executive Pay," 1993).

As this discussion implies, competition seems to be more than a means to an end in the United States and apparently has become a major goal itself. Just as more than half the rules and regulations in professional football deal with protecting and enhancing competition in the league, so U.S. antitrust laws and regulations were essentially created to safeguard competition and equality of opportunity for individuals and groups, and these are deeply rooted in American ideals and values that trace back to European immigrants to the United States. These immigrants represented diverse groups who were basically at war with one another in Europe: The English did not like the Irish, the Germans had problems with the Poles, and so on. Although these hostilities and negative feelings were intense when the immigrants came to the United States, they were not usually displayed through violence because the immigrants were tired of war and bloodshed. Rather these feelings manifested themselves in competition, specialization, and the division of labor. Each geographical area in the United States specialized in a particular category of production: the Northeast in manufacturing, the Midwest in agriculture, and the West in cattle. Even within parts of the country that specialized in agriculture, there was further specialization. The more fertile northern region of the United States (states such as Idaho) specialized in farming crops different than those of the less fertile (but more populated) South. The distinct, highly specialized immigrant communities were still competing with one another economically, but their use of the law of comparative advantage propelled each to focus its efforts on one particular domain of production in which it excelled.

Thus the communities were involved in a new kind of war, one that once and for all was designed to settle the score between Protestant and Catholic, Pole and Jew, English and Irish, German and Dane. Competition prevailed, and the battles of the Middle Ages were refought in the United States, although with new specialized weapons and for new competitive endowments. Each community frequently believed that it carried the burden of proving its own superiority through bigger dams, larger statues, more crops, and greater wealth. The legacy of competition continues to flourish in American society today, although with more legitimacy.

European immigrants, although distinct and dissimilar, shared deep suspicions of authority. They assumed that authority impedes competition and foils specialization, both for individuals and groups. Their main reason for fleeing Europe in the first place was corrupt and oppressive authority or government. Systems of checks and balances were developed in the United States primarily to protect the people from rulers who might control the economy, dictate religion, or dominate political power. Similarly, the NFL is the only league in the world that has used a system of checks and balances during a sporting match. Until recently, there were two sets of referees, one on the field equipped with whistles and flags and the other in a review booth equipped with a videocassette recorder and a color television. If one team did not like a call made by a field referee, it could appeal to the review judges who watched the play on video and made a final judgment.

Technological development is a catalyst to competitive specialization. Technology is the ingredient that provides competitive specialization with the efficiency required in an intensely capitalist society such as the United States. Similarly, technological development plays a key role in the NFL. The weight machines that professional football players use, the cameras and satellites that follow them, and the specialized equipment they wear are integral to the American fascination with tools and machines.

The reason behind this fascination with tools is quite simple: The United States has historically been "short" on labor and "long" on raw materials. To use their abundant raw materials, Americans had to substitute machinery and equipment for unskilled labor. Influenced by the success of their highly mechanized industry in the late 1800s, Americans were shrewdly induced to use the power of machines and technology. To Americans, technology was empirically proven to stimulate growth and success, and their dependence on machines grew heavier with every increase in the number of American patented inventions.

Today, every American seems to carry a gadget of some sort to aid some kind of task; in this way, Americans are quite similar to the Japanese. Look at the football player! He wears a helmet, shoulder pads, neck pads, shin guards, ankle pads, and thigh guards to protect himself; he wraps antistatic nonadhesive tape around his wrists and fingers for support; and he wears state-of-the-art synthetic-rubber shoes for artificial turf or evenly spiked fiber-saturated shoes for grass fields. Then each type of player has his own distinctive equipment: Receivers wear grip-aligned synthetic gloves to catch the football; linebackers wear tinted-glass face masks (shatterproof, of course) to protect their eyes from glare; and cornerbacks wear ultralight reinforced plastic back pads to maximize their speed. Even the coaches have their own specialized gadgets: They use sensitive cellular devices to communicate with the statistician. And even though some sports traditionalists find it hard to believe, some teams are researching a cellular microheadphone to be installed in the quarterback's helmet so that he can hear the coach's instructions.

Americans are typically not influenced greatly by extended kinship or family groups; it is the nuclear family that is the locus of activity and identification. In many ways, American families are like the three squads in football mentioned earlier. A football player relates primarily to his squad and only secondarily to the team. Similarly, Americans relate to society through nuclear families and not kinship groups. As a general rule, American children are taught to relate essentially to their nuclear family at a young age; they learn through the example of their parents that the nuclear family is the integral part of their lives. Americans normally encourage independence, self-reliance, and initiative in their children. A child is raised to believe that a rich, healthy, happy, and fulfilling life can be attained by almost anybody as long as one is willing to follow certain steps and procedures. The American egalitarian spirit is nourished in a child and accentuated in his mind by his eager-to-make-the-child-successful parents. As a result, when that child has matured into the adult stage, he or she tends to believe that success (wealth, health, and happiness) is an individual's responsibility and duty. Any individual who is poor, unhealthy, or unhappy is frequently viewed by Americans as a person who failed in availing him- or herself of the opportunities offered.

As Stewart and Bennett (1991) show, Americans believe in equality, but only equality of opportunity; personal successes and failures are attributed directly to the individual. Many, if not most, Americans tend to see poverty and misery as self-induced, at least to a large extent. Stewart and Bennett also point out that this makes life difficult for the average American, because he or she must constantly achieve in order to meet such high expectations. Americans are not honored for past achievements but for what they are currently accomplishing; in this sense, their personalities tend to be constantly in a state of flux and evolution.

One major result of this orientation is that American managers are generally open to change and are constantly introducing new programs with which they can identify and for which they can claim much of the credit; it is not sufficient for them to build only on the programs of their predecessors (Kanter, 1979). However, they tend to jettison programs just as quickly, and the United States is famous both for the fads that it introduces and the short-term orientation of its managers.

Huddling

There is another characteristic that differentiates football from any other sport in the world: the huddle (how offensive teams group before each play to call a certain plan into action). Within the huddle are different players from diverse backgrounds and with various levels of education. All have agreed that the only way to accomplish a certain task is to put differences aside and cooperate objectively to achieve a certain goal. After the game, every player returns to his own world, living his own life in his own unique way. That is the essence of the melting pot: a diversified group of people who temporarily forget their differences to achieve a common goal. As early as 1832, Alexis de Tocqueville drew attention to this facet of the American perspective:

> These Americans are the most peculiar people in the world. You'll not believe it when I tell you how they behave. In a local community in their country a citizen may conceive of some need which is not being met. What does he do? He goes across the street and discusses it with his neighbor. Then what happens? A committee comes into existence and then the committee begins functioning on behalf of that need. And you won't believe this but it is true. All of this is done without reference to any bureaucrat. All of this is done by the private citizens on their own initiative. (in Miller & Hustedde, 1987, p. 91)

And this melting pot is becoming even more diverse: Between 1980 and 1990, the percentage of the population of Hispanic origin increased from 3.0% to 3.9%; the comparable figures for Asians were 1.5% and 2.9%; for African-Americans, 11.7% and 12.1%; and for European-Americans, 83.1% and 80.3%.

Can a football team afford the luxury of eliminating the huddle? In most cases, no. However, the 1991 Super Bowl, possibly the best one of all, featured the Buffalo Bills, who did not huddle after each play, and the New York Giants, who did. It was a close game that was decided only in the last minutes. The no-huddle Bills were able to use this approach only because of the expertise of their outstanding quarterback, Jim Kelly. Once again an individual was able to shine within the group context. Still, the final result was that the huddling Giants won. Although there is no final verdict on this issue, it seems that all teams, including the Buffalo Bills, will take advantage of the huddle, at least sometimes. Similarly, most, if not all, groups and organizations in the United States use huddling to handle their problems and achieve their objectives.

The American concept of huddling to coordinate activities is quite different from that of the Japanese sense of community within the organization. The Japanese normally socialize with co-workers after work, and if a major problem occurs, they will sometimes go off-site for an evening of drinking, dinner, informal camaraderie, and, finally, discussion of the problem at hand and how to address it. Periodically, they will repeat such sessions until the long-term problem is solved. Americans, on the other hand, tend to huddle together in a business meeting specifically to address and solve the problem at hand, after which they scatter to complete other work-oriented activities. If additional meetings are necessary, they are normally conducted in the same fashion.

As Daniel Boorstin (1965) has so persuasively shown, the lone cowboy or lone frontiersman is a poor metaphor for the United States. Rather, as adventuresome Americans moved westward to pursue a better life, they came together frequently to form temporary associations or teams to solve specific problems. However, given the rapid mobility of American society—a characteristic still dominant today—relationships among members of these groups tended to be cooperative but only superficially friendly; there was no time to develop deep friendships. The United States is the classic "doing" society whose members are primarily interested in building and accomplishing goals; the focus in the United States is on accomplishing present goals to ensure a safe future; little attention is given to past activities and history. Europeans and Asians frequently complain that it is difficult to establish deep, personal relationships with Americans. As a general rule, Americans intensely commit themselves to a group effort—but only for a specified and frequently short period of time. Unlike many Europeans, who live, work, and die within 30 miles of their birthplaces, Americans frequently huddle in temporary groups as they change jobs, careers, geographical areas, and even spouses throughout their lives.

In football, the huddle divides the game into smaller sets of tasks that when accomplished successfully lead to the fulfillment of victory. The game itself is divided into independent jobs that are separated by short periods of position reassessment and fueled by continuous tactics. The huddle phenomenon in American culture—meeting together to subdivide a large task into smaller related jobs that are accomplished one at a time—is illustrated in the way that Americans tackle problems. Any intricacy is broken down to smaller issues addressed one at a time. Americans tend to believe that any problem can be solved, as long as the solution process comprises a specific number of steps to follow and questions to answer. Likewise in football, no matter how complicated a situation may be, teams are convinced that they can overcome the complexities through a standardized planning process.

The American System of Manufacturing (ASM), a system that developed as a result of Frederick Taylor's work on time and motion study at the end of the 19th century, is the "huddle" of American economic history. It reflects how the American mind is tuned. Just as the football huddle allows a standardized planning process for a specific situation, the ASM allows a standardized manufacturing process for different products.

The ASM emphasizes the simplicity of design, the standardization of parts, and large-scale output. Americans introduced the concept and use of mass production as a direct consequence of the intense use of machinery. Whereas a group of German workers took one week to masterfully produce 10 high-quality shotguns in the 1800s, the same number of American workers, with the help of standardized parts and ready-to-assemble components, produced in one day many more shotguns at a cheaper price. American products throughout history have been less known for their elegance than for their utility, practicality, and cheapness. The American culture is one that respects machines and considers them critical to civilization. In fact, one of the United States' major contributions to the development of society has been its emphasis on ingenious tools and giant machines.

American society directly relates standardization to ranking of individuals. There is a great dependency on ranking via a standardized process (often based on statistical analysis) in the United States. Usually there is no time to judge people subjectively. Stewart and Bennett (1991) point out that many "being" or high-context societies rank or rate employee performance in an absolute sense to save face; for example, Jones is a superior or good performer. However, Americans in their "doing" mode typically disagree with this approach and compare individuals to one another when evaluating performance. Standards are relative and not absolute, and an employee may well be replaced when someone else ranks higher than him or her. Even in an academic setting, students in the United States are evaluated and compared relative to one another. The student's grades are plotted on a "curve" of relative performance. Usually, this bell curve determines each student's final grade.

As might be expected, Americans normally want to know what the bottom line is so that they can objectively make a decision. This perspective is particularly disconcerting in U.S. schools and colleges where many students want to know only what will be on the final examinations. The egalitarian character of Americans and the fast pace of life necessitates one or another form of "standardized ranking" when assessing a certain situation.

Although most Americans consider mathematics boring and tedious, all forms of standardized ranking that involve figures and numbers are used. When ranking quarterbacks, for instance, the NFL standardizes the ranking process by defining different numerical categories, often called "numbers," that cover all aspects of the position. Each quarterback has certain numbers and figures ranging from "percentage of pass completions" to "interceptions over touchdowns" to "number of yards passed per game." The quarterback's livelihood depends on those numbers. To negotiate a raise, a quarterback must "improve" his numbers, and when a quarterback is benched it is often because of "unsatisfactory" numbers.

Numbers have an immense impact on the decision-making process in American society, whether in financial market analyses, college recruitment programs, or political decisions. American politicians are very sensitive to polls (which are nothing but numbers), even to the extent that there is always a statistician on any major political staff. Similarly, the dependence on aptitude tests is crucial in the U.S. education system. Academic institutions normally require that students take one or another standardized test. Even though the admission decision is based on a larger number of criteria, the aptitude test score is extremely influential. Just as a college football player's numbers are the arguments on which he is judged for professional recruitment, so the student's aptitude test scores frequently become the decisive factors for college acceptance or rejection.

This whole notion of standardized ranking evolves from the American perception of time, which is not thought of as a continuous and abundant commodity. Frequently there is no time for conducting any specialized or personalized tests when judging recruits. There is only one standard test that is to be taken once every so often because, naturally, time is limited. Analogously, the sport of football is based on the notion that time is limited, and teams are continually trying to beat the clock.

There is almost always a time limit in the United States, and the huddle in football reflects this supposed time shortage. There is a specific time limit for the huddle before each play. One often watches football players rushing into or out of the huddle in a quick attempt to conserve time. Similarly, Americans constantly have a stressful feeling that time is running out, and therefore they must talk quickly, walk quickly, eat quickly, and even rest quickly. When eating, Americans sometimes attempt to consume the largest quantities of food in the shortest time possible. Where else in the world can a mere human being eat a "double whopper with cheese," accompanied by massive amounts of potatoes and a cup of soda so big one cannot lift it, in fewer than 10 minutes?

When talking, an American has mastered the art of developing acronyms for time-consuming words such as *economics* ("econ" for short)! The concept of extended formal names—for example, Herr Professor Doktor—is not only anathema to egalitarian Americans, but also runs against the grain of their time-saving efforts. Any combination of words that forms a name or a title of some sort is promptly diminished to a fewer number of letters to save time when saying them. The National Football Conference and the American Football League are never referred to as such but instead are efficiently called the NFC and the AFL. The grand old party is GOP, madam is ma'am, President Kennedy is JFK, the federal bank is the "Fed," *amplifier* becomes "amp," and, best of all, "Howdy" is the time-conscious way to say "How do you do?"

Because of the American notion of the scarcity of time, when improvident news events occur, especially scandals such as Oliver North's adventures or Marion Barry's sex- and drug-related mischief, they are vigorously discussed and energetically debated in American society—but not for long. Americans do not have much time to dedicate to one news event. As Edward and Mildred Hall (1990) have shown, Americans are monochronic, doing one activity at a time rather than several activities. After intensely analyzing one major event for a short period, Americans become distracted and begin to focus on a new event.

Time is also limited in the United States because there are so many things to do in one's lifetime. The society develops technologically at horrendous speed, and it is difficult to keep up. One must be continuously on the move. This is the United States: There is little time for contemplating or meditating. Ideally, one succeeds at an early age, and success in the United States is often impersonal and lonely. Football provides that sense of belonging and the brotherhood that success lacks, and the huddle is the ideal time-efficient approach for handling problems either in football or at work. The popular belief that the top is often lonely, however, does not inhibit most Americans from pursuing higher levels of achievement because life, they believe, is a test of self-reliance and independence.

Ceremonial Celebration of Perfection

The new immigrants had a somewhat utopian vision for the American land. The ideals that the American concept symbolized were, and still are, considered sacred and perfect. Unlike other major societies, the sources of American values are human-written materials that are believed to be inviolate and perfect, namely, the U.S. Constitution and the Declaration of Independence. American history is an ongoing battle designed to preserve these "perfect" values and utopian ideals as incarnated in these documents. One thus can understand why the United States had a utopian image in the minds of immigrants. Charles Sanford (1961) encapsulates the essence of this image in the following way:

> The Edenic image, as I have defined it, is neither a static agrarian image of cultivated nature nor an opposing image of the wilderness, but an imaginative complex which, while including both images, places them in a dynamic relationship with other values. Like true myth or story, it functions on many levels simultaneously, dramatizing a people's collective experience within a framework of polar opposites. The Edenic myth, it seems to me, has been the most powerful and comprehensive organizing force in American culture. (p. vi)

For centuries, the American continent was "utopianized" by people fleeing persecution, subjection, tyranny, and oppression. America, the concept, was actually an attempt to create utopia. America, the value, encompassed all that is perfect: strength, wealth, philanthropy, family, children, and glory. This is utopia. Analogously, football personifies that unblemished portrait of utopia, and professional football is a symbol of that perfect American utopia.

The Declaration of Independence and the Constitution, the basic written sources of American values, however, were authorized by individual human beings, rather than gods, prophets, sacred apostles, or holy emperors. From this fact one can understand why America ceremonially glorifies the individual. The common belief in the United States is that the individual is capable of anything he or she wants to accomplish. Individual achievements, whether earning a degree or scoring the highest number of field goals for one game, are considered precious human deeds and are entitled to commemoration in one type of ceremony or another. Ceremonial celebrations of more significant accomplishments of American individuals, such as winning the Democratic party presidential nomination or the Super Bowl, automatically reflect the American pursuit of perfection and utopia.

When retired NFL players are selected to the professional football's Hall of Fame, the most prestigious honor in professional football, the induction ceremonies celebrate both the individuals selected and the country that bestowed such perfection. There is a high sense of nationalism in professional football that is ceremonially reflected before the start of each football game. The national anthem is played and sometimes sung by a celebrity, and the fans proudly sing along with him or her; the flag procession precedes every football game, and representatives from the Army, Navy, and Air Force carry the American flag and assemble on the field. Apparently, nothing is worth celebrating more and nothing is more perfect than the United States. Sporting events in general, and professional football games in particular, are in essence ceremonies that celebrate how perfect teams can be, how spectacular the nation is, and how well the system works.

The celebration of nationalism is evident not only in football but in most, if not all, areas of socializing in the United States. On television, which Americans watch while socializing, many commercials are tied directly to nationalism, and innumerable marketable products or services are related to the national culture. In general, Americans perceive the United States to be young, successful, and prestigious. By associating products with the nation, marketers aim to relate the youthfulness, beauty, and sex appeal of the United States to their own products. For example, a Miller beer commercial touts the beer as "made the American way" and consumed by proud U.S. product supporters. The jingle is accompanied by pictures of smiling

American faces and happy American children, all of whom are joined in a dramatic celebration of the perfect beer brewed by the perfect country. In the background, and throughout the commercial, the American flag flies gracefully, symbolizing flawlessness. There is basically nothing stated about this beer other than that it is pure American. That is enough for many American consumers. The utopian American character rubs on success, popularity, and prestige.

Sometimes nationalism generates ethnocentric behavior in the United States. In football, for instance, the Super Bowl is referred to as the "world championship" despite the fact that only American teams compete. To many Americans, the United States is the world, or at least the best part of it. The globe revolves around the United States, and the poorer members of the international community are protected by and fed with American remittances. Nations of the world must therefore follow the American course and act the American way or else suffer the consequences of failure.

Consequently, U.S. economic success and military might often induce egotistical reactions to international events among its citizens. These narcissistic feelings are frequently evoked by news media's persistent portrayal of and fascination with the world's disasters and mishaps. To the American media, "no news is good news," and thus the outside world is often reported as volatile, violent, and miserable. The positive features of foreign countries are rarely highlighted by U.S. media. Because the average American is constantly bombarded with news of famines, wars, violence, and political turmoil from the outside world, he or she is frequently not aware of the pleasant and fascinating features of other nations. This ethnocentrism is so extreme that many Americans believe that the United States is the safest and most prosperous country in the world, even when the facts do not support such a conclusion, as we discussed earlier.

The American utopia is not complete without the practice of religion. More than half of the American population attends church regularly. Only Ireland, with 87% of its population regularly attending church, and perhaps a few other countries such as Poland surpass the United States in this measure. There are more than 4,000 churches in the United States that appeal to all different types of religious beliefs. Although the country is primarily Christian (30% of the population is Protestant and 20% Roman Catholic), there are many other denominations. Also, billions of dollars are spent on church-related activities. For example, it is often said with some justification that the Vatican would be in grave financial difficulties if American Catholics decreased significantly their level of financial support.

In football, the ceremonial pursuit of perfection is blessed by priests who pray for individual teams before and after matches, as noted earlier. Just as team managers try to relate to and identify with the society through religious ceremonies, so Americans participate in religious activities to belong socially to a group. For the early immigrants who left their families and possessions, religion became the basic element that reestablished their social life in the United States. To these new immigrants, moving to a different society entailed rootlessness and a weakened ethnic identification. Religion thus became a means of identification and belonging for Americans, and churches and religious organizations frequently formed political pressure groups to achieve goals that helped their members and that were compatible with their beliefs.

By way of summarizing this discussion of American culture, it is possible to relate this football metaphor to Hofstede's (1980a) four dimensions of culture. Of the 40 countries in Hofstede's original study, the United States ranked first on the importance that its respondents attached to individualism. The United States also clustered with those countries that accepted and even relished a high degree of uncertainty and risk in everyday life and that manifested a high degree of masculinity or aggressive and materialistic orientation to life. Also, Americans demonstrated a preference for informality, low power distance between individuals and groups, and weak hierarchical authority. These findings are not surprising and help to confirm the generalizations put forth in this chapter.

The United States is still viewed by many throughout the world as far better than the countries in which they live, if not necessarily as a utopia. It still attracts large numbers of immigrants who are willing to put up with the glaring problems of American cities because of the opportunities that are available to those who work hard and strive for success. When they arrive, they tend to experience a distinctive form of culture shock that occurs because of the interplay among individualism and competitive specialization, huddling, and the ceremonial celebration of perfection. Much of this culture shock is encapsulated in American common sayings and aphorisms. We end this chapter by highlighting a few of them:

- Life is just a bowl of cherries.
- Let's get together and work on this problem.

- It's lonely at the top.
- Hi! How are you? (asked as one walks past another without any desire for or expectation of an answer)
- You're from Nigeria? Is that a city in Germany?
- Gotta run, man. Maybe we'll talk later.
- America—Love it or leave it, buster!
- Where there's a will, there's a way.
- One step at a time.
- It's never too late.

PART III

EXTENDING
AND INTEGRATING
THE CONCEPTS

17

The Chinese Family Altar

When a Westerner visits a traditional Buddhist temple in Asia, he sees different images of the Buddha such as the Reclining Buddha, the Sitting Buddha, and the Walking Buddha. However, in a Chinese Buddhist temple, these Buddha images are supplemented by a formidable group of statues that seem to represent warriors who are massive in size and strength. These fierce-looking warriors frequently have rough-looking beards and moustaches, and they carry large swords. It is a surprise for many Westerners, then, to learn that these "warriors" are actually representations of important people within extended kinship and family groups, and that they actually lived in Chinese villages 1,000 or 2,000 years ago. The position of honor that these figures have in the temple is but one demonstration of the importance that the Chinese place on the family and kinship group, even to the extent of allowing them to be situated alongside the Buddha images.

Throughout this book, we have given prominent attention to the nation as our unit of analysis. However, as Ronen and Shenkar (1985) demonstrate, it is possible to cluster countries into groups that are similar to one another in terms of language, religion, and geographical closeness. In this book we have used the nation as our unit of analysis, as we found it very difficult to identify metaphors that were appropriate for groups of nations.

The Chinese, however, represent one ethnic group for which one metaphor is appropriate, regardless of the nation in which they reside. This does not seem to be true for other ethnic groups. Thus Joel Kotkin (1993) has described the major ethnic groups—expatriate Chinese, Japanese, Jews, English, and Asian Indians—who have achieved remarkable economic success outside their homelands. However, the metaphors for the non-Chinese groups as described in this book—kibbutzim and moshavim, the Dance of Shiva, the Japanese garden, and the traditional British house—do not apply fully when members of these groups become expatriates.

The importance of the family and kinship group cannot be overestimated for the Chinese, and the metaphor we have selected for the Chinese—the family altar—reflects this fact. One Taiwanese diplomat who lived in several countries had a family altar in Taiwan but carried drawings of his ancestors to whom he and his children prayed when he traveled; Amy Tan's (1991) bestselling novel *The Kitchen God's Wife* includes the concept in its title; many expatriate Chinese travel to their original homeland so that they can visit the burial places of their ancestors at least once in their lives, because in Confucianism living relatives have an obligation to tend such places on a regular basis if at all possible or at least to visit them; and the Chinese family name is traditionally given before the personal name, unlike the Western practice of mentioning the personal name first. These examples—and countless others are possible—indicate the prominent place that family and kinship groups hold in Chinese society.

Of course, some scholars may argue that other ethnic groups also are family oriented. However, Chinese society is neither individualistic nor collectivistic, as are other family-based ethnic groups, but is based on relations (Liang, 1974). Confucians, for example, feel that individuals have roles they must fulfill; in doing so, their individualism can enlarge and enrich them for the greater good of the family and kinship group. The relation-based system of the Chinese in which roles are differentiated is quite different from that of the more collectivist and nondifferentiated system of the Japanese, as Nakane (1973) has pointed out:

> In the Japanese system all members of the household are in one group under the head, with no specific rights according to the status of

individuals within the family. The Japanese family system differs from that of the Chinese system, where family ethics are always based on relationships between particular individuals such as father and son, brothers and sisters, parents and child, husband and wife, while in Japan they are always based on the collective group, i.e., members of a household, not on the relationship between individuals. (p. 14)

Hence the Chinese tend to take seriously their relations with others, whether inside or outside the kinship group. They have separate words for older brother, younger sister, and each aunt or uncle from each side of the family, and they tend to make lifelong friendships that are clearly demarcated from acquaintances. Still, similar to many other high-context ethnic groups, the Chinese usually spend a long time getting to know an individual before doing business with him or her. Other unique characteristics of the Chinese family system are described below.

In addition, like the Japanese and other group-oriented cultures, the Chinese tend to experience difficulty differentiating the individual from the group. There is no equivalent word for privacy in Chinese and some other languages that stress the importance of the group rather than the individual, such as Japanese and Arabic. In fact, the word *I* has negative connotations in Chinese and Japanese, as do many other related characters. From both the Chinese and Japanese perspectives, the individual exists or is someone only when he or she is a member of a group.

Chinese culture is closely associated with Confucianism, Taoism (pronounced "Dow-ism"), and, to a lesser extent, Buddhism. Because we already highlighted Buddhism in Chapter 15, we will treat only Confucianism and Taoism in this chapter, after which we will describe the Chinese altar and its three dimensions: roundness, which symbolizes the continuity and structural completeness of the family; harmony within the family and the broader society; and fluidity, or the capacity to change while maintaining solid traditions. We will then briefly describe the activities of 50 million expatriate Chinese and the countries in which they have been such important economic driving forces.

Confucianism and Taoism

Confucius died in 479 B.C., frustrated that he never was able to become a major advisor to any regional ruler in China. However, his ideas took hold in large part because of the vicious warfare that was occurring between these regional rulers, and his emphasis on forming tradition deliberately in accordance with China's idealized past period of great harmony had wide appeal.

Confucian thought is encapsulated in five terms, the first of which is *Jen*: human heartedness or the simultaneous feeling of humanity toward others and respect for oneself (see Smith, 1958, 1991). Second is *Chuntzu*, "the Superior Man," or someone who is fully adequate and poised to accommodate others as much as possible rather than selfishly acquire all that he can. The third is *Li*—propriety, or the way things should be done. For example, the five relationships involve the appropriate conduct that should occur between father and son, older and younger brother, husband and wife, older and younger friend, and ruler and subject. More specifically, Li reflects the importance that Confucius attached to the family, and it evolved from the earlier era of ancestor worship to include the concepts of filial piety and veneration of age. There is a second meaning of Li—ritual—and it is envisioned as encompassing all of a person's activities during his or her whole life.

Te is the fourth term, and it refers to the power by which men should be ruled, not by force but moral example. Finally, there is *Wen*, which accords a place of prominence to the arts as a means of peace and as an instrument of moral education.

The device for developing tradition deliberately was extreme social sensitivity, and this is still reflected in the Chinese concept of face. As discussed in Chapter 14, *face* is an unwritten set of rules by which people in society cooperate to avoid unduly damaging others' prestige and self-respect. In bargaining, for example, the winner should allow the loser some minor tactical reward, especially when all observers can ascertain the identity of the vanquished. If a father's business becomes bankrupt and he dies suddenly, frequently his sons will work to pay off the debt to maintain face for the family. When an individual loses face, he or she tends to adopt a stony or blank expression as if nothing has happened; generally, face is forfeited through loss of self-control or a display of frustration and anger (Bonavia, 1989, pp. 73-74).

Some experts have argued that Confucianism is not a traditional religion, because it has no concept of a personal God and only an amorphous concept of heaven or a shadowy netherworld in which ancestors live and help to guide the living. Thus the Chinese tend to focus on this world and not the next. David Bonavia (1989) aptly captures the essence of being Chinese in the following description, although he was primarily discussing modern China:

> The most determining feature of the Chinese people's attitude to the world around them is their total commitment to life as it is. . . . In this world view, all human activity—religion, sex, war—consists of functional acts aimed at achieving something. Only the arts are considered to have intrinsic value, and they are chiefly reflections of the real world or an imagined world, not abstract patterns. . . . Action must have a purpose, the Chinese feel; there is nothing ennobling about pain, and death is an infernal nuisance. . . . Most Chinese, seeing a Hindu holy man stick a knife through his cheeks or walk on coals, would conclude that he was either a fool or a fraud. . . . [T]he central concept of Chinese society is functionality. (pp. 56-57)

Taoism is usually considered the primary religion among the Chinese, whereas Confucianism relates to the manner in which an individual is to behave in society. This religion was supposedly created by Lao Tzu, who was born in 604 B.C., and its main tenets were outlined in one small book, *Tao Te Ching* (The Way and the Power).

Tao, or "the way," has three overlapping meanings. First, it can be known only through mystical insight. Second, it refers to the ordering principle behind the universe or all life, and it represents the rhythm and driving force of nature. Third, humans should order their lives to be in balance with the universe.

Power, the second element in the book's title, refers to the belief that a person gains power by leading a life that is in harmony with the dictates of the universe. This approach continues to shape the Chinese character and is manifested in the desire to achieve a state of serenity and grace.

The basic approach of life that is consonant with the universe is *wu wei* (creative quietude). It is simultaneous action and relaxation and letting behavior flow spontaneously. Creative quietude is never forcing or straining but seeking the empty spaces in life and nature and moving quietly and without confrontation through the avenues of least resistance.

Taoists reject all forms of self-assertiveness and competition and seek more of a union with nature and a simplicity of life than materialistic possessions. There is an extreme aversion to violence that verges on pacifism. Taoism also includes the traditional Chinese symbols of yin and yang, which connote that there are no clear dichotomies, but that all values and concepts are relative to the mind that entertains them. Thinking in yin and yang terms means seeing the universe as pairs of interacting opposites, such as shadowed and bright, decaying and growing, moonlit and sunlit, earthly and heavenly, and male and female. Whether something is classified as yin or yang depends not on its intrinsic nature but on the roles it plays in relation to other things, which is consistent with the relation-based system of the Chinese. Clayre (1985) expands on these ideas as follows:

> In relation to Heaven man may be classified as yin, but when paired with Earth he would be seen as yang. Heaven itself is the supreme embodiment of the yang aspects of the cosmos: ethereal, bright, active, generative, initiatory and masculine. Earth is seen as deeply yin: solid, dark, cool, quiescent, growth-sustaining, responsive and feminine. (p. 201)

Men and women are not seen as exclusively yang or yin: Each has a predominance of one aspect or the other, and the balance within and between them may change. The relation of the two elements is always changing, a continuous cycle where each may dominate in responsive sequence. This idea may have evolved from the annual cycle of growth and decay found in agricultural China, and in the rotation of day and night and annual seasons.

Taoists traditionally had little empathy for Confucianists, whom they viewed as pompous and ritualistic. A more fundamental difference is summarized by the Chinese themselves, who say that "Confucius roams within society, Lao Tzu wanders beyond." However, in many ways Taoism, Confucianism, and Buddhism are complementary, and it is commonly said that they are "the Three Faiths in One." Thus many Chinese accept Confucianism as a guide to daily living, have recourse to Taoist practitioners for ritual purifications and exorcisms, and employ Buddhist priests for funerals.

We have only sketched some of the major concepts and values that make up the Chinese value system, and there are wide divergences from it in many situations. Still, this value system has not been stamped out or radically changed for thousands of years as Mao Tse Tung and others would have liked. Instead, it has evolved slowly over time. Ambrose King (in Kotkin, 1993, p. 177) has pointed out that many of the 50 million expatriate Chinese have developed a culture of "rationalistic traditionalism, a combination of traditional filial and group virtues with a pragmatism shaped by the conditions of a new competitive environment." Similar to Italian Catholics who attend church only irregularly, these expatriate Chinese and even those living within the confines of China are more culturally than spiritually influenced by their three faiths.

In a similar manner, Chinese culture is closely linked to language. People in China's various regions are actually a mix from diverse ethnic origins who speak mutually unintelligible dialects. In south-eastern China, where Cantonese is the primary dialect, it is impossible to understand the dialect of northern China, which is Mandarin. Remarkably, all dialects of spoken Chinese can be written in the same way and understood by anyone, regardless of the pronunciation of words. Whereas the English language uses only 26 letters to represent all spoken sounds and written words, the Chinese language is a storehouse with more than 50,000 different symbols or logograms, each standing for a different word. Amazing feats of memory are required to master such a language, which tends to reinforce cultural values. This generalization is also valid for the Japanese language (see DeMente, 1990).

Roundness, Harmony, and Fluidity

The Chinese family altar is the cornerstone of family life for Chinese in many parts of the world. It is the tie that binds a dispersed family and serves as a focal point for viewing an extended family that includes the living, the dead, and those yet unborn. Although it may be thought of as a traditional and ancient aspect of Chinese society, and even as an anachronism in modern mainland China, the Chinese altar is helpful in providing insight into the values, attitudes, and behaviors of the Chinese.

The physical presence of the altar represents the family as a well-knit integrated unit. A house with two altars contains two families; a household with no altar usually considers itself part of another family, and its members will go to the house in which the altar resides for important rituals. In many parts of the world, the Chinese tend to live in family or kinship compounds that have several houses, and frequently each contains a family altar. The altar typically stands in the central room of the house opposite the principal door. Such altars are meant to be publicly seen: Many are visible from the street, and guests usually sit in front of them. There is normally an incense pot on the left side of the altar, because this is the position of honor for any of the animistic gods that the Chinese revere; the ancestral tablets are placed on the right side alongside their incense pot. Most of the altars have a backdrop that depicts some of the more popular deities. The newer, more prestigious backdrops are painted on glass in bright colors that glitter. Varying amounts of religious odds and ends, including written charms and souvenirs of visits to temples, also decorate the altar, and frequently a Buddha image also stands on it. The ancestral tablets affirm the idealized picture of the Chinese family as a patrilineal kinship group and commemorate its immediate patrilineal forebears and their wives. The family also may have a larger ancestral hall housing the tablets of more distant forebears.

Many families worship at the family altar regularly and sometimes every day. A representative of the family, usually one of the older women, burns three sticks of incense. One stick goes into the ancestor's incense pot, another is positioned in the incense pot reserved for the gods revered by the family members, and a third stick is placed outside of the door to welcome the gods and ancestors. As might be expected, the older family members tend to worship more frequently than younger members.

Further, the family tends to commemorate the death days of their closer ancestors or those whom they have personally known. On such occasions, the living members of the family serve its deceased members full meals complete with bowls and chopsticks, rice and noodles, and some of their favorite dishes; food is also provided for the animistic gods in many instances. In this context, people treat ancestors almost as if they were still living kin. Family members typically eat the food after the ancestors have supposedly eaten—that is, once the incense sticks have burned out. Ancestors also receive food offerings during major festivals for the gods; domestic worship of the gods tends to occur on the 1st and 15th of every lunar month.

Roundness, the first of the three characteristics of the family altar, stands for the continuity and structural completeness of the family; it symbolizes that the family is the basic, distinct, and enduring feature of the Chinese culture. The family altar as such represents the critical point of continuity between the natural world and the supernatural world. As indicated previously, Confucianism did not develop a Westernized conception of heaven; it holds that the dead exist in a shadowy netherworld and can communicate with and directly influence living relatives. For the Chinese, there is not a sharp demarcation between birth and death. Rather, all humanity is considered to be part of an organic system; in yin-yang fashion, individuals are continually being born into and processed in it, but they do not experience final separation from it or death in the Westernized sense. To the Chinese, the system, life, and time itself are circular, and all are united with one another because of this circularity. This perspective is consistent with both Buddhist and Taoist beliefs.

According to this rounded viewpoint, what is crucial is that Chinese individuals have descendants who can worship them and provide food and sacrifices; under such conditions, the deceased will lead a contented life in the netherworld. All of the efforts of the living are directed toward obtaining a rounded family in which the descent line is preserved. Thus roundness suggests a unity of the family circle that is related to the structural ideal of flawless Chinese patrilineage. Male children, who are obligated to perform ceremonial and ancestral rites, are preferred over female children. Hence roundness also suggests that men should have wives who can bear sons.

There are some problems with this idealization of roundness. Some women cannot bear sons. Under classical Chinese law, failure to bear a son was grounds for divorce. Some children die before they are of age to produce offspring, and historically it was common for them to be buried unceremoniously and unmourned. Sometimes the father does not live to old age, and his family does not receive the honor accorded to those who have achieved such distinction. However, the premature death of parents does not preclude their participation in the family, because they can be enshrined in ancestral tablets; the premature death of a husband does not weaken his wife's claim to a position in the descent line; and the failure to have children is correctable by adoption.

Such a patriarchal approach has led to the inequality of the sexes. Daughters occupy an inferior position to sons in the family, as do wives to husbands, and the wife assumes a position of relative equality with her husband and authority over her adult sons only when she is old, at which point she is accorded a position of honor and prestige. In such a context, most activities are segregated by sex.

In previous eras, polygamy was common among the Chinese, and it can still be found in isolated instances in rural areas. This practice complicated the familial structure, but the first wife was usually accorded the most honor and authority. In the modern world, it is typical for a Chinese man to marry only one woman, although the practice of having a "minor wife" or mistress is common. Because of the emphasis on the family, the Chinese businessman frequently works alongside his wife, or she will handle office matters while he is in charge of external relations. This pattern has limited the growth of many Chinese businesses, because only the wife and other family members are given positions of authority. Sometimes the husband and wife rarely see one another because of his external activities, but this is acceptable behavior provided that the husband is working hard on behalf of the family.

One Chinese family living in Thailand is typical. Every Sunday the wife of the oldest son hosts all family members at her home, including the younger sons and their families. Even though some of the brothers are not especially competent, the eldest son and CEO of the family business allows them to keep their positions as vice presidents and heads of the family's factories, but nonfamily members actually are the key decision makers in their factories. However, these nonfamily members participate in the Sunday activities only on an irregular basis. Because they are excluded from becoming full members of the familial in-group and can never aspire to become owners of the factories in any real sense of the word, it is common for them to quit after a few years and establish their own businesses.

This rounded perspective leads the Chinese to take a long-term perspective on problems and issues that they face. Unlike Americans, most of whom feel that a long-term plan involves a projection into the future of 3 to 5 years, the Chinese tend to be comfortable with plans that are expressed in 10, 20, and even 100-year increments. Geert Hofstede (1993), whose 40-nation study of cultural values is highlighted in this book, has expanded his four-dimensional framework into five dimensions because of recent research on the Chinese. He calls this dimension the "Confucian dynamic," and it reflects a long-term rather than short-term orientation; it also resembles in some ways the Protestant ethic in that deferred gratification of individual needs is accepted for the purpose of long-term success that helps the family.

This rounded conception of familial relationships is distinctively Chinese, and it encompasses members of the family over space and time. It is the family rather than the individual that has been the basic unit of social organization among the Chinese since the time of the Duke of Chou in the 12th century B.C. He established the system of *bao-jia*, or family and kinship rule and divided society into units of 10, 100, 1,000, and 10,000 families arranged by neighborhoods and districts. Each unit chose a leader from its ranks who was responsible for the behavior and welfare of all families in that jurisdiction, and this leader in turn reported directly to the leader of the next highest bao-jia unit. If a man committed a crime, the head of his own household would be held accountable, followed by the head of his 10-family unit, the 100-family unit, and so on. As a result, minor crimes were rarely reported beyond the smallest unit that had the authority to settle such matters. In one way or another, modern Chinese follow this pattern of collective responsibility, although practices vary widely by the nations in which they reside.

Further, the concept of roundness helps to explain the well-known Chinese practice of *guanxi* (connections). The lifeblood of a Chinese company is guanxi. Penetrating its layers is like peeling an onion. First come connections between people and ancestors, then those between people from the same village, between members of the family, and finally between the family and close associates who can be trusted, such as the competent executives who are not family members but who actually run its factories. All of these relationships are considered to be continual in nature, and obligations go far beyond what can be put into a contract. For example, a Chinese businessman will help a household servant establish her own business after she has served the family faithfully for several years; he will also expect a Western colleague to help his son gain admission into a prestigious Western university after they have worked together on a joint venture for some years.

Typically, the Chinese, similar to many other high-context cultures, are less concerned with what is written in the contract than in the actions that people take to meet their obligations as they emphasize guanxi. For example, the American Chamber of Commerce of Thailand spent two years identifying an American partner for a Chinese-Thai businessman who was seeking to establish a joint venture. At long last, all of the principal parties were to gather for dinner in Bangkok to finalize the arrangements, but the Chinese-Thai businessman angrily stormed out of the room when the American businessman showed up with a lawyer and a written contract, thus putting an end to the potential joint venture. To the high-context Chinese, this was an affront of the highest order.

The Chinese also tend to bypass the use of banks because of this system of guanxi. In fact, banks were unknown in China until the 20th century. Throughout the world, the Chinese establish communal investment and credit associations. Friends, relatives, and colleagues pool their money to form a mutual fund from which each member may take turns borrowing, and the Chinese rely on the personal closeness of the group to inhibit fraud or default. Sometimes these associations will lend money to other Chinese who cannot afford to contribute to the association. Further, the Chinese are well-known for lending their personal funds to their relatives in other nations—for example, Taiwanese investment in Malaysia and Thailand.

The largest Chinese families even establish private social welfare agencies that are open to anyone from the family. For example, the Chinese Lee family—there is also a Korean Lee family—operates a social welfare agency in a large building in New York's Chinatown that helps any Lee of Chinese origin obtain employment or solve any crisis such as dealing with immigration officials who may be trying to deport him or her and family.

Even the conception of the modern Chinese businessman is related to the concept of roundness. Many Chinese businessmen fly around the world so frequently that they have been caricatured as "space-men." They meet regularly with business associates in other nations who are united to one another through guanxi. If they are working with non-Chinese businessmen, they spend a great deal of time getting to know them so that the noncontractual nature of their relationships is prominent.

As explained in Chapter 14, the need for harmony and its development as a cultural ideal seems to have originated in the activities surrounding wet rice farming, and this generalization is also valid for China. Given the need to cooperate closely if subsistence for all was to be provided, the Chinese accorded primacy to harmony rather than to other ideals, such as the Western conception of life, liberty, and the pursuit of happiness. When disharmony infects the relations in the family, supernatural explanations for it are frequently offered, and the support of ancestors and gods is the natural way to reestablish harmony.

Roundness is a necessary but not sufficient condition for harmony, the second characteristic of the family altar. Ideally, the harmonious family is one in which there are few if any quarrels, financial problems, or illnesses. The most common prayer among many devout Chinese is for harmony, and it is frequently printed on door frames, charms, wedding cakes, and even the walls of homes. It is a prayer that is directed both to ancestors and gods. And, as indicated above, the members of the living family offer food and rituals in return for the harmony that they seek.

People make all kinds of requests at the family altar: for example, helping a child pass an examination, curing the sick, and obtaining employment. Although the requests are not always met, devotees often feel renewed hope and comfort, in large part because of the rituals that unite deceased and living family members through the medium of the family altar. Even the skeptical carry out the rituals— just in case.

Although the Chinese seek to achieve harmony, their worldview is not nearly as comforting as that of the Christian who can aspire to a tranquil heaven that is under the supervision of a benign and personal God. The shadowy netherworld represents a degree of uncertainty that the Christian does not have to take into account. It may be for this reason that the Chinese tend to believe in luck and fate, and that they have little if any control over events. In a Chinese Buddhist temple, for example, the worshipper can purchase a set of fortune sticks that he throws on the ground and then rearranges before consulting a book that predicts his future in terms of this rearrangement. Similarly, many Chinese do not use car seatbelts, because they believe that nature will take its normal course no matter what they do.

Also, although other cultural groups like to gamble, many Chinese clearly are attracted to it, seemingly in part because of this sense of uncertainty, luck, and fate. The major sense of security and harmony comes from the rounded family and the all-encompassing family altar. Many times gambling and games of chance reinforce both harmony and roundness. For example, large Asian families, each of which may include 30 or more individuals and several generations, go to restaurants for several hours of convivial conversation and relaxation, during which time they leisurely play cards and other games of chance. Similarly, it is not unusual for a Chinese family of 30 or more members, including several generations and close family servants, to go to the seashore for several days and spend most of their time inside an air-conditioned house talking to one another, drinking, eating sumptuous meals, and playing games of chance in which all participate; sometimes no one even ventures to the beach because of the enjoyment that the family members experience interacting with one another under such circumstances.

The third characteristic of the family altar is fluidity, or the capacity to change while maintaining solid traditions. It reflects the relation-oriented approach of the Chinese: They can be individualistic as long as they meet their many obligations to various family members, including those who are deceased.

So even though the Chinese tend to be conservative, they are frequently innovative and entrepreneurial. The number of Chinese inventions and scientific breakthroughs is startling, and Joseph Needham (1954) has an ongoing project describing them that, when completed, will fill 25 volumes. These include the first suspension bridge, fishing reels, rudders for ships, hang gliders, parachutes, fireworks, lacquer, wallpaper, paper, armor made from paper, wheelbarrows, and the first design for a steam engine. Similarly, as Kotkin (1993) and many others have described, the Chinese have been especially successful in establishing business enterprises, and they are disproportionately successful and entrepreneurial compared to most, if not all, other ethnic groups. This balanced emphasis on conservatism and innovation clearly reflects the concept of fluidity.

In traditional Chinese religion, there is a huge pantheon of gods and goddesses, most of whom are the heroes of Chinese myths, legend, and history and deified either by imperial order or popular choice. Some communities have cult followings that have evolved around a particular historical figure who supposedly protects and guides the town or who may have worked a miracle in it. The reputed powers of the best-known deities have been confirmed by generations of Chinese over the centuries. However, devotees believe that the power of a deity tends to decline with age and eventually loses its efficacy completely. The Chinese generally pray only to gods who have answered at least some of their petitions. When the decline in power occurs, the devotees begin to worship a new god. Thus there is fluidity in that change occurs, although devotion at the family altar continues.

Even the history of China can be interpreted in terms of the three characteristics of the family altar. Han, the largest cultural group, consists of more than 90% of the population. However, given more than 1 billion people in China, it is not surprising that there are more than 60 cultural groups that range in size from millions of people to only a few thousand, and most of them have and have had harmonious relations with one another. Almost all of Chinese history can be divided into periods defined by dynasties. Families or rulers would occupy the throne until another would take power away. History was viewed as endless cycles of renewal and decline, starting with the first dynasty in approximately 1953 B.C. and ending only with the retirement of the last emperor in A.D. 1911. Each ruler was considered to have a mandate bestowed on him by the gods to rule fairly and wisely. When an heir became corrupt or lazy, rebellions would break out and a new emperor would surface. He would typically introduce reforms that were consistent with the underlying cultural values of roundness, harmony, and fluidity. The fact that China was the most developed civilization in the world for a significant portion of this long time period may also be attributed to the emphasis on these three characteristics. As a broad generalization, the dynastic cycle helps to explain, through the mechanism of periodic renewal, how the Chinese were able to retain a consistent and continuous pattern of government for thousands of years (Major, 1989, pp. 46-47). Thus this cycle exemplifies all three characteristics of the family altar: roundness, or continuity and structural completeness of the family and family-based nation; harmony over thousands of years marred only by periodic revolutions; and fluidity, or maintaining the past while accepting change.

Expatriate Chinese

Today there are more than 50 million expatriate Chinese, and many of them have been spectacularly successful in businesses throughout the world when compared to other cultural groups. Initially, these emigrants from China did not come from mainstream Chinese society, which was at times insular and suspicious of foreigners, whose cultures were generally considered inferior. They instead originated from the peripheral southern regions of China where control and subservience to the emperor was less rigid.

In some of the countries in which these expatriate Chinese settled, such as Thailand and the United States, they have integrated themselves effectively and even married non-Chinese in increasingly large numbers. In other countries such as Malaysia and Indonesia, the Chinese have experienced discrimination and resentment, and they tend to be less effectively integrated with the other cultural groups. In Malaysia, for example, a Chinese cannot be the CEO of a company seeking government contracts. To get around this restriction, the Chinese put a native Malay into this position while retaining most of the power.

Some of this discrimination seems to be religious in nature, brought, for example, by Muslims in Malaysia and by Indonesians against Confucians. Whatever its causes, it has divided such countries into Chinese and non-Chinese groups that experience difficulty in developing harmonious relations.

Taiwan, a country of 20 million people, is an interesting example of the success that the expatriate Chinese have wrought. It was established as a separate country after World War II when General Chiang Kai-shek and his followers were driven out of China by the communists. Its rulers realized that the most important resource of Taiwan was its population's Confucian dynamic, so laws were established that fostered entrepreneurship. Taiwanese businesses are generally small and family dominated, and they have been so successful that the country is now one of the richest in the world.

Hong Kong, 95% of whose citizens are Chinese, has a population of 5.7 million people. Although it occupies only a small area of 412 square miles, more than 120 million fly into Hong Kong each year, most of them for business or shopping. Business is so successful that executives have been forced to build "vertical factories" that are housed in tall buildings, and each factory is built on top of the other.

In Singapore, with its population of 2.7 million, there are three ethnic groups: Chinese (77%), Malays (15%), and Indians (6%). Like

Taiwan and Hong Kong, this country has been resoundingly success-ful, in large part because of the herculean efforts of the Chinese, because the country was extremely poor until recent years. These three countries have been so successful that they, along with Korea, have been nicknamed the "Four Tigers of Asia."

Thailand, which is rapidly becoming Asia's fifth tiger, has a pop-ulation of 55 million, and its two main ethnic groups are native Thai (75%) and Chinese (14%). These two groups are quite comfortable with one another and, as indicated previously, intermarriage is com-mon. Whereas the Chinese play their traditional roles as business-men, particularly small businessmen, the Thais tend to control the government, the military, and the banks. Ironically, the Thais contin-ually debate the merits of "Taiwanizing" Thailand, because many of them prefer to keep their long-established and traditional ways of doing business and enjoying life, which are frequently incompatible with modern approaches.

The expatriate Chinese are influential in most, if not all, of the countries in which they reside. Unlike the expatriate Japanese, who tend to separate themselves from the societies in which they reside and eventually want to return to Japan, expatriate Chinese seek integration in the countries in which they reside, although they stay in contact with one another through their far-flung families and the activities of the so-called spacemen who roam the world seeking business opportunities.

In short, the expatriate Chinese are similar to the traditional Chi-nese in that the family is the basic social unit through which all are united in a relation-based system. Roundness (and harmony and fluidity) is emphasized by these families, who form a complex but informal network throughout the world. The Chinese, regardless of their country of residence, tend to exhibit conservative and high-con-text behavior. Although some Chinese may have moved away from the practice of honoring ancestors at the family altar, they typically accept the importance that is attached to the need for roundness, harmony, and fluidity. In this sense, the family altar is not only an appropriate metaphor for the Chinese but one that clearly illustrates the major values of this ethnic group, no matter where they settle permanently.

18

The Metaphors in Perspective

The basic approach in this book has been to describe a nation in terms of a suitable and complex metaphor that could then serve as a guide, map, or beacon for understanding and interacting with its members. We have now described 16 nations in terms of such metaphors. Also, we have used one metaphor, the Chinese family altar, to describe a cluster of nations in which the Chinese influence is significant. In this chapter, we want to integrate some of the major strands of thought associated with each metaphor and put them in perspective.

Specifically, we begin the chapter by focusing on the dimension of individualism-collectivism, which is considered by many experts to be the most important dimension along which societies can be arrayed (see Triandis et al., 1988; Triandis, McCusker, & Hui, 1990). Then, to supplement and enrich our distinction between culture-general and culture-specific understanding (see Chapter 1), we distinguish between culture-creating mechanisms and cultural behavior or the behavior that derives directly from them; we devote the two final sections of this chapter to a discussion of both of these issues.

Types of Individualism and Collectivism

It is quite common to compare and contrast individualistic and collectivistic societies. Geert Hofstede (1980a), whose work has been given prominent attention in this book, pointed out that all of the economically successful societies in his study of nations, with the exception of Japan, were individualistic in nature. He suggested that individualism might be more important to economic development than collectivism, but by 1988 he changed his mind in light of the rise of the four Asian tigers (see Bond & Hofstede, 1988; Hofstede, 1993). Specifically, research by Michael Bond and his colleagues (1987) indicated that these Asians generally subscribe to a Confucian "work ethic" or "dynamic" that is quite similar to the Protestant work ethic, particularly in terms of deferring immediate gratification for the achievement of long-term goals. And, given the competitive economic system that was allowed to operate in these four countries, this Confucian ethic flourished.

As suggested previously, Hofstede's work has been important because it is the only large-scale cross-cultural study in which the type of organization was held constant: All of the respondents worked for the same multinational firm (IBM). His research is also important because it indicates that there are at least four—and now five if we accept the Confucian dimension—dimensions that we should examine when comparing cultures. Thus Ben Kedia and Rabi Bhagat (1988) posit that Japan's economic success may well be the result of the interaction of two of Hofstede's dimensions: collectivism and masculinity or the acceptance of aggressive and materialistic behavior. Although Japan clustered with the 20 countries in Hofstede's study that had a high score on collectivism, it had the second lowest score among them, although it had the highest score of all 40 countries on masculinity.

It is extremely difficult to pinpoint precisely how Hofstede's dimensions interact with economic growth, but his research does suggest that any discussion of societies and their economies should include not only individualism-collectivism but also other value dimensions. And, as our own analysis of metaphors indicates, there are clearly many different types of both individualism and collectivism. Broadly speaking, we can relate our metaphors to individualism in the following way:

German symphony: subordinated individualism
Italian opera: exteriorized individualism
Traditional British house: tradition-bound and iconoclastic individualism

Spanish bullfight: proud and self-sufficient individualism
American football: competitive individualism
Swedish stuga: individualism through nature and self-development
French wine: rationalistic individualism
Irish conversation: religion-focused individualism

We also have identified different types of collectivism, including:

Chinese family altar: relation-based and differentiated family system
Japanese garden: kata-based undifferentiated family system
Dance of Shiva: religion-dominated family system
Israeli kibbutz: democracy-based family system

Further, some of the societies that Hofstede profiles as collectivistic exhibit a high degree of individualism. This orientation is manifested in the Israeli movement from kibbutzim to moshavim. The Thais seem to maintain a group-focused individualism that allows for the dynamic interplay between accepting rigid hierarchical authority and *sanuk*, or fun. Similarly, some of these supposedly individualisic societies are also collectivist, for example, Ireland and its tremendous emphasis on helping others. Thus collectivistic societies can also be individualistic, and vice versa.

One reason why individualism-collectivism has been identified as being so critical may relate to the methodology that is normally used to evaluate cross-cultural differences in values, attitudes, and behavior. Researchers such as Hofstede tend to rely on a factor-analytic and clustering method whereby numerous questionnaire items are reduced to four or five independent factors; individualism-collectivism normally contains the largest number of items. Although this approach is crucial for increasing culture-general understanding, it does tend to neglect the nuances that a more qualitative or ethnographic approach such as the metaphorical method are able to discern. Both approaches are important, although the qualitative approach is especially important in understanding cross-cultural differences along the individualism-collectivism dimension. Without such descriptions, an observer or visitor may well misinterpret behavior that is classified on an a priori basis as either collectivistic or individualistic. From our perspective, the individualism-collectivism dimension must take into account different types of both individualism and collectivism and is subdivided into more precise dimensions so that behavior that might appear totally collectivistic also can be understood as individualistic (although within the context of

the collectivity), and behavior that might seem to be totally individualistic can be comprehended as collectivistic (within the context of
individualism).

Culture-Creating Mechanisms

In many situations it is difficult to understand the dynamics of
culture, but culture is created through only a small number of mechanisms. Ronen and Shenkar (1985) suggested that three are critical in
explaining the emergence of different clusters of societies: Religion,
common language, and geographical closeness (see Chapter 1). Joel
Kotkin (1993) has argued that "tribes" are formed because of a
common ethnicity, a common religion, and an emphasis on the
extended family, as discussed in the previous chapter. In our discussion, we also include the educational system, socialization, the form
of government, history, social class structure, and rate of technological change.

In many nations, religion has declined in importance, at least as
evidenced by regular church attendance. Even our metaphors reflect
this decline: Most are not explicitly religious in nature. However,
religion is still quite important as a cultural force, a fact confirmed
by the large percentage of people in various countries such as France
who identify themselves as Catholic but who rarely attend church. In
Thailand, the numerous wats, or Buddhist temples, are a striking con-
firmation of the value that Thais attach to Buddhism, even though they
citizens tend to frequent the wats irregularly, usually during specific
holy days. In the case of France and Thailand, the religious values of
Catholicism and Buddhism clearly permeate numerous aspects of
daily living, such as what is considered ethical behavior and the
manner in which individuals relate to one another in both private
and public.

Comparatively speaking, the United States has a high proportion—approximately 50%—of citizens who attend church regularly
or at least once a week; the number increases during periods of crisis.
As indicated in Chapter 16, religion represents a vital cultural force:
The many waves of immigrants to the United States have tended and
still tend to cluster together in churches where they protect and help
one another. Probably only Ireland and Poland have larger percent-
ages of people who attend church more regularly than do Americans.

Language is another culture-forming mechanism of vital importance. Sharing a language helps individuals feel comfortable, define

in-groups and out-groups, and communicate both thoughts and emotions. As indicated in Chapter 3, language or voice is so important that it is one of the four key elements of the Italian opera metaphor; for the Irish, language or conversation is the actual metaphor itself. In Japan, the language is used subtly through various word endings and inflections to indicate insider or outsider status, relative status, and even moods. In Belgium, the conflict between the French and Flemish languages is directly related to the controlled or balanced behavior that Belgians manifest. These examples could be multiplied several times to demonstrate the importance of language as a culture-forming mechanism.

Also, geographical closeness tends to allow similar values to evolve in neighboring nations. As Ronen and Shenkar (1985) have demonstrated, only one of their eight clusters of countries did not reflect geographical closeness (see Chapter 1). The Anglo cluster included countries that share religions and language but who have had waves of immigration that reduced geographical closeness.

As our discussion of the various educational systems suggests, many of these nations place a great emphasis on this culture-forming institution. Perhaps the best example is Thailand, which is rapidly becoming the so-called fifth tiger of Asia. Education is so important that the king himself—or, if he is unavailable, a close family relative—personally hands out diplomas for approximately six hours at each university graduation, during which two cameras record the event so that all students can have their pictures taken while receiving their diplomas. It is typical for each university to have two or three large-scale rehearsals before the actual graduation so that no mistakes will occur at graduation; students receive their actual diplomas rather than blank ones, as is the custom in the United States; and Buddhist monks chant continuously throughout the ceremony while collectively holding one string that signifies unity. Further, the king demonstrates the importance he attaches to education by spending 20 days each year handing out diplomas at all major public universities, which in Thailand have higher status than private universities.

Further, as discussed in Chapter 4, Germany allowed the Allies to change its economic, political, and social systems after World War II with the notable exception of education: Its leaders demanded that its educational system be allowed to operate as it had for more than 200 years, and today this educational system serves as a model that other countries are studying closely because of its effectiveness. In the prospering countries of East Asia, excluding Japan and China, 16.9% of government money is spent on education compared to 4.5%

in the West ("Question of Care," 1993). Clearly, these examples suggest that many leading nations understand the importance of education, not only as a culture-creating but also as an income-generating mechanism.

The United States, which has a school year cycle of 180 days, compares poorly to many other countries, including Japan (243 days), Italy (216 days), Thailand (200 days), and Britain (196 days). Although American students have not done well in standardized tests in comparison with students in other countries, attitude surveys indicate that they have a much more positive feeling about their abilities than do those other students. In fact, this feeling may well reflect the cultural metaphor of American football: Even American graduation ceremonies have taken on the air of a football game, with students shouting enthusiastically and even interrupting speakers throughout the event. Education seems to be valued in the United States only if it allows the individual to compete more effectively in the short run—that is, if there is a clear relationship between the education and immediately obtaining a job. This type of value and resultant behavior is in sharp contrast to that manifested in Thailand and other countries where graduation is an exciting but solemn event itself. Although the value of education for obtaining a job is important to these nations' citizens, they seem to feel that education has an intrinsic value that cannot be measured purely in terms of the labor market.

Also, as our discussion of the educational systems of other countries suggests, many nations relate education much more closely to societal goals than does the United States (see, for example, Chapter 4). Once again, the metaphors reflecting the values of these societies provide insight into this phenomenon. In the case of the United States, football emphasizes competitive individualism, as does the educational system that allows a wide range of choice and opportunities to students, even permitting them to major in fields of studies where there is an obvious dearth of jobs. Other countries simply would not countenance this approach.

Education is clearly one aspect of socialization, but several others help to mold the personalities of individuals in different societies. In some European countries such as Belgium and Germany, children form only a few close personal friendships in life, and usually this process occurs during the early years of childhood. Americans, on the other hand, tend to have many friendships but few that are deep and long-lasting. Several explanations for this phenomenon have been offered, including the sheer size of the United States and the rapid mobility of the labor force. Our metaphor of football would suggest that the deeply ingrained cultural value of competitive individualism may lead to such an outcome. For example, Americans tend to recommend people for jobs whom they do not know well, although they are aware that these individuals are competent for the positions and capable of competing effectively. In many other societies, family connections are the best predictor of job referral and placement, and sometimes incompetent individuals are hired simply because of such connections (see Chapter 17).

Perhaps the most dramatic instance of the importance of socialization is the Japanese use of *amae* or the Thai equivalent of *krengchai*. As shown in Chapter 14, Japanese mothers tend to make their children quite dependent on them, encouraging them to focus their attention on the mothers' faces, often carrying them close to their bodies for the first few years of life, and letting the children sleep with their parents until 6 or 7 years of age. The American pattern is quite different: The child is encouraged to explore the world about him or her and to become independent as soon as possible. This Japanese pattern, which is also common in other Asian nations, reflects the metaphor of the Japanese garden: The group and harmony are seen as more important than individuality and independence, which are highly valued by competitive Americans.

Another culture-forming factor that is quite important is the type of government. As Bond and Hofstede (1988) have argued, the Confucian ethic was permitted to flourish in the four tigers of Asia in the past 30 years, and it seems that the form of government allowing for this state of affairs is critical for economic success. While on a trip to China during 1988 when economic experimentation was being encouraged by the government, I visited an open-air food market where merchants were allowed to sell their goods competitively: Salespeople bustled about, not only waiting on customers but also continually encouraging them to visit their stalls. Just a few blocks away was a government-operated market that greatly restricted prices and paid each merchant by the hour regardless of the number of items sold. These merchants seemed to be asleep and were not especially interested in customers, because their pay was predetermined. The contrast between the two markets was startling.

Erwin Helms, Emeritus Professor of American Studies at Göttingen University in Germany, was invited to lecture at universities in the former East Germany after its merger with West Germany. In personal correspondence, he stated the following about the influence of the form of government on values:

> When . . . I lectured there, I noticed how far apart we had become culturally. The mentality of the students in the East is very different from that in the West: The ideological indoctrination beginning in the youth organizations and continued in the army (future students have to serve three years in the army to be admitted to a college) seems to have made them speechless. Used to obeying orders, they are unable to ask questions or to express an opinion. (E. Helms, personal communication, December 1, 1992)

As the East Germans become accustomed to the capitalistic system and the West German educational system that emphasizes freedom of thought and opinion, this situation will change. Still, Professor Helms's brief description aptly encapsulates the influence that the political system can have on culture. And, as our discussion of the Chinese nations suggests (Chapter 17), changing the form of government to allow for competition does bring about a renewed enthusiasm and refocused culture. Although the form of government clearly influences culture, many values survive despite governmental efforts to eradicate them, as the strength of the Chinese family after Mao's onslaught on it during the 1960s and 1970s attests.

Further, the history of a society directly influences cultural values. Italians, for instance, tend to be suspicious of foreigners, in large part because of the many years during which this country was ruled by them. Spaniards tend to cluster together for a similar reason, as the many invasions they experienced motivated them to live and work close to one another while still allowing them to preserve their proud, self-sufficient individualism. Such examples could be multiplied a thousand times to show that it is extremely difficult to consider a nation's culture without examining its history.

An additional culture-forming mechanism is a society's class structure. Many societies have a rigid class structure in which there are only a few members of the upper class, a small middle class, and a large lower class. Some political scientists have argued that this pattern is conducive to revolution, a situation that can be amelioriated by the growth of the middle class and a decline of the lower class. However, some citizens who would define themselves as middle-class in the United States identify with the working class in England, thus suggesting that there is a psychological dimension to the class structure of a society (see Chapter 2).

The United States prides itself on being a middle-class society in which all are allowed to compete and individual performance—for example, football—is rewarded lavishly. Americans do not seem to mind rewarding some individuals such as a quarterback or fullback disproportionately, but they want to see a relationship between performance and rewards. Thus many Americans do not object to the fact that CEOs of large corporations receive more compensation in the United States than their counterparts elsewhere. They are bothered, however, by the fact that the compensation of many poorly performing CEOs is much higher than that of high-performing CEOs.

Finally, the rate of technological change is having a dramatic effect on cultural values. In many Third World countries, television is having a profound influence on cultural values: The viewers see a style of life that is in sharp contrast to their own poverty-driven existence. The ability to communicate rapidly through the use of facsimile (fax) and computer networks is allowing citizens of many nations to integrate their activities and, probably in the long run, their values and outlooks on life. Frequent visits and stays in countries other than one's own also help to facilitate the development of a broader set of values. All of these factors reflect the movement toward a global village in which at least some values found previously in one or a few countries will be shared widely across several nations. In fact, technology may well be the major mechanism for increasing communication across cultures and minimizing cultural differences.

Cultural Behavior

There has been a great and ongoing debate about the utility of most management and psychological theories of motivation, almost all of which have been developed by Americans. For instance, American textbooks in several disciplines tend to emphasize Abraham Maslow's (1970) needs hierarchy, which posits that as individuals grow and mature, and satisfy their lower-order needs, higher-order needs emerge or evolve that then must be satisfied. Thus needs are supposedly satisfied in the following sequence: physiological (food, water, sex, shelter), safety and security, belongingness and love (acceptance and friendship), esteem (self-esteem and the esteem of others), and self-actualization or realizing one's full potential as a productive, creative person. Although Maslow's theory focuses specifically on human development over a lifetime, other theorists have revised and applied it directly to work motivation. But this theory or its revision does not apply directly to many countries in which the key need is not self-actualization but belongingness and love as actualized in familial relations. Many Asians, for instance, think first of what the family wants them to do rather than of esteem or self-actualization. This outlook is much stronger in Asia and in some European countries than in the United States.

In Thailand, for instance, a Western-educated young female manager told an American acquaintance that she was engaged to marry, and the American responded positively to the news. However, she then dejectedly told him that her husband-to-be was spoiled, immature, and irresponsible, and that she did not even want to be near him, let alone marry him. When the American replied that her decision did not seem to follow the logical decision processes taught to her in her MBA program in the United States, her reply was that she had to follow her parents' wishes or never see them again.

Our discussion of motivational theory suggests that a distinction should be drawn between individual behavior and cultural behavior. There are universal patterns of individual behavior that can be found in most, if not all, societies. Thus it is not surprising that some motivational techniques lead to increased performance in both the United States and other countries (for example, see Welsh, Luthans, & Sommer, 1993). However, a good amount of behavior is contingent on the culture in which a person exists. As suggested in Chapter 1, it is reasonable to estimate that between 25% and 50% of behavior is culturally determined. Thus it is important to identify the motivational techniques that are appropriate for each culture, some of which are culture general and some culture specific.

Throughout this book we have emphasized numerous differences in cultural behavior. In this section we focus on the issues of time, work and leisure, hierarchical authority, bureaucracy, sports and rituals, and small-group and public behavior.

Edward Hall's well-known distinction between monochronic and polychronic time is a good starting point for evaluating cultural behavior (see Hall & Hall, 1990). Many societies such as Thailand are polychronic—that is, people do several things simultaneously. Americans and Germans, on the other hand, tend to do things logically and sequentially, completing one activity before going on to another. It is difficult to break away from this cultural behavior. For instance, Thai professors sometimes show visiting American professors the manner in which they teach and personally use the management-by-objectives system that they learned in the United States. This system is sequential in nature: Goals are first stipulated, means are then identified for reaching them, and a time frame is established for accomplishing each of these objectives. However, these Thai professors, after spending a considerable amount of time constructing such a system for reaching particular goals, totally disregard it. Their circular and polychronic notions of time are so ingrained that they move away from such a system as soon as they can, sometimes without consciously realizing it.

In addition, different countries place differing emphases on work and leisure. As indicated in Chapter 9, the Spanish word for work, *negocio*, is literally translated as the absence of leisure—that is, work is to be done only because it provides leisure time during which people really begin to experience life to its fullest. In Thailand the word for work, *ngan*, is also translated as play, and Thais like to punctuate their workdays with periods of sanuk or fun. By contrast, Americans, Germans, and the Chinese tend to view work in a highly favorable manner. One typical Chinese businessman in Bangkok, for example, begins his workday at 10 a.m. and spends 25 of every 30 days working until 1 a.m. or 2 a.m. His only scheduled vacation occurs during a few days in which his family celebrates the Chinese New Year. Seven-day workweeks are the norm rather than the exception, and his wife helps to facilitate his activities by being in charge of his office and staff when he is making his frequent trips to other business firms. This pattern of behavior is widespread among the Chinese.

Of course, devotion to work does not have to be excessive: The Germans work many fewer hours per year than do Americans and have many more holidays, but they are focused and committed when at work. And many Germans would argue that work and leisure should be in balance. The lack of such a balance is, in fact, one of the criticisms that some Americans make of the Japanese, suggesting that they work too hard and in the process injure not only themselves but also other nations by producing so many goods that they must export excessively, thus creating difficulties in maintaining a reasonable balance of trade with other nations.

Also, it is notable that the upper classes of many nations such as Italy and Spain tend to view lower-level occupations negatively, not allowing their children to work and failing to provide them with an empathy that can cross class and occupational lines. In nations such as Italy, the medieval idea that the only valid work is intellectual in nature still holds sway. Americans, on the other hand, tend to feel that work is good for younger members of society, because it provides them with a set of experiences that will make them more mature, empathetic, and competitive. However, there is a point of diminishing returns, and many American students critically injure their careers by spending so much time working that their schoolwork is mediocre.

Further, nations such as France and Thailand have a much more positive view of hierarchical authority than do Americans, who prefer to de-emphasize status and power, at least officially. Still, this authority can be combined with a high degree of employee participation and involvement, as the experiences of both Germany and Japan attest. Whereas Americans tend to view hierarchy negatively, these two nations accept it as a given and work within the constraints that it imposes. Ironically, the gap in total compensation between the CEO, other top-level officers, and workers is greater in the United States than in any other nation.

Several of the societies described in this book have a negative view of a related concept, bureaucracy, particularly governmental bureaucracy. In Spain and Israel, citizens hire people to take their place in the long lines in which individuals wait interminably for the services dispensed by government bureaucracies. Although Americans are not fond of bureaucracy, they typically do not need to take such extreme measures to deal effectively with it, although some wealthy and busy Americans are now following the pattern found in Spain and Israel.

In addition, the concepts of sports and rituals are highlighted throughout this book. Americans in particular enjoy football at least in part because they tend to identify with the winner. The Japanese, on the other hand, schedule each of their professional baseball games for 3 hours and 20 minutes, and many of them end in ties, which makes the face-saving and group-oriented Japanese comfortable. To the Spanish, the bullfight is a ritual in which the bravery of the matador is tested. All of these examples suggest that sports and rituals constitute effective metaphors for describing a society's basic cultural values.

Finally, small-group and public behavior frequently are a direct reflection of culture. Both in Germany and Britain, children are usually left at home when the parents go to a restaurant, most probably because it is felt that they are not mature enough for this type of adult activity and thus will disrupt it. Conversely, Asian restaurants frequently service large multigenerational families who not only eat but also play cards and other games for several hours. Although Americans typically do not have such multigenerational dinners, especially those that last for several hours, parents usually bring their children to restaurants.

These types of small-group and public behavior pale in comparison to the exteriority manifested by Italians and, to a lesser extent, other Latin nations. People in Italy are drawn ineluctably to the piazza so that they can exteriorize their emotions and feelings. All of these societies put a high value on family relations, and exteriorization does occur at home. But it extends to other groups, even to the extent that people visit the piazza on a daily basis to see old acquaintances and friends and make new ones.

In sum, we emphasize that we have highlighted only some of the major cultural behaviors in this chapter; the other chapters in this book go into them in much greater detail. All of these behaviors are a direct reflection of culture and the culture-forming mechanisms that allow them to evolve. We hope the metaphors help to increase our understanding not only of the societies themselves but also of the specific behaviors that flow directly from their culture-forming mechanisms. Other metaphors also may be suitable or supplementary, but it is our feeling that the dynamics of the culture of a particular nation can be best understood through the use of one dominant metaphor that reflects the basic values that all or most of its members accept without question or conscious thought. In the final analysis, it is the dynamics of culture that are of greatest importance, and metaphors constitute one effective means for understanding them in a meaningful and proactive manner.

References

Adler, N. J. (1991). *International dimensions of organizational behavior* (2nd ed.). Boston: PWS-Kent.

Arden, N. (1990, May). Searching for India along the great trunk road. *National Geographic*, pp. 177-185.

Aronson, D. R. (1978). *The city is our farm*. Cambridge, MA: Schenkman.

Banerji, P. (1983). *Erotica in Indian dance*. Atlantic Highlands, NJ: Humanities Press.

Barnlund, D. (1989). *Public and private self in Japan and the United States*. Yarmouth, ME: Intercultural Press.

Barzini, L. (1964). *The Italians*. New York: Atheneum.

Barzini, L. (1983). *The Europeans*. New York: Simon & Schuster.

Beckett, J. D. (1986). *A short history of Ireland*. London: Cresset Library.

Bell, B. (1991). *Insight guides: Ireland*. Singapore: APA Publications.

Benton, W. (Ed.). (1970). *Encyclopedia Brittanica*. Chicago: Encyclopedia Brittanica.

Bettleheim, B. (1969). *The children of the dream*. New York: Macmillan.

Bisbee, S. (1951). *The new Turks*. Philadelphia: University of Pennsylvania Press.

Bonavia, D. (1989). *The Chinese*. London: Penguin.

Bond, M. et al. (1987). Chinese values and the search for culture-free dimensions of culture. *Journal of Cross-Cultural Psychology, 18*, 143-164.

Bond, M., & Hofstede, G. (1988). The Confucius connection: From cultural roots to economic growth. *Organizational Dynamics, 16*, 5-21.

Boorstin, D. (1965). *The Americans: The national experience*. New York: Random House.

Boswell, T. (1990, August 12). What we are talking about when we talk about sports. *The Washington Post Magazine, 12,* 22-28.

Braganti, N., & Devine, E. (1992). *European customs and manners* (2nd ed.). Minneapolis, MN: Meadowbrook.

Brint, S. (1989, July-August). Italy observed. *Society,* pp. 71-76.

Burmeister, I. (Ed.). (1980). *These strange German ways* (14th ed.). Hamburg, Germany: Atlantik-Bruchke.

Burns, A. C. (1963). *History of Nigeria.* London: Allen & Unwin.

Burr, A. (1917). *Russell H. Conwell and his work.* Philadelphia, PA: Winston.

Campbell, J. (1962). *The masks of God: Oriental mythology.* New York: Penguin.

Carroll, R. (1987). *Cultural misunderstandings: The French American experience.* Chicago: University of Chicago Press.

Carson, R. (1962). *Silent Spring.* Greenwich, CT: Fawcett.

Castes adrift. (1992, November 21). *The Economist, 325,* 44.

Clarke, M., & Crisp, M. (1976). *Understanding ballet.* New York: Harmony.

Clayre, A. (1985). *The heart of the dragon.* Boston: Houghton Mifflin.

Coomaraswamy, A. (1969). *The dance of Shiva.* New York: Sunwise Turn. (Original work published 1924)

Crow, J. A. (1985). *Spain: The root and the flower* (3rd ed.). Berkeley: University of California Press.

Crozier, M. (1964). *The bureaucratic phenomenon.* Chicago: University of Chicago Press.

Death among the blossoms. (1991, May 25). *The Economist, 319,* 39-41.

De Gramont, S. (1969). *The French.* New York: G. P. Putnam.

Delany, M. (1974). *Of Irish ways.* Minneapolis, MN: Dillion.

De Mente, B. (1990). *The kata factor.* Phoenix, AZ: Phoenix Books.

Deutsch, E. (1968). *Bhagavad Gita.* New York: Holt, Rinehart & Winston.

Dindi, H., & Gazur, M. (1989). *Turkish culture for Americans.* Boulder, CO: International Concepts.

Dornberg, J. (1975). *The new Germans: Thirty years after.* New York: Macmillan.

Elon, A. (1971). *The Israelis.* New York: Penguin.

Executive pay: It doesn't add up. (1993, April 26). *Business Week,* p. 122.

Fieg, J. (1976). *A common core: Thais and Americans.* Yarmouth, ME: Intercultural Press.

Fieg, J., & Mortlock, E. (1989). *A common core: Thais and Americans* (rev. ed.). Yarmouth, ME: Intercultural Press.

Fisher, G. (1988). *Mindsets: The role of culture and perception in international relations.* Yarmouth, ME: Intercultural Press.

Fisher, M. (1993, March 21). Germany's wimp complex. *Washington Post,* pp. C1-C4.

Friedman, T. L. (1989). *From Beirut to Jerusalem.* Garden City, NY: Doubleday.

Frost, E. (1987). *For richer, for poorer.* New York: Council on Foreign Relations.

Furness, N., & Tilton, T. (1979). *The case for the welfare state.* Bloomington: Indiana University Press.

Galbraith, J. K. (1984). *The affluent society* (4th ed.). Boston: Houghton Mifflin.

Geertz, C. (1973). *The interpretation of culture.* New York: Basic Books.

George, P. (1987). *University teaching across cultures.* Bangkok, Thailand: U.S. Information Service.

Glyn, A. (1970). *The British: Portrait of a people.* New York: G. P. Putnam.

Gopal, R., & Dadachanji, S. (1951). *Indian dancing.* London: Phoenix House.

Graham, R. (1984). *Spain: Change of a nation.* London: Michael Joseph.

Haire, M., Ghiselli, E., & Porter, L. (1966). *Managerial thinking: An international study.* New York: John Wiley.

Hall, E. (1959). *The silent language.* Garden City, NY: Doubleday.
Hall, E. (1966). *The hidden dimension.* Garden City, NY: Doubleday.
Hall, E. (1976). *Beyond culture.* Garden City, NY: Doubleday.
Hall, E. (1983). *The dance of life.* Garden City, NY: Doubleday.
Hall, E. (1987). *Hidden differences.* Garden City, NY: Doubleday.
Hall, E., & Hall, M. (1990). *Understanding cultural differences.* Yarmouth, ME: Intercultural Press.
Haskell, A. (1963). *The Russian genius in ballet.* Elmsford, NY: Pergamon.
Haskell, A. (1968). *Balletomania.* New York: AMS Press.
Haycraft, J. (1985). *Italian labyrinth.* New York: Penguin.
Health party protests Gorbachev lunch menu. (1990, November 8). *The Baltimore Sun,* p. 8.
Heclo, H., & Madsen, H. (1987). *Policy and politics in Sweden.* Philadelphia, PA: Temple University Press.
Hoffman, M. (Ed.). (1991). *World almanac.* New York: Pharos.
Hofstadter, R. (1955). *Social Darwinism in American thought.* Boston: Beacon.
Hofstede, G. (1980a). *Culture's consequences.* Beverly Hills, CA: Sage.
Hofstede, G. (1980b). Motivation, leadership, and organization: Do American theories apply abroad? *Organizational Dynamics, 9,* 42-63.
Hofstede, G. (1991). *Cultures and organizations: Software of the mind.* New York: McGraw-Hill.
Hofstede, G. (1993). Cultural constraints in management theories. *Academy of Management Executive, 7,* 81-94.
Huxley, A. (1951). *Antic Hay.* New York: Modern Library.
Iwao, S. (1990). Recent changes in Japanese attitudes. In A. Romberg & T. Yamahoto (Eds.), *Same bed, different dreams* (pp. 55-73). New York: Council on Foreign Relations.
Japan Productivity Center. (1984). *Managerial behavior in Japan and the U.S.A.: A cross-cultural survey.* Tokyo: Author.
Jenkins, D. (1968). *Sweden and the price of progress.* New York: Coward, McCann & Geohegan.
Johnson, H. (1985). *How to enjoy wine.* New York: Simon & Schuster.
Joyce, J. (1964). *Portrait of the artist as a young man.* New York: Viking.
Kagitcibasi, C. (1990). Family and home-based intervention. In R. Brislin (Ed.), *Applied cross cultural psychology* (pp. 121-141). Newbury Park, CA: Sage.
Kakar, S. (1971). Authority patterns and subordinate behavior in Indian organizations. *Administrative Science Quarterly, 16,* 298-308.
Kakar, S. (1978). *The inner world.* New York: Oxford University Press.
Kanter, R. (1979). Power failures in management curcuits. *Harvard Business Review, 57*(4), 65-75.
Kedia, B., & Bhagat, R. (1988). Cultural constraints on transfer of technology across nations: Implications for research in international and comparative management. *Academy of Management Review, 13,* 559-571.
Keefe, E. (1977). *Area handbook for Italy.* Washington, DC: American University.
Keirsey, D., & Bates, M. (1978). *Please understand me.* Del Mar, CA: Prometheus Nemesis.
Kesselman, M., Krieger, J., Allen, C., DeBardeleben, J., Hellman, S., Pontrisson, J., & Ost, D. (1987). *European politics in transition.* Lexington, MA: D. C. Heath.
Kielman, A. (1983). *Childhood and maternal health services in rural India: The Narangwal experiment* (Vol. 1). Baltimore, MD: Johns Hopkins University Press.
Kightly, C. (1986). *The customs and ceremonies of Britain.* London: Thames & Hudson.
Kluckholn, F., & Strodtbeck, F. (1961). *Variations in value orientations.* Evanston, IL: Row, Peterson.
Kotkin, J. (1993). *Tribes.* New York: Random House.

LaFraniere, S. (1991, January 5). U.S. has most prisoners per capita in the world. *Washington Post*, p. A5.

Lannoy, R. (1971). *The speaking tree: A study of Indian culture and society.* New York: Oxford University Press.

Laurent, A. (1983). The cultural diversity of Western concepts of management. *International Studies of Management and Organization, 13*(1-2), 75-96.

Lessem, R. (1987). *The global business.* London: Prentice-Hall International.

Levine, I. (1963). *Main street, Italy.* Garden City, NY: Doubleday.

Liang, S. (1974). *Chung-kuo wen hua yao-i* [The essential features of Chinese culture]. Hong Kong: Chi-Cheng T'u Shu King Hsu.

The little class game. (1992, September 12). *The Economist,* p. 64.

Major, J. (1989). *The land and the people of China.* New York: J. B. Lippincott.

Marvin, G. (1988). *Bullfight.* New York: Basil Blackwell.

Maslow, A. (1970). *Motivation and personality* (2nd ed.). New York: Harper & Row.

McGoldrick, M. (1982). *Ethnicity and family therapy.* New York: Guilford.

Meyer, L. (1982). *Israel now: Portrait of a troubled land.* New York: Delacorte.

Michon, J. (1992, December 5). Crown and crisis. *The Time Machine,* Arts & Entertainment (television network).

Milbank, D. (1993, March 17). We make a bit more of St. Patrick's Day than the Irish do. *Wall Street Journal,* pp. A1-A8.

Miller, L., & Hustedde, R. (1987). Group approaches. In D. E. Johnson, L. R. Miller, & G. F. Sommers (Eds.), *Needs assessment: Theory and methods* (pp. 105-131). Ames: Iowa State University Press.

Milner, H. (1989). *Sweden: Social democracy in practice.* New York: Oxford University Press.

Mole, J. (1991). *When in Rome . . . : A business guide to cultures and customs in 12 European nations.* New York: AMACOM.

Moore, T. (1859). *The poetical works of Thomas Moore.* Boston: Philips, Sampson.

Morley, C. (Ed.). (1945). *Bartlett's familiar quotations.* Boston: Little, Brown.

Munshi, K. (1965). *Indian inheritance* (Vol. 1). Bombay: Bharatiya Vidya Bhavan.

Nakane, C. (1973). *Japanese society.* London: Penguin.

Narayana, G., & Kantner, J. (1992). *Doing the needful.* Boulder, CO: Westview.

Needham, J. (1954). *Science and civilization in China.* Cambridge, UK: Cambridge University Press.

Negandhi, A., & Prasad, S. (1975). *The frightening angels: A study of U.S. multinationals in developing nations.* Kent, OH: Kent State University Press.

Newman, P. (1987, December 7). A national contempt for the law. *MacLean's,* p. 40.

Nikhilananda, S. (Ed.). (1953). *The yogas and other works.* New York: Ramakrishna-Vivekananda Center.

Nortman, D. (1985). *Population and family planning* (12th ed.). Washington, DC: Population Council.

O'Brien, F. (1961). At swim-two-birds. In U. Mercier & D. Greene (Eds.), *1000 years of Irish prose.* New York: Gross & Dunlap.

O'Brien, F. (1974). *The poor mouth: A bad story about the hard life.* New York: Seaver.

Ouchi, W. (1981). *Theory Z.* Reading, MA: Addison-Wesley.

Pearson, L. (1990). *Children of glastnost: Growing up Soviet.* Seattle: University of Washington Press.

A question of care. (1993, January 30). *The Economist, 326,* 34.

Reischauer, E. (1988). *The Japanese today: Change and continuity.* Cambridge, MA: Belknap.

Richmond, Y. (1992). *From nyet to da.* Yarmouth, ME: Intercultural Press.

Ronen, S., & Shenkar, O. (1985). Clustering countries on attitudinal dimensions: A review and synthesis. *Academy of Management Review, 10*, 435-454.

Ross, A. (1969). *What are u?* London: Andre Deutch.

Rowland, D. (1985). *Japanese business etiquette.* New York: Warner.

Russell, F. (1973). *The Horizon concise history of Germany.* New York: American Heritage.

Ruth, A. (1984). The second new nation: The mythology of modern Sweden. *Daedalus, 113*, 53-96.

Sanford, C. (1961). *The quest for paradise.* Urbana: University of Illinois Press.

Schatz, S. (1987). *Nigerian capitalism.* Berkeley: University of California Press.

Schein, E. H. (1985). *Organizational culture and leadership.* San Francisco: Jossey-Bass.

Shamberg, M. (Producer), & Crichton, C. (Director). (1988). *A fish called Wanda.* Hollywood, CA: Metro-Goldwyn-Mayer Pictures.

Shaw, G. B. (1916). *Pygmalion.* New York: Brentano's.

Smith, H. (1958). *The religions of man.* New York: Harper & Row.

Smith, H. (1991). *The world's religions.* San Francisco: HarperCollins.

Smith, L. (1990, February 26). Fear and loathing of Japan. *Fortune*, pp. 50-60.

Srinivas, M. (1980). *India: Social structure.* Delhi: Hindustan.

Starr, J. (1991). *Kissing through glass.* Chicago: Contemporary Books.

Stening, B. (1979). Problems in cross-cultural contact: A literature review. *International Journal of Intercultural Relations, 3*, 269-313.

Stewart, E., & Bennett, M. (1991). *American cultural patterns: A cross cultural perspective* (2nd ed.). Yarmouth, ME: Intercultural Press.

Stoller, R. (1975). *Perversion: The erotic form of hatred.* New York: Pantheon.

Sundberg, G. (1910). *Det Svenska folklynnet.* Stockholm, Sweden: Norstedt & Soners.

Tan, A. (1991). *The kitchen god's wife.* New York: Ballantine.

Tasker, P. (1987). *The Japanese: Portrait of a nation.* New York: Meridian.

Taylor, S. (1990). *Culture shock!: France.* Portland, OR: Graphic Arts Center.

Thomas, D. (1992, November 9). The French accent on fitness rigeur. *Washington Post*, pp. D1, D2.

Triandis, H., Brislin, R., & Hui, C. (1988). Cross-cultural training across the individualism-collectivism divide. *International Journal of Intercultural Press Relations, 12*, 269-289.

Triandis, H., McCusker, C., & Hui, C. (1990). Multimethod probes of individualism and collectivism. *Journal of Personality and Social Psychology, 59*, 1006-1020.

Tuchman, B. (1962). *The guns of august.* New York: Macmillan.

Tuning in to the future. (1992, September 5). *The Economist*, pp. 61-64.

Vedel, A. (Ed.). (1986). *The Hachette guide to French wines.* New York: Knopf.

Verleyen, F. (1987). *Flanders today.* Tielt, Belgium: Lannoo Editions.

Waters, M. (1984). *The comic Irishman.* Albany: State University of New York Press.

Welsh, D., Luthans, F., & Sommer, S. (1993). Managing Russian factory workers: The impact of U.S.-based behavioral and participative techniques. *Academy of Management Journal, 36*, 58-79.

Wheaton, K. (Ed.). (1990). *Insight guide: Spain.* Singapore: APA Publications.

Willey, D. (1984). *Italians.* London: British Broadcasting Corporation.

Willis, D. K. (1985). *Klass: How Russians really live.* New York: St. Martin's.

Zetterberg, H. (1984). The rational humanitarians. *Daedalus, 113*, 72-79.

Additional Readings

Ajayi, J. F. (1966). *Yoruba warfare in the nineteenth century.* Cambridge, UK: Cambridge University Press.

Ardaugh, J. (1982). *France in the 1980s.* London: Penguin.

Axtell, R. E. (1990). *Do's and taboos around the world* (2nd ed.). New York: Wiley.

Axtell, R. E. (1991). *Gestures.* New York: John Wiley.

Ayandele, E. (1966). *The missionary impact on modern Nigeria, 1842-1914.* New York: Longman.

Barzini, L. (1971). *From Caesar to the Mafia.* New York: Library Press.

Belgium: Unity in diversity. (1987) Tielt, Belgium: Uitgeverij Lannoo.

Binyon, M. (1983). *Life in Russia.* New York: Pantheon.

Boudard, M., Boudard, M., & Bryssinck, R. (1990). *Modern Belgium.* Palo Alto, CA: Society for Promotion of Science and Scholarship.

Christopher, R. C. (1983). *The Japanese mind.* New York: Fawcett Columbine.

Cleeve, B. (1983). *A view of the Irish.* London: Buchan & Enright.

Coote, C., & Batchelor, D. (1949). *Winston Churchill's maxims and reflections.* Boston: Houghton Mifflin.

Danaher, K. (1966). *Irish country people.* Cork County, Ireland: Mercier.

d'Haevens, A. (1980). *150 Years of communities and cultures in Belgium: 1830-1980.* Brussels: Ministry of Foreign Affairs.

DiFranco, A. (1983). *Italy: Balanced on the edge of time.* Minneapolis, MN: Dillion.

Dumont, L. (1985). Are cultures living beings? German identity in interaction. *Man, 21,* 587-604.

Ensurd, B. (1985). *The pocket guide to wine*. New York: G. P. Putnam.

Galef, J. (1987). *Even monkeys fall from trees and other Japanese proverbs*. Rutland, VT: Charles E. Tuttle.

Germany benign: Or malign? (1990, January 2). *The Economist*, pp. 13-14.

Golovkina, S. (1987). *The Bolshoi ballet school*. Neptune City, NJ: TFH.

Green, L. (1974). *Modern migrations in western Africa*. London: Oxford University Press.

Gregory, J., & Ukladnikov, A. (1980). *Leningrad's ballet*. London: Robson.

Gustafsson, M. (1984). The silences of the north. *Daedalus, 113*, 94-103.

Harris, P., & Moran, R. (1987). *Managing cultural differences* (2nd ed.). Houston, TX: Gulf.

Hayden, I. (1987). *Symbolism and privilege: The ritual context of British royalty*. Tucson: University of Arizona Press.

Hingley, R. (1977). *The Russian mind*. New York: Scribner.

Hypes, J. (1937). *Spotlights on the culture of India*. Washington, DC: Daylion.

Insight guides: Israel. (1989). Singapore: APA Publications.

Kakar, S. (1989). *Intimate relations*. Chicago: University of Chicago Press.

Keefe, E. (1982). *The Soviet Union: A country study*. Washington, DC: Government Printing Office.

Kras, E. (1989). *Management in two cultures*. Yarmouth, ME: Intercultural Press.

Library of Nations. (1985). *Britain*. London: Time-Life.

Lieblich, A. (1984). *Kibbutz makom*. Tel Aviv: Schocken.

Lichine, A. (1985). *Alexis Lichine's guide to wines and vineyards of France* (3rd ed.). New York: Knopf.

Life World Library. (1970). *Britain*. New York: Time-Life.

Long, M. (1989). High tech: The future is now. *National Geographic Magazine, 176*(1), 92-101.

Mangione, J., & Morreale, B. (1992). *La storia: Five centuries of the Italian American experience*. New York: HarperCollins.

Morley, C. (Ed.). (1945). *Bartlett's familiar quotations* (11th ed.). Boston: Little, Brown.

Murray, W. (1987). *Italy, the fatal gift*. New York: Dodd, Mead.

Narla, V. (1969). *Traditional Indian culture*. Vijayawada, India: Vijaya.

Nayakaw, M. (1973). *The garden art of Japan*. New York: Weatherhill.

Nichols, P. (1973). *Italia, Italia*. Boston: Atlantic Monthly Press.

Nnoli, O. (1976, July). The dynamics of ethnic politics in Nigeria. *Odu, 14*, 3-25.

Nwabara, S. (1977). *Iboland: A century of contact with Britain: 1860-1960*. Atlantic Highlands, NJ: Humanities Press.

Reischauer, E. (1981). *Japan, the story of a nation*. New York: Knopf.

Rohlen, T. (1974). *For harmony and strength*. Berkeley: University of California Press.

Romberg, A., & Yamamoto, T. (1990). *Same bed, different dreams*. New York: Council on Foreign Relations.

Rowe, M. (1991). *So very English*. London: Serpent's Tail.

Sampson, A. (1982). *The changing anatomy of Britain*. New York: Random House.

Shilling, M. (1988). *Update Belgium*. Yarmouth, ME: Intercultural Press.

Shipler, D. (1989). *Russia: Broken idols, solemn dreams*. New York: Penguin.

Shireen, K. (1988). Belgium: The shape of things to come? *Banker* [UK], *138*, 31-37.

Singha, R., & Massey, R. (1967). *Indian dances: Their history and growth*. New York: George Braziller.

Sinha, J. (1990). *Work culture in the Indian context*. New Delhi: Sage.

Sinha, S. (1972). *Aspects of Indian culture and society*. Calcutta: Indian Anthropological Society.

Smith, H. (1990). *The new Russians*. New York: Random House.

Smith, R. (1978). *Kurusu*. London: William Dawson.

Tanaka, Y. (Ed.). (1985). *Japan as it is*. Tokyo: Gakken.

Thomas, K. (1992, December 10). Formal split caps year of royal scandal. *USA Today*, pp. D1-D2.

Tillier, A., & Beardwood, R. (1991). *Guide to business travel in Europe* (2nd ed.). Chicago: Passport.

Todd, E. (1987). *The making of modern France: Ideology, politics, and culture*. London: T. J. Press.

Trimingham, J. S. (1962). *A history of Islam in West Africa*. London: Oxford University Press.

Waley, A. (1934). *The way and its power*. London: Allen & Unwin.

Waley, A. (1956). *Three ways of thought in ancient China*. Garden City, NY: Doubleday.

Walmsley, J. (1986). *Brit-think, Ameri-think*. New York: Penguin.

Weber, E. (1991). *My France: Politics, culture, myth*. Cambridge, MA: Harvard University Press.

Zeldin, T. (1982). *The French*. New York: Pantheon.

Ziegler, W. (1984). *DuMont guide to Ireland*. New York: Stewart, Tabori & Chang.

Author Index

360

Subject Index

About the Author

Martin J. Gannon (Ph.D., Columbia University) is Professor of International Management and Behavior at the College of Business and Management, University of Maryland at College Park. He teaches in the areas of international organizational behavior and business strategy and has served in this college as Associate Dean for Academic Affairs, Chair of the Faculty of Management and Organization, and Codirector of the Small Business Development Center. He has also been the Senior Research Fulbright Professor at the University of Kassel in West Germany, and the John F. Kennedy and Fulbright Professor at Thammasat University in Bangkok, Thailand.

In 1988 Professor Gannon introduced an innovative course in the business curriculum at Maryland, "Organizational Behavior: A Multi-Cultural Perspective," on which this book is based. He also has taught managers and students in both Europe and Asia.

Professor Gannon has written 75 articles that have been published in such journals as *The Academy of Management Journal, The Academy of Management Review, Journal of Applied Psychology, California Management Review, Journal of Applied Psychology, International Journal of*

Management, and *Industrial Relations.* His eight books include *The Dynamics of Competitive Strategy* (coauthor, 1992), *Management* (1988), *Strategic Management Skills* (coauthor, 1986), and *Organizational Behavior* (1979). Currently he is working on two coauthored books: *Ethical Dimensions in International Management* and *Managing Without Traditional Methods: Innovations in Human Resource Management.*

Professor Gannon is a past president and fellow of the Eastern Academy of Management, and he has been active in the organization's biannual international conferences. He also has been chair of the Human Resource Division of the Academy of Management. Throughout his career he has served as a management trainer and consultant to many private firms and government agencies, including Chemical Bank, Upjohn Company, the U.S. Office of Personnel Management, American Federation of Government Employees, and the U.S. General Accounting Office.